PRINCIPLED ENGAGEMENT

As an early anti-apartheid campaigner I was a very reluctant convert to any kind of dealing with repressive regimes. But experience with Myanmar and elsewhere has taught me that careful, selective engagement can advance human rights in the hardest of situations. The case studies and foreign policy and aid strategies analysed here deserve the attention of all serious-minded policymakers. Principled Engagement *is intelligent, lucidly written and compelling.*

Gareth Evans, Foreign Minister of Australia 1988–96, President of the International Crisis Group 2000–09, Chancellor of The Australian National University, Australia

T0300221

Principled Engagement
Negotiating Human Rights in Repressive States

Edited by

MORTEN B. PEDERSEN
University of New South Wales, Australia

DAVID KINLEY
Sydney University, Australia

LONDON AND NEW YORK

First published 2013 by Ashgate Publishing

Published 2016 by Routledge
2 Park Square, Milton Park, Abingdon, Oxfordshire OX14 4RN
711 Third Avenue, New York, NY 10017, USA

First issued in paperback 2016

Routledge is an imprint of the Taylor & Francis Group, an informa business

British Library Cataloguing in Publication Data
A catalogue record for this book is available from the British Library

The Library of Congress has cataloged the printed edition as follows:
Principled engagement : negotiating human rights in repressive states / edited by Morten B. Pedersen and David Kinley.
     pages cm -- (Applied legal philosophy)
    Includes bibliographical references and index.
    ISBN 978-1-4094-5538-7 (hardback)
1. Human rights. 2. Discrimination--Law and legislation.
3. Civil rights. 4. Political persecution I. Pedersen, Morten B., editor of compilation. II. Kinley, David, lecturer in law, editor of compilation.
    K3242.P75 2013
    342.08'5--dc23

                                                        2013012222

ISBN 13: 978-1-138-25065-9 (pbk)
ISBN 13: 978-1-4094-5538-7 (hbk)

Contents

List of Figures and Tables

Figures

Tables

Notes on Contributors

James Cockayne is a lawyer, strategist and analyst based in New York. Previously head of the Extradition and Transnational Crime Units in the Australian Attorney-General's Department, James has spent the last decade based in New York, helping governments, international organisations, business and civil society deal with violent non-state actors. James spent two years as Co-Director of the Centre on Global Counterterrorism Cooperation and led their work in Africa, after four years as a Senior Fellow at the International Peace Institute. He has also worked in war crimes trials in both West and East Africa, served as Chair of the Editorial Committee of the *Journal of International Criminal Justice*, and was a founding editorial member of the *Journal of International Humanitarian Legal Studies*. Author of over 60 peer-reviewed articles and book chapters on international law, armed conflict and criminal justice, James' books include: *Capitalizing on Trust: Harnessing Somali Remittances for Counterterrorism, Human Rights and State Building* (CGCC, 2012); *Peace Operations and Organized Crime? Enemies or Allies* (edited with Adam Lupel, Routledge, 2011); and *Beyond Market Forces: Regulating the Global Security Industry* (IPI, 2009).

Mac Darrow is the Chief of the Millennium Development Goals Section of the Office of the United Nations High Commissioner for Human Rights (UN/OHCHR), working on policies, programming tools, advocacy and capacity-building strategies to mainstream human rights within the UN system. He has extensive experience on human rights and development issues in policy, operational and academic settings, and has published monographs, chapters in edited volumes and articles in refereed journals on international human rights law, international environmental law, international organisations and development. He has previously worked as a consultant for various United Nations agencies including, in 2010, for the World Bank's Legal Vice-Presidency on the interrelationships between the international human rights and environmental legal regimes relevant to climate change.

Jolyon Ford is the senior Africa analyst at global analysis and advisory firm Oxford Analytica. He received a PhD from the Australian National University in 2011, and holds degrees in history, law and international law from the University of KwaZulu-Natal (South Africa) and the University of Cambridge. He has worked in government, civil society, an intergovernmental organisation (the Commonwealth Secretariat) and academia. He is also a senior research consultant to the Institute for Security Studies, Pretoria.

Pierre Gentile is head of the Protection of the Civilian Population Unit at the International Committee of the Red Cross (ICRC) headquarters in Geneva, where he oversees a project to elaborate and disseminate professional standards for protection work. He began his career with the ICRC in 1996 as a delegate in Vukovar, Croatia, and subsequently spent ten years working in ICRC delegations in Rwanda, Columbia, Afghanistan, Peru, Ethiopia and Israel. Since 2009, he has participated in annual meetings of policy affiliates for the Refugee Studies Centre in Oxford, Great Britain. He holds an undergraduate and Master's Degree in Political Science from the University of Geneva.

Auret van Heerden is President and CEO of the Fair Labor Association and has more than 30 years experience in international human and labour rights. He began campaigning for workers' rights as a young student in apartheid South Africa and co-authored a book in 1976 that called for trade union rights for black workers. He served two terms as president of the National Union of South African Students. After graduating in industrial sociology from the University of the Witwatersrand in Johannesburg, he founded an institute that provided research and training services to trade unions and civil society groups. He was forced into exile in May 1987 after long periods of solitary confinement and torture. In 1988, Auret joined the International Labour Organization (ILO) and worked on its Program of Action against Apartheid in Geneva until 1994 when the new democratic South African government appointed him Labor Attaché in the South African Permanent Mission to the UN in Geneva. He returned to the ILO in 1996, where he worked on labour relations issues in 25 zone-operating countries and established a Swiss-funded project to improve labour relations in Special Economic Zones in China.

Richard Horsey spent ten years working for the ILO on forced labour in Myanmar, including five years as the organisation's representative in Yangon (a book drawing lessons from these experiences was published in 2011 by Routledge). He later worked for the United Nations Office for the Coordination of Humanitarian Affairs (UNOCHA), leading a year-long study on how to improve delivery of humanitarian assistance to conflict-affected parts of Myanmar. Subsequently, he was appointed senior adviser and spokesperson for the UN relief effort in Myanmar following Cyclone Nargis. He is a widely published political analyst, focusing on isolated authoritarian regimes. He is the Myanmar Adviser for the International Crisis Group, and he has also written for Chatham House, the World Bank, the Conflict Prevention and Peace Forum and the Transnational Institute. He is fluent in the Myanmar language, and holds a PhD in psychology.

Ann Kent is the author of *Between Freedom and Subsistence: China and Human Rights* (OUP, 1993); *China, the United Nations and Human Rights: The Limits of Compliance* (University of Pennsylvania Press, 1999); and *Beyond Compliance: China, International Organizations and Global Security* (Stanford University Press, 2007). Formerly an Australian Research Council Fellow at the Faculty of

Law, Australian National University, she has also been a China research specialist in the Commonwealth Parliamentary Research Service and in the Australian Department of External (now Foreign) Affairs. Currently, she is a Visiting Fellow in the ANU College of Law, Australian National University, Canberra. She has also taught in China, in 1975 at Shanghai Teachers' University and, in 2005, at Fudan University in Shanghai.

David Kinley holds the Chair in Human Rights Law at the University of Sydney, and is an Academic Panel member of Doughty Street Chambers in London. He has worked for nearly 20 years as a consultant and adviser on international and domestic human rights law in Vietnam, Indonesia, South Africa, Bangladesh, Thailand, Iraq, Nepal, Laos, China, the Pacific Islands, and Myanmar/Burma. He has worked for a wide range of international organisations, including the UN High Commissioner for Human Rights, the World Bank, the Ford Foundation, AusAID, and the Asia Pacific Forum of National Human Rights Institutions, as well as a number of transnational corporations and NGOs. He has also previously worked for three years with the Australian Law Reform Commission and two years with the Australian Human Rights Commission. His recent publications include *Civilising Globalisation: Human Rights and the Global Economy* (Cambridge University Press, 2009), as well as *Corporations and Human Rights* (Ashgate, 2009) as editor, and *The WTO and Human Rights: Interdisciplinary Perspectives* (Edward Elgar, 2009), and *Human Rights: Old Problems and New Possibilities* (Edward Elgar, 2013) as joint editor. He is currently working on two new books: one examining the intersections between global finance and human rights, and the other, a textbook on economic, social and cultural rights.

Joel Negin is Senior Lecturer in International Public Health at the University of Sydney and a Research Fellow at the Menzies Centre for Health Policy. He lectures on health systems, project management and health and development at the University of Sydney and guest lectures across Australia. Joel's research focuses on multi-sectoral development models, the HIV response, and health systems strengthening in sub-Saharan Africa and the Pacific. He has worked in a number of countries including Botswana, Côte d'Ivoire, Kenya, Liberia, South Africa and Zimbabwe on various health and development projects for UN agencies, government departments and academic institutions. He served as technical adviser to the National AIDS Control Council of Kenya and worked with Botswana's National AIDS Coordinating Agency. He holds a Master's in International Affairs from Columbia University and a first degree from Harvard University.

Justine Nolan is the Deputy Director of the Australian Human Rights Centre and a Senior Lecturer in law at the University of New South Wales. Her research interests are in human rights and corporate accountability. She has worked closely with a broad range of representatives from NGOs, government, companies and the United Nations in consulting on business and human rights issues. Prior to her appointment at UNSW in 2004 she was the Director of the Business and Human Rights Program at the Lawyers Committee for Human Rights (now Human Rights First) in the United States. Justine is a member of the Australian Department of Foreign Affairs and Trade, AusAid's Human Rights Grants Scheme Expert Panel and NSW Legal Aid's Human Rights Panel.

Morten B. Pedersen is Senior Lecturer in International and Political Studies at the University of New South Wales/Canberra (the Australian Defence Force Academy). He previously worked as Senior Analyst for the International Crisis Group in Myanmar (2001–2008), and has held academic positions also at the United Nations University in Tokyo and the Australian National University. He has served as a policy adviser for a number of governments and international organisations, including the UN, the World Bank, the European Commission and the Australian Government. His publications include some 40 titles on Burma/Myanmar, international statecraft and human rights, including *Promoting Human Rights in Burma: A Critique of Western Sanctions Policy* (Rowman & Littlefield, 2008), and (with Anna Magnusson) *A "Good Office"? Twenty Years of UN Mediation in Myanmar* (New York: International Peace Institute, 2012). He is currently working on a book on the dynamics and prospects of Myanmar's democratic transition process.

Chris Sidoti is a human rights lawyer, activist and teacher. He currently works from Sydney, Australia, as an international human rights consultant, specialising in the international human rights system and in national human rights institutions. He was director of the International Service for Human Rights (ISHR), based in Geneva, Switzerland, from 2003 to 2007, and is now a member of the board of ISHR. He has been Australian Human Rights Commissioner (1995–2000), Australian Law Reform Commissioner (1992–1995) and Foundation Director of the Australian Human Rights and Equal Opportunity Commission (1987–1992). He has also worked in non-government organisations, including for the Human Rights Council of Australia and the Australian Catholic Commission for Justice and Peace. In 2007–2008 he was the independent chair of the United Kingdom Government's Northern Ireland Bill of Rights Forum. He is an adjunct professor at the University of Western Sydney, Griffith University (Queensland), University of the Sunshine Coast (Queensland) and the Australian Catholic University, and an Affiliate at the Sydney Centre for International Law at the University of Sydney.

Series Editor's Preface

The objective of the Applied Legal Philosophy series is to publish work which adopts a theoretical approach to the study of particular areas or aspects of law or deals with general theories of law in a way which focuses on issues of practical moral and political concern in specific legal contexts.

In recent years there has been an encouraging tendency for legal philosophers to utilise detailed knowledge of the substance and practicalities of law, and a noteworthy development in the theoretical sophistication of much legal research. The series seeks to encourage these trends and to make available studies in law which are both genuinely philosophical in approach and at the same time based on appropriate legal knowledge and directed towards issues in the criticism and reform of actual laws and legal systems.

The series will include studies of all the main areas of law, presented in a manner which relates to the concerns of specialist legal academics and practitioners. Each book makes an original contribution to an area of legal study while being comprehensible to those engaged in a wide variety of disciplines. Their legal content is principally Anglo-American, but a wide-ranging comparative approach is encouraged and authors are drawn from a variety of jurisdictions.

Tom Campbell
Series Editor
Centre for Applied Philosophy and Public Ethics
Charles Sturt University, Canberra

Acknowledgements

The editors gratefully acknowledge the generous funding provided by United Nations University in Tokyo for this project. Additional financial support was provided by the Sydney Law School, as well as the Australian Research Council under Discovery Grant DP1096521. Preparation of the manuscript would not have been possible without the assiduous editorial attentions of Johanna Stratton, Adriana Edmeades and Samantha Brown.

Acknowledgement

Chapter 1

Introducing Principled Engagement

Morten B. Pedersen and David Kinley

The post-Second World War era has seen impressive progress on institutionalising international human rights norms through an ever-expanding number of multilateral treaties, state signatories and global oversight mechanisms, mostly linked to the United Nations system. Progress on compliance with these norms has been much slower, however, and a huge gap remains between international norms and national practice of human rights. This is particularly the case in the most repressive states that this book is particularly concerned with, where authoritarian rulers not only deny citizens any meaningful say in government, but also terrorise and impoverish the general population (or significant subgroups). We do not need to determine exactly which states belong to this category, except to say that they score at the bottom of most human rights indexes and stubbornly resist both internal and external efforts to alleviate the situation. For the purposes of analysis though, we exclude crisis situations requiring immediate action to stop, for example, a looming genocide, as well as failed states where the government has little control over its territory. Such situations present a different set of challenges, which are more usefully examined through the lenses of humanitarian intervention, peace- and state-building, than human rights per se.

Debates over how to promote human rights in repressive states have tended to pit those seeking to enforce international norms through punitive sanctions, mainly focusing on political freedoms, against others favouring non-interventionist approaches that seek to facilitate longer-term internally driven change by opening such countries up through trade, investment and economic development. Yet neither sanctions nor business have had, or seem likely to have, much effect on the most repressive regimes; in fact, both approaches can have serious perverse consequences for human rights (see Chapter 2 by Pedersen in this volume). Our concept of Principled Engagement delineates a third way, which emphasises engagement with repressive rulers and their agents, as well as broader groups in society, to alleviate concrete human rights violations and improve the structural framework for human rights protection. This approach relies on non-coercive pressure and support rather than punishment, yet works proactively to identify the shortcomings of existing systems, promote better policies and practices and strengthen domestic forces for change.

Principled Engagement is commonly used in transitional states that show at least a rhetorical commitment to democracy and human rights, yet is often derided by mainstream human rights activists as "appeasement" or "self-seeking" when it comes to openly authoritarian states. This is perhaps not surprising given the tendency of Western governments to engage only with those authoritarian states that are too big or otherwise important to be "bullied". However, it is important to distinguish between the practice of self-interest and the principles of Principled Engagement as understood here. The approach elaborated on in this book is a substantially different proposition from, for example, America's "constructive engagement" with South Africa under apartheid, ASEAN's "enhanced interaction" with Myanmar, or the West's current "quiet diplomacy" with China, none of which have in practice been primarily concerned about human rights. We believe that engagement can indeed be "principled" in this regard (i.e. used strategically to promote institutions that respect, protect and fulfil human rights) – and that, properly implemented, Principled Engagement may well be the most effective approach in many of the most repressive states, or at the very least a necessary complement to other approaches. In this introductory chapter, we seek to further flesh out what we mean by Principled Engagement by comparing it to the alternatives. Chapter 2 develops the basic argument for why we believe this strategy deserves greater attention than it currently gets.

International Strategies for Promoting Human Rights

In order to facilitate analysis, we distinguish between three general strategies employed by "sender" states or organisations for promoting human rights in "target" states: Ostracism, Business as Usual, and Principled Engagement. All have the same ultimate goal – the promotion of human rights. Yet the strategic objectives and methods differ, as do, in turn, the use of the main tools of foreign policy. Figures 1.1 and 1.2 illustrate the key differences between these three approaches. The text further elaborates and considers the different theories of change underlying each.

Proponents of *Ostracism* seek to force their will on uncooperative targets. Blaming human rights violations on "bad rulers" and the pursuit of vested interests, they demand regime change. Only democracy is seen to ensure that leaders govern in the interest of the general population. Since no tyrant gives up power and privileges voluntarily, senders seek to coerce targets to comply with their demands by denying them legitimacy, income or other resources. They condemn authoritarian rule and strictly limit diplomatic exchanges; they ban or otherwise seek to restrict trade and investment with the target country; and they reduce aid, usually to purely humanitarian projects implemented without government involvement. In extreme cases, they may seek to expel the target state from international institutions. Usually there will be a gradual escalation from threats to increasingly more serious value deprivation. The theory is that bad rulers will cease their repressive ways when, *and only when*, the perceived costs of maintaining them surpass the perceived benefits – or, failing that, will

Objective \ Method	Democratic government	Just governance	Economic development
Coercion	OSTRACISM		
Mediation		PRINCIPLED ENGAGEMENT	
Facilitation			BUSINESS AS USUAL

Figure 1.1   International strategies for promoting human rights

be overthrown in a coup or popular uprising and replaced by leaders willing to undertake the changes demanded. Ostracism leaves little room for negotiation or compromise since this would amount to bending to illegitimate power and leave in place the perceived cause of the problem.

Business as Usual marks the opposite end of the spectrum of human rights policies. Rather than blame human rights violations on bad rulers, the problem is seen to lie in underdevelopment and isolation. Proponents of this approach celebrate the supposed virtues of globalisation, which is seen to advance economic development, leading to global value convergence. Thus, they support bringing target states into the international community, with a particular emphasis on expanding or "normalising" economic relations. Through foreign aid, trade and investment, target economies will be modernised, people will be lifted out of poverty, and newly empowered modern classes will push for civil and political liberties, eventually bringing about a transformation to rights-abiding states. The role of international actors in this scenario is non-interventionist. Criticism of violations is absent or muted. Senders engage freely with the target country based primarily on commercial decisions and the pursuit of mutual gain. Rather than pressure and demands, Business as Usual relies on what social power theorists have referred to as "ecological control", where senders seek to further compliance by modifying the social or physical environment of the target, on the assumption that this new environment will bring about the desired change in behaviour. The drivers of change, in other words, are essentially internal; the result of natural evolution as countries grow richer.

Principled Engagement spans the middle ground between Ostracism and Business as Usual, combining normative pressure with positive support to effect incremental governance reform. The focus here is on agency: the people, institutions and policies that violate (or uphold) human rights. Proponents of Principled Engagement believe that repressive institutions can be reformed, at least to a degree, to produce better human rights outcomes without demanding regime change or waiting for the slow-moving forces of "modernisation". This does not imply that they are unconcerned with democracy or development, far from it. The focus, however, is less on these overarching structures than on the underlying governance processes and the ways in which human rights can be advanced within existing political and economic systems. From this perspective, it is less the form than the *substance* of the political regime that matters, and less the quantity than the *quality* of economic development.

While Ostracism limits international exchanges with the target country and Business as Usual normalises them, Principled Engagement seeks to actively harness such exchanges to promote "just" or rights-abiding governance. Senders eschew megaphone diplomacy in favour of critical dialogue with those responsible for human rights violations, and in fact increase engagement with the target state on human rights issues. Rather than stopping trade and investment, they try to regulate it to ensure that it benefits human rights, typically through various forms of business "codes of conduct" – or they may seek to influence economic policies or labour practices in the target country to help ensure that international economic exchanges are consonant with human rights values. They use foreign aid proactively to improve human rights through technical assistance and training, support for progressive government programs or "rights-based approaches" to development. Moreover, they encourage target states to join multilateral institutions whose domain includes human rights, seeing such institutions as important platforms for persuasion and socialisation. In sum, principled engagers use positive motivational influences to encourage and support repressive states to change their behaviour in ways consonant with international human rights norms.

	Ostracism	Business as Usual	Principled Engagement
Diplomacy	*condemnation*	*non-interference*	*critical dialogue*
Foreign aid	*political conditionality*	*alignment*	*positive support rights-based approaches*
Trade & investment	*economic sanctions*	*free markets*	*corporate social responsibility*
Multilat. institutions	*exclusion*	*integration*	*standard-setting & monitoring*

Figure 1.2   International tools for promoting human rights

To further draw out the differences between Ostracism, Business as Usual and Principled Engagement, it may be useful to imagine three different conversations with target states. In the case of Ostracism, communications essentially take the form of extortion: "If you don't do what we want, we will hurt you." In the case of

Principled Engagement, by contrast, senders seek to persuade the target to act of its own volition: "It is in your own best interest to do this. If you have difficulties doing it, we can help." The monologue is here replaced by dialogue where senders not only communicate their own preferences, but also seek to understand the target's position and reach common ground. In the case of Business as Usual, sender and target tacitly agree to leave their human rights differences aside and focus on common (commercial) interests.

Ultimately, the three approaches reflect fundamentally different perceptions of the role of international actors and their importance to national human rights progress. Ostracism seeks to *enforce* international norms through punitive measures, much like states enforce domestic laws within their own territory. In the absence of political will within target states to respect, protect and fulfil human rights, the responsibility is seen to fall upon the international community to act as a supranational authority. This contrasts strongly with Business as Usual, where international actors act only to *facilitate* an essentially domestically driven process, leaving state sovereignty intact. Principled Engagement falls somewhere in between. In recognition of the difficulty of enforcing international human rights in the absence of a supreme international authority, it seeks rather to *mediate* the "conflict" between external norms and internal practices by encouraging and supporting the target to reform. This approach is more respectful of national sovereignty than Ostracism but does include normative pressure on the target to conform with international standards, *unlike* Business as Usual which essentially leaves it up to target states to decide whether to reform their human rights practices or not.

These three approaches are, of course, "ideal types". The human rights policy of any given sender will rarely encompass the full range of interactions with the target, and neither objectives nor methods fall into neat categories but rather arraign along a continuum, creating certain "grey zones". In practice though, governments (and other organisations) tend to make a strategic choice between these general approaches. Once the general direction of policy is set, both the internal sender debate and relations with the target state limit the scope for deviations, instead favouring a gradual deepening and expansion of the core approach. Sanctions, for example, establish "moral commitments", which make it difficult to revise the objectives or methods later, lest it be seen as backing down. Also, they tend to breed hostility and distrust between the sender and target, thus further inhibiting any future rapprochement. Our ideal types thus not only serve as analytical devices, but also have practical political resonance and relevance.

Purpose and Structure of this Book

The basic ideas underlying Principled Engagement are not new and as such are more descriptive than innovative. Yet they have rarely if ever been comprehensively applied in the most repressive states – and, perhaps for that reason, their operationalisation and effectiveness in such contexts has been the subject of little systematic scholarly inquiry. These are the limitations with which this book is concerned. While we believe that Principled Engagement provides an important alternative to Ostracism and Business as Usual for dealing also with the worst cases (see Chapter 2), relatively little is known about this approach, including what it looks like in practice, how it works to influence change and what conditions determine success or failure. Chapters 3–11 explore these questions through a series of case studies.

The first two case studies, by former Australian Human Rights Commissioner Chris Sidoti and Protection Officer with the International Committee of the Red Cross (ICRC) Pierre Gentile, seek to draw out the basic principles of Principled Engagement, looking at what is required to make it work and "do no harm". While both are strongly supportive of the underlying assumptions of this approach, they also stress that Principled Engagement is hard and difficult work, requiring commitment, skills, and sometimes a great deal of courage. Sidoti, in Chapter 3, draws on his wide personal experience with human rights work in countries like China, Indonesia, Myanmar and Vietnam to tease out a number of general lessons, or principles, for the execution of Principled Engagement. Engagement, he argues, is the optimal approach in most countries. Yet it is a demanding one, which risks slipping into co-option unless senders are strongly focused on results, and committed, among other things, to transparency, accountability and continuous self-reflection. Gentile (Chapter 4) goes one step further, arguing that for the ICRC, as the guardian of international humanitarian law, engagement with all sides to an armed conflict is "a duty". Constructive and confidential dialogue with *all* belligerents is a crucial element of ICRC's "neutral, impartial and independent approach", which helps the organisation secure access in crisis situations, gain "a proper understanding of the context and all its players", and develop "a network of trusted interlocutors involved in the violence". While public denunciation aimed at ostracising parties to a conflict can become necessary in extreme cases, for the ICRC this is a "last resort" to be exercised only "after Principled Engagement has proved to be impossible or ineffective after repeated attempts". Like Sidoti though, Gentile emphasises that Principled Engagement is "easier said than done", describing the challenges ICRC often faces, in particular, in establishing legitimacy, securing regular access to key interlocutors and agreeing on a legal basis for dialogue.

Each of Chapters 5–9 analyses and assesses a specific case of Principled Engagement, yielding a wealth of insights on different countries (China, Burma, Zimbabwe, Liberia, Chad), different issues (forced labour, HIV/AIDS, workers' rights, violent economies), different agencies (ILO, Fair Labor Association, World Bank), and different tools (diplomacy, aid, trade and investment). Ann Kent, a legal scholar and China specialist with the Australian National University, starts this part of the book off by offering a sweeping assessment of international human rights policies on China since the 1970s (Chapter 5). These policies have encompassed elements of all of the three ideal type approaches discussed above, including perhaps the most substantial case anywhere in the world of Principled Engagement with a significantly repressive state. Kent's conclusions are at once sobering and encouraging. Tracing change and continuity in Chinese government behaviour in the human rights realm over 40 years, she emphasises the overwhelming importance of domestic imperatives. Yet even a major power like China is not unresponsive to international engagement. While neither Ostracism (1949–1979, 1989–1990) nor Business as Usual (1997–present) by the major Western powers has had much success, Principled Engagement has successfully induced the Communist Party to engage with the international human rights regime and undertake some limited reforms. Kent points particularly to the usefulness of persistent "communicative" engagement through multilateral institutions, which has helped overcome sovereignty issues.

In Chapter 6, Richard Horsey, formerly with the ILO in Myanmar, provides a project-level perspective on the dynamics of Principled Engagement. His analysis of the extended and difficult, but ultimately relatively successful, negotiations between the ILO and the, now former, Myanmar military government over the elimination of forced labour offers an example of the potential of Principled Engagement even under very difficult circumstances. The detailed narrative traces the responses of the Myanmar authorities to external criticism from the early days of denial and counter-threats to the incremental establishment over a ten-year period of a cooperative ILO-government complaint system, which contributed to a significant reduction in the use of forced labour. Horsey unequivocally credits the carefully calibrated combination of pressure, dialogue and technical assistance within an overall framework of Principled Engagement for these results. Yet, his analysis also stresses just how demanding such an approach is, and the absolute imperative of staying true to human rights principles. Indeed, he concurs with many of the principles established by Sidoti in Chapter 3. The ILO's work in Myanmar is certainly not a case of "quiet diplomacy" for ambiguous purposes as some recent engagement with China has been, but rather an example of a hard-nosed, strategic approach with unwavering commitment to achieving results, which perhaps falls at the hard end of the Principled Engagement spectrum.

Jolyon Ford and Joel Negin, in their discussion of donor policies and the HIV/AIDS crisis in Zimbabwe (Chapter 7), offer a more cautious assessment of the potential Principled Engagement. While dismissing both Ostracism and Business as Usual as feasible options for dealing with Mugabe's post-2000 regime, the authors also question whether responsible assistance is in fact possible in cases like Zimbabwe (2000–2008), where the government lacks any real policy other than power maintenance and self-enrichment. Contrary to senior international aid officials at the time, who strongly criticised donors for doing too little to help the victims of the HIV/AIDS epidemic, Ford and Negin stress the significant risk that additional funds channelled through the government would simply have been misappropriated by corrupt officials for other ends or used to boost the legitimacy of a bad regime. By contrast, they applaud the cautious re-engagement by donors since the agreement in 2009 on a power-sharing arrangement between the government and the opposition, which they believe "can help fortify or inspire reformist elements at crucial periods, hold open political space, and engender popular belief in an alternative and viable future". This raises the uncomfortable possibility that there may be cases where international actors keen to promote human rights may have little option but to wait for domestic opportunities to open up.

Auret van Heerden and Justine Nolan address the emerging field of business and human rights in Chapter 8. Their analysis of the work of the Fair Labor Association (FLA) to alleviate violations arising from supply-chain production has strong parallels with Horsey's earlier chapter on forced labour. Like the ILO in Myanmar, the FLA is engaging against a backdrop of threatened sanctions (in this case consumer boycotts and the potential loss of contracts), which has helped motivate companies to take human rights seriously. Yet van Heerden and Nolan believe that the FLA, again much like the ILO, has made a critical contribution to the mix, acting as a trusted third party to convene and moderate discussions, providing practical proposals for action and contributing technical assistance where needed. Importantly, deeper engagement appears to be producing more lasting results. While the FLA's initial reliance on a top-down "audit-based policing model" produced a "veritable industry of falsification", clearly failing to change the culture of non-compliance, sustainable compliance is now being sought through a new "partnership model" that emphasises needs assessments and capacity building for companies, along with empowerment of their workers. Like other principled engagers, the FLA has faced criticism for conferring legitimacy on business and, ultimately, making little difference. Yet, as the authors show, companies that join the FLA are effectively agreeing "to help regulate unregulated jurisdictions; they establish rights in workplaces that would otherwise not enjoy them." Reducing corporate violations of workers' rights may be a process of progressive realisation, but it is progressing.

In Chapter 9, James Cockayne steps outside the traditional realm of human rights promotion to look at international efforts to reform the violent economies that sustain repressive regimes and contribute to human rights violations. In such economies (of which depressingly many Cockayne provides a survey), "predatory and parasitic activities, such as graft, drug production and trafficking, and illicit traffic in natural resources" are typically employed as means to sustain organised coercion. As, ordinarily, neither the approaches of conducting business as usual nor threats of ostracisation make much headway in changing such dire circumstances (because they often fail to confront the economic aspects of endemic human rights abuse), Cockayne turns his attention to the possibilities of Principled Engagement in addressing the problem. The focus of his analysis is on whether and how Principled Engagement can "transform the *mediating institutions* that sustain such regimes' control of illicit revenues" by breaking the incentive structures that reward violence with greater power and riches. Acknowledging the especial difficulty posed by the fact that as such oppressive regimes mature, so economically motivated entrepreneurialism becomes intermingled with politically motivated human rights abuses, he suggests that for it to do so effectively, the engagement pursued must be both highly strategic and deeply communicative, and while its impetus may be internationalised, the instruments and agencies of change must be internalised. Whereas the business as usual approach tends to launder dirty deeds, and ostracism drives them underground and beyond reach, Cockayne sees Principled Engagement as a combination of *both* approaches, with the art being when and how to employ them (separately or together) and the aim being to change the cost/benefit calculations facing those exercising oppressive power to release it, and those subject to oppression to resist it. By following the good example of this approach in Liberia (and learning from the bad example of Chad), Cockayne concludes with a set of policy directives that he argues are essential to constructing a strategy of Principled Engagement that takes seriously "the economic underpinnings of violent regimes" by seeking to change them.

Chapters 10–11 shift the focus to the sender side of the equation, looking at some of the opportunities and challenges that exist in the contemporary international environment in engaging in a principled way on human rights. In Chapter 10, David Kinley reflects on how development can act as a vehicle for Principled Engagement within the specific context of the contemporary shifts in the nature and purpose of aid and development. He analyses four of these "New Aid" formats: (i) the existential debates over whether aid's failures are such that it should be dispensed with altogether; (ii) the rise of the private sector's direct participation in development work; (iii) the agenda-setting encroachment of the militarisation of aid; and (iv), the known and unknown developmental and human rights impacts of the rise of China's inscrutable aid program and attendant expansion of its trade relations with (other) developing nations. He examines how each of these blurs such traditional boundaries as between trade and aid, the public and private, and the military and the pacific, as well as how and to what extent human rights can be ingratiated into the methods and goals of development. While noting that both development and human rights are more art than science, he argues that it is imperative for developmental economists, human rights activists, policy analysts, politicians, and international lawyers alike to engage with these features of New Aid in order "to formulate the regulatory frameworks (domestic and international) that enhance its potential and mitigate its human rights contradictions and detriments". To this end, Kinley concludes his essay by offering a set of broad "projections" that he suggests might guide these agenda-setters: to balance public/private developmental inputs; to engage more directly with non-Western donors; to more surely represent the combination of development and human rights goals in key global fora (such as the G20 and the Doha Round of trade talks); and to be both robust and realistic about what added value international human rights regimes bring to achieving development objectives, and vice versa.

Aid is in many ways a quintessential barometer of sender/target country relations. It is withdrawn when cold-shoulder punishment is being meted out, and it flows through business as usual channels when reward, sympathy, or seizing opportunity are in order. The modern history of development thinking has indeed oscillated between these two poles, and it is upon this platform that Mac Darrow mounts his analysis of the utility of Principled Engagement in the context of so-called "new aid modalities" in Chapter 11. Darrow offers a critical perspective on the 2005 Paris Declaration, which by "entrenching an unduly technocratic, managerialist and de-politicised development policy agenda" is essentially committing donors to move aid closer to business as usual approaches. While the new modalities that flow from this may be positive from a purely aid efficiency perspective (which he is careful to acknowledge as a notable benefit), there is the distinct prospect that aid effectiveness may suffer, in the sense that such risk aversion will undermine human rights guarantees. This is especially problematic, Darrow argues, in country situations where the threats to human rights are greatest – the very situations in which the need to adopt a rights-protecting approach, however configured, is correspondingly utmost. Notwithstanding that the UN was itself a signatory to the Paris Declaration, Darrow investigates the fact the UN has, in recent years, formulated a human rights advocacy agenda in its development work (more akin to old-style "donorship", conditionality approaches that the Paris Declaration was in part introduced to combat) and examines how this has been reconciled with the new aid modalities using a number of country case studies (including Cambodia, Mozambique, Tanzania, Vietnam, as well as in harder cases such as Uzbekistan, Iran and Myanmar). Concluding that there has been more incoherence than reconciliation between the two approaches, Darrow maintains that the Paris Declaration Principles need adjusting to arrest the slide towards uncritical support for target government priorities when human rights guarantees are at risk, and that the UN – despite its own Behemothian incongruities – is the appropriate (indeed mandated) organ to take the lead on this enterprise. Darrow makes clear that while he is cognisant of the danger of "overreacting" to human rights problems in the face of other pressing national concerns and circumstances, he highlights the need for "human rights bottom lines" that is provided by Principled Engagement.

In recognition of the necessity of making Principle Engagement practicable, Darrow concludes the chapter with a series of suggestions aimed at assisting the UN in undertaking its leadership role, including: building a better understanding of how to do human rights advocacy; greater collaboration (i.e. "mainstreaming') among different parts of the UN; more effective UN engagement in human rights policy dialogue with other donor agencies; and enhancing the technical guidance employed to assess national situations, including investing greater authority in Resident Coordinators. In this way, Darrow believes, the Paris Declaration Principles can be made to work *for* human rights, rather than against them or indifferent to them.

Given its wide scope and complexity, this book necessarily can only be a first foray into the subject of Principled Engagement. Our approach is deliberately eclectic, aimed at shedding light on a broad field of issues rather than reaching final conclusions. Yet it is our hope that by beginning to explore key questions, we can help facilitate more strategic policy thinking as well as encourage further systematic analysis in this area.

Chapter 2

The Theoretical Case for Principled Engagement

Morten B. Pedersen

The strategic choices underlying international human rights policies are inherently uncertain and highly case sensitive. We can rarely predict with any great confidence how particular targets will react to particular policies, since each case differs on numerous dimensions. There are, however, some general patterns in these influence attempts that, coupled with detailed knowledge and analysis of specific situations, can help guide decision makers. In this chapter, I seek to identify some of those general patterns, and in the process begin to build a theoretical case for Principled Engagement with repressive states.

The effect of any human rights policy depends on the characteristics of the target, including its position in the international system, the balance of power between pro- and anti-rights constituencies and, not least, the root causes of existing violations, all of which can vary greatly from place to place and time to time. In some cases, there may be little the international community can realistically do to help the victims of repression. Indeed, one of the underlying premises of this book is the need for greater realism about the ability of external actors to promote human rights, especially in the most repressive contexts. Yet, as we shall see, serious limitations as well as costs are commonly associated with both ostracising and normalising relations with repressive states, underscoring the need to explore alternative approaches. As one such alternative, Principled Engagement has, at least theoretically, several notable virtues and few downsides, assuming that it is properly designed and implemented.

Ostracism

Ostracism, to some degree or another, has become the default approach by Western governments to highly repressive states in the post-cold war era (except in countries like China or North Korea where other interests than human rights take precedence and demand engagement). Yet, empirically, this apparent faith in the civilising potential of coercive democracy promotion is on shaky ground. While proponents cite supposed successes in countries like South Africa and Poland, the spectacular failures in Cuba, Myanmar and Haiti, among others, demonstrate the limitations of Ostracism as a global strategy for promoting human rights in the more entrenched cases, as well as the significant risks it entails.[1] The increasing use of "smarter" targeted sanctions is a step forward, but provides only a partial solution to the fundamental problems with coercive measures that motivated this shift in the first place.

Limitations

Some limitations of Ostracism are intrinsic (i.e. general across all cases). Most importantly perhaps, since no international consensus exists on democracy as an international norm, this approach suffers from fundamental legitimacy problems. This makes it harder to gain broad international cooperation than if the objective is framed in the language of international human rights law.[2] It also increases the risk that the target will dismiss the efforts as just another "neo-imperialist ploy", especially if the sender is a major power. Many non-Western states resent both the implicit priority given to political rights and the use of coercive means. Already 25 years ago, Jan Egeland warned, "For Third World governments it is of particular importance that external criticism is founded on what the United Nations has established as internationally recognized human right standards ... Attempts to westernize human rights have only one effect: The international climate is further polarised."[3] With the decline in Western normative and material power since then, this is a growing problem that could ultimately defeat 60 years of efforts to build a viable international human rights regime, unless a new consensus can be built based on a higher degree of transnational dialogue and accommodation of different political and cultural perspectives. China, in particular, but also other rising powers, is increasingly challenging Western hegemony in many areas of international affairs, including human rights.

The problem of legitimacy is compounded by a lack of policy consistency. Because Ostracism disrupts senders' relations with the target state, bilateral human rights policy along these lines invariably becomes hostage to broader national security and economic interests and therefore tends to be pursued in a selective manner. The resulting double standards not only leave the citizens of some states largely without international protection, but also further weaken the perceived legitimacy of interventions when they do take place.

The limitations of Ostracism are drawn out clearer once we consider who the targets are. Ostracism rests on two core assumptions, both of which are deeply problematic for the group of highly repressive states that we are mainly concerned with in this book: (1) external pressure can induce authoritarian leaders to democratise; and (2) democratisation leads to broad improvements in human rights.

The first assumption finds little support in the academic literature, whether one looks to studies of sanctions as a general phenomenon or of democratisation more particularly. Although the conventional academic wisdom that "sanctions don't work" may overstate its case,[4] the conditions under which coercion is most likely to succeed are quite restrictive, providing little ground for optimism about the type of cases that we are concerned with in this book. There is near consensus in the literature that sanctions work better the higher the costs they impose on the target, the more democratic the regime is, and the more limited the objectives are.[5] To this, we might add the common-sense notion that coercive pressure works best when it builds on and reinforces strong internal pressure for change. Looking at our target group of highly repressive states, few if any of these conditions are likely to be satisfied.

First, in order to impose significant costs on the target, the senders must be an essential source of trade, investment, aid or other valued resources.[6] This condition is rarely satisfied for today's most repressive states, nearly all of which are located in non-democratic regions and have other authoritarian states as their neighbours and main allies and trading partners. Even if Western democracies can agree to apply coercive measures, it will in most cases be fairly easy for the targets to circumvent them and thus lower the costs of non-compliance.

Secondly, since authoritarian political power is typically accompanied by highly centralised economic control, leaders are often able to divert the economic costs imposed by sanctions away from themselves and their supporters and on to politically weak groups.[7] In fact, studies show that authoritarian elites are frequently able to exploit economic scarcities in a restricted economy to increase "rents" and thus, paradoxically, may actually benefit from sanctions.[8]

Thirdly, the political economy of authoritarianism makes such regimes resistant to the destabilising effects of sanctions, even in the case of fairly large economic losses.[9] Unlike democratic governments whose survival depends on providing public goods for the general population, authoritarian regimes normally rest on a fairly narrow support base, which can be bought off with private goods. Since the majority of people have no political voice, the overall economic welfare of society matters little. In other words, authoritarian regimes lack the "transmission belts" required to translate economic costs into political effects.

Fourthly, the potential costs of complying with demands for democracy are very high for the most repressive rulers. Not only do they stand to lose power and privileges, but they also risk being held accountable and punished for past abuses. Even if sanctions imposed significant costs, it is unlikely that any of the governments in our target group would willingly comply with the demand to subject their rule to genuinely popular elections, never mind institute the kind of substantive democratic reforms required to make elections work in the ways intended. For sanctions to be successful in such cases, they would likely have to induce an actual overthrow of the existing regime. This, however, is unlikely to happen under conditions of high repression, which significantly increase the costs of both opposition to and defection from the regime.

Many governments will make *some* concessions to try to undercut the push for international isolation, such as signing human rights treaties, releasing individual political prisoners, or even going as far as stage-managing nominally "democratic" elections (while ensuring that the incumbents win). Any reforms undertaken under duress are likely, however, to be largely cosmetic. Governments that have not internalised the underlying values (or do not at least see an intrinsic value in reforms), but comply with international norms for instrumental reasons only, are bound to "cheat" or revert to their old ways as soon as the pressure is released. Indeed, sanctions encourage such ritualistic behaviour by reducing human rights compliance to a mechanical cost-benefit calculation.

The related literature on international influence and democratisation reaches similar conclusions. While Levitsky and Way, for example, believe that Western pressure *can* influence democratic transitions, they argue that this depends on a high degree of "linkage" (i.e. social and economic interdependence between the sender(s) and the target).[10] Similarly, Kopstein and Reilly find that the diffusion of Western norms, resources and institutions depends on geographical proximity, as well as a country's openness and receptiveness to external influence.[11] Such studies may help explain why democracy has advanced in Europe or Latin America, but by the same token inspire little optimism about the prospects in much of Africa, the Middle East or Asia, where most of today's most repressive regimes are located and where key mediating factors of international influence are largely absent.

Importantly, even if international pressure can in some cases help induce democratic transitions, it is of little relevance to "the longer-term pouring of democratic content into a nascent democracy, necessary for high quality, liberal democracy".[12] This point is underscored in studies of externally enforced democracy. While foreign powers, for example, have overseen the establishment of formal democratic institutions in a number of countries, including Afghanistan, Cambodia, East Timor and Iraq, the end result has often been disappointing.[13] Indeed, Charlesworth dismisses as lacking any empirical basis the common assumption by democracy builders that international interventions "can act as a decisive break between a problematic traditional order and the clean and shiny new world of modern democracy".[14] If this is the case in situations where international agencies are in place to encourage the process, help establish basic security and support institution building and economic development, there is even less reason to believe that distant pressures can bring about meaningful and sustainable democratic outcomes in more insular and isolated countries.

Ultimately, the main conclusions emerging from the sanctions and democracy literatures are much the same: political change depends primarily on domestic factors. When these are hostile, international pressure is likely to be ineffective, or of limited enduring importance. In Przeworski's words: "Democracy cannot be exported; at most it can be imported ... the political impetus must come from within."[15]

The second assumption underlying Ostracism – that democratisation will be accompanied by broad advances in human rights – may at first glance appear to be on firmer ground. Democracy in itself represents a bundle of political and civil rights. Moreover, numerous studies have found democratic government to be strongly, and positively, correlated also with physical integrity rights,[16] and socio-economic rights.[17] This apparently promising picture fades quickly, however, once we disaggregate the *process* of democratisation. While the older (mainly Western) democracies, generally, score highly on respect for human rights, this is much less the case for the newer third and fourth wave democracies, many of which continue to suffer from illiberal governance, endemic corruption and crushing poverty.[18] This is consonant with Davenport and Armstrong's finding that positive effects of democracy on state repression are visible only at a relatively high level of "institutionalization" of democracy,[19] as well as with studies showing that development depends not on regime type as such, but rather on "good governance" (another institutional dimension).[20] Importantly, many new democracies do not appear to be in transition to more substantive, higher quality (liberal) democracy, but rather seem to be stuck in a twilight zone of mixed democratic and autocratic features with little prospect of reaching democracy's full human rights potential. This empirical problem resonates with the concerns expressed by students of international democracy building about the unlikelihood of imposed democratic institutions taking root in countries that lack key attributes, thus raising further questions about the appropriateness of Ostracism for our target group, which by definition are deeply hostile environments for democracy and human rights. In fact, some scholars warn that the instability of democratic transitions in such contexts can lead to more, not less, human rights violations.[21] This is particularly likely to happen in countries emerging from civil war, where the imposition of political (and economic) competition risk overwhelming weak institutions, leading to increased violence.[22]

A fundamental limitation of Ostracism is that it treats symptoms, not causes. Democracy is only indirectly, and often weakly, linked to the major causes of human rights violations, including armed conflict, underdevelopment and weak state capacity, never mind cultural foundations such as patriarchy. Similarly, as Uvin argues, sanctions "only scratch the surface of much deeper issues related to attitudes, interests, distribution of power, the nature of institutions and deficient knowledge".[23]

Importantly, and deeply paradoxical for a strategy that is rooted in a commitment to popular participation, the pursuit of democracy can be entirely divorced from the immediate concerns of local communities. This is especially the case in conflict-ridden and deeply impoverished countries where basic security or simply putting food on the table necessarily has greater immediacy for many people than, for example, the right to vote. Senders may argue that democratisation advance both peace and development, but this is at best a long-term, roundabout route, the relevance of which is often not perceived by those whose main concern is finding the next meal.[24] Alas, Ostracism by its very nature means that senders often have limited understanding of popular preferences in the target country (aside from what English-speaking dissidents or exiles may claim they are). This approach tends to be driven by external values and aspirations rather than those of the intended beneficiaries.

None of this implies that it is wrong to promote democracy; it does, however, underscore the need for more subtle and locally informed approaches to human rights and cautions against unrealistic expectations.

Counter-Productive Effects

If limitations were the only problem, Ostracism might still be justified as a means of bolstering international human rights law or simply standing up for "what is right". However, sanctions and isolation often have counter-productive effects, which raises serious questions about how moral this supposedly "moral approach" really is. While few systematic studies of the counter-productive effects of human rights sanctions exist, anecdotal evidence from the general literature suggest that they can take at least five broad forms: reactance, "rallying around the flag", defensive violations, collateral damage and domestic opposition cost.

International pressure often backfires. Like people in general, authoritarian leaders resent attempts by others to limit their behavioural freedom. Threatening demands therefore tend to produce an opposite effect, prompting the target to resist for the sake of resistance – or more precisely, to assert its freedom to choose. Psychologists refer to this phenomenon as "reactance" or "anti-conformity".[25] In an international relations context, it is particularly evident in post-colonial states where the experience of imperialism has bred xenophobic forms of nationalism, making resistance a matter of personal face as well as national pride. In such contexts, no self-respecting leader can be seen to give in to outside pressure. Indeed, any concessions might well undercut their personal authority and position of power within the ruling elite. Thus, rather than motivate repressive rulers to reform, sanctions may actually cause "a further 'hardening' of the regime around core bases of support, a preoccupation with showing resolve, and a declining willingness to make tradeoffs".[26]

Reactance is not limited to authoritarian leaders, but can take the form of a broader nationalistic backlash against the sender. In national security states, coercive interventions can feed into founding ideologies revolving around the need to defend the country's sovereignty and integrity against external influences, thus causing domestic groups to rally around the authoritarian leadership and actually strengthening the regime internally.[27] This effect was famously observed by Galtung in his early, seminal study of Rhodesia in the 1960s[28] and is fairly common, especially in countries with a high level of state control of the media, which can be used to "whip up" nationalistic fervour and scapegoat the foreign threat for home-grown problems.[29] Rallying around the flag is particularly likely to happen among security forces and other groups closely associated with the state, including privileged economic groups, yet can also extend to broader segments of the population. Recent documented examples include China after the Tiananmen Square massacre (see Chapter 5) and the Federal Republic of Yugoslavia during the Bosnian War.[30]

In addition to these negative motivational reactions, outside pressure often provokes defensive measures by the target to shore up regime stability. Sanctions are inherently threatening; they aim to strengthen the opposition, induce social unrest and encourage defections from the regime. Target regimes, therefore, frequently respond defensively in ways that negatively affect human rights. First, they ramp up political repression to impede any mobilisation of anti-regime forces.[31] This may involve a tightening of censorship, pre-emptive crackdowns on any signs of dissent, including increased use of extra-judicial arrests and torture, or a general reduction in political space. Secondly, they take steps to shield regime supporters from the adverse economic effects of sanctions and increase their rewards for loyal behaviour. The costs of sanctions are shifted downward to the general population, especially the politically weakest and economically most vulnerable, and scarce state resources are redistributed away from general development and social services.[32] Finally, target regimes strengthen controls of foreign influences, for example by further restricting international media, travel and other communications, as well as humanitarian agencies which typically come under suspicion of supporting the political agenda of their governments. This, in turn, reduces the ability of such actors to help the victims of bad and repressive governments. One of the most dramatic examples of this was the efforts by Myanmar's military rulers in the aftermath of Cyclone Nargis, which killed more than 100,000 people in 2008, to block access for foreign humanitarian efforts which they feared might mobilise popular anti-government sentiment.[33]

Sanctions can also cause major direct harm to the population. By denying the population the benefits of normal trade, investments, aid and other international exchanges, the measures taken to ostracise the regime invariably hurt many of the intended beneficiaries. As former UN Secretary-General Boutros Boutros-Ghali argued in his influential 1995 *Supplement to an Agenda for Peace* report, sanctions are "a blunt instrument that inflicts suffering on vulnerable groups, complicates the work of humanitarian agencies, [and] causes long-term damage to the productive capacity of target nations".[34] Subsequent research has provided ample evidence of just how serious such humanitarian consequences can be, especially in the case of comprehensive sanctions. The direct loss of jobs, income or aid is a major concern. To give another example from Myanmar, the imposition of a US import ban on Myanmar products in 2003 caused the immediate closure of around 200 garment factories and the loss of an estimated 75,000 jobs. This came on top of long-standing formal and informal aid sanctions that over two decades cost the country 10–15 billion aid dollars compared to similar least-developed countries.[35] Yet the most debilitating effects arise over time as the cumulative effects of international isolation and bad governance insidiously erode target countries' economic and social infrastructure, causing long-term damage that can only be reversed with great difficulty and at great expense. The international sanction regimes against Cuba (1960–present), Haiti (1991–1994), Iraq (1991–2003) and Burundi (1996–1999) are all tragic examples of these wider negative dynamics.[36] Although sanctioning governments may attempt to alleviate such harm through increased humanitarian assistance, this is a "fool's errand". Humanitarian assistance at best provides a Band-Aid for selected groups (and not necessarily those hardest hit by sanctions). Moreover, humanitarian actors are frequently caught between international sanctions regulations, which complicate the deliverance of aid, and local authorities who further restrict humanitarian space out of fear that foreign aid organisations might engage in subversive political activities. In theory, any short-term deterioration in human rights will give way to longer term improvements as authoritarian leaders are forced to concede or transfer power to a more rights-abiding government. However, for the poor who suffer double victimisation by their own and foreign governments, there may be no long-term future and the supposed benefits, as noted, often do not emerge.

Each of the counter-productive effects discussed here also tends to weaken domestic pro-democracy groups and human rights defenders who work to bring about change and protect the population. Once democracy and human rights become associated with foreign demands and pressure, these values are (further) delegitimised within the local context. This weakens moderates within the regime who risk being dismissed as unnationalistic, casts suspicion about opposition groups that come to be viewed as "fifth columnists", and generally makes it harder for domestic pro-rights constituencies to argue for change. At the more material level, increased repression and the weakening of the socio-economic basis of civil society also make it harder for opposition groups to organise and mobilise against the authoritarian regime. This is essentially a matter of increased risk – risk of suffering serious harm at the hands of security agencies, and risk of losing livelihoods. While economic stagnation in more affluent societies may produce social unrest, in already impoverished countries further scarcity is more likely to strengthen state control as people become more dependent on the state for their survival needs or simply do not have the time and resources to engage in politics. Sanctions also more directly weaken opposition groups by restricting opportunities for linking up with the outside world.

In sum, the effect of sanctions is often the opposite of what is intended. Rather than creating doubts and internal division in the ruling elite, coercive pressure may strengthen regime cohesion and rally broader groups behind the authoritarian leadership; and rather than strengthening pro-rights constituencies, it may make it harder to advocate and mobilise for change. Meanwhile, countries under sanctions often see an increase in political repression and deterioration in the socio-economic conditions of life for the general population. This, of course, describes a worst-case scenario, and the overall impact in many cases will be more ambiguous, with a mix of negative and positive effects, but the risk of making the situation worse is significant, especially in our target group of highly repressive, recalcitrant states.

Opportunity Costs

The opportunity costs of sanctions are harder to measure but potentially of major concern. They arise from senders' loss of ability to pursue alternative or complementary policies which might otherwise have helped to improve the human rights situation. International disengagement from the target country leads to a loss of knowledge and contacts needed to develop effective policies of any kind; it undercuts important long-term drivers of value change, such as international exposure and economic modernisation; and it restricts opportunities to work with reformers within the authoritarian regime, as well as with dissidents and human rights defenders, to bring about incremental change. It also limits the ability of senders to assist in areas where weak state capacity rather than deliberate state policy is the main cause of violations, and to help the victims of state repression directly. In pursuing human rights through isolation of the target regime, senders effectively abandon all non-coercive ways and means to improve the situation. Thus, human rights policy is reduced to an often illusive quest for regime surrender, while pro-rights constituencies within the target country, and not least the many victims of repression, are left to their own devices. As we shall see below, engagement, too, is likely to have only limited effect in the most repressive states, yet it may be the only real possibility of beginning to break down the stranglehold of the state on society.

"Smart" Sanctions

Over the past decade and a half, growing recognition of the political limitations, and especially the humanitarian cost, of comprehensive sanctions regimes have seen both an intellectual and a practical shift towards the use of so-called "smart" or targeted sanctions. Targeted sanctions are "the precision munitions of economic statecraft".[37] They include measures such as travel bans, freezing of financial assets, arms embargos and limited economic sanctions on sectors monopolised by the state.

The theory is that by targeting the interests of leaders of the offending states and their closest supporters rather than the general economy, sanctions can be made more effective and collateral damage can be minimised. The experience so far, however, is mixed at best. Targeted sanctions have proven very hard to implement effectively,[38] and often to be little more than a nuisance to decision makers.[39] In a study of 11 UN sanctions regimes between 1990 and 1999, Cortright and Lopez found that seven out of eight cases of smart sanctions had little or no effect.[40] Since they "spare" the broader population, they may be particularly ineffective as tools of regime change, which will generally require undermining the material basis of regime power, thus forcing the authoritarian leadership's hand.

Targeted sanctions do help reduce collateral damage and opportunity costs. Yet they do little if anything to overcome other perverse effects, such as reactance, defensive violations and domestic opposition costs which arise from threats to the ruling elite. It might be argued that the very concept of *targeted* economic sanctions is in fact a misnomer in highly centralised states since any reduction of the available resources, no matter what its cause, will lead to a redistribution of the remainder based on power; the authoritarian elite will serve itself first and the weak will suffer. Ultimately, as Bull and Tostensen conclude,

> it may very well turn out that smart sanctions are simply not smart enough to achieve the stated objectives, and remain a blunt instrument which will continue to cause violation of economic and social rights on a large scale. They

are probably an inappropriate instrument for the purpose of bolstering human rights.[41]

The key to more effective sanctions may lie less in "targeting" than in more flexibility and greater use of complementary policies. A number of scholars highlight the importance of bargaining. The effectiveness of sanctions, Rose argues, "comes not from [their] ability to punish or coerce, or from the severity of the economic hardship and social dislocation [they] may cause, but from [their] ability to encourage bargaining with the expectation of reducing or ending conflicts".[42] Rather than bludgeoning the target into compliance, the idea here is to use sanctions to nudge it towards a mutually acceptable agreement.

This "bargaining model" of sanctions requires a fundamentally different approach from the "punishment model" underlying Ostracism. First, bargaining depends on dialogue and therefore is hard to combine with diplomatic sanctions or other strongly condemnatory practices, which cut communications links and generate hostility between the parties. Secondly, there can be no bargaining without some willingness to compromise over policy goals. No authoritarian leader can afford to be seen to back down to international pressure, never mind to surrender power. In order to avoid an impasse, senders must be willing to "temper their demands [for regime change], either by offering face-saving outlets for the target state, or, if necessary, by making concrete concessions in exchange for compliance with a modified, but still meaningful, set of demands."[43] Thirdly, research shows the importance to successful bargaining of complementing threats with incentives (i.e. a "carrot and stick approach"). This may simply mean gradually lifting sanctions in response to partial concessions. However, it can also involve more "positive" incentives such as security guarantees (for example, amnesties for past rights violations) or economic or other assistance. In the most difficult cases – where targets are highly insular, or sender and target have a history of hostility – it may even be necessary to offer incentives without asking or expecting any immediate concessions in return, but rather to establish the basis for future "good faith" negotiations.[44] Like all other strategies, bargaining needs to be context sensitive. However, any sender who seeks agreement with the target rather than its defeat and surrender must be prepared to engage, negotiate and compromise. This is fundamentally at odds with Ostracism, and in fact has significant overlap with our concept of Principled Engagement.

None of the problems with Ostracism are universal. There have, however, been very few cases of sanctions bringing about democracy, and seeming success stories, such as South Africa and Poland, were relatively "easy" cases in that the target regimes were heavily dependent on the West, politically, economically, culturally or all of the above. Many, if not all, of the most repressive states today are much harder cases. They typically have highly insular, nationalistic leaders, are relatively isolated from the outside world (and prefer it that way), and are located in non-democratic regions. Meanwhile, Western normative and economic power is in decline globally, weakening the prospect that effective sanction regimes can or will be erected in the future for the purpose of promoting democracy. The best-case outcome of coercive pressure in many of these cases is likely to be superficial reforms, which in practice leave autocrats in power and broader human rights problems largely unaddressed.

There is a need also for greater realism about what the introduction of democratic institutions can achieve in the most repressive states, which often have no prior experience with democracy and tend to lack the social, economic and cultural underpinnings for the effective functioning of participatory institutions. If political reform heightens instability and elite fears of losing their socio-economic privileges, it may in fact result in increased repression and economic controls, to the detriment of human rights.

Even if we accept that democracy is ultimately required to guarantee human rights, it does not follow that this must be the immediate priority. Not only are incremental improvements in human rights possible within less than democratic structures, such improvements may in fact help to build the basis for a stable transition to a more meaningful, higher quality democracy down the road. This observation is particularly relevant to the group of highly repressive states that we are primarily concerned with in this volume. The more demanding and complex the human rights problems are, the greater the need to moderate the immediate ambitions. These are cases where idealism must probably give way to realism.

Business as Usual

Business as Usual, as a strategy for promoting human rights, essentially rests on a positive story of economic globalisation. Considering the costs of isolating repressive and often impoverished states, the opposite strategy of normalising international trade and investment can seem immediately appealing – and indeed states such as Chile, South Korea, Taiwan, China and Indonesia have made major strides in important areas of human rights, in part at least, as a result of their growing participation in the world economy. Whether these positive experiences are transferable to the countries in our target group is questionable, though. Like sanctions, the effects of foreign trade and investment on human rights depend critically on conditions in the recipient state, which in our cases are more likely to produce negative results.

Limitations

The positive story of economic globalisation runs something like this: (1) foreign trade and investment spur economic growth; (2) economic growth advances human development (socio-economic rights); and (3) human development generates popular pressure for civil and political rights. Each of these causal links is elaborated in the relevant theoretical literatures and supported empirically by quantitative studies. Yet in each case there are also important exceptions; in other words, any potentially positive effects are contingent on certain mediating conditions. Three counter-stories will serve to highlight the limitations of foreign trade and investment as a force for human rights, particularly when it comes to the most repressive regimes and weakest states.

Foreign trade and investment, theoretically, spur growth by increasing investments, transferring technology and expanding markets. Empirically, there is a clear and positive correlation between countries' economic openness and economic growth.[45] Yet not all forms of trade and investment are equally beneficial. While foreign involvement in manufacturing, for example, tends to conform to this positive story, that is much less the case for natural resources extraction, particularly oil and gas.[46] Unlike manufacturing, which tends to be privately owned, labour intensive and have significant positive up- and down-stream effects, the oil and gas sector is typically monopolised by the state and has weak links with the broader economy. It therefore does little to spur wider growth, unless state revenue is strategically reinvested to build the country's physical and human infrastructure and increase productive capacity in other areas. On the contrary, access for state elites to "easy wealth" tends to fuel corruption and diminish the need for sound economic management, resulting in less, or even negative, growth. It also increases the stakes of the political competition for control of the state and weakens the reliance of the state on society for taxation purposes, conditions which tend to increase conflict and fuel political repression within a context of weakened state accountability.[47]

The second part of the positive story of economic globalisation theorises both a direct and indirect link between growth and human development. Growth expands employment and income. It also increases government revenue, thus supporting increased public spending on social services. The overall result is better access for people to food, shelter, health and education. This, however, assumes that the benefits of growth are spread widely across the population, something which cannot be taken as given, especially in states which lack leadership commitment to human rights in the first place. Unless economic openness to the outside world is accompanied by economic freedom within recipient countries, the direct benefits of growth will be monopolised by the state and other economic elites. Under such circumstances, economic growth is unlikely to lead to human development and the expansion of social and economic rights unless the state itself has a strong redistributive focus. In sum, the developmental and human rights benefits of foreign trade and investment depend crucially on the degree of economic liberalisation and government commitment to poverty reduction and social services, which, in both cases, tend to be weak in our target group.

Even in countries where the benefits of growth are widely spread, political development does not necessarily follow. Although scholars have persuasively argued that the broader social processes associated with economic development and modernisation tend to undermine authoritarianism,[48] the empirical evidence for this theoretical proposition is ambiguous. While some quantitative studies show a strong positive link between economic development and democratisation,[49] others find only a weak link,[50] or none at all.[51] Scholars have also questioned the nature of any correlation; some say that development, rather than bring about democracy, simply sustains it once it is already in existence.[52] Theoretical arguments and statistical probabilities aside, authoritarian regimes in China, Vietnam, Singapore and elsewhere have proven adept at short-circuiting any causal links between economic and political development, using a mix of co-option and selective repression.[53] The more repressive a state is from the outset, the more likely it is that the government will act to curtail the scope for opposition and the less likely that growth will have a democratising effect. It may be, as some scholars suggest, that it is only a matter of time before the "dam will burst",[54] but certainly the political benefits of modernisation can be long delayed.

Given the complex and conditional nature of the link between foreign trade and investment and human rights, it should come as no surprise that the literature offers no conclusive answers to the general question of whether economic globalisation supports (or damages) human rights. Importantly for the present analysis though, this ambiguous overall picture hides systematic differences between different types of state which do not bode well for our target group. The human rights effects of foreign trade and investment are not arbitrary or indeterminate, but depend in large part on state policies and practices, in particular the presence or absence of conscious efforts to ensure that international economic exchanges, and economic growth more generally, benefit not only a narrow elite, but the population as a whole. As Dunoff observes, "Through the policies they enact, the practices they adopt and the safety nets they provide, states have a major role in determining whether globalization will, in the end, turn out to be more friend than foe of human rights."[55] Since the states with which we are primarily concerned tend to have highly centralised economies, to invest little in broad-based economic development or social services, and to repress those that threaten their power, the latter is much more likely than the former. This problem is compounded by the strong tendency for foreign economic involvement in countries that suffer from political instability, weak rule of law and low levels of development to be concentrated in the extractive sector, which has few direct benefits for the poor. In sum, there is little basis for confidence in the theories underlying Business as Usual strategies for promoting human rights in the most repressive states.

Counter-Productive Effects

In light of these limitations, the risk of serious counter-productive effects weighs heavily in any general assessment of Business as Usual. These take three broad forms. First, foreign trade and investment which overwhelmingly benefits the state can be used by an unpopular government to finance repression or co-opt support, thus potentially helping to prop up the regime. Secondly, foreign economic engagement may actually motivate an authoritarian elite to increase repression in order to capture the benefits. The prospect of huge windfalls from foreign investment in agriculture or export of agricultural products, for example, can be a strong incentive for economic elites to displace small landowners and further consolidate landholdings under their control. Similarly, governments keen to attract foreign direct investment in manufacturing might use repression to enforce industrial peace in situations of low wages and bad working conditions. Foreign companies contribute directly to such practices by entering into joint ventures with state-owned or crony companies, or forcing down prices in the supply chain.[56]

At the project level, foreign investments can harm human rights when, for example, abusive agents of the state are hired to provide project security, local communities are displaced to make room for new investment projects, or the environment is damaged. These are all too common occurrences in countries where local governments fail to take their responsibility to protect human rights seriously. Although steps are often taken, especially by Western companies and organisations, under the rubric of corporate social responsibility, to alleviate any such negative externalities, this only serves to underscore the need for any credible human rights policy to go beyond purely economic thinking. Indeed, the latter falls under the rubric of Principled Engagement.

Like democracy, there is no doubt that economic development is an important base and driver of human rights progress. Yet foreign trade and investment is not intrinsically beneficial; rather, it needs a "civilizing" element or influence.[57] Ideally, this would be provided by the recipient state in the form of investments in broad-based growth, protection of labour and environmental rights, redistribution of national revenue through social welfare programs, and so on. Yet, if national governments fail, the responsibility falls on the source of international trade and investment to ensure that it benefits human rights rather than harming them.

Ultimately, the problems with Business as Usual mirror those of Ostracism. It is asking a lot of international actors to affect fundamental structural changes in sovereign countries, whether political or economic, especially where domestic conditions for such changes are fundamentally weak. Further, the links between overarching political and economic structures and human rights are generally weak. In either case, domestic governance presents a critical intervening variable. For those committed to promoting human rights, this suggests a need for more nuanced approaches closer to the ground that seek to grapple with the more immediate, and often unique, causes of human rights violations. This is no less important in the most difficult and repressive contexts than elsewhere, and might in fact be particularly prudent in countries where structural change is strongly resisted.

Principled Engagement

Since Principled Engagement has rarely, if ever, been comprehensively applied in highly repressive states,[58] there are relatively few comparative experiences to draw on and little existing analysis (Chapters 3–11 in this volume begin to redress that lacuna). The serious limitations and costs frequently associated with both

Ostracism and Business as Usual, however, make a "negative" case for Principled Engagement (or at least for exploring alternative policy options). More positively, there are several theoretical reasons why we may have some general confidence in this approach, as laid out below.

Focusing on the Immediate Problem

The focus on agency, or governance, is a core strength of Principled Engagement. While policymakers and scholars alike tend to focus on the simpler world of macro-structures, it is the people within those structures that make policy, protect rights, or violate them. The problem with structural approaches such as Ostracism and Business as Usual is that they ignore the degree to which processes such as democratisation and development are given content by people, policies and institutions. There are big variations in the human rights situation among authoritarian regimes, and among poor countries. It stands to reason that improvements can be made without changing the structures. Conversely, changes in structures are no guarantee of improvements in human rights. Unless elections are accompanied by broader political freedoms and people are able to use them to hold rulers accountable, they may make little difference to who is in power and how they govern. And unless development is widely shared, the political and broader human rights benefits will remain limited. It would therefore seem prudent to focus on governance issues that have an immediate impact on people's lives and can help give substance to longer-term structural changes.

Overcoming Collective Action Problems

Another virtue of Principled Engagement is its potential to overcome collective action problems. The more difficult a policy objective is (and few are more difficult than promoting human rights in recalcitrant states), the greater the need for policy consistency *within* and coordination *across* senders. Yet, when it comes to international human rights promotion, one often looks in vain for either. Senders frequently struggle to maintain a clear and persistent commitment to human rights within their broader dealings with target states. Moreover, it is rare for different senders to agree on how to deal with highly repressive regimes. The gap is particularly pronounced between Western and non-Western governments, which tend to have not only different perceptions of national interests, but also different basic foreign policy orientations.

The problem of internal consistency is rooted in the priority given by *most* states in *most* situations to national security and economic interests over other people's human rights. Although promoting human rights is consonant with, and indeed necessary for, advancing international, and thus national, peace and prosperity, this general fit often breaks down when it comes to specific countries and policy choices. Human rights sanctions negatively affect security and economic interests, either directly by severing existing links between states or indirectly by creating hostility. Conversely, a single-minded pursuit of national interests often meets resistance from normative institutions and constituencies within sender states. Principled Engagement allows for a better calibration of otherwise conflicting objectives and thus facilitates greater policy consistency by governments committed to promoting human rights.

The problem of inter-state coordination is intrinsic to global governance. Yet, by charting a middle course between interventionist and hands-off approaches, Principled Engagement offers an opportunity to strengthen international consensus and cooperation on human rights. While Western governments may prefer Ostracism for ideological as well as symbolic (domestic political) reasons, they should appreciate the opportunity that a softer approach, less threatening to traditional notions of state sovereignty, offers to co-opt rising non-Western powers into an international order that continues to put a premium on human rights. For these rising powers, support for Principled Engagement provides an opportunity to gain international legitimacy within the existing liberal world order without sacrificing cherished values and interests of their own. In other words, Principled Engagement provides the most promising platform for building a truly global human rights regime and thus for optimising human rights outcomes across all states, including those that have fallen through the cracks in the current regime. This does not require that everyone does the same thing, only that policies are complementary.

Alleviating Sovereignty Concerns

Consistent and comprehensive pressure is a good starting point, but ultimately of course success depends on the ability of senders to get traction with those who are to be convinced to change their behaviour. This is no easy feat in a world of sovereign states where resistance to foreign "interference" in domestic politics remains high, especially among states which perceive human rights as Western-centric and subject to abuse by powerful nations pursuing vested interests. However, Principled Engagement alleviates such sovereignty concerns, for several reasons. First, its objectives are explicitly defined in terms of international human rights norms, which have been established primarily through the United Nations and to which most states in the world have committed themselves. This increases the legitimacy of sender concerns and pressure, making it harder for targets to outright reject cooperation. Secondly, Principled Engagement eschews the exercise of overt, coercive power and thus weakens the spectre of neo-imperialism. Less likely to raise nationalistic resistance, it helps move "negotiations" beyond the bluster often associated with coercive approaches and reduce resistance for resistance's sake. Thirdly, by emphasising governance reform over regime change, Principled Engagement leads with the thin end of the wedge, thus increasing the chances that it can break through the wall of political resistance that highly repressive regimes often erect around themselves. Once the "outer wall" is breached, the challenges of securing reform become more practical in character. National pride is less of an issue, and the focus moves to more objective interests. Governments are probably no more likely to be persuaded than coerced to concede power, but many human rights violations do not serve vital regime interests and are therefore open to negotiation under the right circumstances.

Dealing with Complex Causes

The causes of human rights violations are complex and varied. It is not simply a matter of government ill-will as proponents of Ostracism tend to assume, or of weak state capacity as Business as Usual advocates maintain. It may be both, or it may be rooted in factors outside the control of the state – and the cause, or causes, is unlikely to be the same in different countries and for different types of rights. The range and diversity of rights, as well as the multiple levels of government (and non-government) involved, calls for discrete, targeted approaches to different rights, not broad-stroke solutions. At issue here are not just the immediate causes of rights violations, but also the underlying causes. Given the weak status of human rights norms in our target group, reducing rights violations depends to a high degree on alleviating the reasons why they take place in the first place. Among other things, this means addressing issues of national (in)security and elite economic interests, which breed "rules of exception" and mobilise pro-violation constituencies.[59] These, again, are highly complex issues, which do not lend themselves to hands-off approaches such as Ostracism and Business as Usual.

The comparative advantage of Principled Engagement in this respect is clear. It is a much broader, multi-pronged and multi-layered strategy, which incorporates a greater range of influence mechanisms and directly engages a greater mix of actors both internationally and within the target state. This makes it possible to tailor policies to specific problems and supports a more in-depth approach that engages with the varied causes of human rights violations, both immediate and underlying. By giving up coercion, principled engagers are open to the use of a range of other influence mechanisms, including incentives, persuasion, socialisation and state capacity-building, as well as empowerment of the victims of rights violations. Importantly, this does not happen at the expense of pressure for change; rather, pressure is exerted in other, more context-sensitive ways. Business as Usual does potentially exert similar influences to Principled Engagement, but these are less "directed" and therefore more uncertain.

In addition to the greater number of influence mechanisms supported by Principled Engagement, this strategy harnesses a greater variety of senders with different comparative advantages. Unlike Ostracism and Business as Usual, which both require a high level of, especially economic, exchanges with the target state to be effective, and therefore tend to provide a meaningful role only for the most powerful or neighbouring states, Principled Engagement is an "equal opportunity" strategy. Bigger states may be able to offer greater incentives or material assistance. Yet, smaller states with fewer global interests often have greater moral authority and therefore greater persuasive power. The same goes for inter-governmental organisations (IGOs) and non-governmental organisations (NGOs), which also tend to have highly specialised skills and a strong on-the-ground presence.[60] Transnational corporations (TNCs) are a relatively new and controversial member of the club of human rights actors. Yet in repressive states they often have unique access to authoritarian elites. As buyers and investors, they also have the ability to directly influence workers' rights. Importantly, since IGOs, NGOs and TNCs are usually engaged in projects which have significant benefits for the target country, they are well placed to build long-term relationships and trust with local authorities and communities alike, which increase their potential influence in other areas, such as human rights. Not all of these actors are comfortable adopting a human rights agenda, yet if mobilised they can significantly broaden and deepen international influences in multiple, complementary ways. The greater number of senders also enhances the legitimacy of the whole exercise.

Mobilising Domestic Constituencies for Reform

The multi-fibred fabric of Principled Engagement is further enriched by the potential for building international–domestic partnerships for reform. Pro-rights constituencies exist even in the most repressive states, yet have demonstrably been unable to make progress on their own. At the same time, international actors have limited direct influence on critical governance processes. Principled Engagement offers a solution to this conundrum by facilitating direct linkages with soft-liners, technocrats, business owners and local communities, as well as traditional advocates of human rights such as opposition parties and human rights defenders. It may seem counter-intuitive to work with people within repressive regimes to promote human rights. Yet these are often the best placed to make a difference. Soft-liners, if co-opted, can provide protection for progressive programs, and technocrats often have a genuine commitment to public service (or at least to doing their job the best they can). Business owners will do what benefits their bottom line and may be persuaded to pay higher salaries or improve working conditions in their factories in order to attract responsible international buyers or investors. On the demand side, too, it behoves senders to look beyond the political opposition which may in fact be less effective than civil society groups or informal groupings of villagers that can push for human rights without threatening the power of existing elites. By working with these domestic pro-rights constituencies, international groups can actively support positive internal developments while at the same time pushing the boundaries of change. This also has the added advantage that change driven by domestic actors is more sustainable.

In sum, Principled Engagement is a more complex strategy for a very complex problem. It is also a more flexible strategy, which allows adjustments to be made and new elements to be added in response to changing circumstances on the ground. Principled Engagement may exercise less overt pressure on leaders than Ostracism, and contribute fewer resources than Business as Usual, but what it lacks in "strength" it makes up for in speed and agility.

Substituting the State

Typically, international human rights strategies aim, in different ways, to generate *domestic* will and capacity to institutionalise human rights in national law and practice. This, however, is often a long-term process, and in the meantime principled engagers have the ability to substitute for national mechanisms. By acting as witnesses to day-to-day abuses, foreign human rights and other organisations present on the ground in repressive states are often able to dissuade local agents of the state from abusing their power.[61] Aid organisations also help expand access for vulnerable groups to food, health and education, while companies provide jobs and income. This, of course, is not a sustainable solution to human rights problems, which must be respected, protected and fulfilled locally. But it helps bridge the gap between aspirations and reality, and it can make all the difference to victims of violations. Importantly, victories in these small skirmishes can contribute toward the overall war effort. Doing things right puts pressure on local authorities to do better, and provides models for how to do so. For individuals and communities, receiving help can be a novel and empowering experience, as they come to realise that repression is not natural. Foreign aid projects can also give the recipients practical experience of organising to promote common interests. The importance of this type of "modelling" should not be underestimated, especially in closed societies where knowledge of different ways of living and doing things is often limited.

Downsides?

Critics might argue that engagement provides legitimacy for bad governments or funds repression. This is indeed a risk in any form of engagement. Yet, for senders committed to *principled* engagement minimising any such benefits for the repressive regime is at least an integral part of the tactical decisions on how to engage (see Chapter 3 by Sidoti in this volume). Principled Engagement incorporates criticism of human rights violations where criticism is due (tempered only by the overriding priority of getting the target to stop such violations). Moreover, any assistance provided under a strategy of Principled Engagement would be subject to high standards of transparency and accountability. This is, of course, not a guarantee that no benefits can be derived by a cunning government, but it is worth noting that many repressive states in fact seek to restrict any foreign presence, which they fear could destabilise the authoritarian equilibrium. Such states clearly do not perceive benefits from being engaged, but rather must be persuaded or cajoled to open up. As the project director for a recent study on North Korea concluded: "We in the U.S. need to stop thinking of economic engagement as a carrot. It's more like some very bitter, foul-smelling medicine."[62]

Sceptics might further argue that efforts to promote reform within existing power structures have little prospect of producing major improvements in human rights. This is a potentially more serious concern. But the key question that we need to ask here is not how big the potential improvements are in absolute terms, but rather how big they are relative to those associated with alternative strategies. Principled engagers are likely at least to be able to pick the "low-hanging fruit". If, in addition, they can substitute in some small way for the state's failure to protect and fulfil basic rights and thus help people stay alive, the significance of their efforts should not to be easily dismissed. Importantly, small changes may be what are needed to open for broader changes in the medium to longer term. The potential benefits of expanding the horizons of insular leaders and perhaps alleviate their siege mentality are many. In countries suffering from armed conflict, a peace deal can dramatically change both the immediate human rights situation and the longer term prospects for demilitarisation and democratisation. Improved education has positive ripple effects across the political and economic spheres. Even if Principled Engagement does not produce major results immediately, it provides a vehicle for helping build the basis for quicker and more sustainable reform once the domestic political situation allows it.

Small, incremental changes may seem insignificant to activists fired up by moral indignation and deeply committed to saving the victims of human rights violations. However, there is something to be said for cooler heads to prevail when it comes to strategising. If Ostracism is in fact harmful, a policy of Principled Engagement that produces relatively small or delayed benefits may still be the better option. The reality is that, in some countries, there is only limited space for influencing the human rights situation. In these, the most difficult contexts, the alternative to incremental change will often be no change at all.

Like all "critical" approaches, the argument for Principled Engagement starts from a dissatisfaction with existing or mainstream ways of looking at and doing things. Few highly repressive regimes are vulnerable to defeat by coercion, and not many are sufficiently successful economically, or blind politically, to allow themselves to become obsolete. The argument here is not that Principled Engagement is the best strategy for dealing with all repressive states all of the time. Often, the optimal approach may be some combination of these or other strategies which have not been discussed here. Yet, a more prescriptive conclusion might be that Principled Engagement should be the strategy of *first* choice in the most repressive contexts, just as it is in more open or transitional societies.

Compared to the alternatives under consideration here, Principled Engagement has three clear theoretical advantages. First, it provides important insights into the outlook, power dynamics and abilities of the target regime, which helps assess the prospects of different strategies of promoting human rights. As Sidoti argues in Chapter 3 in this volume:

> Principled Engagement is an opportunity to "probe" the space for human rights change in countries that may, from afar, seem closed to such discourse, i.e. to look behind the wall of resistance that is often erected in response to international condemnation (or the veil of apparent indifference that may exist under conditions of normal cooperation).

Secondly, it establishes a direct link between international actions and human rights conditions on the ground, in both directions. While Ostracism and Business as Usual both rely on broad structural changes to advance human rights, Principled Engagement directs senders to identify priority problems affecting people in their daily lives and respond more immediately. As such, it is less likely that ongoing violations will be ignored and more likely that some form of relief will be forthcoming. This is something that ordinary people suffering from repression are bound to appreciate. Thirdly, Principled Engagement is less likely than the alternatives to do significant harm to the intended beneficiaries, provided it is done properly. Thus, one could argue that Ostracism or Business as Usual should be considered only once sufficient knowledge has been gained to assess their likely impact (through a period of Principled Engagement), and *if* Principled Engagement proves ineffective or insufficient.

In conclusion, Principled Engagement at the very least provides a theoretically compelling strategic framework for dealing with the manifold and complex challenges of international human rights promotion, not only in the easy cases where it is usually applied, but also in the more difficult and urgent ones with which we are concerned in this book. Whether it works, whether it works *better*, and under what conditions, are empirical questions, but certainly there is a need to further explore the potential of this strategy in particular cases.

Endnotes

1   Even in South Africa, the supposedly most clear-cut case of sanctions success, country specialists have voiced doubts about the conventional wisdom that sanctions forced the National Party government to the negotiation table. External pressure, they argue, was only a small part of a complex process of change that included also the high level of internal conflict and violence, the changing demands of the South African economy, and the demise of the threat of Communism. Philip I. Levy, "Sanctions on South Africa: What Did They Do?", *The American Economic Review* 89, no. 2 (1999), 415–20. Former South African President F.W. de Klerk argues that sanctions, by stymieing economic development, in fact delayed change and had little to do with his decision to dismantle apartheid. Willem de Klerk, *The Last Trek – A New Beginning: The Autobiography* (Basingstoke: Macmillan, 1998). For a similar analysis of the ambiguous impact of Western sanctions on Poland's Communist regime, see Gregory F. Domber, "Evaluating International Influences on Democratic Development: Poland 1980–89", CDDRL Working Papers No. 88, July 2008. Importantly, the conditions for democratisation were more favourable in both South Africa and Poland than they are in most, if not all, of the remaining highly repressive states. For a comparison of South Africa and Myanmar, see Morten B. Pedersen, *Promoting Human Rights in Myanmar: A Critique of Western Sanctions Policy* (Denver: Rowman & Littlefield, 2008), 259–61.

2   Contrary to democracy, few governments today openly reject the universality of core human rights standards, and the great majority of states have signed most of the major human rights covenants and treaties.

3   Jan Egeland, "Human Rights – Ineffective Big States, Potent Small States", *Journal of Peace Research* 21, no. 3 (1984), 210.

4   For a sweeping critique of sanctions as a tool of international statecraft, see, for example, Richard N. Hass, "Sanctioning Madness", *Foreign Affairs* 76, no. 6 (Nov/Dec 1997), 74–85; Ramesh Thakur, "Sanctions: A Triumph of Hope Eternal over Experience Unlimited", *Global Dialogue* 2, no. 3 (Summer 2003), 129–41. According to the most comprehensive study of sanctions success, economic sanctions have succeeded (i.e. contributed significantly to the partial or full achievement of the foreign policy goal) in about one-third of the cases over the past century. Gary Clive Hufbauer et al., *Economic Sanctions Reconsidered*, 3rd edition (Washington, DC: Peterson Institute for International Economics, 2007). This number, however, is strongly debated. See Robert A. Pape, "Why Sanctions Do Not Work", *International Security* 22, no. 2 (Fall 1997), 90–136; Kimberley Ann Elliott, "The Sanctions Glass: Half Full or Completely Empty?, *International Security* 23, no. 1 (Summer 1998), 50–65; Robert A. Pape, "Why Sanctions *Still* Do Not Work", *International Security* 23, no. 1 (Summer 1998), 66–77.

5   The argument outlined below draws mainly on the numerous studies of economic sanctions. However, very similar conclusions can be found in the related literature on aid conditionality and legal sanctions. Peter Uvin, *Human Rights and Development* (Bloomfield, CT: Kumarian Press, 2004), 56–82; Katarina Tomasevski, *Between Sanctions and Elections: Aid Donors and Their Human Rights Performance* (London: Pinter, 1997); Mark J. Osiel, "Why Prosecute? Critics of Punishment of Mass Atrocity", *Human Rights Quarterly* 22 (2000), 118–47; Martin Mennecke, "Punishing Genocidaires: A Deterrent Effect or Not?", *Human Rights Review* 8, no. 4 (July 2007), 319–39; Kenneth A. Rodman, "Dafur and the Limits of Legal Deterrence", *Human Rights Quarterly* 30 (2008), 529–60.

6   T. Clifton Morgan, Navin Bapat and Valentin Krustev, "The Threat and Imposition of Economic Sanctions, 1971–2000, *Conflict Management and Peace Science* 26, no. 1 (2009), 92–110; Elena V. McLean and Taehee Wang, "Friends or Foes: Major Trading Partners and the Success of Economic Sanctions", *International Studies Quarterly* 54 (2010), 427–47.

7   Kim Richard Nossal, "The Limits of Linking Aid and Trade to Human Rights", in Mark Charlton and Elizabeth Riddle-Dixon, eds, Cross-Currents: International Relations in the Post-Cold War Era (Toronto: Nelson Canada, 1993).

8   William H. Kaempfer, Anton D. Lowenberg and William Mertens, "International Economic Sanctions Against a Dictator", *Economics and Politics* 16 (2000), 29–51; David Lektzian and Mark Souva, "An Institutional Theory of Sanctions Onset and Success," *Journal of Conflict Resolution* 51, no. 6 (December 2007), 848–71.

9   Kim Richard Nossal, "Liberal-Democratic Regimes, International Sanctions, and Global Governance", in Raimo Varynen, ed., *Globalization and Global Governance* (Lanham, MD: Rowman & Littlefield, 1999), 127–49; David Cortright and George Lopez, *The Sanctions Decade: Assessing UN Strategies in the 1990s* (Boulder, CO: Lynne Rienner, 2000); Risa A. Brooks, "Sanctions and Regime Type: What Works and When?," *Security Studies* 11, no. 4 (Summer 2002), 1–50; Susan Hannah Allen, "The Determinants of Economic Sanctions Success and Failure," *International Interactions* 31 (2005), 117–38. Abel Escriba-Folch and Joseph Wright, "Dealing with Tyranny: International Sanctions and the Survival of Authoritarian Rulers", *International Studies Quarterly* 54 (2010), 335–59, modify this argument slightly, showing that, among authoritarian regimes, personalist regimes are relatively more susceptible to the loss of external revenue, while sanctions have little effect on single-party and military regimes.

10   Steven Levitsky and Lucan A. Way, "International Linkage and Democratization", *Journal of Democracy* 16, no. 3 (2005) 20–34.

11   Jeffrey S. Kopstein and David A. Reilly, "Geographic Diffusion and the Transformation of the Postcommunist World", *World Politics* 53, no. 1 (October 2000), 1–37.

12   Amichai Magen, "Evaluating External Influence on Democratic Development", CDDRL Working Papers No. 111, March 2009.

13   Karin von Hippel, *Democracy by Force: US Military Intervention in the Post-Cold War* (Cambridge: Cambridge University Press, 2000); Andrew J. Enterline and J. Michael Greig, "Against All Odds? The History of Imposed Democracy and the Future of Iraq and Afghanistan", *Foreign Policy Analysis* 4, no. 4 (September 2008), 321–47.

14   Hilary Charlesworth, "Building Democracy and Justice after Conflict", Cunningham Lecture 2006, Academy of the Social Sciences, 2007. See also Andrew J. Enterline and J. Michael Greig, "Against All Odds?".

15   Adam Przeworski, "No Democracy Without Free Competitive Elections", 29 April 2011, available at http://www.afronline.org/?p=14539 [accessed 18 July 2011].

16   Christian Davenport, "Constitutional Promises and Repressive Reality", *Journal of Politics* 58, no. 3 (1996), 627–54; Christian Davenport, "Human Rights and the Promise of Democratic Pacification", *International Studies Quarterly* 48, no. 3 (2004), 539–60; Linda Camp Keith, "Constitutional Provisions for Individual Human Rights", *Political Research Quarterly* 55, no. 1 (2002), 111–43; Bruce Bueno de Mesquita et al., "Thinking Inside the Box: A Closer Look at Democracy and Human Rights", *International Studies Quarterly* 49, no. 3 (2005), 439–57.

17   Morton H. Halperin et al., *The Democracy Advantage: How Democracies Promote Prosperity and Peace* (New York: Routledge, 2005).

18   Fareed Zakaria. "The Rise of Illiberal Democracy", *Foreign Affairs* 76, no. 6 (1997), 22–43; Joel D. Barkan, "Protracted Transitions Among Africa's New Democracies", *Democratization* 7, no. 3 (2000), 227–43; Marina Ottaway, *Democracy Challenged* (Washington, DC: Carnegie Endowment for International Peace, 2003).

19   Christian Davenport and David A. Armstrong, "Democracy and the Violation of Human Rights", *American Journal of Political Science* 48, no. 3 (2004), 538–54. See also Bruce Bueno de Mesquita et al., "Thinking Inside the Box".

20   The World Bank, *The East Asian Miracle: Economic Growth and Public Policy* (Washington, DC, 1993); Ashutosh Varshney, "Why Have Poor Democracies Not Eliminated Poverty?", *Asian Survey* 40, no. 5 (September–October 2000), 718–36. Larry Diamond, "Moving Up Out of Poverty: What Does Democracy Have to Do with It?", CDDRL Working Papers No. 4, 11 August 2004. Statistical studies by both the World Bank and the UN Development Programme (UNDP) fail to establish a link between regime type and the rate or distribution of economic growth: The World Bank, *World Development Report 2001* (Washington, DC, 2001); UNDP, *Human Development Report 2002* (New York, 2002), p. 4.

21   Helen Fein, "More Murder in the Middle: Life Integrity Violations and Democracy in the World", *Human Rights Quarterly* 17, no. 1 (1987), 170–91; Patrick M. Regan and Errol A. Henderson, "Democracy, Threats and Political Repression in Developing Countries: Are Democracies Internally Less Violent?", *Third World Quarterly* 23, no. 1 (2002), 119–36.

22   Roland Paris, *At War's End: Building Peace After Conflict* (Cambridge: Cambridge University Press, 2004).

23   Uvin, op. cit., 65–7.

24   Ardeth Maung Thawnghmung, *Behind the Teak Curtain: Authoritarianism, Agricultural Policies and Political Legitimacy in Rural Myanmar* (London: Kegan Paul, 2004).

25   S.S. Brehm and J.W. Brehm, *Psychological Reactance: A Theory of Freedom and Control* (Academic Press, 1981).

26   Stephan Haggard and Marcus Noland, "Engaging North Korea: The Role of Economic Statecraft", East-West Center Policy Studies No. 59, 2011.

27   George A. Lopez and David Cortright, "Economic Sanctions and Human Rights: Part of the Problem or Part of the Solution?", *The International Journal of Human Rights* 1, no. 2 (Summer 1997), 9–10; Ernest H. Preeg, *Feeling Good or Doing Good with Sanctions* (Washington, DC: CSIS Press, 1999), 7–10; Robert A. Pape, "Why Economic Sanctions Do Not Work", *International Security* 22, no. 2 (Fall 1997), 106–7; Reed M. Wood, "A Hand Upon the Throat of the Nation: Economic Sanctions and State Repression, 1976–2001", *International Studies Quarterly* 52 (2008), 495.

28   Johan Galtung, "On the Effect of International Economic Sanctions: With Examples from the Case of Rhodesia", *World Politics* 29, no. 3 (1967), 378–416.

29   Zachary Selden, *Economic Sanctions as an Instrument of American Foreign Policy* (Westport, CT: Praeger, 1999); Marla Tannenbaum and William Rose, "When and Why Economic Sanctions Strengthen the Target Regime: A Constructivist Examination of the Impact of State Control of the Media in Serbia". Paper presented at the Annual Meeting of the International Studies Association-Northeast, Philadelphia, 6 November 2003.

30   Ibid.

31   Dursun Peksen and A. Cooper Drury, "Economic Sanctions and Political Repression: Assessing the Impact of Coercive Diplomacy on Political Freedoms", *Human Rights Review* 10 (2009), 393–411; Emilie M. Hafner-Burton, "Sticks and Stones: Naming and Shaming the Human Rights Enforcement Problem", *International Organization* 62 (Fall 2008), 689–716.

32   Reed M. Wood, "A Hand Upon the Throat of the Nation: Economic Sanctions and State Repression, 1976–2001", *International Studies Quarterly* 52 (2008), 489–513. For a more general account of the association between perceived threats and increased state extraction of resources from society, see David Lektzian and Brandon C. Prins, "Taming the Leviathan: Examining the Impact of External Threat on State Capacity", *Journal of Peace Research* 45, no. 5 (2008), 613–31.

33   International Crisis Group, *Myanmar After Nargis: Time for Normalising Aid Relations*, Asia Report No. 161, 20 October 2008. Another example is the move by the Sudanese government, after the issuance by the International Criminal Court in 2009 of an arrest warrant for President Omar al-Bashir on war crimes charges, to expel 10 foreign aid agencies. Government officials justified this by reference to what they saw as collusion between these agencies and hostile governments. Peter Martell, "Sudan Expels Aid Agencies after ICC Warrant", *AFP*, 4 March 2009.

34   Boutros Boutros-Ghali, *Supplement to an Agenda for Peace*, A/50/60, 3 January 1995, p. 16.

35   Morten B. Pedersen, *Promoting Human Rights in Myanmar: A Critique of Western Sanctions Policy* (Denver: Rowman & Littlefield, 2008).

36   For a good summary of the relevant research on Cuba, Iraq and Burundi see Marc Bossoyt, *The Adverse Consequences of Economic Sanctions on the Enjoyment of Human Rights*, report prepared for the United Nations Economic and Social Council, E/CN.4/Sub.2/2000/33, 21 June 2000. On Haiti, see Elizabeth Gibbons and Richard Garfield,

"The Impact of Economic Sanctions on Health and Human Rights in Haiti, 1991–1994", *American Journal of Public Health* 89 (1999), 1499–504; Elizabeth Gibbons, *Sanctions in Haiti: Human Rights and Democracy under Assault* (Westport, CT: Praeger, 1999).

37 Daniel W. Drezner, "Sanctions Sometimes Smart: Targeted Sanctions in Theory and Practice", *International Studies Review* 13 (2011), 96–108.

38 Joy Gordon, "Smart Sanctions Revisited", *Ethics & International Affairs* 25, no. 3 (2011), 315–35.

39 Michael Brzoska, "From Dumb to Smart Sanctions? Recent Reforms of UN Sanctions", *Global Governance* 9 (2003), 531–2.

40 David Cortright and George A. Lopez, *The Sanctions Decade: Assessing UN Strategies in the 1990s* (Boulder: Lynne Rienner, 2000).

41 Beate Bull and Arne Tostensen, "Bolstering Human Rights by Means of 'Smart' Sanctions", in Hugo Stokke and Arne Tostensen (eds), *Human Rights in Development Yearbook 1999/2000* (The Hague, Kluwer Law International, 2001).

42 Euclid A. Rose, "From Punitive to a Bargaining Model of Sanctions: Lessons from Iraq", *International Studies Quarterly* 49 (2005), 472. See also Michael Chaitkin, *Negotiation and Strategy: Understanding Sanctions Effectiveness*, Center on International Cooperation, New York University, 2009; David Cortright, "Powers of Persuasion: Sanctions and Incentives in the Shaping of International Society", *International Studies* 38, no. 2 (2001), 113–25.

43 Chaitkin, op. cit., 12.

44 Cortright, op. cit., 120. See also David Cortright, "Incentive Strategies for Preventing Conflict", in David Cortright (ed.), *The Price of Peace: Incentives and International Conflict Prevention* (Lanham, MD: Rowman & Littlefield Publishers, Inc., 1997), 275–80.

45 Jeffrey L. Dunoff, "Does Globalization Advance Human Rights?", *Brooklyn Journal of International Law* 25 (1999), 125–9.

46 Andrea Mihalache-O'Keef and Quan Lin, "Modernization vs. Dependency Revisited: Effects of Foreign Direct Investment on Food Security in Less Developed Countries", *International Studies Quarterly* 55 (2011), 71–93.

47 This phenomenon is often referred to as the "resource course", typified by such oil-rich states as Nigeria.

48 For an overview of the modernisation thesis, see Ronald Inglehart and Christian Welzel, "How Development Leads to Democracy", *Foreign Affairs* 88 (2009).

49 According to a recent survey, the level of development (measured as GDP/capita) explains 40 per cent of the variation in democracy, or 60 per cent if one includes a dummy variable for oil wealth, which increases GDP but often inhibits democratisation. The Economist, "The Economist Intelligence Unit's Index of Democracy 2008", 2009, available at http://graphics.eiu.com/PDF/Democracy%20Index%202008.pdf [accessed 16 December 2012].

50 John B. Londreagan and Keith T. Poole, "Does High Income Promote Democracy?", *World Politics* 49 (October 1996), 1–30.

51 Adam Przeworski and Fernando Limongi, "Modernization: Theories and Facts", *World Politics* 49 (January 1997), 155–83.

52 Ibid.

53 According to Bruce Bueno de Mesquita and George Downs, "Development and Democracy", *Foreign Affairs* 84 (2005), 78, "Authoritarian regimes are getting better and better at avoiding the fallout of economic growth – so good, in fact, that such growth now

tends to increase rather than decrease their chances of survival." They explain this by the ability of such regimes to impede political coordination among opposition groups without seriously affecting the economic coordination needed to deliver growth.

54   Daniel Deudney and G. John Ikenberry, "The Myth of the Autocratic Revival: Why Liberal Democracy Will Prevail", *Foreign Affairs* 88 (2009), 77–93; Inglehart and Welzel, op. cit.

55   Dunoff, op.cit., 137–8.

56   In addition to the direct effects of foreign trade and investment, pressure by the World Trade Organisation (WTO) (and the international financial institutions) on developing countries to undertake neo-liberal economic reforms have been widely criticised for harming the poor.

57   David Kinley, *Civilising Globalisation: Human Rights and the Global Economy* (Cambridge, UK: Cambridge University Press, 2009).

58   China probably comes closest, but human rights have not been a significant focus of the China policies of, for example, the US and the EU.

59   Sonia Cardenas, *Conflict and Compliance: State Responses to International Human Rights Pressure* (Philadelphia: University of Pennsylvania Press, 2007), 28, defines "rules of exception" as historically conditioned myths that justify violations of international human rights in particular national contexts.

60   Contrary to diplomats who tend to be generalists, those working for IGOs and NGOs are often experts in areas such as human rights law, mediation, community development or malaria prevention.

61   Mark Duffield, "On the Edge of 'No Man's Land': Chronic Emergency in Myanmar," Centre for Governance and International Affairs, University of Bristol, Working Paper No. 01-08, 2008.

62   *North Korea Inside Out: The Case for Economic Engagement*, Report of an Independent Task Force convened by Asia Society Center on US–China Relations and The University of California Institute on Global Conflict and Cooperation, December 2009.

Chapter 3
Ten Principles for Engagement

Chris Sidoti

I have been engaged with human rights since the 1980s. I worked with human rights non-government organisations in the Philippines during the Marcos dictatorship. I was a member of the first two Australian human rights delegations to China, in 1991 and 1992, in the aftermath of the Tiananmen Square massacre. I was also a member of the first Australian human rights delegation to Vietnam in 1995. I worked with the Indonesian National Commission on Human Rights during the Suharto dictatorship in the 1990s. Most controversially, I conducted human rights training programmes for government officials in Myanmar between 2000 and 2003. And so on. I hadn't fully appreciated it until now, but what I have been trying to do for the better part of three decades has been Principled Engagement.

Principled Engagement by definition must be based on principle. To ensure that its practice is clear it is important to articulate what those principles are. Drawing on my many years of experience of what I now know is Principled Engagement, I propose ten principles for this approach to human rights work.

Three Experiences

Let me first say a little about the three principal experiences I will refer to in this discussion. They are examples at the hardest end of the Principled Engagement spectrum, relating to human rights work in some of the most difficult contexts. The results were questionable and limited in two of the three cases. I have selected them on the basis that, if Principled Engagement has something important to offer in these situations, then it has wide application to human rights work generally.

The Australian Human Rights Delegations to China

In 1989, the Chinese government and the People's Liberation Army used extreme force to disperse large peaceful demonstrations in and around Tiananmen Square in central Beijing, killing a significant but unknown number of people and arresting many thousands of others. The repression came as a shock to many governments and to human rights advocates, who were expecting far better of the reforming Chinese regime.

For two years after Tiananmen, China was shunned by many states, though not by all by any means. It faced unusual criticism in the United Nations Commission on Human Rights but, with the support of its friends, who formed a majority, China was able to prevent the Commission from adopting any critical resolution against it throughout the 1990s.

Most states that were critical of China realised that the isolation of China was not possible, even if it had been desirable as a strategy. By the early 1990s they had begun to explore ways to establish a relationship with China that included engagement on human rights. The Australian government sought and obtained the agreement of the Chinese government to hold a bilateral human rights dialogue.

The first official Australian human rights delegation visited China in July 1991 and the second visited in November 1992. The delegations were formally parliamentary delegations as they were led by members of parliament. Each of the delegations included three members of parliament, one from the governing Labor Party, one from the opposition Liberal Party and one from the Australian Democrats, which then held the balance of power in the Australian Senate. The delegations also included human rights experts, China scholars, interpreters (including interpreters of Tibetan and Uighur) and foreign ministry officials. The mix of expertise in the delegations enabled them to cover wide areas of knowledge so that they were able to enter into very detailed discussions of critical issues with their Chinese counterparts.

The delegations visited China for two weeks each time. The visits included discussions with government officials and academics, visits to prisons and other places of detention, and other types of government activity relevant to human rights. The first delegation went to Tibet and the second to the Xin Jiang Autonomous Region, two regions where there was significant opposition to Chinese control. The delegations were not, and did not pretend to be, on an investigatory mission. They did not have the mandate for that and it was not their role. Their purpose was dialogue but their mere presence, which was well known at times in some places, brought attention to human rights that would not have been possible otherwise. The dialogues were always frank, very direct and often challenging to both sides. Certainly the Australian delegations obtained and released far greater knowledge of Chinese law and the legal system, and of human rights in China, than had previously been available.

On both occasions the delegations invited the Chinese government to reciprocate with delegations to study human rights in Australia and to continue the dialogues here. The Chinese government responded but showed little interest. Senior ministers said, almost this bluntly, that China had many challenges in developing and modernising and was not all that concerned about the human rights situation in a small, rich country like Australia. However, at the same time, many of the interlocutors showed considerable knowledge about and interest in the position of indigenous people in Australia.

There was a gap of some years after these two delegations before bilateral human rights dialogues between Australia and China resumed. On their resumption, the dialogues were undertaken on a very different basis: as annual meetings between officials, usually in Beijing or Canberra, without visits to remote or troublesome regions or to prisons and places of detention, and with little contact with experts beyond the foreign ministries.

The Indonesian National Commission on Human Rights

General Suharto took control of Indonesia in October 1965 and remained in power for over 30 years. He led a dictatorship that was based on military repression but which increasingly became a personal and family business. During these decades the Indonesian military waged lengthy wars without restraint in East Timor, West Papua and Aceh. People throughout the country were subjected to serious violations of human rights. For most of the time, however, Suharto and his government were concerned about their international image and credibility and sought to find ways to look better than they were.

In 1993 the United Nations (UN) convened its second world conference on human rights, in Vienna, Austria. The then Foreign Minister of Indonesia, who faced some pressure at the conference due to the human rights situation under the Suharto dictatorship and Indonesia's long-standing occupation of East Timor, announced his government's intention to establish a national human rights institution. There was no doubt that this was done to improve Indonesia's image before an international audience. The National Commission on Human Rights (Komnas HAM) was established in 1994.

The new Commission had good leadership with high-level access within the government, including at times to President Suharto himself. Although much scepticism was expressed at the time of its establishment, it quickly proved itself to be a serious and independent institution through the conduct of inquiries into incidents of serious human rights violation. The Suharto regime had little tolerance at the time for work by Indonesian human rights NGOs. In fact it often arrested, intimidated, tortured and sometimes "disappeared" human rights defenders. Komnas HAM had the space to act, with relative freedom, because it was an official state institution established by a Presidential decree. While its status was not secure and it lacked many important guarantees of its independence, its leaders were serious, innovative and courageous in driving a human rights agenda, particularly in investigating incidents of serious violations.

Very early in the life of Komnas HAM, the Australian Human Rights Commission had to decide whether and, if so, how, to relate to it. The then Australian Human Rights Commissioner, Brian Burdekin, decided on engagement. Komnas HAM presented a unique opportunity for serious human rights work in Indonesia, the first significant opportunity for many years and an opportunity too important to pass up. I continued that approach when I succeeded Brian Burdekin in 1995. The following year, when the Australian Commission convened the first regional meeting of national human rights institutions, Komnas HAM was invited. At the July 1996 regional meeting, it became a founding member of the Asia Pacific Forum of National Human Rights Institutions. The Australian Commission became heavily involved in supporting Komnas HAM, through human rights training programs, Commissioner and staff exchanges and study tours, and participation in the Asia Pacific Forum.

When the Suharto dictatorship became embroiled in crisis in early 1998, the leaders of Komnas HAM played important roles. It undertook investigations of serious incidents of disappearance and violence and reported fearlessly. In May it played a leading role in encouraging the President to resign and promoting a peaceful transition to democracy. Then during the transition period it continued its work of investigating human rights violations and again demonstrated its integrity through thorough reporting.

Komnas HAM has continued under the democratic system in Indonesia. Its legal status has been strengthened, now having a constitutional basis in the place of the original presidential decree. It has more staff who are now working in a large number of regional offices. And it makes a great contribution to the establishment and strengthening of other human rights institutions in the region, through the Asia Pacific Forum.

The Myanmar Human Rights Training Project

In 1999, after almost ten years of stalemate in dealing with the Myanmar military regime, the then Australian Minister for Foreign Affairs, Alexander Downer, commenced a low-profile initiative to engage senior leaders of the regime in a bilateral human rights project. His hope was to see the regime establish a national human rights institution that might prove to be an actor in bringing change to Myanmar, as Komnas HAM had done in Indonesia. He had raised the possibility of establishing a human rights institution with his Myanmar counterpart in the margins of a meeting of the Foreign Ministers of the Association of Southeast Asian Nations (ASEAN). Surprisingly, the Myanmar Foreign Minister expressed interest and agreed to a visit by an Australian expert for discussions.

I was the Australian Human Rights Commissioner at the time and, through the regional association of national human rights institutions, the Asia Pacific Forum, I had been working with states in the region to establish and strengthen national institutions. The Minister asked me whether I would be prepared to make a short visit to Myanmar for the discussions agreed at the ASEAN meeting. After some consideration and consultation I agreed and stopped in Yangon for two or three days after an Asia Pacific Forum workshop that year in Sri Lanka. I met with General Khin Nyunt (then the de facto Prime Minister and later formally appointed as Prime Minister until being purged by the regime in 2004), several ministers (most of whom fell with General Khin Nyunt in 2004) and senior officials. The establishment of anything approaching even a partially independent national human rights institution seemed a long way off but there was far more openness than I had expected to engaging in joint work on human rights, initially through human rights training for government officials.

The human rights training project began in October 2000 and continued until April 2003. The project leader was Professor David Kinley, then at Monash

University's Castan Centre for Human Rights Law. I contributed to many of the courses, along with academics from the Castan Centre.

We were assured that all participants would be encouraged to speak freely and they were so encouraged in our presence at the beginning of each course. At first there was little evidence that the participants took this encouragement seriously, but over the three-year period they gradually became more relaxed and developed confidence in our seriousness. In time, many participants were quite open and at times critical in their comments – at least in private conversations. These years were times of increasing speculation about the intentions of the regime. There was evidently a slightly reformist group under General Khin Nyunt that saw a need for at least some change in the system. The extent of their influence was unknown but the discussions in the courses always came round to the possibilities for change.

At first, participants were all officials regarded by their superiors as safe but the range of backgrounds of participants widened over the project's three years. The courses came to include local academics, including legal academics who had never before had an opportunity to learn about human rights and who began to teach in the universities what they were learning from us, using the course materials. They came to include representatives from organisations that were outside the government, even though tightly controlled by the regime. Towards the end, there were representatives from ethnic minority groups and organisations. We asked many times for invitations to be issued to political parties, including the National League for Democracy, the party of Daw Aung Suu Kyi, but we were told that the time was "not yet right" for that.

Throughout the three years, on each visit we continued to meet ministers and senior officials and discussed with them not only the courses but broader questions of human rights in Myanmar and Myanmar's engagement with the international human rights system. On my first visit, I asked to see Daw Suu Kyi, who was then under house arrest, if she was willing to see me. I was permitted to meet her on the next visit. In 2001, the following year, she was released from house arrest. I discussed with the regime's leaders the request of the Special Rapporteur on Myanmar of the United Nations Commission on Human Rights to make an official visit to Myanmar. Following these discussions, the then recently appointed Special Rapporteur, Paulo Sergio Pinheiro, was permitted to visit on several occasions whereas his predecessor had not been able to make a single visit. I am not claiming that the engagement with Myanmar was the cause of these positive developments, only that it may have played some part.

In April 2003, David Kinley and I visited Myanmar again to discuss the next stage of the project. It was agreed with the Myanmar authorities that the next stage would widen further the range of participants and take the training into new areas of the government. Then, in May, Daw Suu Kyi's convoy was attacked and many of her colleagues killed. She herself was returned to house arrest. The project could not continue in such circumstances and so it was first suspended and then, when a year later there was no sign of improvement, it was cancelled. The brief period when some change seemed possible came to an end in October 2004 when General Khin Nyunt and his group within the regime were purged.

Drawing on these three experiences and many others, I propose my ten principles for Principled Engagement.

Ten Principles

Principle 1: Principled Engagement must be principled, directed towards the full enjoyment of all human rights by everyone

The first principle provides the direction or orientation for the engagement. Principled Engagement is a strategy, not an objective, and so of itself it provides no values basis for work. But it cannot be directionless. There must be clarity about the purpose of the engagement and its objectives. For human rights engagement the purpose is the full enjoyment of all human rights by everyone.

The full enjoyment of all human rights by everyone recognises both the universality of human rights and their comprehensive nature. Human rights touch every aspect of a person's life and of the life of the community. In all countries human rights are compromised in one way or another. Some countries are committed to meeting economic and social rights, for example, while ignoring or even opposing civil and political rights. Others do the reverse. Principled Engagement respects and promotes all human rights. We need to be clear about this.

While engagement may be cooperative and even friendly, those with whom we cooperate must be aware of our values and objectives. There should be no equivocation or ambiguity. We are prepared to cooperate, indeed to engage, but our values and objectives are not compromised. On the contrary, anyone wishing to know the basis upon which we engage should have no doubt of the commitment to the full realisation of all human rights for everyone. This can lead to difficult conversations and can even threaten the relationship at times. Nonetheless, without this basic principle, Principled Engagement is not possible.

In fact, in my experience, clarity about human rights objectives is possible without making cooperation impossible. During the human rights delegations to China and Vietnam, those with whom we spoke were of no doubt where we stood. They knew of our national and individual positions of support for human rights. During the human rights training project in Myanmar, leaders of the military regime entered into discussions with us about human rights and our views on the universality of human rights and their applicability to all nations. In neither context did our openness on this end the engagement. On the contrary it enabled very frank discussions, including serious disagreements, about critical issues.

Principle 2: Principled Engagement must be engaged, directly involving and challenging state authorities to ensure better compliance with human rights obligations

Principled Engagement is not a strategy of staying remote but one of being actively involved. It means sitting and talking, sometimes with people who are personally responsible, directly or indirectly, for human rights violations. It requires exchanging views, expressing opinions, acknowledging both achievements and deficiencies, debating and at times arguing.

The engagement needs to be respectful and honest. There are some regimes whose human rights records are such that any praise is impossible. The regime in North Korea comes immediately to mind. The great majority of governments, however, are neither all good nor all bad. They lie along a spectrum of human rights performance. Even those whose records are appalling often have significant human rights achievements that have to be acknowledged. Unless their achievements are acknowledged, criticism of their deficiencies is easily dismissed as unfair, unbalanced, political rather than legal, and motivated by objectives other than human rights.

There is no doubt that the human rights performance of China falls far short of international legal standards. At particular times and in particular places it has been appalling. Nonetheless, the Chinese government can rightly claim some great achievements in human rights promotion and protection. The most important is that China now feeds more than a fifth of the world's population, an extraordinary human rights achievement by any standards. Criticising China's human rights performance without acknowledging such an achievement is truly unbalanced and unfair. The human rights delegations to China in 1991 and 1992 were always careful to acknowledge this achievement and other similar human rights achievements of the Chinese government. The Chinese government has certainly advanced economic and social rights in China over the last 30 years, although there has been little advance in civil and political rights. The delegations were sharply critical of events such as those in Tiananmen Square in 1989 and the continual repression in Tibet. Because they were fully engaged with their Chinese dialogue partners, they were able both to praise and to criticise as appropriate. In doing so, there was more legitimacy in the criticism and a greater willingness on the part of the dialogue partners to engage in return. Most of all, however, recognising the achievements was simply right and proper.

Principled Engagement with the Myanmar military regime was no doubt pushing the limits of the strategy for promoting and protecting human rights. When I was involved in the human rights training project there, I felt at times that I was literally supping with the devil. I dined on many occasions with the Minister for the Interior who was responsible for the police and prisons. I drank whisky on many occasions with the head of the national police. These social occasions were difficult but they provided opportunities for Principled Engagement – opportunities to express my views informally but unequivocally, to argue for changes in regime policy and practice, including in relation to particular people who were imprisoned, and to explore ways in which the engagement could be extended to new areas. I attempted to ease my conscience by declining invitations to sightseeing and by flying on airlines and staying in hotels that were not owned by the regime. Engagement is complex. It is not easy. It is risky.

Principle 3: Principled Engagement must be strategic, seeking and pursuing the most effective means of promoting and protecting human rights

There are many strategies for the promotion and protection of human rights. Principled Engagement is simply one. It arises from an examination of the full range of strategies as they might apply to a particular country or situation. The examination seeks to identify all possible strategies and from among them choose the ones that are most likely to be most effective.

Principled Engagement can be pursued in some circumstances at the same time as other strategies. In fact it often provides an important complement to other strategies. Take the Myanmar work as an example. Many human rights groups were strongly advocating a policy of total isolation of the Myanmar regime, including through the imposition and enforcement of international sanctions against it. I did not see it necessary to choose exclusively one strategy over the other. In fact, the campaign for isolation of the regime made the strategy of Principled Engagement possible. The regime may have had no interest in human rights training had it not been for the isolation campaign. The human rights training may also have added strength to the isolation campaign. It was one of the very few cooperation projects being undertaken in Myanmar at the time and some in the regime feared that if the project were stopped, support for the isolation campaign would increase. At the time I welcomed the criticism that the training project received and I was glad of the strength of the campaign for isolation. In that context there was room to manoeuvre through Principled Engagement.

If different strategies are to be pursued to best effect, there must be dialogue, even argument, among human rights advocates. Different strategies can complement each other but they can also undermine each other. Human rights advocates will not and need not always agree on the best strategies to pursue. Nonetheless, they themselves must engage with each other on a principled basis. They should share information and analysis and explore together the strengths and weaknesses of each strategy. Principled Engagement seeks involvement not only with rights-violating regimes but also with the divergent strands of the human rights movement.

Principle 4: Principled Engagement must never tolerate human rights violations or deny their occurrence

As well as being clear about our human rights objectives we should be clear about our views on violations. Human rights violations occur in all countries but they are never justifiable and should never be tolerated. Nor should their occurrence be denied. Engagement has no firm foundation when the parties to the engagement keep silent on human rights violations or deny their existence.

Dealing with violations need not occur in an atmosphere of embarrassment or anger. Of course, raising the situation of human rights violation with the concerned country will always be sensitive, especially when the country concerned is your host. The issue will need to be addressed sensitively. But there is no point in engaging in human rights work if critical issues are never raised, if everyone pretends that a situation of serious human rights violation simply does not exist.

When the Australian human rights delegations visited China in 1991 and 1992 the situation of human rights in Tibet was raised. The delegation raised many human rights issues with our Chinese hosts but none was more sensitive than human rights in Tibet. Those discussions were quite heated at times. After each delegation returned to Australia, it reported to the Australian Parliament. Those reports included significant discussion of the situation in Tibet. When the second delegation went to China in 1992 it was confronted quite sharply in relation to its report of the first visit the previous year. The comments on Tibet in that report were taken very seriously by the Chinese government and rejected. Our Chinese government counterparts strongly criticised the delegation, particularly the delegation leader, Senator (at the time) Chris Schacht. After a robust exchange, it was made clear to us that our request to make a second visit to Tibet would not be granted and that the basis of the refusal was the comments we had made the previous year. The human rights situation in Tibet is very serious and it would have been unacceptable not to inquire into it and comment on it. Although that resulted in the refusal of a further visit, the comments were justified and had to be made. Principled Engagement requires that. Nonetheless, the Chinese government did not refuse the second visit itself, only the proposed Tibet component of it, and it did not refuse engagement with the delegation. On the contrary, it granted our request to visit Xin Jiang, another region in which there had been conflict between the local people and the Chinese government.

Similarly, the human rights delegation to Vietnam in 1995 raised sensitive human rights issues with the Vietnamese government. We asked for an opportunity to meet dissident Buddhist leaders in Hue. We were aware of the Vietnamese government's particular hostility towards these leaders. This request was more sensitive than any other request we made, including a request to visit a prison. The request was granted, the meeting took place and our engagement was strengthened because of that.

Principle 5: Principled Engagement must be respectful of victims of human rights violations and their situations and views

Much of the controversy surrounding some aspects of my human rights work has arisen because victims of human rights violations and their supporters demanded a more confrontational strategy in dealing with countries with bad human rights records. The victims were sceptical about any possibility of improving the human rights situation merely through engagement. They feared in fact that the engagement would strengthen the hand of the repressive government, give it greater international credibility and set back progress towards better human rights compliance. Some countries also were of this view and argued for a far stronger response.

The perspectives and the views of victims of human rights violation must be respected. Victims are entitled to justice but most of them never receive it. They are the ones who are most expert about their own situations and their own experiences and often about the overall human rights situation in the country. However, they are not necessarily the best informed about strategies to improve human rights or even the best informed about the contemporary situation in the country. Often they have been in exile for many years and have lost contact with the reality on the ground. Often their focus is limited to one situation or one area. Many have been forced by their experiences to adopt uncompromising positions in relation to the regime in control of their country and so see any engagement with that regime as undermining their efforts and the human rights struggle generally.

During the four years of my work in Myanmar I met often with Myanmar refugee groups, both in Bangkok and in Sydney, to discuss the project, at least before and after each visit to Myanmar. Many were generally negative and sometimes extremely hostile towards the project, both privately and in the public media. Some were totally sceptical of the prospects of the project making any progress in improving human rights in Myanmar but thought the effort worth a try. That was my view too. In our discussions we were able to exchange different perspectives and, while not convincing each other of our own positions, we were able to work together because of our common objective of improving human rights in Myanmar.

Although the views of victims must be respected, those views are not necessarily correct and they are not necessarily the best approach. Principled Engagement requires us to make our own decisions based on the best possible information and advice. It would be wrong and foolish not to seek, respect and take into account the views of victims, but that does not mean that those views have to be accepted and acted upon.

Principle 6: Principled Engagement must be a long-term commitment to incremental improvement in the enjoyment of human rights

Human rights work is long-term work even if we are impatient for improvement and anxious to end violations. Its urgency does not alter the fact that rapid progress in human rights rarely occurs. Usually progress comes step by step over a lengthy period of time. For that reason, Principled Engagement requires long-term commitment. It does not set unreasonable or utopian deadlines and it does not commit merely to one encounter or to one period of time.

The problem with incrementalism is that it is slow. It can sometimes involve two steps forward and one step back, or even at times one step forward and two steps back. Principled Engagement needs to understand this and, however unhappily, deal with it. Nothing will change overnight but everything may change over a period of years. Through Principled Engagement we seek to influence the direction of change positively and accelerate the process of change as much as possible.

Nonetheless, events can make Principled Engagement impossible, at least for a time. During the four years of my activity in Myanmar, small improvements occurred. Most notably, when I was first involved, Daw Aung San Suu Kyi was under tight house arrest. I asked on my first visit to meet her, if she was willing to see me, and was told that I would be permitted to do so on my next visit. That promise was kept and in October 2000 I was able to have a lengthy meeting with the opposition leader at her residence. She was released in 2001 and travelled extensively in Myanmar over the next two years. However, in May 2003, after her convoy was attacked and many of her colleagues killed, she was again placed under house arrest. At that point the human rights training project was suspended and a year later it was ended. This was disappointing because in April 2003, a little before Daw Suu Kyi was again arrested, a further stage of the project had been agreed and it would have moved into important new areas, seeking to influence the state social welfare sector more broadly than had previously been possible and to involve for the first time a number of organisations outside the formal government structure. Nonetheless, it was impossible at that time to continue the project under the circumstances of Daw Suu Kyi's return to house arrest.

Sometimes Principled Engagement has to be placed on hold.

Principle 7: Principled Engagement must do no harm

In accepting that progress will inevitably be slow, we must be certain that at the very least no harm is done. Principled Engagement that itself results in human rights violation, or contributes to human rights violation, or condones human rights violation, is unjustified and unsustainable. Being patient and committed in the long term is not the same as causing harm.

This difficult issue confronted me in relation to both the human rights delegations to China in 1991 and 1992 and the human rights training project in Myanmar. In both cases opponents of the activities argued that the delegations/ training project would actually harm human rights. So far as the China delegations were concerned, the argument was that by undertaking the visits, the actions of the Chinese government during the Tiananmen protests would be condoned, its international reputation would be restored and, as a result, it would be emboldened in its policies and practices that violated human rights. A similar argument was made in relation to the Myanmar project, that simply undertaking the project would enhance the reputation of the Myanmar military regime and in that way both reduce pressure on it to change its practices and encourage it to continue them. These arguments had a good basis in experience and in the situation at the time. Both governments had been and were serious human rights violators and both at the time were subjected to measures of international isolation. There was certainly a risk that the engagement could reduce the external pressure and could encourage those governments to persist in their ways.

Human rights work is never without risk. There is always the risk of causing harm; making a bad situation worse. But the presence of risk does not excuse inaction. If it did, we would never act in response to human rights violations. We would never take any initiative to address a bad human rights situation in case we made it worse. What is required is not inaction because of risk but careful, intelligent, evidence-based assessment of the extent of the risk, of the likelihood of the activity doing harm. That assessment must be accompanied by an assessment of the potential for progress and of alternative strategies. And it should seek to identify strategies to minimise the risk if the engagement were to proceed.

The most compelling fact in relation to Myanmar in 2000 was that other strategies had been tried, and were still being tried, and had achieved nothing. Western states were imposing economic sanctions but there was no evidence that they were having any impact whatsoever in improving human rights in Myanmar. On the contrary, the evidence was that the military regime in its isolation was becoming more intransigent and more uncompromising. Though sceptical, many Myanmar human rights advocates agreed with this analysis.

So far as China in 1991 was concerned, it had been subjected to intense international criticism at the time of the Tiananmen massacre and during the two years following. But China was too big and even then its economy was too powerful for there to be a realistic way in which isolation would work. In fact isolation had already been tried and failed, from the time of the success of the Communist revolution in 1949 until the mid 1970s (see Chapter 5 by Kent in this volume). A return to isolation offered no solution to China's human rights performance. A short period of partial isolation after events as serious as those in Tiananmen was justified as an expression of international condemnation of the actions of the Chinese government. But it was not a permanent solution. There were risks in undertaking the human rights delegation visits in 1991 and 1992 but the limited period of isolation was coming to an end. There was an opportunity to seize the moment to commence a serious dialogue about human rights, before the pressure was lifted entirely.

It is easy to be wise in retrospect, but even in retrospect I cannot see any harm that resulted from these initiatives. On the contrary, looking back I can see some marginal gains – temporary in the case of Myanmar, very limited in the case of China. The risks were assessed and they were worth taking. The results, however, were less than I had hoped.

Principle 8: Principled Engagement must be directed towards the development of strong independent institutions that are able to promote and protect human rights effectively

Principled Engagement should be directed towards building local capacity for the protection and promotion of human rights. Human rights work is best done locally. Human rights obligations are obligations primarily of governments towards their own people. Principled Engagement should not be based on the replacement of local responsibility and local action by the intervention of external activists or experts. So, Principled Engagement seeks to develop strong, independent institutions locally. These institutions can be courts and law enforcement agencies, parliaments and other mechanisms to check and balance the executive, civil society and NGOs. Most importantly, they include national human rights institutions, independent state institutions with a strong legislative basis and a broad mandate for the promotion and protection of human rights.

Over the last 20 years I have worked with national human rights institutions in many countries in the Asia-Pacific region, including Indonesia, the Philippines, Thailand, Palestine and the Maldives. These institutions are often established in situations of human rights crisis or political transition. In some cases they have played a role in the process of transition, as key actors for human rights in societies in turmoil.

Komnas HAM in Indonesia was established in 1994 as a sop to international opinion. Yet it was able to do good work and make notable achievements, including in playing a role in the removal of the Suharto dictatorship. In Palestine, the Independent Commission on Human Rights is a strong, credible organisation that monitors and investigates actions of the Palestinian National Authority and its various agencies. In the Maldives, the Human Rights Commission is helping to steer a democratic course in a very difficult transition after 30 years of dictatorship. In Thailand, the Human Rights Commission works in a situation of political turmoil, demonstrating its independence from both political factions, the Red Shirts and the Yellow Shirts, and advocating universal standards of human rights as the basis on which the actions of the government and the opposition should be investigated and judged.

The development of strong, credible, independent national human rights institutions is one of the direct results of work based on Principled Engagement. These and other national institutions can have permanent impacts on countries' human rights performance. They can contribute to the development of human rights respecting societies, in which the protection and promotion of human rights is a national priority.

Principle 9: Principled Engagement must be transparent and accountable

When the strategies for human rights work are discussed, there is always debate about whether advocacy is better done behind closed doors or in the open. Diplomats invariably argue that quiet diplomacy is the most effective means of human rights promotion and protection. Activists always prefer a more public approach that is also generally more confrontational. The choice of strategy is portrayed as a choice between cooperation and confrontation. Principled Engagement does not accept this choice but takes a different path.

Principled Engagement values cooperation but does not reject confrontation out of hand. It uses both cooperation and confrontation at different times, and sometimes at the same time, but its work is always transparent. Transparency ensures that the engagement is principled. It allows public scrutiny of what is said and what is done so that the activity itself can be challenged and the strategy behind it debated. Transparency also has the benefit of increasing knowledge of the particular human rights situation, thereby enabling others to act on the situation, perhaps using different but complementary strategies.

The contrast between the two approaches is evident in the different stages of Australia's human rights dialogue with China (see also Chapter 5 by Kent in this volume). The two delegations in which I was involved operated transparently with comprehensive reports tabled in the national parliament on each occasion. The reports not only described what the delegations had discussed and done but also provided a great deal of information about and analysis of the human rights situation in China. Human rights dialogues between Australia and China occur now on a regular basis, generally annually. For some time no public reports of the dialogues were issued. More recently a report of each dialogue is released but it is brief and generally descriptive rather than analytical. It lacks the depth of information and analysis that characterised the earlier reports. In part this is due to the changed nature of the delegation involved in the dialogue. The Australian human rights delegations in 1991 and 1992 were mixed delegations led by members of Parliament and including human rights experts and China experts. Delegation members operated in the public sphere and were used to research, analysis and advocacy in public forums. The members of recent delegations have been public servants. They typically work behind closed doors, writing confidential briefings and advice. They rarely venture into the public sphere with their own opinions and analysis. The differences in the reports reflect the differences in the delegations.

Transparency ensures the integrity of the engagement itself and provides opportunities for broader engagement by actors in other contexts. Transparency is a principle that lies at the heart of Principled Engagement.

Transparency leads to accountability. Alongside transparency, accountability helps to ensure that engagement remains principled and that it is effective in promoting human rights and avoiding harm. The lines of accountability, however, are usually unclear. Where the engagement is undertaken by a parliamentary delegation, as in the China delegations of 1991 and 1992, there is a clear line of accountability to the Parliament itself and more immediately to the minister who appointed the delegation members. However, most Principled Engagement is undertaken by individuals and groups that do not have this kind of clear accountability. Nonetheless, the first line of accountability is to the person, institution or organisation that authorised the engagement and appointed those involved in it.

This kind of accountability is, however, insufficient. There must also be some form of accountability to the broader community and particularly to the victims of human rights violation. Establishing the mechanisms for this is difficult. Transparency is one mechanism. Where what is said and done is generally known, those involved expose themselves to comment, including criticism, in response. They have the opportunity of entering into public debate on the effectiveness and integrity of the engagement, on alternative strategies that may be more effective, and on the future of the engagement itself.

Between 2000 and 2003, when I was engaged in the human rights training in Myanmar, I met regularly with Myanmar exile groups in Sydney and Bangkok. I reported to them on each of my visits to Myanmar and heard their views in response. I also adopted the practice of commenting in the media after each visit. I not only gave media interviews but also took part in live discussions on radio and television, sometimes with well-informed experts on Myanmar, both critics and commentators, and sometimes with rabid, ill-informed, non-Myanmar campaigners. These were not formal mechanisms of accountability but they ensured that my work was subjected to scrutiny and at times criticism. Ultimately no one was responsible for my decisions and actions in relation to Myanmar except me, but the comments of others, especially those most entitled to comment, Burmese refugees, helped enormously to keep me on the right track. Accountability mechanisms of some kind like these have to be built into all exercises of Principled Engagement.

Principle 10: Principled Engagement must be monitored and evaluated

Monitoring and evaluation are key components of any human rights work. We need to know how effective our work is and what can be done to make it more effective. Monitoring and evaluation are the means for this. I mean here not the informal accountability mechanisms described above but more systematic methods by which we set objectives, plan results and identify indicators by which those results can be measured. This is standard methodology in development work and it is especially important in human rights work where the risks are great. However, monitoring and evaluating human rights work is very difficult, for many of the reasons I have already described. It is long-term work; there can be gains and losses over short periods of time; there are many people involved; and it is difficult to understand what impact our specific actions have had, positively or negatively.

Monitoring and evaluating human rights work based on Principled Engagement can be especially difficult. It is such intangible work. And I have no easy answers. Certainly the projects in which I have been engaged that could be characterised as Principled Engagement lacked good measurable indicators of effectiveness. Some of them had formal project documents that incorporated much of the ordinary methodology of development projects – goals, objectives, imports and outcomes, log frames and so on. Other projects were far more informal. The human rights delegations to China, for example, were not standard development projects, but the training programmes in Myanmar were. The difficulty with monitoring and evaluation on the basis of individual projects is that the projects are usually short term. They may relate to a single activity or a couple of activities over a short period of time, say one year. Proper evaluation requires a longer time span and a high level of analytical evaluation. Human rights projects rarely have either.

I can point to some examples of reasonable evaluation in which I been involved. On several occasions I have evaluated the human rights work of the Independent Commission on Human Rights and human rights NGOs in Palestine. I have also evaluated human rights projects undertaken by UN agencies. I have evaluated human rights training programs conducted by academic and other organisations. Each of these experiences has raised the problems I have described. It has been possible to paint a broad-brushed picture of the work of the project evaluated and to provide anecdotal evidence of effectiveness. It has been possible to count the number of activities undertaken and the number of people who have been involved in them and to assess what those people have thought about the activities in which they engaged. This is useful information and helps to develop new projects that integrate lessons learned and have a better prospect of being more effective. But these evaluations failed to answer the most basic question we want answered: how effective has the project been in improving the promotion and protection of human rights in a particular country?

I have not encountered any evaluation methodology that satisfactorily answers this basic question. That is not an excuse for not trying. We need to know how effective our human rights work is. We need to know whether it is improving the situation, having no impact whatsoever, or causing harm. We need to know how to do it better. These needs apply as much to activities of Principled Engagement as to any other area of human rights work. Seeking better means of monitoring and evaluation is part of Principled Engagement.

Conclusion

Principled Engagement is an important and effective option among the range of strategies available for the protection and promotion of human rights. If national situations and appropriate strategies for human rights are properly assessed, Principled Engagement is likely to be the strategy of choice in dealing with most countries.

When I reflect on my own experience, I see the choices that have confronted me, and the results of the choices I have made. I can accept that I have made compromises even though I would argue that I have always attempted to advance human rights. I can see how my own activities frequently fall within the scope of Principled Engagement.

The ten principles I have proposed seek to place Principled Engagement on a proper footing so that it does not sink into a form of co-option. They are tests to determine when bilateral cooperation is Principled Engagement and when it is not. They are also strategic choices that are made, consciously or unconsciously, whenever we do human rights work. The principles make those choices explicit so that they can be properly analysed and rationally made.

The ten principles point Principled Engagement in the right direction, ensure that the relationships are quite clear and proper, and give due respect to victims. They provide accountability and enable increasing effectiveness. They are not the last word on Principled Engagement but they may be helpful.

Chapter 4

Engaging with All Actors of Violence: Necessity, Duty and Dilemmas from an ICRC Delegate's Perspective

Pierre Gentile[1]

The International Committee of the Red Cross (ICRC) works to promote better respect of international humanitarian law (IHL) and other legal norms protecting civilians and people *hors de combat* and, for that purpose, seeks to establish direct dialogue with *all* actors in situations of armed conflict or other situations of violence, *regardless* of their ideological stance or human rights record. In this respect it can be considered a 'principled engager' as defined in the present volume.

This chapter argues – in line with the ICRC's institutional position – for the necessity for the ICRC to be able to access and engage meaningfully with all actors in situations of violence, including with opposition armed groups. This is a long practice that derives from the organisation's unique mandate and from the fact that IHL binds all parties to an armed conflict (including non-state actors), as opposed to human rights laws which are binding only on states parties.[2] Nevertheless, it must be recognised that the ICRC's stance is not always an easy one to maintain. Thus, I also detail some of the dilemmas and challenges that ICRC delegates encounter in the field.

Background: How Neutrality Came to Be Seen as Political Engagement

For the past 150 years, the ICRC has worked to protect the lives and dignity of victims of armed conflict and to provide them with assistance. When confronted with the humanitarian consequences of violence, the ICRC seeks to have access to the areas directly affected, as well as to health infrastructure receiving and treating the wounded, and to people arrested in connection with the violence. It needs to be able to assess independently the needs of communities and individuals, both in terms of assistance (economic security, access to health, access to water) and in terms of protection. The present chapter focuses on protection activities (see Figure 4.1)[3] conducted *intra-muros*, in favour of people deprived of their liberty, or *extra-muros* in favour of the general population, including Internally Displaced Persons (IDPs), the wounded, the sick or any group that might be exposed to particular risks of abuse in a given situation.

Protection aims to ensure that authorities and other actors respect their obligations and the rights

of individuals in order to preserve the safety, physical integrity and dignity of those affected by

armed conflict and other situations of violence.

Protection includes efforts to prevent or put a stop to actual or potential violations of international

humanitarian law (IHL) and other relevant bodies of law or norms.

Protection relates firstly to the causes of, or the circumstances that lead to, violations – mainly by

addressing those responsible for the violations and those who may have influence over the latter –

and, secondly, to their consequences.

This definition of protection also includes activities that seek to make individuals more secure and

limit the threats they face by reducing their vulnerability and/or their exposure to risks,

particularly those arising from armed hostilities or acts of violence.

Figure 4.1   ICRC's working definition of protection
Source: ICRC, "ICRC Protection Policy: Institutional Policy," *International Review of the Red Cross* 90, no. 871 (September 2008), 752, available at http://www.icrc.org/eng/resources/documents/article/review/review-871-p751.htm [accessed 15 May 2012].

The ICRC's commitment to engage all sides in situations of armed conflict dates back to its founding in 1863, and is in line with the Geneva Conventions (common article 3, and the second additional protocol of 1977), as well as a large number of customary IHL rules, which explicitly bind non-state armed groups that are parties to an armed conflict.[4] In parallel with the development of IHL, the ICRC in its field practice has devoted more and more resources to extending and maintaining networks of interlocutors, including in periods of transition, in order to better engage all key actors when violence erupts.

The ICRC's strategy is not without its critics. Today, the will to actively engage all actors involved in armed conflict, or in other situations of violence, is seen by some as an outdated and a somewhat *poussièreux* principle. Especially after the US-led intervention in Afghanistan in 2001, many among the humanitarian community argued that renewing contacts with the Taliban was "morally contestable, old-fashioned and inappropriate for the new contexts of today".[5] Critics are of the view that seeking to stay neutral and engage all parties to a conflict is obsolete, especially in asymmetrical conflicts where the weakest party often adopts tactics that run counter to the principles and rules of IHL. This argument suggests that we have entered a new era of disrespect for international law in which violations are so gross that any attempt to establish a dialogue with some non-state actors based on the notion of respect for international obligations or the protection of civilians is naïve and doomed to failure.

Yet, is this really the case? At the time the Red Cross was founded, were the different European imperial armies that much more respectable when it came to their behaviour towards the population on whose soil they fought? When, in the early 1930s, the ICRC engaged delegates in a major operation for the first time in Africa, were the Italian forces invading Ethiopia showing respect for IHL rules by using poisonous gases and bombing field hospitals? The reality is that disrespect for civilians, the wounded or imprisoned, is not new. Neither is such disrespect limited to dictatorships or to rebel groups fighting asymmetric wars. Even armies with 'good causes' have committed war crimes and atrocities. During the Second World War, the Allies resorted to bombing cities and killing hundreds of thousands of civilians to instil a sense of fear and break the morale of the enemy nations.

Another argument sometimes advanced against a position of neutrality is based on the re-emerging notion of "just war". As Haroff-Tavel notes, "Those who believe they have good reasons to wage war tend to misunderstand the motives of those who, owing to their neutrality, do not support them. If a cause is just, they feel, then war is legitimate and the ends justify the means. That being the case, everyone should take part in their struggle."[6] In the ICRC's view, however, the notion of "just war" makes neutrality all the more necessary for an organisation whose aim is to bring assistance to conflict victims on the ground.

For the ICRC, engaging all sides is not a political statement or a naïve inheritance from its past history turned into dogma. Rather, it is necessary for the organisation's own security and for its own credibility. It is also a duty in seeking to fulfil the ICRC's mission of protection and serving as a guardian of IHL. As Harroff-Tavel argues,

> There are few belligerents who do not consider their war as just, but this does not make it just for their adversaries. The ICRC must not fall into the trap of stating that some wars are just and others not, which would be tantamount to ruling on issues of *jus ad bellum* – the law governing recourse to force – whereas its mandate requires it to ensure respect only for *jus in bello* – the rules that apply in wartime.[7]

Engaging with all sides is an inevitable corollary of the ICRC's principles of neutrality, impartiality and independence.

In situations where violence and abuses prevail, it is a constant struggle to reach all victims and ensure that the voice of humanity is heard by all. Yet, even in the case of Afghanistan, a few years down the line, few would contest how crucial it was for the ICRC to re-establish direct contact and some level of trust with the Taliban in order to carry out its activities, to play the role of a neutral intermediary in situations of hostage taking, and to secure access for health staff conducting a polio eradication campaign in remote areas.

Engaging everyone is, however, not always straightforward. Several dilemmas arise. The last part of the chapter looks at some of these dilemmas, but before debating them it is necessary to understand the logic behind the ICRC's approach when working in the midst of violence. It is important to grasp how dialogue with armed actors about abuses that have been documented by ICRC delegates influences efforts to promote the integration of IHL into national laws and, beyond that, into the military's rules of engagement.

Dialogue with Armed Actors: A Central Component of any Protection and Prevention Strategy

In conflict, or in other situations of armed violence, the ICRC favours direct engagement with all actors involved. It does so for several reasons: to explain its activities, to get access to areas and people of concern, to receive security guarantees but, importantly, also to enhance protection for the population, for the detainees, or for the wounded and the sick, through direct dialogue. The ICRC reminds the authorities of their obligations, and discusses pragmatically the recommendations its delegates make after monitoring respect for IHL and other rules by armed actors, and after observing the humanitarian consequences of the violence on the population. This dialogue is set within the framework of an agreement of confidentiality to allow for more transparent and direct exchanges.

The ICRC will, in principle, never disclose the reports it submits to the authorities or an armed group, nor disclose the content of the discussions it has with them. In turn, the authorities cannot use part of the reports they receive, taking sentences or passages out of context, without risking the ICRC speaking out publicly. The ICRC might, exceptionally, express publicly its concerns when its delegates observe serious humanitarian consequences of violence that need to be addressed swiftly by the parties engaged in the violence. As Dominik Stillhart, Deputy Head of Operations, explained, "For example, we might write a news release about the overall rights of detainees or the humanitarian impact of insecurity and displacement, but we will not speak publicly about individual allegations of abuse or specific violations of international humanitarian law."[8] Even in today's interconnected world with its highly active media, confidential dialogue as described in this paper can be pursued alongside the issuance of public pronouncements on protection concerns in certain humanitarian situations as assessed by ICRC delegates, or on clarification of IHL rules to be respected in a given situation.

This way of interacting with authorities has become somewhat of a trademark of the ICRC over the decades. But it is important to understand that this dialogue is not a standalone activity. It is usually part of a series of activities, deployed within a structured and multi-disciplinary strategy that is adapted to each context and, in principle at least, regularly revised.

To simplify, when adapting its protection strategy to a given context, the ICRC calls upon five modes of action (Figure 4.2):

1. persuasion (based on a confidential dialogue with the authorities concerned);
2. support (direct or indirect support provided to the authorities by giving them technical or financial assistance to fulfil their legal obligations);
3. substitution (acting wholly or partially in lieu of defaulting authorities which are incapable of fulfilling their obligations to end violations or to rescue the victims of violations);
4. mobilisation (generating interest among other entities – States, NGOs, institutions of civil society, international or regional organisations – which are likely to influence the authorities/weapons bearers to prevent or put a stop to a violation);
5. denunciation (public denunciation under exceptional circumstances only).

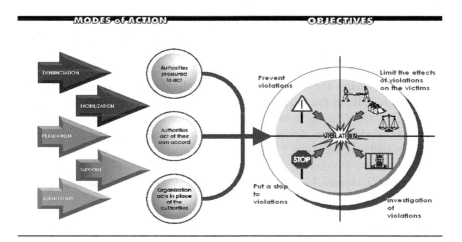

Figure 4.2   Five modes of action for the same objectives
Source: ICRC, "Enhancing Protection for Civilians in Armed Conflict and Other Situations of Violence", October 2008, available at http://www.icrc.org/eng/resources/documents/publication/p0956.htm [accessed 15 May 2012].

Principled Engagement as described in this book relates to three of the five modes of action used by the ICRC: Persuasion, Mobilisation and Support. These modes of action are often combined within a protection strategy: persuasion with substitution (such as when the ICRC convinced the Israeli Defense Forces to improve real-time coordination mechanisms used daily to obtain the green light for the Palestinian Red Crescent to evacuate wounded civilians during

Israeli offensives in Gaza), or support with persuasion and mobilisation (for example, after the fall of the Taliban, the ICRC prepared, in agreement with the new Afghan national authorities, a report based on its technical assessment of the state of the prison infrastructure throughout the country; this report was intended to support the Ministry of Justice in identifying priorities for the rehabilitation of prisons and to contact potential donors interested in supporting prison reform in Afghanistan).

The ICRC's commitment to establishing a constructive and confidential dialogue is based partly on maintaining a neutral, impartial and independent approach, but also on gaining a proper understanding of the context and all its players, and on developing a network of trusted interlocutors involved in the violence. Denunciation could mean putting at risk relationships of trust built over time, or even having to leave a country for years (in today's world, returning once having left can be another challenge). Public denunciation aimed at ostracising one of the parties to a conflict is therefore a last resort only, when persuasion, mobilisation and support have clearly failed. In other words, denunciation is an option left open when Principled Engagement has proved to be impossible or ineffective after repeated attempts. It is extremely rare in the history of the ICRC to resort to such public denunciation, knowing that its access to interlocutors and to conflict zones might be seriously reduced as a result. The most well-known case, among the very few that were actually recorded over the last 25 years, relates to the genocide in Rwanda. At the time the ICRC, which did not leave the country but set up a clinic on its premises in Kigali, made public calls in the international media describing the dramatic situation its delegates were facing to inform public opinion and mobilise humanitarian actors and world leaders. Even so, maintaining a capacity to engage all parties on the ground was necessary.[9]

Confidential Dialogue: A Key Item within a Wider Catalogue of Possible Activities

Combining different modes of action requires being able to implement different sets of activities simultaneously. As the ICRC's former Director-General Angelo Gnaedinger said,

> Speaking more specifically about the ICRC's protection work, it is worth mentioning that in an effort to prevent or put an end to violations the ICRC engages in a wide range of activities which can be placed in two main categories:
>
> 1. Activities aimed at those responsible for violations: I am talking here first of all about the representations on behalf of people at risk with the authorities, in charge but also about the support we provide for the improvement of national legislation, incorporating international humanitarian law in the training given

to the armed forces, and liaising with and between warring parties on specific humanitarian issues.[10]

2. Activities aimed directly at reducing the vulnerability of individuals or their exposure to violence. These include registering the persons concerned, tracing those who have disappeared, occasionally arranging for the evacuation of individuals, organizing mine-awareness activities, and carrying out assistance programmes designed to reduce exposure to risk.[11]

Bilateral confidential dialogue is one of a series of activities. Arguably it is the central one for the ICRC. No strategy will do without direct dialogue with the parties, or at least not without attempting to establish such dialogue. Dialogue is nevertheless not to be seen as an aim in itself but rather as a means to reinforce protection for the population concerned. Therefore, direct bilateral and confidential dialogue is never the only protection activity delegates implement in a given context.

As Figure 4.3 shows, different ICRC activities require different skills; however, political and contextual analysis, incident documentation and sensitive information management are required in all cases. Strong legal expertise is needed to work with the authorities towards domestic implementation of international IHL obligations whenever a discrepancy exists, as any gap may otherwise contribute to an environment in which violations are more likely to occur. Military and legal expertise is often needed to discuss protection concerns related to the conduct of hostilities with armed forces, and to have the necessary credibility to work with them, if required, to adapt their rules of engagement and training to diminish the chances of documented abuses recurring. Communication skills come into play when addressing protection concerns publicly and also when designing a media campaign for populations exposed to particular risks (for example, to the risks posed by ordnances in the open, such as unexploded cluster bombs in Southern Lebanon after the armed conflict of 2006 between Hezbollah and Israel).

Principled Engagement

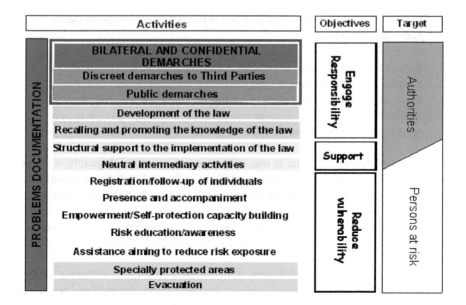

Figure 4.3 Protection activities implemented by the ICRC

Source: ICRC, "ICRC Protection Policy: Institutional Policy," *International Review of the Red Cross* 90, no. 871 (September 2008), 766, available at http://www.icrc.org/eng/resources/documents/article/review/review-871-p751.htm [accessed 15 May 2012].

One of the difficulties is to ensure that all activities carried out in a given context are connected and form part of a real multi-disciplinary strategy. There must be a certain level of coherence between, on the one hand, the confidential dialogue with authorities to whom representations are made about documented incidents and abuses and, on the other hand, activities promoting knowledge of IHL within the army, or activities helping communities to reduce their exposure to risks. Without such coherence, synergies between these activities are difficult to achieve. At worst, prevention activities that disregard the context in which they are implemented could prove damaging to the organisation's credibility.

Exploring Some Practice-Based Dilemmas

Establishing a fruitful dialogue with all armed actors and their allies is easier said than done. Contrary to what some may think, pursuing neutrality by engaging all actors meaningfully is certainly not choosing the easy option. To illustrate the difficulties, I discuss here three of the main challenges the ICRC confronts in the field: establishing its legitimacy, securing regular access, and agreeing on a legal basis for dialogue.

Legitimacy

Legitimacy is an important part of any serious dialogue. If the authorities or the leaders of an armed group see no legitimacy for the ICRC to discuss sensitive matters related to abuses, establishing the basis for a confidential dialogue will prove almost impossible.

In situations of international armed conflict, the ICRC has been given a strong mandate by the international community, with clear obligations for states to cooperate with its activities.[12] In situations of non-international armed conflict, the ICRC has a conventional right of initiative as provided in Article 3 common to the four Geneva Conventions. Finally, in other situations of violence not reaching the threshold of armed conflict, the ICRC has a right of initiative that is derived from the statutes of the International Red Cross and Red Crescent Movement (approved by the states). The legal framework determines, to some extent, how the legitimacy of the ICRC may be perceived in any given situation. It is nevertheless not the only source of legitimacy for the ICRC, and is often not enough to establish a solid base for a confidential dialogue on abuses.

Authorities agree to engage with the ICRC in dialogue in large part because they see an interest in discussing its observations and recommendations rather than because they are acting on a legal obligation to do so. There is therefore more to legitimacy than the legal framework. In fact, the ICRC's legitimacy is plural: it comes from its mandate, its legal expertise and its expertise in other fields, which it can use or share with the authorities in question. Its legitimacy is also derived from a long history of field presence and knowledge of the context of armed conflict based on implementing relevant protection activities.[13] One example of such expertise, which is recognised by many states, is in the field of detention. The ICRC has developed and tested working modalities over a number of decades and has acquired a practical knowledge of how prisons and penitential administrations function in a variety of countries. Another example is the management of missing persons' files. The ICRC has collected and managed files of missing persons in numerous countries and actively worked with the authorities and armed groups to establish the whereabouts of people unaccounted for, often in situations of violence. It has developed *ante-mortem* and *post-mortem* databases for forensic work, expertise in the handling of mortal remains due to large-scale killings or disasters, and also strong experience in working with the families of missing persons. Finally, experience has shown that pre-existing, long-term activities related to the dissemination and integration of IHL and/or rules on the use of force in law enforcement operations, with the security forces, can also help build the necessary legitimacy to discuss sensitive issues with them.

It is no surprise that armed actors have, in different countries and at different times, contested the ICRC's legitimacy to engage in a dialogue on protection issues using a variety of arguments. Challenging, but not uncommon, is the situation in which an armed group engaged in conflict denies the applicability of IHL by arguing that it is a legal framework agreed on by states only, and furthermore that it places unfair constraints on opposition groups. In such a case, legitimacy deriving from proximity with the victims and communities at risk might turn out to be more compelling for the ICRC to rely on than its legal expertise. As ICRC President Jakob Kellenberger said:

> The potential range of 'new actors' whose actions have repercussions at the international level is of course vast. While many of these 'new actors' have in fact been around for some time, they have called into question – and will continue to call into question – some of the more traditional assumptions on which the international legal system is based. The spectrum of these actors is still very broad, encompassing a range of identities, motivations and varying degrees of willingness, and ability, to observe IHL and other international law standards. Certain organized armed groups, private military and security companies, transnational corporations, urban gangs, militias and the huge variety of transnational criminal entities – including 'terrorist' groups and pirates – all require scrutiny in this regard. Identifying and understanding these actors and their characteristics is a fundamental prerequisite to better addressing the challenges arising from their involvement in modern armed conflict. It is also important to recognise how complex the reality is in order to avoid falling into the trap of misleading categorisation that does not serve the interests or increase the protection of people affected by contemporary conflict.[14]

The ICRC's legitimacy to engage in a constructive dialogue with armed groups can also be challenged by the formal authorities. This can happen, for example, when trying to establish contact with an armed group that is emergent, or that the authorities consider to be a delinquent or terrorist organisation that is not a party to a conflict. National authorities may fear that ICRC interaction with such a group confers it a status it does not deserve. This is a misinterpretation as the ICRC is in no way giving legal or political status to the groups it engages with, or to their agendas. In addition, IHL itself is very clear in providing that the application of its rules "shall not affect the legal status of the Parties to the conflict".[15] It is nevertheless a matter of perception that can affect the way authorities encourage or discourage the ICRC to maintain contact with all actors in a situation of violence. This is especially true in situations of violence that do not meet the threshold of an armed conflict, in which the legitimacy for the ICRC to engage with non-state actors is often challenged, especially by authorities with whom the ICRC has a relationship based primarily on its role as guardian of IHL.

Operationally, it is one of the first tasks of any delegate to establish the ICRC's legitimacy in dealing with protection issues, while developing or consolidating its network of interlocutors.

Regular Access

Access is, without doubt, the main challenge today for many humanitarian organisations. When it comes to protection, access has different dimensions:

- to first hand sources: the victims, individuals and communities, and to the place where violence erupts, in order to collect first-hand information on which to base the dialogue;[16]
- to secondary sources: media, local leaders and associations, diplomats and people who might have influence over the actors involved in the violence;
- to the correct interlocutor with whom to establish a protection dialogue with a view to addressing concerns.

Obtaining access to the most appropriate interlocutors with whom the ICRC wishes to develop a confidential dialogue on protection issues involves considerable confidence building. It is not the kind of sporadic or "one-off" contact often reported in the media. Considerable time needs to be invested: time to meet and understand each party's perceptions and constraints; time to meet frequently enough for the ice to be broken and for sensitive issues to be discussed openly and frankly.

One of the first difficulties lies in identifying and then establishing regular contact with the correct interlocutor within a government ministry (or within the armed forces or a non-state actor) – an interlocutor who is positioned to take the action required. Regular access is often a challenge as key interlocutors may – unless they have a strong interest in meeting you – appoint someone else to deal with humanitarian organisations on a regular basis and become almost unreachable. You might end up meeting an interlocutor who has extremely limited power. This, for example, was the case for a while with the Israeli Defense Forces (IDF) in the Palestinian Occupied Territories. The IDF asked all humanitarian organisations to go through its Civil Affairs section where it had appointed liaison officers at the local and regional levels. On the one hand, this route improved day-to-day contact in the field at a local level. It allowed the discussion of concrete issues relating to specific families or communities whose problems were often linked to the restriction of movement and which could be handled by junior liaison officers working for Israeli Civil Affairs. On the other hand, it made it more difficult to establish regular contact with the operational units or with the chief of staff level, with whom the ICRC wanted to discuss broader issues that could not be resolved at a lower level.

Establishing privileged contact takes time and a genuine understanding of the local context and the way that decisions are made. It is of great importance to understand what issues need to be addressed and with whom in order to gain trust and be efficient. To discuss certain topics, the ICRC has seen the need to gain more and more professional expertise: in responding to the specific needs of victims, the ICRC may rely on legal, forensic, or weapons and de-mining expertise. Doing so has often proved indispensable to making meaningful recommendations and consolidating the dialogue with parties engaged in armed conflicts or other situations of violence. Being careful not to become trapped in a dialogue that ends up being too technical and removed from the real decision makers is an important consideration.

It is often more complicated to maintain regular access to non-state actors than to established authorities. In general, international ostracism of non-state actors is higher today than it is for state actors. Very few rebel groups are seen, on the international scene, as legitimate and many are listed, or at least labelled, as "terrorists". Such labelling is often intended to deny legitimacy to the group and to render any contacts with it illegal. Even groups relying on large and established political organisations with a long-term presence in local politics can be ostracized.

The three challenges that are most common when it comes to regular access with non-state actors are:

- Access to people who are being looked for by the authorities and who fear for their safety if they meet ICRC delegates directly. The use of more and more efficient surveillance technology has only accentuated this challenge in recent years. During the height of violence, even the leadership of well-established non-state actors might become hard to contact. This was the case with the military wing of Hezbollah in Lebanon in 2006 and Hamas in Gaza in 2009.
- Access to regions where insecurity is high as a result of violence between a non-state actor and the authorities, or owing to banditry capitalising on a lack of law enforcement. Insecurity related to criminality tends to increase at a time when opposition armed groups start to lose their grip on a region and former members or petty criminals take advantage of the absence of effective authority and the availability of weapons to rob or kidnap people.
- Access to people who have a negative perception of humanitarian workers and who can even be a threat to the delegates in the field.

Insecurity that affects humanitarian workers can also be created by the authorities or armed opposition in order to prevent outsiders from reaching areas where military operations are being carried out. But to some extent it is easier, or at least more straightforward, when the leadership is clearly identified and security guarantees can be obtained through persuasion. Far more complex in terms of access are situations in which responsibilities are diluted and meaningful guarantees hard to obtain. At the end of 2009, two ICRC colleagues were kidnapped, one in Chad and one in Darfur, in situations where banditry was hindering humanitarian access. They both stayed in captivity for several months before being finally released by their captors on two separate occasions. In early 2009, three ICRC colleagues were kidnapped in the Philippines by an armed group. They, too, were released, although Eugenio Vagni, the last to recover his liberty, remained hostage for six months. In all cases, the ICRC's operations had to be cancelled, suspended or reduced for several months in the areas where these incidents happened. Since then, several other colleagues were taken hostage for weeks or months. In 2012,

ICRC health worker Khalil Dale was murdered in Quetta, Pakistan, four months after his abduction. This tragic event deeply shocked the ICRC.

Legal Bases for Dialogue about Violations and Abuses

The legal obligations of a party to an armed conflict compared with those of an actor in a situation of violence vary. Namely, the legal framework that applies depends on whether the party's armed forces are engaged in hostilities (where IHL applies) or in law enforcement operations only. When an armed conflict erupts, it is crucial that the relevant authorities and the ICRC have a shared understanding of the applicable framework. With the formal authorities of a state, this is usually relatively straightforward, although there are some situations where, for political reasons, the authorities may wish to deny that they are engaged in an armed conflict despite the intensity and regularity of armed confrontations (and thus would contest the applicability of IHL, at least publicly). Such situations might complicate the ICRC's dialogue with high-level political authorities but in general not with the army and the security forces which are involved in the military operations.

Gaining a similar understanding of the applicability of IHL by the leadership of non-state actors engaged in armed conflict can be difficult initially, especially if the group sees IHL as a framework defined by states *for* states. Experience shows, nevertheless, that most non-state armed groups engaged in an armed conflict do refer to the Geneva Conventions with regularity. This does not mean that they will not disregard or even consciously violate some of the rules laid down in these conventions. However, when an armed group recognises the applicability of international laws it becomes easier for ICRC delegates to engage in a protection dialogue to discuss these violations and the measures that can be taken to limit them. A pragmatic approach is then often required to convince armed groups to abide by rules they previously disregarded. In recent years, many armed groups operating in Chad or in Sudan have publicly committed themselves not to recruit minors into their ranks; some have even agreed upon demobilisations and reinsertion plans. Minors are still recruited locally, but it has become a topic that can be discussed with the leadership of the groups. The dialogue has evolved from denial to constructive exchanges of views, and some individual cases have been resolved.

Situations of violence that do not meet the legal criteria for armed conflict present additional challenges. In such cases the legal framework covering the actions of a group resorting to violence is the national legislation, not IHL. Invariably, this means that violence by non-state groups is illegal, making it hard to conduct a dialogue with them on protection issues based on their legal obligations. Instead, the ICRC refers to "principles of humanity". Often, local customs and traditions can be referred to in order to underline similarities with the principles of humanity.

Such a parallel can be drawn rather informally, as it was in 2005 when the ICRC office in Awash, Ethiopia, established contacts with local elders in Afar, a region where tensions were running high between two major clans in the region, the Afar and the Issa. The delegates, having compiled information on several cattle raids and incidents between the two communities, initiated discussions with respected elders about the necessity for them to emphasise respect for women and children who were being increasingly harmed in the raids. An awareness and prevention campaign was put in place locally in cooperation with the Federal authorities, which encouraged the ICRC to decrease tensions between the clans. The campaign ended when accompanying assistance projects implemented by the ICRC in health and road infrastructure were seen as controversial and lacking a sound understanding of land ownership. Such an experience illustrated the difficulties in addressing communal violence in an integrated project.

More convincing and somewhat more formalised is the recent experience in Papua New Guinea. In order to enlist the views of the people of the Pacific, the ICRC assigned a group of law students from the University of the South Pacific with the task of examining traditional warfare practices in the Pacific and possible similarities with contemporary principles of humanitarian law. The researchers established that a number of practices during times of violence in the Pacific constituted clear limitations imposed on warfare. Further, these practices, in use prior to European contact, have direct correlation with modern laws regulating war. The study was published and disseminated by the ICRC in areas where communal violence still occurs, to increase the ICRC's acceptance in the eyes of the actors of violence. The objective was to reinforce a message of humanity and hopefully reduce the level of violence against the most vulnerable members of the communities.[17]

Both these examples are taken from confrontations with a strong community-based component, which have facilitated discussion of principles of humanity and customary respect for the most vulnerable. But what about urban situations that have developed recently, such as the Maras or gangs phenomena in Central and South America? An interesting experiment was conducted after the fall of President Aristide in Haiti and the rise of armed gangs in some of the poorest part of Port-au-Prince from 2004 to 2007. The ICRC established regular contact with armed gangs in Cité Soleil and Martissan, two of the most violent areas at the time. ICRC delegates were able to convince the gangs to facilitate access to certain public services for the community. For example, the gangs allowed the Water Board (whose representatives, for some time, entered these neighbourhoods accompanied by ICRC delegates before feeling comfortable enough to go on their own) to repair and improve the water distribution network to ensure that the most vulnerable had free access to water. They also permitted the opening of small offices of the Haitian Red Cross in the affected neighbourhoods that served to evacuate the wounded and sick to hospitals. ICRC delegates, in this case, emphasized humanitarian principles and the respect for the communities' basic needs without referring to a specific legal framework. The dialogue was probably also facilitated by the fact that ICRC delegates at the same time were visiting places of detention and monitoring the conditions in which fellow gang members were detained.

Conclusion: Diversity as Complementarity

Direct dialogue with all parties to an armed conflict or another situation of violence is central to the operational identity of the ICRC. When it comes to protection work, confidential bilateral dialogue is a central component of any of the organisation's strategies. I do not claim that such a *modus operandi* is the only way to do protection work. Nor do I propose that the ICRC's choice to remain neutral, impartial and independent, and to seek a constructive dialogue with all actors, is an example that other humanitarian organisations should follow. On the contrary, complementarity between different humanitarian and human rights actors in the field is based on diversity of expertise, methodology, access, and also of corporate identity and strategies.

This chapter shows how difficult it can be to establish a constructive dialogue with authorities and armed groups, especially when the aim is to push them to assume their responsibilities in preventing IHL and/or human rights abuses. Identifying the relevant interlocutors, gaining legitimacy to discuss protection issues, referring to a shared legal framework and maintaining regular access to them, are among the main challenges in the field. These difficulties only grow when the international community ostracises one or more of the relevant actors. Actively pursuing a confidential dialogue with all parties is therefore often a difficult, and sometimes an impossible, task. It is certainly not the easy way out, as some critics tend to depict. Is it, then, really worth the effort?

The fact is that in a protracted conflict, as well as at the height of an emergency, families continue to approach the ICRC to report missing relatives. Detainees imprisoned for years keep discussing their problems with delegates during lengthy private talks that might expose them to the authorities, or in front of fellow detainees. Communities facing discrimination or clear threats continue to welcome the ICRC's regular visits as they allow them to voice their concerns. Those are small, but clear, signs that from the perspective of people affected by conflict or violence the answer is, "yes, it is worth the effort".

Endnotes

1   The views expressed in this chapter are those of the author alone and do not necessarily reflect the position of the ICRC. The analysis benefited from advice and input, notably on the legal background, from Thomas de Saint Maurice who works as a legal adviser in ICRC headquarters in Geneva.

2   There is a growing tendency among experts and practitioners to consider non-state actors with 'quasi-state' organisations and capabilities to be bound by human rights norms.

3   For more details on how the ICRC understands protection, the following document defines key notions and describes the framework for action: ICRC, "ICRC Protection Policy: Institutional Policy," *International Review of the Red Cross* 90, no. 871 (September 2008), available at http://www.icrc.org/eng/resources/documents/article/review/review-871-p751.htm [accessed 15 May 2012].

4   In 2005, the ICRC published a major international study into current state practice in international humanitarian law in order to identify customary law in this area. Presented in two volumes, the study analyses the customary rules of IHL and contains a detailed summary of the relevant treaty law and state practice throughout the world. In the absence of widespread ratification of numerous important treaties in this area, the ICRC publication is of major importance given that it identifies the common core of international humanitarian law binding on all parties to all armed conflicts. Jean-Marie Henckaerts and Louise Doswald-Beck (eds), *Customary International Humaniarian Law* (Cambridge: ICRC and Cambridge University Press, 2005), available at http://www.icrc.org/eng/resources/documents/publication/pcustom.htm [accessed 15 May 2012].

5   Fiona Terry, "Research Project on the ICRC Practice of Neutrality," *ICRC Internal Report* (Geneva: ICRC, March 2009). Terry herself contested this perception.

6   Marion Harroff-Tavel, "Principles Under Fire: Does it Still Make Sense to Be Neutral?" *Humanitarian Exchange* December (2003), available at http://www.icrc.org/eng/resources/documents/misc/5vueea.htm [accessed 27 April 2013]. In this article Harroff-Tavel discusses five arguments frequently advanced against neutrality.

7   Harroff-Tavel, Ibid.

8   Interview with ICRC Deputy Director of Operations Dominik Stillhart, "Confidentiality: Key to the ICRC's Work but not Unconditional", 20 September 2010, available at http://www.icrc.org/web/eng/siteeng0.nsf/htmlall/confidentiality-interview-010608 [accessed 15 May 2012]. According to Stillhart, confidentiality is an essential tool that enables the ICRC to reach out to people affected by insecurity, violence and armed conflict. It allows the ICRC to build trust, communicate and influence change. He underlines that as a result of the ICRC's long-standing practice of confidentiality, states cannot ask the ICRC to testify or serve as a witness before their domestic courts. This testimonial immunity has been confirmed by a number of domestic and international tribunals, such as the International Criminal Tribunal for the former Yugoslavia, the International Criminal Tribunal for Rwanda and the Special Court for Sierra Leone. More than 80 countries have specifically recognised this immunity by treaties or legislation. In addition, Rule 73 on Privileged Communications and Information in the Rules of Procedure and Evidence of the International Criminal Court stipulates that the ICRC retains the final say on the release of its information. No other organisations were granted this privilege and the ICRC feels that its testimonial immunity underscores the importance of confidentiality as the cornerstone of its work.

9   "Engaging in dialogue means first and foremost listening to the other side, especially if despair is what has driven them to your door. It means acting as a reference point, even without speaking, perhaps above all without speaking. Holding a dialogue means grasping how the other person understands your words, providing that he is still capable of understanding anything at all. From this point of view, the ICRC delegation had been engaged in a constant dialogue in Kigali, even or especially at the worst times. Dialogue makes a far better cornerstone for security than armoured vehicles or bullet-proof vests. Dialogue is a sign of openness and trust. An armoured vehicle is the physical expression of fear, withdrawal and the wrong kind of strength, aggressive strength. Dialogue is the

expression of a calm strength which sometimes recharges the batteries of the person you are talking to." Excerpt from speech by Philippe Gaillard, ICRC head of delegation in Rwanda 1993–94, on 18 October 1994 at the International Museum of the Red Cross and Red Crescent, Geneva, entitled *Rwanda 1994: La vraie vie est absente* ("Real Life is Elsewhere" – Arthur Rimbaud).

10   The ICRC often plays a crucial role as neutral intermediary between the parties by helping to settle humanitarian issues. For example, the release of six Congolese soldiers by two armed groups in January 2010. During the same week, in two different locations, soldiers were handed over to the ICRC after its delegates spoke with each of the six men in private to make sure that they freely accepted their transfer back to the Congolese armed forces.

11   Address by Angelo Gnaedinger, ICRC Director-General, "Protection of Civilians in Conflict – The ICRC Perspective", Humanitarian and Resident Coordinators' Retreat, Geneva, 9 May 2007.

12   The Geneva Conventions, in particular Article 126 of International Committee of the Red Cross (ICRC), *Geneva Convention Relative to the Protection of Civilian Persons in Time of War (Fourth Geneva Convention)*, 12 August 1949, 75 UNTS 287 and Article 143 International Committee of the Red Cross (ICRC), *Geneva Convention Relative to the Treatment of Prisoners of War (Third Geneva Convention)*, 12 August 1949, 75 UNTS 135, available at: http://www.icrc.org/eng/war-and-law/treaties-customary-law/geneva-conventions/index.jsp [accessed 15 May 2012].

13   ICRC, *Overview of Operations 2011*: "the relevance of the ICRC's response refers to meeting the most pressing needs of people affected by armed conflict and other situations of violence in an evidence-based, result-oriented and timely manner, and using the ICRC's traditional modes of action (support, substitution, persuasion, mobilization, denunciation)", available at http://www.icrc.org/eng/assets/files/reports/2011-overview-operations-rex2010-611-final.pdf [accessed 15 May 2012]. Its commitment to remain impartial, neutral and independent when responding to needs is a key element of ICRC's credibility, and in the end to its legitimacy to act in a given context. As long as ICRC is effectively perceived as neutral and impartial in its action and not deviating from such a core principle, it increases the trust put in it by all, therefore boosting its legitimacy.

14   ICRC President Jakob Kellenberger at the Conference on Challenges for IHL Posed by New Threats, New Actors and New Means and Methods of War, organised by the Swiss Federal Department of Foreign Affairs in cooperation with the ICRC, Geneva, 9–10 November 2009.

15   Common Article 3 to the Geneva Conventions.

16   From an assistance point of view, immediate access to victims and affected communities is critical in order to assess their needs and respond efficiently and independently. In an emergency situation, it is of paramount importance that protection teams are deployed rapidly in order to intervene while violence is ongoing so as to integrate a protection perspective into any humanitarian large-scale response (in a "do no harm" perspective, but also in view of maximising multi-disciplinary synergies when programming is being done).

17   ICRC Regional Delegation in the Pacific, Suva, "Under the Protection of the Palm: Wars of Dignity in the Pacific", 21 July 2009, available at http://www.icrc.org/eng/resources/documents/misc/wars-of-dignity-pacific-210709.htm [accessed 15 May 2012].

Chapter 5
Engaging China on Human Rights

Ann Kent

China is no longer the 'pariah state' it once was. While it has highly nationalistic leaders, some still insular, and operates in a non-democratic environment, it is now reasonably well integrated into the international community, even though with growing power its behaviour has become increasingly exceptionalist. China's post-1971 history, however, provides a useful basis for a comparative study of the effectiveness of the three types of engagement under consideration in this book: Ostracism, Principled Engagement and Business as Usual. A focus on China as a state in transition from pariah status helps identify the best ways in which the international community may attempt to influence that transition, and possibly those of other authoritarian states.

The human rights situation in China remains serious. The award of the 2010 Nobel Peace Prize to Chinese dissident Liu Xiaobo, still languishing in prison, was symptomatic not only of the parlous treatment of peaceful dissent in China, but also of the international community's gradual loss of patience with China for its failure to improve its human rights conditions over the two decades since 1989. Recently, China has made some progress in due process rights and the idea that development is compatible with welfare, or that market economies can combine a free market with care for those it disadvantages. As former Premier Wen Jiabao acknowledged during his press conference at the 2010 National People's Conference, "We should pay attention to unequal income distribution and judicial unfairness".[1] However, it is notable that, while an improvement in selective civil rights may have been an outcome of engagement with UN bodies, and even with bilateral technical assistance programmes, it has not helped stem the current and ongoing repression. Indeed, with the onset of revolution in the Arab world in 2011, Chinese repression of domestic dissent has become even more severe and wide-ranging. The leaders' nervousness in the face of anonymous calls in China for a "jasmine revolution" has led to the criminal detention and disappearances of a number of activists and lawyers, as well as to the manhandling of foreign journalists.[2] Even an elite and internationally renowned artist like Ai Weiwei was subjected to harassment and detention, while the case of blind activist Chen Guangcheng, beaten while in house detention after a term of imprisonment, captured the attention of the world when he fled from his home town of Linyi to obtain sanctuary in the US Embassy in Beijing. Indeed, the 2011 Annual Report of the US Congressional Executive Commission on China concluded that "official rhetoric notwithstanding, China's human rights and rule of law record has not improved ... it appears to be worsening in some areas". A particular concern was the government's "misuse of the law to violate fundamental human rights".[3]

International concerns are not just based on humanitarian considerations: they are also justified by reason of normative self-interest. As China has become more powerful economically, particularly since the global financial crisis and its Olympics debut in 2008, it has had some success in its ongoing attempts to co-opt the human rights debate and to export its own value system. It has done this with a combination of hard and soft power tactics.[4] Thus, prior to the 2008 Beijing Olympics, it caused an international outcry when it organised thousands of Chinese nationals studying or working in foreign countries to disrupt demonstrations supporting Tibet during the transit of the Olympic flame, thereby temporarily impairing the rights to association and demonstration in those countries through which it passed. Already, for some years, China has challenged the right of foreign governments to receive the Dalai Lama, even though the Dalai Lama resides outside China. When Liu Xiaobo was awarded the Nobel Peace Prize, China warned other states not to send representatives to attend the ceremony, and refused permission for Chinese intellectuals to travel to Norway to receive the prize in Liu's place. It threatened economic retaliation against the Norwegian government for a decision made independently by the Nobel Prize Committee and arrested or confined Liu's relatives and fellow dissidents.[5] Its new assertiveness has also been demonstrated in the arrogance bordering on contempt with which it responded to criticism during the Universal Periodic Review (UPR) of its human rights by the UN Human Rights Council in February 2009, and its evident satisfaction when its record was praised by some of the states with the worst human rights records. Both reactions could only be compared with its early responses to the multilateral critique in the months after the government crackdown on democracy protesters in Tiananmen Square in June 1989. They represented a definite regression from China's increasingly internationalist and mature responses to international human rights engagement since 1991. If the international community wishes to uphold the legitimacy of the international bill of rights, it must now act to defend it more resolutely. As Freedom House pointed out in the summary of its 2011 report, "the increasing truculence of the world's most powerful authoritarian regimes has coincided with a growing inability or unwillingness on the part of the world's democracies to meet the authoritarian challenge, with important consequences for the state of global freedom".[6]

Even without this external impact, while China's human rights activists and lawyers are working tirelessly and perilously from within the country to rectify its human rights problems, the key question remains whether the international community has employed, and is employing, the most effective means to support them.

The question of Principled Engagement is thus at the core of the problem which the world faces with China on human rights. How can we engage China on the basis of principles which, despite constitutional guarantees, it does not support in practice? If to date that engagement has not been effective, or has not been sufficiently principled, in what ways can it be improved? This study will hopefully help confront the basic problem faced in this volume, which is how the international community can engage an authoritarian state on the basis of human rights principles whose legitimacy that state largely rejects.

Principled Engagement, as defined by Pedersen and Kinley in this volume, relies on non-coercive means, yet works proactively to identify the shortcomings of existing systems and promote better policies and practices by directly engaging repressive governments. It targets specific issues based on the international bill of rights, is critical, transparent, compromise-seeking, and aims to persuade and encourage. In the context of understanding China, I would like to further distinguish between two sub-categories of Principled Engagement: 'strategic' and 'communicative'. As defined by Marc Lynch, both can be principled. But while *strategic* engagement "rests on a strategic mode of action, in which the building of interdependencies and dialogues [a]re instrumental policies to change the target state", a *communicative* mode of action is one where "states enter into public dialogues in order to more effectively communicate, discover and shape preferences, and arrive at mutually acceptable institutions". Communicative engagement is "designed to allow for the free exchange of reasoned argument under conditions which minimise the direct application of power". However, if it is to be effective, he states, it must also be public.[7] An emphasis on communicative rather than strategic engagement has the benefit of mitigating extreme challenges to a state's sovereignty, and pre-empting hostile reactions, always a hazard in the case of authoritarian states. It is more typically a feature of multilateral engagement on human rights, but can also under specific conditions be practised by individual governments and by NGOs and private organisations. At the same time, it must be stressed, in real life situations there is an overlap between strategic and communicative engagement, so that the two form a continuum rather than constituting polar opposites.

Neutralisation of the sovereignty issue is particularly important in relation to human rights, since rights are such a politically sensitive issue. External efforts to influence a country's human rights, unlike efforts, for instance, to alter their policies on nuclear disarmament, directly engage with the target country's legal, political, economic and social systems, and therefore represent a direct threat to its sovereignty. Authoritarian states are by their very nature insecure, suspicious of human rights, and highly protective of sovereignty. One must therefore ask at the outset: what are the reasons that such states might be prepared to engage on human rights and, more specifically, civil and political rights? For some states, like North Korea, the reasons may be economic. For others, such as China in the 1980s and 1990s, they may not only be economic, but may also stem from a concern to enhance their international status and reputation, as well as from an instrumental wish to influence the human rights debate. Other states, unfortunately, may care neither about economic goals nor reputation. By contrast with civil and political rights, economic and social rights are less of a problem, since some authoritarian states, particularly socialist or former socialist ones, may have a genuine commitment to social justice.

In recent years a scholarly literature has begun to emerge questioning the effectiveness or otherwise of different kinds of external pressure on China's human rights.[8] Apart from addressing the issue of Principled Engagement, it has progressively questioned the effectiveness of sanctions, of a tough United States (US) policy, and even of a US "diplomacy of shame". However, the results of such studies have been limited, in part because, with some notable exceptions, this literature has primarily reflected the concerns of US scholars about the impact of American policy on China, and has thus focused on bilateral policies which are highly vulnerable to sovereignty objections by the target state, rather than taking the whole picture into account.

In attempting an overview of the different sources of pressure, multilateral, bilateral and international nongovernmental, this chapter acknowledges from the outset the difficulty of distinguishing between pressures applied internationally and those emerging from within China.[9] The most one can conclude is that certain human rights outcomes in China may be closely associated with particular types of external and domestic pressures. The following qualitative analysis distinguishes between the different phases of the international community's human rights engagement with China since 1949 and attempts to assess their effectiveness, while taking into account both international and domestic pressures. Thus, it compares and contrasts the effectiveness of periods of Principled Engagement with periods of Ostracism and of Business as Usual against particular domestic environments. From this case study it then seeks to reach conclusions about the most effective international approaches to China, which may also be applicable to other authoritarian states.

1949–1989: From Pariah Status to International Acceptance

Between 1949 and 1971, many Western states ostracised the People's Republic, despite ongoing attempts by some non-Western states to support its replacement of the Republic of China as "China's" representative in the United Nations. After 1971, when these attempts finally succeeded, the world gradually moved away from the two decades of ostracism which had utterly failed to bring China into the international fold.[10] Beijing, in turn, gradually increased its cooperation with the international community and, in particular, with the international human rights regime.

In the early years of its UN membership, China limited its human rights involvement to issues of collective human rights that it had supported since 1949, such as the right to self-determination and opposition to apartheid.[11] For this reason, it refused to participate in the work of the UN Commission on Human Rights but joined another Economic and Social Council (ECOSOC) functional committee, the Commission on the Status of Women. It was also wary about the Universal Declaration and the two International Covenants, emphasising as they did the rights of the individual as well as of the collective.[12] Since it did not become party to any of the conventions relating to human rights, it was not subject to monitoring by the relevant bodies.

It is notable that China's more proactive involvement in the international human rights regime, especially from the late 1970s, coincided not with international pressures but with the end of the Cultural Revolution and the beginning of its economic modernisation programme, which encouraged its greater international openness, its increased interest in participation in the global community and stronger domestic pressures for improved human rights. Even though there was no direct international pressure on it, China would also have been influenced in this period by the international context, which was highly favourable to human rights. Beginning with Ostpolitik in 1970 and the Helsinki Accords in 1975, the West exchanged recognition of the legitimacy of Eastern European countries and the Soviet Union for an improvement in their human rights.

Within this confluence of internal pressures and a growing international human rights consciousness, China sent observer delegates to the UN Human Rights Commission's sessions in 1979, 1980 and 1981.[13] By 1981, it had been elected by ECOSOC as a member of the Commission and in 1982 sent an official delegation. It had then joined the Sub-Commission on Prevention of Discrimination and Protection of Minorities, a panel of human rights experts, in 1984. From 1980 to 1989 it successively signed, or signed and ratified, seven human rights conventions and one protocol.[14] It also participated in the working group to draft and formulate the Convention against Torture and Other Cruel, Inhuman or Degrading Treatment or Punishment.[15] Rounding off this move to ratify human rights treaties in the 1980s, China's ratification of the Convention against Torture on 4 October 1988 made it subject to the obligation in Article 2 to "take effective legislative, administrative, judicial or other measures to prevent acts of torture in any territory under its jurisdiction".[16]

1989–1990: Renewed Opprobrium

In 1989, China's democracy movement was only one part of a worldwide stirring of peoples within socialist states seeking greater human rights and democracy.[17] The Chinese government's armed suppression of the movement in June 1989, unlike the later opening up and political transformation of other socialist states, put an end to the period of relative human rights openness in China, and saw a brief return to a mix of international ostracism and sanctions in response to the killings near and around Tiananmen Square, as well as in other parts of the country. International NGOs soon commenced a critique, while many international organisations and national governments imposed sanctions on China and, in some cases, partially ostracised it. China's immediate reaction was one of hostility and denial. It was not until some six months afterwards, when the mutual hostility had to some extent diminished, that the rest of the world began for the first time to pursue a policy of principled multilateral and bilateral human rights engagement with China.

1990–1997: Principled Engagement

From 1990, human rights were at the forefront of much of China's international relations. The international community sought Principled Engagement with China at both bilateral and multilateral levels, which on the whole fell into the sub-category of communicative, rather than strategic, engagement. In addition to sustained activity by UN human rights treaty bodies, Special Rapporteurs and the International Labour Organization (ILO), the early 1990s opened the era of bilateral parliamentary or human rights delegations to China. These published public reports, delivered criticisms of China's human rights and were constituted by academic specialists, international NGOs, public servants and politicians. The US was still wielding its strategic bilateral weapon of most favoured nation (MFN) sanctions, but this was combined with engaging China in close human rights dialogue and in multilateral forums. The result was a "selective ostracism", wherein the threat of closing off access to MFN served to open up, rather than close down, opportunities for dialogue. It was also the era dominated by the UN Human Rights Commission and Sub-Commission and annual draft resolutions, or, in two cases, resolutions, critical of China's human rights.

In this period, engagement was multi-pronged and public; it came from the UN, from governments and from international NGOs and academics; it focused on the international bill of rights, on governance and reform; and it targeted specific issues. It was critical but compromise-seeking. It sought to persuade, encourage and socialise China on the question of human rights, to strengthen state capacity, and to empower internal forces for change. In the same period too, China took its own steps to build up its academic expertise and human rights capacity, the better to take on the external critique. That is, while the outside world was operating on the basis of Principled Engagement, China tended to respond strategically. Despite its principled objection to the involvement of NGOs in human rights monitoring, it even mimicked international practice by establishing its own human rights NGO, the Human Rights Study Society, although at the UN Human Rights Conference in Vienna in 1993 this was generally known as a GONGO (government organised non government organisation).[18]

Multilateral Engagement

The most dramatic UN response to the killings around Tiananmen Square took the form of a resolution on China by the UN Human Rights Sub-Commission in August 1989. This was followed in August 1991 by the passage of a second resolution, despite China's call for a "no-action" motion. Between 1990 and 1997, several draft resolutions on China were also co-sponsored at the UN Human Rights

Commission. Both Sub-Commission resolutions were rejected angrily by China, but because the Sub-Commission was comprised of human rights experts rather than, as in the case of the Human Rights Commission, states representatives, the shaming effect of such a resolution was less than if the resolution had been adopted in the Commission. It was closer to the monitoring effect of expert-based treaty bodies, such as the Committee Against Torture, as well as of Special Rapporteurs and UN Specialised Agencies such as the ILO, which engaged in "reintegrative shaming", by investigating, documenting and publicising state behaviour which offended human rights standards.[19] Theirs was a longer-term, subtle operation of communicative engagement, reiterating, remonstrating, persuading, patiently arguing, praising evidence of progress, reinforcing norms, communicating and demonstrating procedural requirements.

Between 1989 and 1997, from its initial position of denial and refusal to cooperate with UN bodies, China became increasingly compliant procedurally and began to fulfil its reporting obligations and to cooperate more fully with UN treaty bodies and UN Special Rapporteurs.[20] Multilateral and NGO pressures also stimulated the despatch overseas of many Chinese legal experts to study the application of international human rights law, and the incorporation of human rights standards in new Chinese legislation.[21] If these developments did not impact directly on the repression of dissent, at least they brought a gradual change in laws governing due process in ways that more closely approximated international practice, and therefore promised a fairer court process. Over the years, China also began to reconsider the practice of torture, widespread use of the death penalty and the common practice of administrative detention.

International NGO Engagement

From 1989 until 1997, the main form of engagement with China undertaken by international advocacy NGOs such as Amnesty International, Human Rights Watch and Human Rights in China was Principled Engagement, combined with shaming.[22] This policy was a universal one, which did not vary according to the nature of the political system of the target state. However, it tended to be more strategic than communicative, unless the NGOs were working through the UN human rights treaty bodies, which operated in a more communicative fashion. Their chief raison d'être was to supply hitherto hidden information, often denied by China, as well as well-researched analyses and reports, and that strength was intensified when working in association with multilateral organisations. The latter gave NGOs an authoritative platform from which to publicise their work.

By contrast, the main work being conducted within China, undertaken by a single individual, John Kamm, who later established the NGO the *Duihua* ("Conversation") Foundation, was based on communicative principles. His approach was one of "tough love", mixing friendship with criticism.[23] His work, conducted mainly in private, was critical to the release of countless prisoners of conscience in China from 1989.

Bilateral Engagement

Bilateral monitoring of China's human rights has had a more chequered history and a more controversial role than that of multilateral bodies and NGOs, primarily because, in attempting to impose the will of one state upon another, it has involved challenges to the latter's sovereignty. In other words, it has been more strategic than communicative. It has also been more susceptible to policy changes in response to the strategic environment, and therefore to inconsistency in approach. An evaluation of the active monitoring of China's human rights undertaken from 1989 to 1994 by the US and Australia, as well as of the passive, post-1994 "quiet diplomacy" phase, shows that, of the two, US monitoring was more strategic, and Australia's more communicative.[24]

This evaluation also suggests that, contrary to general belief, China did indeed comply with many of the specific conditions laid down for the renewal of MFN at different periods, at least on paper. Over a period of five years, as the 1993 executive order and previous congressional bills had required, Chinese authorities released political prisoners;[25] agreed to ensure that no goods made with prison labour were exported to the US; arranged the emigration of political prisoners; and agreed to discuss Red Cross visits to Chinese political prisoners. They also claimed adherence to the Universal Declaration of Human Rights and agreed to look into the issue of the jamming of Voice of America, as well as to consider the issue of Tibetan prisoners. Aside from these specific concessions, the publication of China's three human rights White Papers and the invitation to foreign human rights delegations also appear to have been motivated by concern to be seen to respond to the MFN challenge.

However, these changes in China's policies were mainly strategic ones that had limited practical, or at least systemic, impact and were subject to change when the power balance shifted. US linkage policy clearly did not lead to any meaningful internalisation of human rights norms. That this was not achieved is suggested by the continued excessive use of the death penalty, repeated reports of torture and the continued detention and imprisonment of political prisoners, documented between 1989 and 1994 by a range of international NGOs.[26] The failure of MFN to effect a change in the basic administration of justice was also indicated in the 1992 report of the second Australian human rights delegation and in a 1993 report by the Lawyers Committee for Human Rights, *Criminal Justice with Chinese Characteristics*.[27] The unsatisfactory state of overall human rights was indicated by China being rated 82nd on the 1991 Human Freedom Index, and above only Burma, Iraq and North Korea in Charles Humana's *World Human Rights Guide* of 1992.[28]

From the evidence, it is clear that China was prepared to allow curbs on its sovereignty in a highly formalised sense, such as in the release of prisoners on set dates, or in areas where the concessions would not receive publicity. Its leaders were also prepared to concede sovereignty in areas which proved to be non-threatening. For instance, after the initial refusal to allow Fang Lizhi to leave the country, Chinese authorities discovered that the emigration of dissidents had the effect of neutralising them politically. They therefore adjusted their policy, allowing Han Dongfang, Shen Tong, Wang Xizhe, Wei Jingsheng and, later, Chen Guangcheng to leave China, but not to return. The principal issues on which the Chinese were impervious to both multilateral and bilateral monitoring were those regarded as challenging the integrity and legitimacy of the Chinese state or endangering political stability, such as a resumption of dialogue with the Dalai Lama on Tibet, abortion and forced sterilisation, and religious persecution. The limits of compliance were thus defined by China's internal imperatives.

The pattern of Chinese compliance with MFN monitoring, moreover, revealed neither progressive improvement nor progressive decline, and thus differed from the steadier progress observable in some multilateral forums.[29] China's behaviour was contingent on the waxing or waning of its comparative power vis-à-vis the US, both in the foreign policy and domestic senses, on its influence within the international community, and on the degree of its internal political stability. By 1993, the 2000 Olympics had been awarded to Sydney, and another variable, strong presidential leadership, had waned. Henceforth, brinksmanship tactics became less dangerous for China, because there was both less to win and less to lose.[30]

The active phase of Australian human rights diplomacy with China from 1991 to 1993 demonstrated most aspects of principled, communicative engagement. It targeted specific issues, was critical, transparent, compromise-seeking, and sought to persuade and encourage China; moreover, it was accountable and established benchmarks for human rights progress. By contrast with the US, Australia set more modest goals, as was in keeping with the limited, if flexible, mechanisms open to a middle power, and its engagement was less coercive. From mid 1991, separated by a space of one and a half years, its human rights delegations placed pressure on Chinese authorities, while providing a measuring stick of progress over the period.[31] They also established the model for subsequent delegations from Europe and the United Kingdom (UK). Members of the second delegation noted progress in China's human rights and in China's readiness to accept international engagement since the visit of the first delegation. Chinese officials were even beginning to consider that the rights not to be tortured or arrested without cause might be universal.[32]

An important aspect of this early human rights diplomacy was its two-track character. At the same time as it pursued bilateral human rights diplomacy, from 1989 to 1996 Australia co-sponsored draft resolutions on China in the UN Human Rights Sub-Commission and UN Human Rights Commission, two of which were adopted. However, because the human rights delegations had been conceived as joint enterprises, Australia was ultimately dependent on Chinese goodwill to continue its monitoring role, and therefore, indirectly, on the pressures exerted by MFN. For this reason, as China became increasingly immune to US pressure from 1993, Australia proceeded to demote human rights in its overall political relationship with China, rather than regarding them as integral to its own strategic and even commercial relations.[33]

By 1994, individual states had already moved from active Principled Engagement with China to a more passive "quiet diplomacy". This was less effective than the active phase, since it brought an end to open and transparent dialogue. However, because of its two-track character, it still maintained some of the aspects of Principled Engagement. The abandonment of the two-track policy in 1997 spelt the end of this period of strong Principled Engagement with China, which was replaced by an uneasy and ambiguous mix of weaker engagement and a Business as Usual approach.

Overall, the total international engagement with China on human rights between 1971 and 1997 was marked by the following associations ($\Rightarrow$) between international and domestic pressures and outcomes:

- 1971–1979: Weak application of the UN regime, little attention from states and NGOs, combined with little internal pressure $\Rightarrow$ little Chinese interest in, or compliance with, the regime.
- 1979–1989: Weak application of the UN regime, little attention from states and NGOs, yet a favourable international environment for human rights and increasing internal pressures $\Rightarrow$ voluntary Chinese participation in the regime.
- 1989–1990: Strong and sudden application of the multilateral regime through international economic sanctions, combined with China's repressive internal measures and weakened internal pressures $\Rightarrow$ China's resistance and non-compliance.
- 1990–1992: Consistent and strong application of the UN regime and ongoing US threat to remove China's MFN status, combined with China's weak bargaining power and the revival of internal pressures $\Rightarrow$ selective Chinese compliance, including the release of political prisoners.
- 1993–1996: Continued strong application of the UN regime, but gradual weakening application of the overall regime as a result of the delinkage of MFN and human rights, combined with China's improved international economic bargaining position and domestic and social instability $\Rightarrow$ China's reiteration of principles of sovereignty and weakening of compliance with bilateral pressures, though improved procedural compliance in multilateral forums and at the level of improved domestic implementation of international standards of labour, administrative and criminal law.
- 1996–1997: Continued weakening in effectiveness of overall regime, due to loss of bilateral pressures, combined with China's stronger financial bargaining position, stronger domestic political situation but heightened social instability $\Rightarrow$ China's new foreign policy of peace and "cooperation rather than confrontation" in human rights, its continued reiteration of principles of sovereignty and non-interference and its increasingly assertive human rights diplomacy.[34]

In sum, China was more likely to improve its human rights when the international community interacted with China consistently and cooperatively in combined multilateral, bilateral and NGO activity, and when international priorities and China's domestic priorities coincided. By contrast, China was only responsive to bilateral pressures when its strategic interests required it, before 1993, whereas it became more compliant with the standards of the more communicative and authoritative UN human rights bodies over time, and particularly after 1993, even though its enhanced economic status had empowered it to reject bilateral pressures.

1997–Present: Bilateral Business as Usual

The year 1997 was a defining period because it brought an end to consistency and cooperation in the international approach to China's human rights and not only compartmentalised human rights from other aspects of China's bilateral relationship with individual states, but also ended cooperation between states on the question of China's human rights. By this time, China's improved international status within the international community and its increasing economic power had emboldened it to step up its political pressure on states members of the UN Human Rights Commission through a mixture of commercial threats and inducements of bilateral dialogue offered to potential opponents of the China resolution. Australia, along with a number of European states, succumbed to these tactics.[35] In this way, China successfully bilateralised a multilateral process, undermining the ability of the UN Human Rights Commission and Sub-Commission to monitor its human rights effectively. Australia's excuse that it had to withdraw its annual co-sponsorship of the resolution on the grounds of the alleged ineffectiveness of the exercise had a hollow ring, particularly in view of its subsequent co-sponsorship of a resolution on Burma in the same forum.

By a process of divide and rule, China had altered the whole momentum of international human rights engagement with it. By adopting the slogan of "cooperation rather than confrontation", it was co-opting part of the notion of "communicative engagement". The other essential part, "public" communication, however, now became "private and secret". Thus, the bilateral dialogues no longer fitted into the category of genuine communicative engagement. Moreover, the decision as to what kind and degree of engagement should occur had thereby been transferred from the international community to China.

While UN treaty bodies, UN Special Rapporteurs, UN specialised agencies and, for the most part, NGOs, maintained their principled, communicative standards, individual states were now less concerned to pressure China to accept international human rights standards, arguing instead that human rights would improve gradually and naturally in China as a result of the "trickle-down effect" and the evolution of a Chinese middle class demanding improved civil and political rights. This market creed conformed to Pedersen and Kinley's concept of Business as Usual. The new post-1997 bilateral human rights dialogue was premised on the explicit disavowal of any further international critique and an end to transparency and the establishment of benchmarks. This undermined the quality of the previous engagement and the overall effectiveness of international efforts. Interaction was now more market-driven, and aimed at China's GDP, rather than its all-round development. It was primarily cooperative, opportunistic, and non-critical, emphasising the importance of enhancing state capacity and economic structures.

Multilateral Engagement

With the exception of the UN Human Rights Commission, multilateral monitoring of China's human rights continued to be characterised by rigour and consistency. A snapshot of the nature and effectiveness of the post-1997 engagement of UN human rights treaty bodies and UN Special Rapporteurs with China on civil, political, economic and social rights is provided in the 2008 UN summary of reports of treaty bodies, special procedures and other relevant official UN documents, compiled in preparation for China's UPR in the following year.[36] The summary showed areas of progress in China, such as legal reforms, the promotion of gender equality, the restoration of Supreme Court review for all death sentences, and the reduction of poverty. However, by combining the findings of so many UN expert bodies on China's implementation of specific human rights, it also revealed the consistency of their concerns, in particular in relation to the continuing practice of torture, administrative detention, forced labour and human rights violations against human rights activists and petitioners. Other multilateral institutions like the World Bank, the International Monetary Fund (IMF) and the ILO also maintained their steady, communicative, yet critical, engagement, enlarging China's capacities and providing vital assistance and advice.[37] In particular, the branches of UN agencies or UN specialised agencies established within China itself, like those of the ILO and the World Bank, helped encourage slow, incremental changes in China's labour and social policies.

Nevertheless, the new UN Human Rights Council, set up in 2006 partly in reaction to the gradual emasculation of the UN Human Rights Commission by authoritarian states like China, continued to experience similar problems to its predecessor in monitoring China's human rights. This was because, even though its UPR was now comprehensive in its application, and appeared to involve more communicative strategies, it was still constituted by states members rather than human rights experts.[38] It therefore risked the same problem of potentially challenging the sovereignty of authoritarian states. As a protective strategy during the reviews, such states simply organised a united front against their critics.

A perfect demonstration of the difficulties facing UN human rights bodies composed of states members rather than human rights experts occurred in February 2009, on the occasion of China's UPR in Geneva. At the conclusion of the interactive dialogue, China rejected all recommendations from Switzerland, the UK, France, Mexico, the Czech Republic, Italy and Hungary, and the majority of recommendations from Australia, Canada, the Netherlands, Germany, Finland, New Zealand, Sweden, and Brazil.[39] All the latter countries had combined some commendations with strong criticism, particularly on aspects of China's civil rights. Among the recommendations China rejected was that it investigate reports of harassment and detention of human rights defenders, including alleged mistreatment while in police custody (27g) and that it ratify the International Covenant on Civil and Political Rights (ICCPR) as soon as possible and bring its legislation into line with its provisions (30b). China did not reject any recommendations from the countries which had primarily lauded its achievements, such as India, Iran, Singapore and the Philippines.[40] Most of these states, which were either authoritarian states or developing and/or neighbouring states, praised it for its progress in economic and social rights, but some also expressed support for its abuse of civil rights in the interests of maintaining state control. It was a case of *noscitur a sociis*. This process demonstrated the validity of the complaint by Freedom House that in the UN Human Rights Council, "too many of the world's democracies – particularly in Africa, Asia and Latin America – follow the lead of highly repressive countries like Egypt, China and Cuba".[41]

The 2009 proceedings were a testimony at once to China's success in manipulating the human rights politics of the actual forum and to the immense distance it still had to travel before it could satisfy international human rights standards. In many ways it appeared as if China had co-opted the international dialogue in this new forum and was now determining the values and direction of its human rights interaction with the international community. Yet, despite these failings, this new process at least brought some transparency to China's behaviour. It revealed the extent and consistency of UN concerns, highlighted the contribution of NGOs and, most important of all, returned China to the table of comprehensive, international, public scrutiny and accountability, as it did in the case of every other state.[42]

Apart from attempting to influence the norms of the UN Human Rights Council, China has continued to lobby UN human rights treaty bodies, to cut back the mandates of the Special Procedures, and to oppose the accreditation of key NGOs at the UN. As Andrew Nathan and Andrew Scobell have pointed out, "China's goal in all this appears not to be to get rid of the international human rights regime (which would be difficult and unnecessary), but to cap its growth and expansion, freeze its effectiveness at the current level, shape its institutions so that they are deferential to states, and shade the norms to fit Chinese priorities."[43] Chinese diplomats have done this, in the words of prominent UN human rights expert Felice Gaer, not only by threatening their critics, but by "work[ing] to make the instrumentalities that monitor them toothless – to render them into almost powerless entities, for example, creating a committee that cannot speak out, a procedure that cannot name names, or instruments that can't promote compliance".[44]

Bilateral Engagement

Since 1997, the US, the UK, Canada, Australia, Brazil, Norway, Sweden, Germany, Switzerland, Austria and the European Union have all conducted active human rights bilateral dialogues with China. Most have been subjected to similar criticisms by NGOs and politicians of lacking transparency, and of failing to coordinate with other dialogue partners and set a timeframe and clear benchmarks for progress.[45] For instance, the Australia–China human rights dialogue, which began in Beijing in August 1997, was not as transparent as the human rights delegations of the early 1990s, nor did it publish a report.[46] It was not public, representative or accountable, being conducted entirely *in camera*. Although China has sent reciprocal human rights dialogue delegations to Australia, their achievements have been more symbolic than real.

By contrast, the technical assistance or Technical Cooperation Programme (TCP) that Australia, like the US and Europe, offered, theoretically in conjunction with the dialogue, was more meaningful. The Australian TCP was focused largely on civil and political rights, with emphasis on legal issues. By 2004, 40 TCP activities had been implemented, and Australian funding had risen to A$1.6 million per year.[47]

While much of the technical assistance fell into the category of principled and communicative engagement, at the formal governmental level, the actual dialogue since 1997 was scarcely able to match the achievements of the 1991–1992 human rights delegations. In comparison with the US, which continued to hold regular talks on human rights through its embassy in Beijing, and which maintained its public accountability through regular, public human rights reports, Australia emphasised the style of its dialogue at the expense of content and outcome. While the money and effort directed to technical assistance were useful, the dialogue itself, as Australian Foreign Ministry submissions on Australia–China relations have made clear, made no discernible progress. Moreover, until the establishment of the UPR by the new Human Rights Council in 2007, it narrowed Australia's tactical options, as it did those of European dialogue partners, because of China's ownership of the process and its insistence that continuing bilateral dialogue was conditional upon states refraining from co-sponsoring a China resolution in the then UN Human Rights Commission.

International NGO Engagement

While the main focus of advocacy NGOs has remained the critique of China's human rights, since 1997, as part of the "dialogue and cooperation" agreement, an increasing number of developmental NGOs have had access to the country to pursue human rights projects. Thus, by 2006, there were about 250 to 300 international NGOs operating in China.[48] They act as intermediaries between donor governments, the Chinese government and Chinese partners. Since China has never accepted the right of international NGOs to criticise its human rights, some NGOs, such as the Ford Foundation and the Danish Institute of Human Rights, have chosen a more inclusive type of collaboration, at the risk of providing apparent legitimacy for China's human rights policies.[49] Since there are relatively few local NGOs for them to relate to, they claim that often cooperation with the government is their only option.[50] While engaging with Chinese authorities in a communicative fashion, they have therefore opted to avoid politically sensitive issues, politically sensitive places, such as Tibet and Xinjiang, and politically sensitive language.[51]

Even in the case of legal projects, international NGOs have to mediate the tension between politics and their development assistance goals. In jointly devising programmes, they face not only lack of political will on the part of the Chinese government authorities, but also their Chinese partners' fears of accepting projects that could have political implications.[52] In the face of these obstacles, implementing agencies, such as those working on legal projects, acknowledge the limited scope of their achievements in comparison to the enormity of the issues they seek to address.[53] As one scholar of China's "rule of law" programmes put it, "A key question is how much legal professionalism and institution building can achieve in the absence of adherence to the normative values that are the stated or unstated objectives of donor programmes."[54]

Many recommendations have been made to improve the communicative process. A Chinese academic has called for the establishment of a comprehensive international NGO working body through the UN, which would incorporate significant international resources and local representatives:

> The Chinese case reveals an ethical dilemma for INGOs: there is a pressing need to make a concerted lobbying effort that might integrate public monitoring of China's human rights situation and the quiet diplomacy associated with dialogue ... [Because the prestige of the UN in China is high,] cooperating with the UN human rights mechanisms is crucial so that all countries engaged in a human rights dialogue with China build on and reinforce positive results generated by the work on UN procedures.[55]

Sophia Woodman has called for greater commitment on the part of aid donors, improved contextual knowledge, improved cooperation allowing Chinese "ownership" of projects, enhanced coordination between donors, and engagement with the political obstacles placed in their way as a means of opening up space for domestic human rights advocates – "arguably the most crucial aspect of achieving practical change on the ground".[56]

Michael Santoro has also focused on the importance of foreign support for China's embattled domestic human rights advocates, and particularly for China's budding rule of law. An expert on the foreign business community in China, he argues that foreign companies and their lawyers, who are too ready to accept China's *guanxi* ("personal connections") system, have an important role to play in the establishment of a genuine rule of law in China. As he points out, "A number of

NGOs such as the Ford Foundation, the American Bar Association and academics both within and outside China have devoted extensive resources to tilling the soil for legal transformation in China ... Only the business community and its lawyers have failed to do their part."[57] He argues that,

> To the extent that they attempt to resolve commercial disputes through the judicial system and insist on fairness and justice from that system, foreign businesses could positively influence the trajectory and pace of legal reform. Conversely, to the extent that foreign firms continue to rely on personalized power relations, foreign firms are slowing the emergence of the rule of law.[58]

Thus, he calls on foreign companies to show "some moral courage and conviction" by using China's Administrative Litigation Law (ALL), as they are entitled to do under the WTO, to protect their interests in the Chinese courts, just like thousands of courageous ordinary citizens who have used the ALL to challenge government actions in the courtroom. Second, by investing their substantial legal resources in the ALL system, foreign companies can help to build a set of legal precedents for administrative review of actions. Should this fail, they can use international trade law to obtain China's compliance by utilising the transitional review mechanism set up under the Accession Protocol, pursuant to which the WTO may review China's compliance with the protocol for the first eight years of operation. They can also pressure China to implement an independent judicial review system via the WTO Dispute Settlement Body. Finally, they could support the professional independence and liberties of Chinese lawyers. He recommends that businesses adopt a "tough love" approach by communicating "forcefully but in a culturally sensitive manner ... that shows respect and admiration for China's many accomplishments and qualities", and that they work collectively with NGOs and their own governments.[59]

Most of these recommendations have been characterised by calls for greater publicity to be given to collaborative projects, and for political pressure to be used in conjunction with communicative approaches. It is significant, for instance, that, after over 20 years of successful advocacy for Chinese dissidents, during which much of his work has been conducted in private, John Kamm has also supported greater publicity for Chinese prisoners of conscience. In 2009, he called on the US authorities, who for almost two years had been working quietly but unsuccessfully, to secure the release of Chinese American Xue Feng,[60] to change their approach: "Under difficult and dangerous circumstances, Dr Xue made it clear that he wanted the American people to learn of his ordeal. I have little doubt that had his wishes been respected, his case would have already been resolved."[61]

The Current Balance Sheet

Since China's opening up in 1978, poverty has been drastically reduced. In its 2010 progress report for China, *China's Progress towards the Millennium Development Goals*, the UN system in China and the Chinese Ministry of Foreign Affairs noted that "China has made remarkable achievements towards the MDGs, particularly in poverty reduction", although it still faced challenges in the promotion of gender equality, reversing the spread of HIV/AIDS and stopping the loss of environmental resources.[62] Thus, "in 2009, China adopted per capita net income RMB1,196 as the new national poverty line, upon which basis its rural poor population dropped from 0.25 billion in 1978 to 35.79 million in 2009".[63]

However, in terms of redistributive goals and the equality of rights affecting the lives of individual citizens, contrary to expectations, Business as Usual based on the ideology of the "trickle-down effect" has not promoted human rights in China, whether civil, political, economic or social. As foreign investment flooded in and joint ventures proliferated, China's cities were increasingly transformed into vast industrial and construction sites, serviced 24 hours a day by pitifully paid migrant workers flocking in from the countryside.[64] New problems of inequality, corruption, exploitation and subsistence, reminiscent of the 1920s,[65] were fuelled in part by the investment and joint enterprises of those same Western powers professing concern for China's human rights. By 2003, a new leadership in China began to realise that the policy of suppressing civil and political rights had not succeeded in stemming the tide of discontent, and to turn its attention to improving citizens' economic, social and cultural rights. This was to be achieved not by reintroducing the "iron rice bowl" of the socialist system, but by establishing a system which was closer to the welfare state model common in developed Western economies. Thus, the leaders introduced policies to redress economic and social imbalances by expanding the basis of social welfare and social insurance and improving labour conditions.[66] The introduction of the Labour Contract Law in June 2007 and the increase in the minimum wage were important steps in this direction. So was the pledge by Chinese Premier Wen Jiabao at the 2010 National People's Congress that he would increase social spending by 8.8 per cent and spending on rural programmes by 12.8 per cent, whereas spending on national defence would be only increased by 7.5 per cent. As he observed in an earlier online chat, a society was "doomed to instability" if wealth was concentrated in the hands of a few.[67]

This change in policy was primarily the outcome of domestic pressures building up within China itself. While it was also associated with the ongoing efforts and advocacy of multilateral organisations such as the UN Economic, Social and Cultural Rights Committee, the ILO, the World Bank, the IMF and the UN Development Programme, as well as some NGOs, it certainly was not an outcome of bilateral dialogue, which has focused very little attention on economic, social and cultural rights. The social consequences of economic and social inequality had their corresponding impact on the situation of civil and political rights. The denial of vital civil rights, such as the freedoms of association, assembly and collective bargaining, the persistence of the system of administrative detention and the energetic utilisation of a rapidly expanding public security system were just some of the mechanisms used by the Chinese government to maintain social control in a context of widespread discontent. Others were the extensive and wide-ranging resort to the death penalty, the practice of torture and the arrest and sentencing of political dissidents, whether Han Chinese or minority peoples. By 2009, some civil reforms had been introduced, such as an improvement in due process rights and greater judicial controls over the death penalty, leading to a modest reduction of death penalty cases.[68] In the long term, such reform promised an improvement in the treatment of dissidents. In the short term, however, they were more than offset by the government's continuing suppression of dissent. Thus, in 2009 Freedom House reported that,

> Despite expectations that it would enact at least symbolic human rights improvements during its year as host of the Olympic Games, the Chinese government in 2008 increased restrictions on online writers, human rights lawyers, democracy activists, migrant workers, and individuals seeking to petition the central government on abuses by local officials. Religious and ethnic minorities were also subjected to stepped-up repression, including a number of high-profile deaths. While it passed promising labor legislation and extended regulations allowing greater freedom of movement for foreign journalists, the ruling Communist Party generally sought to tighten control over the judiciary and domestic media coverage. Grassroots activists and intellectuals defied this government hostility, raising increasingly bold calls for reform during the year.[69]

In its report, Freedom House identified China as one of the 42 countries out of 193 which were "not free", and as containing 60 percent of the world's population living in a Not Free state. It gave China a political rights score of seven (the lowest score) and a civil liberties score of six (the third lowest score). This placed China into a cohort of nine states, just above the lowest cohort of eight states including Burma and North Korea. Tibet, on the other hand, was one of eight states and two territories receiving the lowest possible ranking for both political rights and civil liberties.[70] In its 2011 report, China's score remained unchanged; the report even described "a broader trend of Communist Party efforts to tighten control over the media, the judiciary and civil society, and to strengthen its repressive apparatus in the face of growing rights-consciousness among the public".[71]

At the international level, the positive impact of UN human rights bodies' Principled Engagement with China on its human rights was reflected in the details of China's 2009 National Human Rights Action Plan.[72] Whereas the international section in China's first human rights White Paper in 1991 was primarily defensive, and while it placed emphasis on the importance of state sovereignty and on the right to development, the 2009 Plan reflected China's increasing involvement in international human rights bodies and focused on its efforts to engage and cooperate with those bodies. The very existence of the 2009 Plan was expressive of China's cooperation with the UN-sponsored movement encouraging all states to establish one. In particular, the Plan emphasised the reports China had made to UN human rights committees on its implementation of its various human rights obligations under each convention, its declared intention, repeated over many years since it signed the treaty in 1998, to accede to the ICCPR and its participation in the first UPR for China in the UN Human Rights Council in 2009. In line with other Asian states, China was also planning to establish its own National Human Rights Institution.[73] However, the subsequent National Human Rights Action Plan (2012–2015), published in close conjunction with the 12th Five-Year Plan for National Economic and Social Development, failed to mention any developments in this area.[74]

On the other hand, such formal compliance existed side by side with China's attempt to co-opt the international human rights discourse, so clearly evinced in the proceedings of China's UPR in 2009. It illustrated the gap between China's support for the human rights regime at a formal level and its actual empirical efforts, whether by use of its hard or soft power, to control it.

What, apart from the particular methods adopted by the international community, were the specific obstacles to Chinese progress? The clear contradictions in China's behaviour with respect to human rights have their origins in conflicting pressures within China itself. Domestic pressures encouraging human rights reform have included the increasing role of Chinese NGOs, the heroic actions of Chinese lawyers and labour rights activists working for the expansion of popular access to civil and labour rights, and other more abstract domestic political pressures, such as China's concern for its international status and good international reputation, the moral focus of its self-image, and, finally, more material economic policy priorities leading it to attempt to woo international friends and allies.

However, to date, international and domestic pressures for reform in China have been trumped by domestic pressures for continuity in its human rights policy. At best, China exhibits a selective compliance, or "selective adaptation",[75] which applies primarily to those international norms which would have little substantive, systemic political impact. The chief barriers to an improvement in China's human rights situation have been the leaders' three priorities: to preserve political power at all costs; to safeguard state security; and to defend China's right to develop. These are familiar defences of authoritarian states. Particularly in the context of the global financial crisis, in China these barriers have created not only the perceived need to assuage popular economic hurt but also to suppress any challenges to the leaders' political authority.

In other words, as in the pre-1997 period, the limits of China's compliance with international human rights standards continue to be defined by China's domestic imperatives. While the reach of the Chinese state may have retreated, it still extends to the strategic centres of power. Even fears of a threat to China's international status and reputation will, in the final analysis, be trumped by its concerns about sovereignty. The priority of sovereignty explains why, for instance, despite the belief of many commentators that, by focusing attention on China, the holding of the Olympics in Beijing would lead to an improvement in its human rights, China's determination to appear strong and in control led it to further repress civil rights both domestically and internationally, whatever the cost to its international reputation.

Conclusion

Notwithstanding the importance of such domestic pressures, the China case bears out many of the arguments of this book. The most consistently effective international approach to human rights, as Pedersen and Kinley hypothesise, has been Principled Engagement. China's human rights progress has also normally been associated with communicative, not strategic, forms of Principled Engagement, working primarily through persuasion, socialisation, capacity building and empowerment. The most effective form has also been public, based on a holistic, consistent and coordinated approach between multilateral, bilateral and NGO mechanisms. This has pre-empted divide-and-rule policies from being adopted by the target state.

Multilateral human rights treaty bodies composed of human rights experts and special expert rapporteurs have, to date, borne the burden of consistent communicative engagement with China. By contrast, engagement at a government-to-government level has generally been less effective because, in a coercive or strategic form of engagement, it has challenged China's sovereignty and has eventually succumbed to China's tactics to dilute its effects. In line with Lynch's argument that engagement must be public, bilateral engagement can only become more effective if it returns to a public, transparent and accountable communicative process which coordinates with other states and with multilateral organisations and international NGOs. Likewise, if a multilateral body like the UN Human Rights Council is to be effective, it should ideally replace its current state-based peer review system with an expert-based one, thereby obviating sovereignty issues. Finally, there is clearly an important role for international NGOs, business people and other professional individuals to directly and indirectly influence China's human rights. Although these efforts can be private, they, like multilateral and bilateral efforts, are arguably more effective if they are also public and transparent. They are most effective if their activity helps empower the domestic human rights advocates on whom the ultimate burden for an improvement in China's rights falls.

International engagement with China has, on occasions, involved elements of coercion in the form of sanctions. However, sanctions have had more impact as a distant or imminent threat rather than once they have been imposed, and when they have been mild rather than when they have been severe. The resort to unmediated coercion between 1949 and 1971, and again in 1989, has exhibited three drawbacks: perverse effects, strategic adaptation effects and power shift effects. First, when it has been too strong, coercion has risked perverse effects, such as when many states reacted with horror to the killings in China in June 1989 and after, by imposing coercive sanctions. Generally, these brought an angry backlash throughout China which only served at the time to unite the government and its citizens against outside pressure, if only as the result of the latter's fears. It also led China to begin to defensively construct its own human rights principles which it counter-posed to the international bill of rights, and to organise a supportive constituency of like-minded states within the UN. Second, although it complied with the US on the specific issue of prisoner release, China soon began to exploit the need in Western liberal democracies for accountability by playing a game of chess with political prisoners. China would initially release some prisoners of conscience at strategic points or dates as they affected the US–China relationship, and then, quite unaccountably, would detain others. Moreover, the drama and publicity surrounding such releases obscured China's failure to undertake meaningful human rights reform. Third, as China has become more powerful by manipulating both its hard and soft power, coercion has become both less relevant and less effective. Moderate coercive pressures may therefore be useful at certain periods, but must be utilised flexibly, with a consciousness of how effective they will be in specific circumstances.

By contrast, the problem with Business as Usual has been that although China has now overtaken Japan as the world's second largest economic power, the "trickle-down effect" has clearly not led to the emergence of a Chinese middle class calling for greater civil and political rights.[76]

There are other longer-term lessons which flow from the China case. To be completely effective, Principled Engagement needs to be linked with a dominant international human rights culture. One of the reasons that Principled Engagement with China was more effective in the early 1990s was that a human rights culture was more influential internationally then than it is in today's market-driven world , and that it was facilitated by unified coordinated policy between multilateral, bilateral and NGO bodies. The source of that stronger human rights culture was the clarion call for human rights issuing from within a range of socialist states, sweeping though China, the Soviet Union and the states of Eastern Europe. It was this call that energised the international community, although it had different outcomes in each state. It is to be hoped that the clarion call for freedom issuing from the Arab world may help to reinvigorate that international spirit. In the meantime, unlike other socialist states, China continues, as it did in 1989, to retreat from the human rights challenge.

However, the fatal weakness in the international human rights system has been the retreat of individual state members, awed and intimidated by China's rise, from Principled Engagement. It has been responsible for China's success in bilateralising a multilateral human rights system. In this context, China's increasing efforts in recent years to export its current human rights value system to the rest of the world, as exemplified in its approach to the UPR and its assertive policies before and during the 2008 Olympics, and to reshape UN human rights bodies to become more deferential to states, have become a threat to human rights globally.

It is clear from the China case that Principled Engagement can help reframe the human rights culture in which authoritarian states operate. UN human rights bodies, and international NGOs in particular, have helped achieve that. On the other hand, as the recent review of China by the UN Human Rights Council shows, they on their own cannot hope to be successful unless their efforts are also supported by the individual state members that comprise them. A revival of genuinely coordinated action at the three levels of international engagement, multilateral, bilateral and nongovernmental, will not in itself bring about major human rights reform in authoritarian states, but it will provide the most congenial and enabling environment for that reform once significant pressures again emerge from within those states for change.

Endnotes

1   The full text of the press conference is available at http://www.maximsnews.com/news20100318ChinaWenJiabopress11003180101.htm [accessed 16 December 2012].

2   China Human Rights Defenders (CHRD), "China Human Rights Briefing Weekly, 23–28 February 2011", available at http://www.chrdnet.com/2011/03/01/china-human-rights-briefing-february-23-28-2011 [accessed 12 May 2012]; Didi Kirsten Tatlow, "Arab Revolts Seen Through Chinese Eyes: Letter from China", *International Herald Tribune*, 24 February 2011.

3   Congressional Executive Commission on China, *Annual Report 2011*, 10 October 2011, 1.

4   Andrew Nathan and Andrew Scobell, "Human Rights and China's Soft Power Expansion", *China Rights Forum* 4 (2009), 1023.

5   Freedom House, "Freedom in the World 2011: The Authoritarian Challenge to Democracy", available at http://www.freedomhouse.org/report/freedom-world/freedom-world-2011 [accessed 12 May 2012].

6   Ibid.

7   Marc Lynch, "Why Engage? China and the Logic of Communicative Engagement", *European Journal of International Relations* 8, no. 2 (2002), 187.

8   Chronologically, see Peter Van Ness, "Analysing the Impact of International Sanctions on China" (Working Paper, Department of International Relations, Australian National University, Canberra, 1989); Lawyers' Committee for Human Rights, *Beyond Linkage and Engagement: A New Approach to US China Policy* (1998); Ann Kent, *China, the United Nations and Human Rights: The Limits of Compliance* (Philadelphia: The University of Pennsylvania Press, 1999); Gregory J. Moore, "Human Rights and United States Policy Toward China", *Crossroads Monograph Series on Faith and Public Policy* 27 (1999); Michael A. Santoro, *Profits and Principles: Global Capitalism and Human Rights In China* (Ithaca: Cornell University Press, 2000); Ann Kent, "States Monitoring States: The United States, Australia and China's Human Rights, 1990–2001", *Human Rights Quarterly* 23 (2001); Alan M. Wachman, "Does the Diplomacy of Shame Promote Human Rights in China?," *Third World Quarterly* 22, no. 2 (2001), 258–9; James de Lisle, "Pressing

Engagement: Uneven Human Rights Progress in China, Modest Success of American Policy, and the Absence of Better Options", Testimony to US Congress; and Michael A. Santoro, *China 2020: How Western Business Can – and Should – Influence Social and Political Change in the Coming Decade* (Ithaca: Cornell University Press, 2009).

9   See also Sonia Cardenas, "Norm Collision: Explaining the Effects of International Human Rights Pressure on State Behaviour", *International Studies Review* 6 (2004), 227; and Dinding Chen, "Explaining China's Changing Discourse on Human Rights, 1978–2004", *Asian Perspective* 29, no. 3 (2005), 155–82.

10   Roberta Cohen, "People's China: Human Rights Exception", *Human Rights Quarterly* 9, no. 4 (November 1987), 447–559.

11   According to *Zhongguo waijiao gailan 1989* [Survey of China's Foreign Relations 1989], (Beijing: Shijie zhishi chubanshe, 1990): 459–60, China believed the UN should give priority to issues of racism, colonialism, foreign aggression and occupation, national self-determination and development.

12   UN Doc E/AC.7/SR.748 (13 May 1974), 156–7, cited in Samuel S.K. Kim, *China, the United Nations and World Order* (Princeton: Princeton University Press, 1979), 486.

13   For this account, see Pang Sen, *Dangdai renquan ABC* [Contemporary Human Rights ABC] (Sichuan: Sichuan renmin chubanshe, 1992), 210.

14   Following is the chronological order of signature [Key: **Y**: China accepted (ratification, accession, or succession); **S**: China signed but not yet ratified; **R**: China made reservations]: *Convention on the Elimination of All Forms of Discrimination against Women*: **Y** (1980), **R** (Paragraph 1 of Art. 29); *International Convention on the Elimination of All Forms of Racial Discrimination*: **Y** (1981), **R** (Art. 22); *Protocol Relating to the Status of Refugees*: **Y** (1982), **R** (Art. 4); *Convention Relating to the Status of Refugees*: **Y** (1982), **R** (Art. 14. 16); *Convention on the Prevention and Punishment of the Crime of Genocide*: **Y** (1983), **R** (Art. 9); *International Convention on the Suppression and Punishment of the Crime of Apartheid*: **Y** (1983); *International Convention against Apartheid in Sports*: **S** (1987); *Convention against Torture and Other Cruel, Inhuman or Degrading Treatment or Punishment*: **Y** (1988), **R** (Art. 20, Para 1 of Art 30). See United Nations, *Multilateral Treaties Deposited with the Secretary-General. Status as at 31 December 1989* (New York: United Nations, 1990), ST/LEG/SER.E/8. For discussion of China's position on these treaties, see Xie Qimei and Wang Xingfang (eds), *Zhongguo yu Lianheguo: Jinian Lianheguo chengli wushi zhounian* [China and the United Nations: Commemorating the 50th Anniversary of the Founding of the People's Republic of China] (Beijing: Shijie zhishi chubanshe, 1995), 343–53.

15   Pang Sen, op. cit., 210.

16   See Article 2.1 in *Convention against Torture and Other Cruel, Inhuman or Degrading Treatment or Punishment*, in UN Centre for Human Rights, *Human Rights: A Compilation of International Instruments* (New York: United Nations, 1993), Vol. 1, Part 1, 294.

17   Bao Pu, Renee Chiang and Adi Ignatius, *Prisoner of the State: The Secret Journal of Zhao Ziyang* (New York: Simon & Shuster, 2009).

18   Li Baodong, the Society's representative at the NGO Conference which preceded the official UN Conference, is now China's UN Ambassador in New York and led China's delegation to the Universal Periodic Review in the UN Human Rights Council in February 2009.

19   This placed pressure on China and other defaulting states to bring their domestic human rights conditions into conformity with international human rights standards, yet

credited them with reform efforts. See theory in John Braithwaite, *Crime, Shame and Reintegration* (New York: Cambridge University Press, 1989).

20   Kent, 1999, op. cit.

21   Ibid., 194–215.

22   Kenneth Roth of Human Rights Watch has stated that "the core of our methodology is our ability to investigate, expose and shame. We are at our most effective when we can hold governmental (or, in some cases, nongovernmental) conduct up to a disapproving public." Cited in Daniel A. Bell, *Beyond Liberal Democracy: Political Thinking for an East Asian Context* (Princeton: Princeton University Press, 2006), 96.

23   As Kamm has stated, "I try to convince my counterparts that releasing someone the government sees as an enemy holds benefits for China, being as specific as possible. I approach the enterprise with respect and in a spirit of friendship and trust. I am results oriented. I never criticise senior officials and when the Chinese government does good, I find ways to recognize it." Cited in Santoro, 2009, op. cit.,141.

24   Kent, 2001, op. cit.

25   The correlation between the release of dissidents and the decision-making dates for MFN is particularly indicative of the effectiveness of MFN in this respect.

26   These included Amnesty International, Asia Watch, and the International League for Human Rights and Human Rights in China.

27   See *Report of the Second Australian Human Rights Delegation to China, 8 20 November 1992* (Canberra: Department of Foreign Affairs and Trade, 10 March 1993); *Visit to China by the Delegation led by Lord Howe of Aberavon: Report* (London: HMSO, 1993); and Lawyers Committee for Human Rights, *Criminal Justice with Chinese Characteristics* (New York, May 1993).

28   See Freedom index cited in *South China Morning Post*, 24 November 1991; and Charles Humana, *World Human Rights Guide* (1992), 725. For a general assessment of China's human rights before 1992, see Ann Kent, *Between Freedom and Subsistence: China and Human Rights* (Hong Kong: Oxford University Press, 1993).

29   Kent, 1993, op. cit., 232–50.

30   Kent, 2001, op. cit., 602–3.

31   Department of Foreign Affairs and Trade, *Report of the Australian Human Rights Delegation to China, 14–26 July 1991* (Canberra: Australian Department of Foreign Affairs and Trade, September 1991), 13.

32   Interview in Kent, 2001, op. cit., 615.

33   Ibid., 614–5.

34   Kent, 1999, op. cit., 248.

35   For detailed analysis of European, Brazilian and Australian dialogue delegations, see Human Rights in China, *From Principle to Pragmatism: Can Dialogue Improve China's Human Rights Situation?* (New York, 1998), available at http://www.hrichina.org/what-we-do/research-and-publications/reports [accessed 12 May 2012].

36   UN Doc. A/HRC/WG.6/4/CHN/2 (16 December 2008).

37   Ann Kent, *Beyond Compliance: China, International Organizations and Global Security* (Stanford, CA: Stanford University Press, 2007), 103–43, 181–202.

38   See comments by Felice D. Gaer in "The UN Human Rights Council's Review of China's Record: Process and Challenges", *Roundtable before the Congressional-Executive Commission on China,* 111th Congress, First session (16 January 2009), 24.

39   UN Doc. A/HRC/11/25 (March 2009), 114–18.

40   The full list of supportive states was Singapore, the Philippines, Algeria, Bhutan, Egypt, Libya, Sri Lanka, South Africa, Sudan, Cuba, Ghana, Mozambique, Angola, Viet Nam, Morocco, Oman, United Arab Republic, Nicaragua, India, Yemen, Jordan, Iran, Bahrain, Zimbabwe, Indonesia, Benin, Mali, Gabon, Palestine, Qatar, Pakistan, Venezuela, Senegal, Colombia, Thailand, Myanmar, and Malaysia.

41   Freedom House, *The UN Human Rights Council Report Card: 2007–2009* (Washington, DC: Freedom House, 2009), 19.

42   The view of the UPR bringing greater transparency to China's human rights was also expressed by Canadian Falonggong advocate David Matas at his seminar "From the UN Universal Periodic Review to an Asia Pacific Human Rights Institution", Centre for International and Public Law, ANU College of Law, Canberra, 25 November 2009.

43   Nathan and Scobell, 2009, op. cit., 20.

44   Felice Gaer, "Engaging China on Human Rights: The UN Labyrinth," *China Rights Forum*, no. 3 (2010), 14, available at http://www.hrichina.org/crf/article/3261 [accessed 16 December 2012].

45   See, for example, International Centre for Human Rights and Democratic Development, *Bilateral Human Rights Dialogue with China*, January 2001, 68. Occasional attempts to hold meetings between states to discuss their dialogue experiences, known as the Berne Process, have been rejected by China as unfriendly. See Nathan and Scobell, 2009, op. cit., 18.

46   The only publication issuing from it was a brief report, containing an itinerary and a short list of issues raised, by the first parliamentarian to take part in the dialogue, Peter Nugent, who was obliged by parliamentary rules to issue a personal report. See *Report of the Parliamentary Representative on the Australian Delegation to the Third Round Australia–China Bilateral Human Rights Dialogue, Beijing, 14–21 August 1999* (18 October 1999), 15.

47   Caroline Fleay, "Australian Foreign Policy, Human Rights in China and the Spiral Model", *Australian Journal of Political Science* 41, no. 1 (March 2006), 82–3.

48   Sun Zhe, "Normative Compliance and Hard Bargaining: China's Strategies and Tactics in Response to International Human Rights Criticism", in Daniel A. Bell and Jean-Marc Coicaud (eds), *Ethics in Action: The Ethical Challenges of International Human Rights Nongovernmental Organizations* (New York: Cambridge University Press, 2006), 152.

49   Daniel Bell and Jean-Marc Coicaud, *The Ethical Challenges of International Human Rights NGOs. Policy Brief No. 9* (Tokyo: United Nations University, 2006), 3–4, available at http://unu.edu/publications/research-policy-briefs/2000-2006/the-ethical-challenges-of-international-human-rights-ngos [accessed 12 May 2012].

50   See Birgit Lindsnaes, Hans-Otto Sano and Hatla Thelle, "Human Rights in Action: Supporting Human Rights Work in Authoritarian Countries", in Bell and Coicaud, 2006, *Ethics in Action*, op. cit., 124.

51   Ibid., 125.

52   Sophia Woodman, "Driving without a Map: Implementing Legal Projects in China Aimed at Improving Human Rights", in Bell and Coicaud, 2006, *Ethics in Action*, op. cit., 137.

53   Ibid., 148.

54   Sophia Woodman, "Bilateral Aid to Improve Human Rights", *China Perspectives* 51 (Jan–Feb 2004), 8.

55   Sun Zhe, 2006, op. cit., 166–7.

56   Woodman, 2004, op. cit., 723.

57   Santoro, 2009, op. cit., 125.

58   Ibid., 122.

59   Ibid., 138–41.

60   Xue Feng was detained by Chinese authorities in 2007 on the charge of promoting foreign business interests.

61   Cited in Charles Hutzler, "China Holds, Mistreats US Geologist", Associated Press, 21 November 2009, available at http://www.guardian.co.uk/world/feedarticle/8818171 [accessed 12 May 2012].

62   "UN Foreword" in Ministry of Foreign Affairs of the People's Republic of China and United Nations System in China, *China's Progress Towards the Millennium Development Goals 2010 Report* (2010), 3.

63   Ibid., 10.

64   See, in particular, Philip P. Pan, "China's New Laborers Forced to Work Till They Drop", *Washington Post* in *Guardian Weekly*, 23–29 May 2002, 37.

65   For contrast with the early 1970s and similarity to the 1920s, see Priscilla Roberts (ed.), *Window on the Forbidden City: The Beijing Diaries of David Bruce, 1973–1974* (Hong Kong: The Centre of Asian Studies, University of Hong Kong, 2001), 56.

66   For details, see Ann Kent, "Chinese Values and Human Rights", in Leena Avonius and Damien Kingsbury (eds), *Human Rights in Asia: A Reassessment of the Asian Values Debate* (New York: Palgrave Macmillan, 2008), 92–3.

67   Tania Branigan and agencies, "Beijing Pledges to Close Poverty Gap", *Guardian Weekly*, 12–18 March 2010, 12.

68   Freedom House, *Freedom in the World: China* (2009), 6, available at http://www. freedomhouse.org/report/freedom-world/2009/china [accessed 12 May 2012].

69   Ibid., 1.

70   Ibid.

71   Freedom House, 2011, op. cit., 8.

72   Information Office of the State Council of the People's Republic of China, *National Human Rights Action Plan of China (2009–2010)*, available at http://news.xinhuanet.com/english/2009-04/13/content_11177126.htm [accessed 12 May 2012].

73   For further details, see Kent, "China's human rights in 'the Asian century'", in Thomas Davis and Brian Galligan (eds), *Human Rights in Asia* (Cheltenham: Edward Elgar, 2011).

74   State Council Information Office, National Human Rights Action Plan (2012–2015) (Beijing, 2011), available at http://www.china.org.cn/government/whitepaper/node_7156850.htm [accessed 28 May 2013].

75   Sun Zhe, 2006, op. cit., 162.

76   The secrecy shrouding bilateral human rights dialogues means that any specific achievements arrived at by this process cannot be measured, or even estimated, since they are by definition non-transparent, to the point where those who might claim achievements, cannot.

Chapter 6

The ILO and Forced Labour in Myanmar

Richard Horsey

This chapter looks at the efforts of the International Labour Organization (ILO) in addressing the very serious problem of State-imposed forced labour in Myanmar. Through a strategic combination of pressure, dialogue and technical cooperation, the ILO managed to gain traction on a very sensitive issue and achieve some impressive results. The fact that it managed to do this not only while Myanmar was going through a phase of greater openness, but also in a subsequent phase of deeper isolation, suggests that the ILO's strategy was an inherently effective one.

A detailed understanding of how this strategy was implemented, and the challenges that it faced, can shed light on the mechanics of Principled Engagement. After setting out the necessary background, the chapter provides a fairly in-depth account of the ILO's efforts. It then assesses the strategy, both in terms of its effectiveness in furthering the ILO's aims, and more broadly from the perspective of the Principled Engagement framework.

Background to the Problem

In March 1997, the ILO established a Commission of Inquiry to investigate the use of forced labour in Myanmar. This was only the tenth time in the ILO's 78-year history that such a step had been taken, reflecting the gravity of the allegations as well as the long-standing nature of the issue.

An ILO Commission of Inquiry is an independent, quasi-judicial body, with a mandate to ascertain all the facts of a case, including through "on the spot" visits and witness hearings, and to make recommendations on steps necessary to remedy a situation. A Commission may set time limits for the implementation of its recommendations. The recommendations are binding, and a member State has three months to indicate whether it accepts them, or whether it wishes to appeal to the International Court of Justice (this has so far never happened). If a State fails to implement the recommendations within the time limit specified, the ILO is empowered to take "such action as it may deem wise and expedient to secure compliance therewith"[1] – including the possibility of economic sanctions.

There were three features of the Myanmar situation that made it distinctive:

- *The longstanding nature of the case.* The ILO had first addressed the issue of forced labour in 1964, requesting changes to Myanmar legislation that were never made.
- *The gravity of the allegations.* In the 1990s, allegations suggested that forced labour was widespread across the country, and was accompanied by other serious human rights abuses.
- *The fact that forced labour was State-imposed.* According to these allegations, it was the government authorities themselves – the army and local government officials – who were imposing forced labour. This made it very different from most other serious cases of forced labour around the world, such as debt bondage, which are generally imposed by the private sector or private landowners.

The roots of the problem can be traced back to laws from the British colonial period – many of which remain valid to this day – authorising government officials to impose forced labour in certain circumstances. In practice, however, the Myanmar army had for decades forced villagers to work as porters during counter-insurgency operations, without any reference to those laws. And after the State Law and Order Restoration Council (SLORC) junta came to power in 1988, it embarked on a massive infrastructure programme – building roads, railways and irrigation schemes using the forced labour of hundreds of thousands of people – something that was completely outside the scope of the colonial legislation.[2]

After challenging the Myanmar government for several years about the situation, the ILO was led to determine that "far from acting to end the practice of forced labour, [the Government] is actively engaged in its promotion".[3] The decision was therefore taken to appoint a Commission of Inquiry. The Government refused to cooperate with the Commission, not allowing it to visit Myanmar, and declining to participate in its formal hearings in Geneva. This did not, however, prevent the Commission from completing its work, and after spending almost 18 months assessing some 10,000 pages of documentary information and taking testimony from 250 witnesses, its 400-page report was damning. It concluded that the Forced Labour Convention "is violated in Myanmar in national law … as well as in actual practice in a widespread and systematic manner, with total disregard for the human dignity, safety and health and basic needs of the people of Myanmar".[4] Its recommendations were that the Government take action without delay to amend the offending laws, stop imposing forced labour in practice, and prosecute anyone who continued to do so.

But in the Report's final paragraphs, the Commission went much further. Disturbed by the lack of cooperation from the Government, and shocked by the scale and gravity of the violations it had found, the Commission concluded its report by essentially calling for regime change:

> This report reveals a saga of untold misery and suffering, oppression and exploitation of large sections of the population inhabiting Myanmar by the

Government, military and other public officers. ... The Commission hopes and trusts that in the near future the old order will change, yielding place to the new where everyone in Myanmar will have an opportunity to live with human dignity and to develop his or her full potential in a freely chosen manner and there will be no subjection or enslavement of anyone by others. This can happen only if there is restoration of democracy where people as a whole can wield power for their common good.[5]

The Government reacted by continuing to ignore the procedure – merely stating in its official response that since there was no forced labour problem in the country, they did not see any difficulty in implementing the Commission's recommendations.

Enforcement Efforts

The Government had clearly not accepted the findings of the Commission, but neither did it appeal to the International Court of Justice. Thus, for the first time in its history, the ILO had to consider how it should deal with a situation where a member State was refusing to implement the recommendations of a Commission of Inquiry.[6] There had been previous cases where governments did not accept such recommendations, but in these cases – Greece under the Colonels or Poland under Jaruzelski, for example – the problem had resolved itself through the fall of the regime responsible for the violations. The ILO's Constitution contained a normative option: article 33 provided for the ILO to impose unspecified "measures" on defaulting member States, with trade measures being one of the intended possibilities. But the ILO was cautious. Article 33 had never been invoked before, and had always been intended as an important deterrent, but one that would rarely if ever need to be invoked in practice. If taking measures under article 33 proved ineffective, this would show that the ILO did not have the power to enforce the standards that it set, potentially undermining its entire system for supervising those standards.

It seemed preferable, therefore, to push the regime to recognise that its behaviour was incompatible with the fundamental principles of the ILO, by effectively showing it the door (there is no possibility for the ILO to expel a member). In 1999, the ILO passed a resolution declaring that "the attitude and behaviour of the Government of Myanmar are grossly incompatible with the conditions and principles governing membership of the Organization" and prohibiting all further technical assistance to Myanmar. Importantly, however, the ILO also left the door open to cooperation. The Resolution contained an explicit exception allowing technical assistance for the elimination of forced labour, and the Director-General had already written to the Government to urge them to accept such assistance.

Myanmar reacted strongly to the 1999 Resolution, saying that it found it "impossible to accept such deplorable and unscrupulous action" and stating that it would cease all cooperation with the ILO on this matter.[7] But it gave no indication that it would renounce its membership of the ILO. The ILO therefore had little option but to pursue article 33 measures. This was uncharted territory, and posed a real dilemma. The measures had to be strong enough to be credible and to have a tangible impact on Myanmar. But they also had to be acceptable to the majority of the ILO's members. The ILO's credibility was at stake either way: if the measures were perceived to be weak or ineffectual, this would show that the ILO ultimately did not have many teeth, which would weaken its whole labour standards system. But if the measures went further than the majority of members were comfortable with, they might fail to be adopted – not only a political victory for Myanmar, but also a serious blow to the credibility of the ILO.

The solution that was decided on was an elegant one. Rather than specifying a detailed set of economic or other sanctions that members were to apply against Myanmar, the decision on what action was appropriate to take was to be left up to the members themselves: they were asked to review their relations with Myanmar in light of the forced labour situation and take appropriate action (international organisations were asked to do likewise, and the United Nations Economic and Social Council (ECOSOC) was also requested to take up the matter). While it ran the risk of appearing indecisive, this solution had its advantages. It meant that members uncomfortable with applying trade sanctions would not be obliged to do so, and therefore would be less likely to vote against the proposed action. At the same time, it provided those members who were ready to take such action with a legal justification for doing so.

In addition, the very weakness of this solution – the fact that members were not obliged to take any specific action – actually provided an advantage, in that it made it difficult for Myanmar to be certain about what the impact of the measures would be. Assuming that Myanmar was ready to shift its position if sufficient pressure was applied – the underlying assumption in invoking article 33 in the first place – then the more uncertainty the better. The alternative would have been to elaborate a set of specific measures that were weak enough to ensure approval at the ILO's annual Conference, the impact of which it would have been easier for Myanmar to assess, and which would therefore have been unlikely to represent much threat. Efforts to construct this kind of "creative uncertainty" were to become a defining feature of the ILO approach in the Myanmar case, and a key element in its effectiveness.

The article 33 measures were put for adoption to the ILO's annual Conference, which was to meet in June 2000. At the same time, the ILO again offered Myanmar technical assistance to help it meet its obligations. There had initially been no response to such offers, but as it became clear that the ILO would proceed with the measures, Myanmar began to change its position of non-cooperation. Starting in October 1999, the ILO and Myanmar began long and difficult negotiations – initially through the Myanmar ambassador in Geneva – on the conditions under which ILO technical assistance on forced labour could be provided; these discussions culminated in the first visit of an ILO mission to the country in May 2000.[8]

This change in attitude was significant, and it marked the beginning of a fundamental change in relations between the Myanmar and the ILO. But to what extent was this change attributable to ILO action? The ILO process was not taking place in a vacuum. Human rights and political issues in Myanmar were the subject of condemnation and action in other United Nations fora, and in the international community as a whole. The UN Commission on Human Rights had invoked special procedures against Myanmar in 1992, by appointing a Special Rapporteur to monitor the human rights situation in the country, and the General Assembly had adopted a resolution on the situation each year since 1991. The European Union, having already put in place an arms embargo, adopted a "common position" in 1996 extending the range of sanctions, including a visa ban on senior Myanmar officials, as well as a suspension of high-level diplomatic contacts; shortly after, it decided to withhold trade preferences. A number of countries had also put in place bilateral sanctions, including the United States. So while it is tempting to see Myanmar's change in attitude towards the ILO as being a result of moves to apply article 33 measures, might this not have been part of a more general shift in attitude, as a result of factors external to the ILO?

It is certainly true that around the time that the change took place, Myanmar began to adopt a more open attitude towards the international community as a whole. The aftermath of the 1997 Asian financial crisis had undermined the notion that Myanmar could share in the fruit of regional economic growth while retaining an autocratic and abusive system of military rule. It had become increasingly clear that in order to develop the economy and the country, Myanmar would have to re-engage with the world at large, and that this would require certain concessions on issues of international concern.

In the late 1990s Myanmar's powerful Office of Strategic Studies – led by one of the "triumvirate" of junta leaders, Lieutenant-General Khin Nyunt – began taking a number of moves to improve the country's international image. Notable developments around this time included the granting of access for the International Committee of the Red Cross to Myanmar's prisons in May 1999; a series of fruitful visits to Myanmar by the United Nations Secretary General's Special Envoy, Razali Ismail, starting in June 2000; an Australian Government human rights training programme for Myanmar officials that started in 2000, following negotiations the previous year; and a series of visits starting in 2001 by the newly-appointed Special Rapporteur on the Situation of Human Rights in Myanmar, Paolo Sérgio Pinheiro (his predecessor, Rajsoomer Lallah, had never been given permission to visit the country). These moves by Myanmar were given additional impetus by the United States presidential elections in late 2000. The previous (Clinton) administration had adopted a very critical approach, and the Myanmar authorities had hoped that they might be able to forge a more positive relationship with a new administration (particularly a Republican one).

Thus, developments in the ILO certainly cannot be viewed in isolation; they were part of a broader shift taking place in Myanmar that had nothing to do with the ILO. At the same time, the fact that the change in attitude towards the ILO was one of the first concrete expressions of this new approach by Myanmar is instructive. It strongly suggests that the threat of article 33 measures was effective given the political context prevailing in Myanmar at the time. And ultimately, the fact that the regime would make significant concessions to the ILO demonstrated the effectiveness of the ILO's strategy of combining pressure with engagement.

Engaging the Regime

So began a series of ILO missions to Yangon to try to bring about tangible improvements in the forced labour situation. The first mission arrived in May 2000, as the ILO's annual conference was poised to decide on the adoption of article 33 measures. The mood was tense. On the day the mission arrived, the official English language newspaper carried an editorial entitled "Pity ILO!" which referred to the 1999 resolution as "disgusting" and declared: "the result is that ILO has lost its dignity".[9] In its first meeting with government interlocutors (and with copies of the newspaper on the table in front of it to reinforce the point) the mission was careful to clarify its role. It pointed out that any decision on sanctions would be made by the Conference, and that the mission had been sent to explain the process involved, and help the Government to formulate a credible and effective set of measures to address the forced labour problem. This helped to clear the air a little, and although there were still suspicions on both sides, the mission was able to have frank and constructive discussions.

Maintaining a clear division of roles between the organisation (the Governing Body and the Conference) and its secretariat (the Director-General and his staff) was important for the success of the mission. If the authorities felt that the role of the mission was to issue threats of sanctions unless its demands were met, this would likely trigger a response based on pride and nationalism, and would lead nowhere. Rather, the mission had to make clear that its role was to offer advice about what action was expected of the Government and the likely consequences, and to report objectively on its discussions. It would then be for the Conference to draw the consequences. This natural "division of labour" between the organisation and its secretariat would be critical for the success of the ILO's efforts in the coming years. But for this to work, successive ILO missions would have to establish a degree of trust with the authorities, not by watering down the message, since this would be counterproductive for the ILO and the Government, but by giving frank and accurate assessments, while at the same time negotiating the maximum possible concessions. Ultimately, the ILO's success in achieving this delicate balance was one of the key elements in making progress in the Myanmar case.

The ILO's first priority was to obtain a change in the legislation, followed in due course by a monitoring presence in the country. It was recognised that a legislative change alone would likely have a minimal impact on forced labour – given weak rule of law, and the fact that in any case most forced labour was imposed with no reference to the offending legislation. But it was nevertheless considered to be an important and necessary first step: it would be a concrete sign of political will from the regime, would signal a change in policy on forced labour, and would (crucially) open the way to prosecutions of people who violated the new policy. The regime had already taken a step in this direction when, in an unsuccessful effort to avert the 1999 resolution, it had issued an executive order in May 1999 ("Order 1/99") directing the relevant authorities "not to exercise the powers conferred on them" to impose forced labour "until and unless any further directive is issued".[10] The order also contained numerous exceptions that permitted the continued exaction of forced labour in violation of the Convention. This was a completely unconvincing step, but the mission was unable to convince the Government to do more – and any mention of an ILO monitoring presence provoked an almost allergic reaction.

At the same time, the ILO was getting some positive signals. For example, in a meeting with the mission, Lieutenant-General Khin Nyunt gave the first explicit acknowledgement of a forced labour problem in the country, and indicated that there was a willingness to cooperate further with the ILO.

The difficulty that the ILO had in obtaining a change in the legislation – something they felt should have been a relatively easy step – reflected the fact that within the regime there was a range of views about how engaged Myanmar should be with the world, and what price, in terms of concessions, it should be ready to pay for improved international relations. Khin Nyunt was the architect of a broad and ambitious programme, then in its early stages, of renormalising Myanmar's relations with the world. He had been given a certain latitude to carry out this programme, but it is clear that there were grave doubts on the part of other members of the regime, including his two superiors (Than Shwe and Maung Aye). Khin Nyunt was therefore being extremely cautious not to overreach and jeopardise his entire programme, and changing Myanmar's laws at the behest of an international organisation was something that in the context of the regime's intensely nationalistic political culture could have easily been portrayed by hardliners as unacceptable.

The ILO Conference recognised that there was a new and more constructive attitude from the regime, which held out the possibility that further progress could be made. But it was also felt that, in the absence of any concrete steps forward, the ILO's credibility would be damaged if it failed to go ahead with the article 33 measures. In the end, a compromise solution was worked out, whereby the Conference adopted a resolution applying the measures, but delayed their implementation for six months – at which point a review of progress was made, with the possibility that the measures could then be shelved. The ILO Director-General played an important role behind the scenes in pushing for the compromise solution. This approach seemed to be the wisest, for a mixture of strategic and pragmatic reasons. Strategically, it would have been a mistake to ignore the shift in the Government's position and apply the measures immediately. Not only would it have likely cut off the nascent process of cooperation with Myanmar, it would also have removed the "Sword of Damocles" which was the reason for Myanmar's change in attitude in the first place. Once the measures had been applied, there would be no pressure for Myanmar to continue cooperating with the ILO, particularly if they turned out to have a limited impact. Of course, the decisions of international organisations are driven more by politics than strategy, and the ILO is certainly no exception. The pragmatic reason for choosing the compromise solution was simply that it seemed to represent the strongest position that the Conference would adopt – all the indications were that any immediate implementation of the measures would not have majority support, and a vote in Myanmar's favour would be a major blow not only for the ILO's efforts to resolve the present issue, but also to the credibility of the Organization as a whole.

A second mission visited Yangon in October 2000, shortly before the review of progress would be made. The Director-General had written to the authorities the month before, outlining what would be expected in order for the measures to be shelved: necessary legislative changes so that forced labour was made illegal in national law; specific instructions to state authorities, particularly the military, on the practical steps to be taken to implement the legislative changes; adequate information on these changes to the entire population; and concrete action to ensure that anyone who illegally imposed forced labour would be prosecuted (possibly to be monitored by the ILO). This was an extremely ambitious agenda, but one dictated by the recommendations of the Commission of Inquiry.

The atmosphere in the discussions was good, but from the outset the mission became bogged down in detailed discussions on government drafts of proposed legislative changes. These drafts appeared to fall far short of what was required. One among several problems was the fact that they took the form of an order supplementing the original Order 1/99 – that is, an order amending another order which was itself a directive suspending the exercise of powers under the Towns Act and Village Act. This was obviously a terribly convoluted solution that would be hard for anyone to follow, and therefore lacked credibility. And beyond this, discussions on credible enforcement mechanisms or an ILO presence remained inconclusive.

In the end, the issuing of an "Order Supplementing Order 1/99" and a set of corresponding administrative instructions was all that the mission managed to obtain. While it was recognised that this could be an acceptable legal basis for prohibiting forced labour if applied in a bona fide way, this step fell far short of expectations. A decision was taken by a very large majority of ILO members at the annual Conference in June 2000 that article 33 measures should be implemented. From a strategic point of view, this outcome was far from optimal. While it may have satisfied a desire in some quarters to finally be able to punish Myanmar for its years of recalcitrant behaviour, it would do little to further the cause of eliminating forced labour in the country. The point had been stressed by the Chair at the start of the debate:

> When considering sanctions which are always a last resort, the objective is not to punish nor to express moral indignation, but rather to induce a change in the behaviour of the State concerned so that a concrete result – in this case the termination of forced labour in Myanmar – can be achieved in a manner that will bring satisfaction to the Governing Body and the Organization as a whole.[11]

If, just at the moment when Myanmar appeared to be taking concrete (albeit inadequate) steps for the first time, the response was to impose the measures, there was a good chance that this would end the process of cooperation; the Government had warned as much at the start of the debate. A key question was whether the Commission of Inquiry's gloomy assessment that there could be no change in the forced labour situation without regime change was correct, or whether it might be possible to make at least limited progress under prevailing circumstances, even if a final resolution of the issue would require broader social and political changes. The outcome of the mission, while not representing any major step forward, did at least hold out the prospect of achieving meaningful concessions through negotiation.

Ultimately, however, the political calculus was the following. Concrete action had been taken by Myanmar, but the progress was not sufficient. If the ILO nevertheless went ahead and shelved the measures, this would ease the pressure on Myanmar and would run the risk that no further action would be taken by the junta, which could undermine the credibility of the ILO. Alternatively, allowing the measures to come into force might bring an end to Myanmar's cooperation, but would preserve the ILO's credibility (and, incidentally, would allow members to present themselves to their constituencies back home as having taken a tough and principled position, a somewhat cynical but highly relevant consideration for many). In the final analysis, it is perhaps not surprising that the majority decision was that there was insufficient basis to block the measures.

And so it was that on 30 November 2000, the article 33 measures against Myanmar came into force. At the same time, the Governing Body had stressed that this decision did not preclude further cooperation and assistance from the ILO in tackling forced labour. The challenge for the ILO at this point was how it could try to persuade Myanmar to continue to cooperate. Following the Governing Body's decision, Myanmar had announced that it would cease cooperation with the ILO on forced labour, but would continue with its own efforts to eliminate the practice. The Director-General's offers of technical assistance were rejected, prompting him to point out to the Government that:

> Myanmar cannot expect to receive credit for [its efforts to address forced labour] in the absence of an objective assessment of their practical implementation and actual impact. The ILO alone is in a position to provide such an assessment with

the authority necessary to carry legal, practical and political consequences at the international level.[12]

The Director-General's proposal of an assessment mission raises the question of why it would be in the regime's interests to continue its cooperation with the ILO, when the latter had just imposed sanctions. Part of the inescapable logic of sanctions is that they can bring about the desired policy changes in essentially one of two ways: through the threat of their imposition (such that the target country takes action to avoid the sanctions being implemented),[13] or through the prospect of their removal (such that the target country takes action after the sanctions have been implemented in order to obtain their withdrawal). Of course, it is impossible to maintain a credible threat of sanctions if the decision to apply them is repeatedly deferred; in the Myanmar case, there was a general feeling at the time of the Governing Body discussion in November 2000 that that point had been reached, and that considerations of credibility demanded the imposition of the measures. This appeared to leave the prospect of removing the measures as the sole remaining lever available to the ILO – a process that would likely be just as slow and uncertain as applying the measures in the first place, by which time it was very possible that Myanmar would have become accustomed to any impact they had had and therefore unlikely to feel the need to take radical measures in order to have them removed. In fact, however, another intriguing possibility emerged, as we shall now see.

Following the decision to apply the measures, the Director-General wrote to all ILO constituents – that is, member States, and the national employer and worker organisations in those countries – as well as other international organisations, requesting them to review their relations with Myanmar, and inform him of what action they had taken. The impact of these measures can be judged from the responses received, summarised by the Director-General in a March 2001 report.[14] By this time, 47 member states had responded (which meant that 128 had not). Most noted simply that they had no relations with Myanmar that could be taken advantage of to perpetuate or extend the practice of forced labour. Importantly, none of Myanmar's neighbours in the region – its major economic partners – took any concrete action. And those member States that provided detailed responses were, not surprisingly, Western countries which took a strong position on the political and human rights situation in Myanmar and which had been most in favour of the imposition of the measures in the first place. However, these countries had already taken the strongest measures that they were willing and able to take, and for the most part, had only very limited economic relations with Myanmar in any case. In fact, it was only the United States that gave any explicit indication that it might be ready to impose additional trade sanctions on the basis of the ILO resolution.

Thus, the response to the ILO's call to action was muted, to say the least, and it was tempting to conclude that the article 33 measures had had little tangible impact. This would be negative not just in the Myanmar case, but would undermine the ILO's labour standards system as a whole. As the *Financial Times* put it at the time, "the lack of action will fuel long-standing criticisms that the ILO, despite its strong words, remains incapable of mustering sustained pressure on countries".[15] The *New York Times* was more blunt, saying that the ILO's "fruitless effort to take a strong stand against Myanmar has shed a harsh light on its lack of enforcement power".[16] But such conclusions were premature. For the measures to be effective in pushing for policy changes, the key question was not their actual impact, but Myanmar's perception of what the impact could be. And there were indications that they were extremely concerned. A "restricted" memorandum prepared by the Myanmar Ministry of Foreign Affairs in December 2000 (a leaked copy of which was sent to the ILO) set out in detail what the likely impact of the ILO measures might be:

> ... some governments and trade unions of western nations as well as some trade unions within the region which are independent of government control may instigate a blockade of trade and investments, hinder Myanmar's import and export transport routes, impose restrictions on job opportunities for Myanmar seamen, and refuse services to Myanmar missions abroad.

> Myanmar's main trading partners are Asian countries, and as the volume of trade with western nations is negligible, it will have little effect on trade. However, if Myanmar import and export goods are declared 'affected cargo', and if loading and unloading is refused at seaports, it will have considerable effect, especially on beans export which earns about USD 300 million per year, and garment export to western nations sold on a quota basis.[17]

The concern that there would be some kind of blockade of Myanmar trade was well-founded. The ILO, of course, is made up not only of governments, but also of workers' and employers' organisations, to whom the measures were also addressed. Many seaports in South Asia, the main destination for Myanmar's lucrative beans exports, had strong and independent unions which had already demonstrated that they were willing to take action against Myanmar vessels – for example, a cargo ship had been temporarily detained by dock workers at the port of Calcutta in August 2000 in protest at the workers' rights situation in Myanmar.[18] And there had been other cases in the past of such "blacking action" by port workers in response to grave labour rights issues in particular countries, particularly apartheid South Africa (as it turned out, no widespread action of this sort ever materialised, in part because it may have violated rules on what is known as "secondary action"; but Myanmar could not have predicted this).

So, despite the fact that the activation of the ILO measures did not have immediate and concrete impact, Myanmar certainly remained worried. And, although the measures were now in force, in many ways their true impact was as uncertain as ever. This was not just because there may have been action in preparation that had not yet been implemented (such as the feared blacking action), but also because many countries had indicated that they were adopting a "wait-and-see" approach – that is, because of tentative openings in the broader political situation in Myanmar, they were holding off on any decision on further sanctions. This provided the ILO with a vital negotiating tactic: pointing out to the regime that there was still time to demonstrate progress on the issue and thereby avoid additional sanctions. This opened up an interesting "third option" in the logic of sanctions: even when it was no longer possible to take advantage of the threat of ILO measures being imposed, and when the prospect of having the measures formally lifted still seemed a distant possibility, the threat that the measures would be "strictly applied" could still be used.

The crucial point, however, is that this "third option" was only available because the ILO remained fully engaged with the Myanmar regime. The prospect that further sanctions could still be avoided, together with the persistent offers from the Director-General of technical assistance to help resolve the issue, produced the desired effect. After several months of disengagement and strong rhetoric from the regime, they quietly resumed discussions with the ILO. In March 2001, the Deputy Minister for Foreign Affairs made a discreet visit to ILO headquarters and indicated that Myanmar was ready to accept the proposed mission to verify what progress had been made by the government in eradicating forced labour.

Conducting such an assessment seemed particularly important at this point. The authorities had taken steps to outlaw forced labour, and there were indications that the forced labour situation in the country had genuinely improved. But it was clear that there was still a very long way to go. A detailed assessment of the progress made, and of the steps still needed to resolve the issue, could both give Myanmar some credit for any progress, as well as take advantage of the prevailing "wait-and-see" attitude to obtain an agreement on further steps – in particular, on a permanent ILO monitoring presence in the country. The fact that the regime and Aung San Suu Kyi were in direct talks had been publicly announced at this point, and there had been a significant number of political prisoner releases. There was a strong sense that political change was coming to Myanmar, and the ILO wanted to develop a compelling vision of how this could translate into progress on the forced labour issue – and, just as important, how progress on forced labour could reinforce the process of political change. An agreement was reached with the Government for the ILO to appoint a "high-level" team to conduct the assessment.

The team was headed by Sir Ninian Stephen, former Governor-General of Australia. It was given remarkable freedom to meet whomever it wished (including Senior General Than Shwe, and two meetings with Aung San Suu Kyi, at that time under house arrest) and to travel wherever it wanted (it flew around the country for two weeks in a private charter plane, meeting villagers, members of civil society, and local officials). Its key recommendations were that some independent and effective complaint mechanism for forced labour cases be established, such as a form of international ombudsperson, as well as the establishment of an ILO office in the country, which could provide credible information on the ongoing trends in the situation, as well as technical advice to the government on ways to make further improvements.

But the strength of the team's report lay not so much in its specific recommendations as in the broad vision that it presented. It expressed its "deep conviction" that the modernisation of the economy could be a decisive factor in ending forced labour, but at the same time recognised that such modernisation would require the engagement of the international community, which was unlikely under present circumstances. It suggested a way out of this dilemma, by noting that the very existence of forced labour was part of the reason why economic relations with Myanmar were so limited, and suggesting therefore that if Myanmar cooperated with the ILO in eliminating forced labour, this could help convince the world to re-engage economically with the country. Of course, the forced labour issue was only one of many reasons for Myanmar's pariah status, but the team felt that clear progress in resolving this issue – in the context of the broader political and socio-economic developments taking place – could be an important signal, and might trigger significant changes in international policy.

Although the findings of the team showed that there had only been a "very moderate" positive evolution in the forced labour situation since the Commission of Inquiry, the very different attitude of the authorities – including their acceptance of the team's visit and their willingness to give it complete freedom to operate – as well as the evolving political context in the country, gave it much more optimism. Its concluding observation contrasts starkly with that of the Commission of Inquiry:

> The elimination of forced labour thus represents not only the discharge of a moral and legal obligation for Myanmar, but also offers an historic opportunity for this country to accomplish its modernization ... The high-level team is confident that there are many in the leadership of the country who have fully grasped the historical dimension of the challenge and the need to respond to it. The basic conviction that the high-level team expressed to the leadership of the country ... remains unshaken: its faith in the capacity of the country and its people to occupy the place they deserve in the international community, and its hope that the international community, thanks in part to the patient and consistent efforts of the ILO, will be of assistance in the process.[19]

Developments over the following year suggested that this optimism was not misplaced. The ILO was allowed to establish an office in the country six months later, headed by a "Liaison Officer" (although it required very difficult negotiations), and on the political front, there were increasingly concrete signs that a deal with the opposition was within reach. However, in the year following the establishment of the office, things began to change. Signs of discord within the regime began to emerge. The political reconciliation process – which had received a boost with the lifting of Aung San Suu Kyi's house arrest and the release from prison of a number of her senior party officials – had begun to stall, the United

Nations envoy had been unable to visit the country for months, and the Special Rapporteur for human rights had had to cut short a visit after discovering a crude listening device during an interview with political prisoners.

Further progress in such a context was slow and difficult. It took another year of negotiations to finalise a "plan of action" that could have a concrete impact on forced labour. This plan – which included the establishment of an independent complaint mechanism and a series of practical efforts to address forced labour – was finally agreed on 27 May 2003, and was to be presented to the ILO's annual conference the following week. But on 30 May, a shocking premeditated attack on Aung San Suu Kyi's motorcade left scores dead or seriously injured, changing everything.

Crisis and Re-Engagement

With hindsight, the events of 30 May 2003 represented the beginning of a fundamental crisis in the engagement process that the ILO was pursuing. The incident raised serious questions about the political fortunes of the Khin Nyunt faction and the future political direction of the country. It was also doubtful whether the complaint mechanism on forced labour could be implemented effectively given the climate of fear created by the incident. These doubts were shared by the donors who were scheduled to provide financing for the plan of action. Under such circumstances, the ILO had no other option than to suspend the implementation of the plan.

Khin Nyunt moved quickly to try to recover the momentum of his political programme, announcing a seven-step "roadmap to democracy" in August that year, and pushing ahead with political reconciliation talks with Aung San Suu Kyi, who remained in detention. After conducting a detailed assessment of the situation, and obtaining renewed commitments from the authorities as well as explicit encouragement from Aung San Suu Kyi, the ILO decided that it should go ahead with the plan of action. However, just when the ILO was to formally take that decision, there was another blow to cooperation.

In early March 2004, it emerged from a leaked court judgement that two people had been convicted of high treason and sentenced to death on the basis that they had had contact with the ILO (a third person had been handed a similar sentence for using an illegal satellite phone to contact exiled labour rights organisations). In one case, the "incriminating" evidence was possession of the author's business card, and in the other case, possession of a publicly available ILO document. It is difficult to imagine a more damaging blow to relations between Myanmar and the ILO. There were clearly considerable tensions within the regime at that time about the future political direction of the country,[20] and there was also considerable unease – particularly within the Attorney-General's office – at the prospect of having an ILO complaint mechanism that was seen as external interference in Myanmar's legal system. It seems likely that the ILO element in the high treason case was a deliberate attempt by spoilers within the regime to undermine relations with the ILO and scupper the plan of action.

The Khin Nyunt faction attempted some damage control by quickly giving the ILO access to the three people in prison, and providing assurances that the references to the ILO were a mistake by the judge. The Supreme Court promptly heard an appeal, but the Attorney-General's office pressed for the death sentences to be upheld (although the expectation was not for these to be implemented, as Myanmar has a longstanding moratorium on judicial executions). It took two appeals and nearly six months before the ILO elements in the case were removed, together with a clear statement that any person in Myanmar could have contact with the ILO without fear of action being taken against them. It was a further three months before the individuals were released from prison.

At this point, it would once again have been possible to go ahead with the plan of action. But the simmering tensions within the regime had finally boiled over. Between late October and early November 2004, Khin Nyunt and most of the officials, ministers and intelligence officers close to him were arrested, and his entire military intelligence apparatus was dismantled. All of the ILO's main interlocutors had been removed at a stroke, and Khin Nyunt's programme of greater openness and political reconciliation was stopped dead in its tracks. Once again, the future for the ILO process looked decidedly uncertain.

In the meantime, however, the cooperation had started to produce some important results on the ground. In January 2004, when it had seemed likely that the plan of action could soon go ahead, two people from the Irrawaddy Delta region approached the ILO Liaison Officer to report an incident where five families had been prosecuted and fined for refusing to perform forced labour. The individuals agreed for this information to be passed to the authorities in Yangon, without identifying them, in order that it could be investigated. The Liaison Officer suggested to the authorities that this was an important opportunity for them to demonstrate their willingness to tackle forced labour (up to now, they had professed a willingness to do so, but no complaints had come through official channels). Somewhat unexpectedly, a team of senior officials from Yangon went to investigate the case, with the result that the forced labour stopped and the district officer responsible was sacked.

The local people were amazed. The idea that it was possible to complain somewhere about a government abuse, and that something would be done to redress it, was unheard of. News of the incident quickly spread, with the result that more people began to approach the ILO Liaison Officer with complaints. In this way, an ad-hoc complaint mechanism evolved. The Liaison Officer would conduct a preliminary assessment – usually by talking to the complainants at his office – to determine that the allegation constituted forced labour (many people came with unrelated grievances), that it was recent, and that there were sufficient details to enable the authorities to conduct an investigation. If so, the Liaison Officer would refer the case to an inter-ministerial committee for action.

As news of this mechanism and its effectiveness spread, more and more complaints were lodged. In 2004 there were approximately 80 complaints, about half of which were sent to the authorities for investigation. The result in most cases was that the particular incident of forced labour – which could involve dozens of villagers – was ended, and a warning was given to the authorities concerned; several children who had been forcibly recruited into the army were also released. A number of government officials were subsequently prosecuted and imprisoned for illegally imposing forced labour, and some of these cases were publicised in the state media. (There were also some problems: not surprisingly, there were attempts at retaliation by local officials against individuals who had lodged complaints against them, but it usually proved possible to resolve these at the Yangon level.)

The authorities were of the view that the benefits of demonstrating their readiness to tackle cases of forced labour outweighed the costs of taking action in a limited number of cases. For its part, the ILO anticipated that action in a small number of cases would be enough to undermine the sense of impunity among local government officials, and that even limited action could therefore have an impact on the levels of forced labour across the country. But as the numbers of complaints began to increase dramatically, the authorities started to become alarmed, and their responses became slower and less convincing.

Following the purge of Khin Nyunt and his faction, the ILO was faced with a new set of interlocutors who saw the ILO process as unacceptably intrusive and of no benefit to the country. The ILO therefore made a bold attempt to engage them. In February 2005 it sent a "very high-level team" to Myanmar, once again led by Sir Ninian Stephen, this time joined by Ruth Dreifuss (former President of Switzerland) and Eui-yong Chung (former Chair of the ILO Governing Body, and a leading figure in South Korea's ruling party). The ILO considered that engaging directly with Than Shwe was the only way to achieve two critical and interrelated objectives: first, to convince Myanmar of the value of continued cooperation with the ILO, and second, to convince the ILO membership to continue that cooperation, by obtaining a sufficiently clear commitment from the regime.

But this effort backfired badly. What the ILO had seen as a valuable opportunity for the regime to demonstrate its political commitment to continued engagement with the ILO, the regime saw as a tool by the ILO to apply more political pressure. On arrival in Yangon, the team was presented with a programme of meetings far more limited than that informally agreed to before its departure. No meetings had been scheduled with the leadership, only with ministers.[21] This in itself was a fairly clear answer to the question of whether the post-Khin Nyunt regime was committed to continued engagement with the ILO. The team used its initial meetings to explain the negative consequences of such a signal, and pressed for a meeting with the leadership. When it was clear that this would not be forthcoming, it cut short its visit, since it was obvious that without such a meeting, there was nothing to be gained from further "technical" discussions.

The result was predictable. In March 2005, the article 33 measures against Myanmar were reactivated. The Government then tried to undermine the complaint mechanism, by announcing that people making "false" complaints of forced labour would be prosecuted as a "deterrent"; a number of such prosecutions were initiated. In response to the deterioration in the situation, in June the ILO Conference indicated that the organisation's members should "intensify" their action against Myanmar, including with respect to "foreign direct investment in all its various forms" and "relations with State- or military-owned enterprises in Myanmar".[22] Over the next few months, relations hit new lows. A series of mass rallies around the country condemned the ILO, and called on the Government to withdraw its membership. Then, the ILO Liaison Officer began to receive a series of graphic death threats, delivered to his home. It was clear that this was a deliberate attempt by the authorities to force him to leave the country, thereby "neutralising" the ILO presence, without the need for the Government to take the diplomatically more costly steps of closing down the office or withdrawing from the ILO.

The situation was now at a crisis point. The ILO Director-General had continued throughout the year to offer to address the situation through dialogue, but this had not produced any positive response. The ILO membership felt that it had no option other than to return to a policy of sanctions, and the Myanmar authorities were apparently ready to call the ILO's bluff – even to the point of threatening to quit. It was clear that an approach based on sanctions and condemnation would have little impact on Myanmar, while at the same time removing any incentive for them to continue demonstrating progress in addressing forced labour. It would also jeopardise the ILO presence in the country, which was achieving tangible results. A return to dialogue and cooperation was therefore indispensible for making continued progress, but the question was how to push an unwilling dialogue partner to come to the table. The situation was analogous to that faced by the ILO following the Commission of Inquiry, except that the ILO's ultimate enforcement option, article 33, had already been used.

The strategy pursued by the ILO at this point involved three elements: preserving the ILO presence, persuading the regime to remain in the ILO, and pushing the regime to resume dialogue and cooperation. All involved the same basic approach: increasing the (perceived) cost to the regime of continuing its policies, to the point where the alternative course of action became more appealing. In the case of the death threats, after appropriate consultations with the United Nations security system it was decided that the ILO would not withdraw its Liaison Officer from Myanmar.[23] The ILO did not shy away from laying the responsibility squarely on the Government, describing it as "a campaign of intimidation orchestrated by the authorities" and warning the Government of its international legal obligations. The matter was raised formally with the UN Secretary-General, and was brought up in the Security Council.[24] The ILO also went public, and the threats received widespread press coverage and were raised in the UK Parliament.[25] Having failed to achieve its objective, and with negative publicity and international scrutiny increasing, the threats against the Liaison Officer stopped.

As regards the threat to withdraw from the ILO – which seemed all the more likely to be acted upon, given that the intimidation of the Liaison Officer had failed to achieve its objective – it was pointed out to the authorities that not only would they have to give two years' advance notice, they would also continue to be bound by their obligations under the Forced Labour Convention even after withdrawal, unless they took the additional step of denouncing the Convention – something they could not do until May 2007 in any case. It was also pointed out that leaving the ILO did not imply that the Organization would stop scrutinising the situation – in fact, the scrutiny would probably only increase, as it had when apartheid South Africa had left the ILO in the 1960s. It thus became clear to the regime that a decision to quit would not take effect for some time, and that it would come at no small diplomatic cost, since it would undoubtedly be interpreted as a signal that they wished to continue to make use of forced labour. In November 2005 the Government announced that Myanmar would not leave the Organization after all.

Nevertheless, the authorities still showed no willingness to resume substantive cooperation with the ILO. In particular, they continued to prosecute people who had complained about forced labour, and two individuals were imprisoned on this basis. This policy of targeting complainants had forced the Liaison Officer to suspend the functioning of the complaint mechanism. The Government claimed that the prosecutions were within their sovereign right and consistent with domestic law, and therefore not a violation of the Convention. It was this dispute that was to form the basis for ILO action. The ILO Constitution provides that disputes over the interpretation of Conventions "shall be referred for decision to the International Court of Justice". While the ILO, as an international organisation, could request an advisory opinion of the Court, this would not be enforceable. What was needed was a binding decision of the Court that would be enforceable through the UN Security Council.

The most straightforward way to achieve this would be for an ILO member State to request the Court to decide the matter. This they could do on their own initiative at any time, but there was little appetite among members to take such a step. An alternative, and in many ways preferable, option would be for the ILO itself to obtain a decision (rather than an opinion) from the Court. This possibility hinges on an obscure legal argument that has never been tested: that the wording of the ILO Constitution could open the way to a "binding advisory opinion".[26] This sounds like a contradictory notion, but in essence the argument is that as a party to the ILO Constitution, Myanmar had voluntarily agreed that opinions of the Court on ILO matters would be taken as binding, and therefore that the enforcement mechanisms provided for in the Statute of the Court would apply. This option provided some potentially strong leverage to the ILO, but raised many legal questions.

The answers to these questions were not clear to the ILO; however, they were no clearer to the Myanmar authorities. Irrespective of what the Court would eventually decide, it was clear to Myanmar that it faced the prospect of a long, difficult and embarrassing international legal process, where it would be seen as trying to defend its right to prosecute victims of its abusive practice of forced labour. This, together with other action being contemplated by the ILO (including as regards the International Criminal Court), and in a context where the United States was pushing for Security Council action on different grounds, convinced Myanmar that a path of cooperation would be less costly than continued confrontation. The Labour Minister was sidelined (and eventually replaced), and a new Deputy Minister was appointed with a brief to mend relations with the ILO. Prosecutions of complainants were ended, those who had been imprisoned were released, and in February 2007 an agreement was reached with the Government establishing a formal complaint mechanism. This mechanism continues to operate, and while there have been some difficulties it has proved successful in resolving many cases of forced labour and forced recruitment. Forced labour remains a serious problem in Myanmar, along with numerous other human rights abuses, but incremental progress continues, and the situation in most parts of the country has considerably improved in the ten years since the Commission of Inquiry. After a new reformist government took over in 2011, progress on these issues has accelerated markedly.

Assessing the ILO's Strategy

The fact that the ILO had a degree of success in tackling a human rights abuse in an authoritarian context such as pre-2011 Myanmar is striking. Progress on human rights issues in such contexts is difficult, and the ILO would not necessarily be the most obvious candidate for achieving such success. It does not have a particularly strong track record in enforcing its standards in authoritarian contexts.[27] Indeed, in the normal range of situations that the ILO faces, that of promoting technical standards among generally cooperative States, dialogue is the most appropriate tool. So in the ILO context, the Myanmar experience can be seen as extreme rather than typical.

It thus seems that success in this case is attributable not to the strengths of the ILO per se, but rather to the particular strategies it adopted. These strategies changed over time, and three distinct phases can be identified:

- *Supervision.* In the period 1964 to 1990, in the absence of any evidence of de facto violations, the ILO used its regular supervisory procedures, requesting that certain Myanmar laws be amended to bring them in line with the Forced Labour Convention. Since the only consequence of failing to do this was a follow-up letter the following year, and a one-paragraph observation in the ILO's 500-page annual standards' report, there was little reason for Myanmar to act.
- *Ostracism.* From 1991, as evidence of widespread violations emerged, the case began to assume much greater prominence. Concern was expressed

in increasingly robust terms, culminating in the strong condemnation of the Commission of Inquiry. Then, in the absence of any response from Myanmar, technical assistance was cut off and Myanmar was implicitly invited to withdraw its membership.

- *Pressure and engagement.* From late 1999 until 2010, the threat to apply article 33 measures was combined with robust engagement with the Government to identify and support concrete actions that could have a meaningful impact on forced labour.

For a regime that was not really susceptible to moral suasion, and which was being widely criticised on a range of political and human rights issues in any case, the first two strategies failed to bring about any discernible progress. To the extent that sanctions worked, it was by pushing the regime to begin engaging with the ILO. The shift from ostracism to a combination of pressure and engagement provides a striking demonstration of the strengths and weaknesses of the two approaches. Confrontation did not achieve much, not only because the regime had a high level of tolerance for criticism and isolation, but also because the immediate elimination of forced labour was not something it would have been able to achieve, even if it had had the political will to do so.

This implied that the only way forward was an incremental one. It hinged on the recognition that – *pace* the Commission of Inquiry – it was possible to make tangible progress on forced labour even within the prevailing political context in Myanmar. The Commission had certainly been correct to point out that a final solution to the forced labour problem would require wholesale reforms of the nature of governance in the country. But this was not a precondition for making *any* progress. Incremental progress could be made, but it required two things:

- *Sufficient pressure* in order to overcome the "political inertia" of the regime, without which it is doubtful that they would have felt the need to make any concessions at all (as the failure of the ILO's earlier efforts at persuasion demonstrates), and
- *Detailed negotiations* to define incremental steps that the regime was willing to take, and which would be regarded as meaningful by the ILO's constituents. Without such engagement it is doubtful that the regime would have been able to come up with steps that were regarded as meaningful to the political organs of the ILO (proposals for such steps always came from the ILO, not the regime).

Combining pressure and engagement in a credible and effective way was not straightforward. Like most authoritarian regimes (or indeed, governments in general), the Myanmar regime did not respond well to threats. The risk, therefore, was that the regime would view the ILO missions as presenting ultimatums rather than giving advice. Indeed, the tensions around the first mission in May 2000 demonstrated this very well: it was not until the government interlocutors understood that the mission was offering objective advice about the consequences of their choices (rather than threats) and constructive suggestions about possible steps forward (rather than ultimatums) that productive negotiation became possible. This could only be achieved by drawing a clear distinction between the political organs of the Organization (its Governing Body and annual Conference) and the Director-General and his secretariat.

The key to carrying out such an approach successfully was accurate *calibration*. That is, it was essential that the steps being demanded by the ILO were always seen by the regime as less "painful" than the likely consequences of failing to take the steps. This required the ILO missions to make an accurate assessment of how powerful the Organization's threats really were, and to be able to come up with proposals for action that would be seen as preferable by the regime – but also regarded as meaningful by the Organization's membership. Again, it would have been impossible to do this without engagement and negotiation. In this respect, it was extremely helpful to have in Geneva two experienced and well-connected Myanmar ambassadors, in succession, both of whom were committed to trying to make the path of cooperation work. And the ILO was fortunate to have two senior officials with exceptional diplomatic and legal skills taking charge of the case in Geneva;[28] their involvement only came about because the issue was such a political priority for the Organization.

It is worth dwelling for a moment on another precondition for such an approach to be successful. Being able to accurately calibrate pressure with demands assumes that the regime in question is making its policy decisions on the basis of rational realpolitik. Like other authoritarian regimes, the Myanmar junta has often been accused of being irrational – for example, in its decision to build a new capital in an isolated and desolate patch of scrubland; for its putative fears of invasion by the United States; for its initial reluctance to give free access to aid workers following Cyclone Nargis. In fact, there is no reason to assume that the regime is irrational. Its decisions are perfectly well accounted for on the basis of a skewed set of priorities and objectives (together with a measure of incompetence); all of the cases mentioned can be accounted for as a rational consequence of the regime's extreme focus on State security.[29]

This in turn implies that the regime derived some benefits from the ILO presence. The benefits were of two kinds. First, the regime was able to avoid stronger measures from the ILO – although, as we have seen, that benefit may have been illusory given the uncertainty surrounding the realistic impact of such additional measures. Second, and more important, the regime could point to the presence as evidence that it was cooperating with the ILO on the elimination of forced labour. This would be unproblematic if such cooperation really was forthcoming, but there were periods during which it was yielding few tangible results (such as during the long negotiations on the plan of action), or even absent altogether (such as during 2005). A constant judgement call had to be made as to whether the (actual or potential) value of the presence outweighed the benefits to the regime. The strong support from many sectors of Myanmar society helped to convince ILO officials on the ground that, on balance, it did.

The incrementalist approach of the ILO was not without its critics. There were those – within the organisation and outside it – who felt that complete and immediate elimination of forced labour, as required by the Commission of Inquiry, was the only acceptable outcome. To be sure, no other outcome is legally or morally acceptable, and therefore complete elimination of the practice must be the objective of ILO action. But to criticise the strategy for failing to achieve this implies that an alternative strategy could have been more successful. But it is not clear what alternatives there were given the political realities and the ILO's limited leverage. And even if it were assumed that the ILO had (or could have had) much stronger leverage than it imagined, it is far from clear that the regime could have ended the use of forced labour, even if it had wanted to do so.

There is a tendency to see abuses in authoritarian states as deliberate policies of a Machiavellian regime. But this is almost always an over-simplification. In the case of forced labour in Myanmar, it can be useful to make a three-way distinction:

- In some cases, forced labour can be a *deliberate policy*. Examples include the legal provisions that at one time permitted certain forms of forced labour, or the huge infrastructure programme in the 1990s to which the population was expected to contribute its labour.
- In other cases, forced labour is an *indirect effect* of other policies. For example, there is no deliberate policy to enlist children into the army, but the extreme pressure on army recruiters to meet quotas results in children being forced to sign up. Similarly, forced labour on small local projects arises from a combination of high expectations of higher authorities and a lack of budgetary resources.
- In many cases, forced labour arises from *individual corruption and abuse* enabled by a climate of impunity. Local-level officials often have a feudalistic view of governance, regarding the labour of the local population as a resource at their disposal. And there is money to be made: by requisitioning more labour than they require for the task at hand, local officials can demand cash in lieu of work.

It is reasonable to assume that the regime has the power to quickly stop its deliberate policies, and these areas are indeed where the initial progress was made. But it is clearly much more difficult for it to address the other two categories of abuse, which require broader governance reform, effective anti-corruption efforts and strengthened rule of law – all of which represent huge challenges in most developing countries.

This is one example of a broader phenomenon. Criticisms of an incrementalist approach to human rights are often based on a fallacy: that the alternative to incrementalism is more rapid progress. In fact, the alternative is usually no progress at all. But it is often difficult to convince stakeholders of this, and thus one of the biggest challenges facing the proponent of incrementalism is how to bridge the gulf between expectations and results. In the present case it was a constant challenge faced by the ILO secretariat, and in a number of cases it led to decisions that were of questionable strategic value – for example, the decision to impose article 33 measures at a time when the regime was beginning to cooperate with the ILO.

A related challenge is that incrementalism is difficult to implement in a political context. It is in the nature of political processes that results are expected within the "political cycle". But incremental progress through Principled Engagement usually comes more slowly. The political cycle in the ILO was particularly compressed, with three key meetings each year at which progress in Myanmar was discussed by the membership.[30] This provided an important level of scrutiny that helped to keep the process moving, but it also helped to foster the unrealistic expectation that evidence of further progress could be presented at each meeting. Not surprisingly, such progress was often intangible, leading the head of the Worker's group in the ILO to complain at one point that, "the danger sometimes with long journeys is that ... you can see steps and progress and then find that in relation to the journey as a whole the progress is nothing like the progress you imagined it to be".[31] (There is an important flip side to this: just as it was hard for the ILO's members to judge whether a succession of small steps represented progress overall, there was also a tendency for the regime – like the apocryphal frog in slowly heated water – to see each step as unimportant, even if the aggregate effect was significant.)

But if lack of tangible progress led to frustration, then a backward step could threaten the whole approach, as it would invariably lead to calls for a return to sanctions. This made the process particularly vulnerable to the vagaries of Myanmar's domestic political situation (the Depayin incident, for example), and particularly susceptible to spoilers – who found they had the power to easily upset the process by manufacturing a crisis (the high-treason prosecutions, for example). Extremely serious though these incidents were, the concerns that they raised for the ILO process were able to be resolved relatively quickly, but the very regular scrutiny by the ILO's governing organs meant that in each case the impact of these events was a suspension by the ILO of important initiatives. This is not to question the decisions themselves, which were entirely appropriate in the circumstances. But it demonstrates that while regular scrutiny can be necessary to maintain the momentum of incremental progress, it is not without its risks.

In the end, though, whatever complexities there were in implementing the approach, in essence it was rather simple. To put it in terms of the clichéd "good cop" and "bad cop", the ILO avoided the usual problems with this approach in international diplomacy – that the engagement-oriented good cop and the sanctions-oriented bad cop fail to coordinate their actions and often have contradictory objectives in any case – by conducting the operation in-house. This ensured that there was no disagreement on the ultimate objective, and allowed the actions of the Organization's political organs (the bad cop) to be reasonably well coordinated with the actions of the Director-General and his secretariat (the good cop), even if there were sometimes divergences in approach. Success required the issue to be a political priority for the Organization, and it required a fairly strong and independent secretariat, which the ILO does have. The tripartite structure of the Organization also helped to avoid G-77 or "like-minded-group" dynamics that are often seen in other multilateral contexts. But ultimately its success is attributable more to the effectiveness of the Principled Engagement strategy adopted by the ILO than it is to the inherent powers of enforcement at the disposal of the Organization.

The Recent Reforms in Myanmar

In 2011, power was transferred to a new semi-civilian government. The wide-ranging reform process that was initiated by President Thein Sein and other leaders completely changed the environment in which the ILO was operating. Myanmar was now shifting decisively away from the its authoritarian past – introducing political freedoms and striving to rebuild the economy and end armed conflict in the ethnic borderlands.

In such a context, the ILO no longer needed pressure to push a recalcitrant regime to take steps that it would have been otherwise disinclined to. Indeed, the legacy of the ILO's years of Principled Engagement meant that it was very well placed to capitalise on the reforms in order to pursue its workers' rights agenda. There were two key aspects to this.

First, long engagement by the ILO meant that the government was well aware of the issues of concern, and what it had to do to meet international standards, even if in the past it had been unwilling to put in place the fundamental reforms needed to comprehensively address them. Its close working relations with the Liaison Officer and officials at headquarters also meant that it was comfortable reaching out to the ILO for further technical advice. The ILO was familiar with all the key domestic actors, and had a detailed knowledge of the legal and procedural situation, as well as the realities on the ground, so that it was well-placed to provide such advice.

Thus, among the first legislative changes to be introduced by the new government was a new freedom of association law, which conforms to international standards and was drafted with detailed technical inputs from the ILO.[32] Few countries have moved so quickly from a situation of lack of freedom of association to compliance with international best practice as enshrined in the relevant ILO convention.[33] This was followed by the repeal of the towns and village acts and their replacement with a new law that removed the offending provisions that had allowed imposition of forced labour by government officials.[34] Strong political commitments were also given by the president and by the commander-in-chief of the armed forces to ending forced labour, and a new plan of action was agreed with the ILO for achieving this at the latest by 2015.[35]

The situation was rather different in other sectors. For example, bilateral sanctions, particularly those imposed by the United States, had led to the disengagement of the international financial institutions from Myanmar for many years. (Similarly, the United Nations Development Program was prevented from engaging with the government or having a regular country programme.) This meant that much of the detailed analytical and diagnostic work on the economy, needed prior to the launch of any significant technical assistance or country programme, was not done.[36] Nor were there capacity development opportunities for government officials. Now that the political context allows the international financial institutions to reengage, considerable time could be lost before they are in a position to provide concrete advice in support of the government's economic reforms, as well as to put in place the major support programmes that are needed.[37] The opportunity cost of isolation and disengagement can now be clearly seen.

Second, the success of the ILO in keeping forced labour and freedom of association at the forefront of the international political debate on Myanmar, and the fact that the quality of engagement with the ILO was seen as a key barometer of the political situation in the country, provided strong incentives to the new government to prioritise reforms that would address long-standing ILO concerns. A normalisation of relations with the ILO, and the removal of ILO sanctions, could be a powerful signal internationally of the extent and credibility of the reforms. This is one explanation for the fact that the new government prioritised labour reforms and strengthened engagement with the ILO so early in the reform process.

Thus, a further benefit of Principled Engagement can be seen. It is not just that in difficult contexts it holds out the possibility of incremental progress. Beyond this, it can contribute to accelerated change when the situation opens up, by maintaining institutional linkages and a technical understanding of the situation, so that reforms can be quickly supported with technical advice and assistance programmes once the political will exists to change the situation.

Endnotes

1   Article 33 of the Constitution of the International Labour Organization.

2   For example, the Government stated in 1993 that over a period of two years almost 800,000 local people had "volunteered" their labour for the construction of the railway from Aungban to Loikaw. "Forced Labour in Myanmar (Burma). Report of the Commission of Inquiry appointed under article 26 of the Constitution of the International Labour Organization to examine the observance by Myanmar of the Forced Labour Convention, 1930 (No. 29)", ILO, *Official Bulletin*, Vol. LXXXI, 1998, Series B, Special supplement, 156.

3   Ibid., paragraph 1.

4   Ibid., paragraph 536.

5   Ibid., paragraph 543.

6   For an illuminating discussion of the effectiveness of the ILO's enforcement mechanisms in light of the Myanmar experience (up to 2003), see Francis Maupain, "Is

the ILO Effective in Upholding Workers' Rights?", in Philip Alston (ed.), *Labour Rights as Human Rights* (Oxford: Oxford University Press, 2005).

7   Myanmar Ministry of Foreign Affairs. Press Release, Yangon, 17 June 1999.

8   That is, the first ILO mission since the Commission of Inquiry. Up until 1996, the ILO had had some limited technical assistance activities in Myanmar and there had been occasional visits to the country in that connection.

9   "Pity ILO!" (parts 1 and 2), *New Light of Myanmar*, 23 and 24 May 2000.

10   "Order Directing Not To Exercise Powers Under Certain Provisions of The Towns Act, 1907 and the Village Act, 1907", Myanmar Ministry of Home Affairs Order No. 1/99, 14 May 1999.

11   See ILO Governing Body, 279th Session, provisional verbatim of the fourth sitting, Thursday, 16 November 2000, morning.

12   Letter to the Myanmar Minister for Labour dated 1 March 2001, reproduced in appendix 5 of ILO document GB.280/6, Geneva, March 2001.

13   The Myanmar Ambassador in Geneva, who was a disarmament expert and chaired the UN General Assembly's First Committee on disarmament and international security in 2000, compared sanctions to the nuclear deterrent: "The best sanctions are those that are never used and never carried out. Sanctions are like nuclear weapons. Their value lies in their deterrent effect, not in their actual use." See International Labour Conference, 89th Session, Geneva, 2001, *Provisional Record* 19, part 3, p. 2.

14   See ILO documents GB.280/6, GB.280/6(Add.1), and GB.280/6(Add.2), Geneva, March 2001.

15   Frances Williams and Edward Alden, "Forced Labour in Burma Tests ILO's Will to Uphold Global Standards", *Financial Times*, 27 March 2001.

16   Elizabeth Olson, "Myanmar Tests Resolve of ILO on Enforcing Standards", *New York Times*, 4 June 2001 (actually written in March 2001, but published later with little updating).

17   "The Question of Steps to Respond to Sanctions which Might Be Imposed by the ILO", restricted memorandum, Myanmar Ministry of Foreign Affairs, 2 December 2000, paragraphs 6 and 7. (While the authenticity of this document cannot be confirmed, it appears likely to be genuine.)

18   See "Union Activists Hold up Burmese Ship at Calcutta Port", Mizzima News Group, 21 August 2000; and Krittivas Mukherjee, "Myanmarese Vessel Freed after Federal Intervention", *India Abroad News Service*, 22 August 2000.

19   See ILO document GB.282/4, Geneva, November 2001, paragraph 86.

20   See, for example, Larry Jagan, "Divisions Widen among Burma's Senior Generals", *Bangkok Post*, 31 March 2004, where it is speculated that the tension between Khin Nyunt and Than Shwe came to a head in December 2003; the judgement in the high treason case was handed down on 28 November 2003 but was only leaked three months later.

21   Under the Myanmar military regime, ministers had a relatively low status. They were not decision makers, but implementers of the decisions taken by the ruling junta.

22   See International Labour Conference, 93rd Session, Geneva, 2005, *Provisional Record* No. 22, part 3, page 9.

23   As the government would have been aware, the normal response of the UN system to such threats is to transfer the staff member out of the country.

24   Briefing by Under-Secretary General Ibrahim Gambari to the Security Council on the situation in Myanmar, New York, 16 December 2005.

25   See, for example, Michael Sheridan, "Briton who Probed Forced Labour in Burma Faces Death Threats", *The Sunday Times* (UK), 6 November 2005; see also *House of Commons Hansard*, 15 November 2005, Column 1180W.

26   See R. Ago, "'Binding' Advisory Opinions of the International Court of Justice", *American Journal of International Law* 85, July 1991, pp. 439–51.

27   While the ILO did confront regimes in Greece, Chile, Poland and Nigeria about their labour abuses, the regimes in question fell before the limits of ILO action were really tested. See Francis Maupain, "Is the ILO Effective in Upholding Workers' Rights?", in Philip Alston (ed.), *Labour Rights as Human Rights* (Oxford: Oxford University Press, 2005).

28   They were Kari Tapiola, Deputy Director-General of the ILO, and Francis Maupain, Special Adviser to the Director-General, and formerly the ILO's Legal Adviser.

29   For a more detailed discussion of some of these issues, see Andrew Selth, "Even Paranoids Have Enemies: Cyclone Nargis and Myanmar's Fears of Invasion", *Contemporary Southeast Asia* 30, no. 3 (December 2008).

30   That is, discussions in the Governing Body each March and November, and a discussion in the Committee on the Application of Standards at the annual Conference each June.

31   Lord Brett, ILO Governing Body, 282nd Session, "Transcript of recorded debate of the fourth sitting, Thursday, 15 November 2001, morning", 4.

32   *The Labour Organizations Law*, 2011.

33   That is, *The Freedom of Association and Protection of the Right to Organise Convention*, 1948, No. 87.

34   *The Ward or Village Tract Administration Act*, 2012.

35   For details, see International Labour Conference, 101st Session, Geneva, May–June 2012, *Provisional Record* No. 2-2, "Report of the Officers of the Governing Body".

36   Engagement was mostly limited to the annual International Monetary Fund's Article IV consultation, which included a World Bank staff member. Myanmar also continued to attend the World Bank's annual meetings. The Asian Development Bank included Myanmar in a limited way in some regional programs (such as the Greater Mekong Sub-region initiative), but had no bilateral technical assistance.

37   For an indication of some of the initial assessments that will be needed to support the development of a future country program, see World Bank, "Interim Strategy Note for Myanmar for the Period FY13–14", 2012.

Chapter 7

Principled Engagement and Public Health: Donors and HIV/AIDS in Zimbabwe

Jolyon Ford and Joel Negin

International responses to Robert Mugabe's repressive rule in Zimbabwe after 2000 provide an important setting for considering the theory and practice of Principled Engagement. This chapter examines the ways in which donors in the field of HIV/AIDS responded to concerns about the Zimbabwean government's misuse of donor funds and violation of democratic and human rights principles. We assess the impact and appropriateness of these responses in the context of the human rights and humanitarian imperatives that such a serious public health situation raises.

The main rationale for any change in approach towards oppressive regimes is to extract a change in conduct or motivational posture.[1] In our view, "normal" donor engagement with such regimes may represent the influence of vested interests, a lack of concern for affected populations, or a utilitarian calculation that scaled-down engagement will cause disproportionate adverse consequences. Similarly, there are perhaps two motivations generally informing donor disengagement: attempts to send powerful messages and create pressures that deter or dissuade the regime from the offending conduct, and concerns about donor funding being misused (including to directly or indirectly sustain the regime, as well as concerns about funding not reaching intended recipients). These political and aid-effectiveness concerns are interlinked. Along with these "negative" perspectives are certain "positive" ones partly underpinning ideas of Principled Engagement: the opportunities in such contexts to bring about a change in wider policies (or at least protection and fulfilment of human rights in the meantime) through engaging conditionally with undesirable regimes.[2]

In the context of these broad preliminary considerations, in this chapter we assess the extent to which relevant donor conduct in Zimbabwe may be understood to have constituted Ostracism, Business as Usual or a form of Principled Engagement. After setting the context (the wider political international isolation of Zimbabwe, the scale of the HIV/AIDS problem, and applicable human rights principles), we suggest that while donors did not totally ostracise Zimbabwe on this issue and often faced intractable governmental indifference, those interactions that did occur could not be considered examples of Principled Engagement.

This entails us engaging with two related questions: what might, and perhaps should, have been done differently (and whether this might have manifested or "counted" as Principled Engagement); and whether donor re-engagement after 2008 has revealed incipient elements of Principled Engagement. In doing so, we hope to contribute towards a clearer understanding of Principled Engagement. In conclusion, we also offer some general thoughts on ways the Zimbabwe experience, and public health issues more generally, might inform evolving Principled Engagement theory and practice.

We distinguish between two periods. From 2000 until early 2009, Zimbabwe's isolation increased. Although donors did not disengage entirely from the HIV/ AIDS sector, funding was substantially reduced and largely directed through international agencies and local civil society groups, thereby avoiding the government. What were the objectives of those controlling external funding for HIV/AIDS programmes? What issues of principle arose in decisions by donors to engage or disengage? What scope might there have been for continued donor engagement that reconciled (principled) political objections or financial governance concerns with (principled) concerns for those living with HIV and AIDS in a climate of political oppression and economic collapse? Was the form and level of engagement effective and appropriate, and at what cost in terms of "collateral damage"?

These issues are complicated when one considers the HIV/AIDS pandemic, since external responses intended to end violations of civil and political rights (the classic scenario of engagement) also raise other rights issues. The evolving international human rights legal framework on issues of health provides part of the relevant normative backdrop against which to judge interventions. In addressing the themes of this book, we explore whether on certain public health issues in grossly repressive states, a more nuanced "third way" might be traceable that balances transparency concerns and the need to send clear political messages of disapproval, with imperatives and mandates to assist vulnerable groups.

During the second period under consideration – after February 2009 – donors tentatively re-engaged a transitional "unity" government in Zimbabwe that retained strong elements of the former regime.[3] This second period provides an opportunity to consider issues of Principled Engagement during formal political transitions, where the urge to seize a perceived window of opportunity for change and to re-engage (thus providing momentum to reform), is balanced with concerns about the risks that early re-engagement may provide a disincentive for real transformation and have a legitimating effect on still-undesirable political actors.

Context

The Politics: Zimbabwe's Isolation

Twenty years after Zimbabwe's 1980 independence, Robert Mugabe's ruling nationalist party was under pressure from a robust urban constituency and trade union movement, as well as "war veterans" who had not tasted the levels of enrichment of the ruling party Zimbabwe African National Union – Patriotic Front (ZANU-PF) elites.[4] Despite donor support and goodwill over two decades, the government failed to pursue land reform and redistribution effectively. After defeat in the 2000 referendum on changing the constitution, Mugabe appeared to encourage land invasions and an accelerated land redistribution "policy", partly to gain local political capital and appease elites and mass constituencies. Capital flight, food shortages and unprecedented economic decline resulted. Increasingly tough legislation and violent suppression of political dissent accompanied self-enrichment by political elites in a climate of worsening basic services and food supply.

The role of the party-controlled state apparatus in the destruction, decline and despair in Zimbabwe led to widespread international condemnation. After the 2002 elections were adjudged not to be free and fair amid intimidation and violence, Zimbabwe was suspended from, and then unilaterally left the Commonwealth. The US, UK, EU and Australia, among others, imposed autonomous ("bilateral") targeted sanctions on the ZANU-PF leadership. Many donors also scaled back or pulled out of operations in the face of strong state interference in programming, politicisation of food aid distribution, or sheer theft of donor funds. Large Western donors ceased direct support to government ministries. The International Monetary Fund (IMF) and World Bank suspended support. These responses took place alongside – and often at loggerheads with – the policies of "quiet diplomacy" of regional African states, led by then South African President, Thabo Mbeki.

Under both internal and external pressure, and in the face of mass human exodus and severe shortages, the ZANU-PF regime finally entered a "power-sharing arrangement" with the opposition Movement for Democratic Change (MDC) by an agreement in September 2008. A "national unity" government, under which the treasury and some service-delivery ministries were nominally under the control of the opposition, came into effect in February 2009. These steps have prompted a moderate increase in international aid, yet while in early 2012 the EU reduced the number of persons subject to travel bans and asset freezes, the broader raft of sanctions on ZANU-PF actors remain in place.

The Problem: HIV/AIDS in Zimbabwe

After 1980, Zimbabwe experienced significant progress in social indicators including life expectancy, under-five mortality and literacy. Zimbabwe reached the turn of the millennium with a remarkably strong public health system. The first HIV case in Zimbabwe was reported in 1985 and was followed in 1987 by the establishment of the National AIDS Control Programme, which delivered an intensified awareness campaign and epidemiological surveillance programme. Successive five-year Medium Term Plans focused on strengthening behaviour change, prevention and management of sexually transmitted diseases and care and support for people living with HIV and AIDS. In 1999, Zimbabwe established a

3 per cent levy on taxable income which represented one of the most creative and forward-thinking resource mobilisation initiatives towards HIV control.[5]

However, HIV in Zimbabwe has been a major public health challenge,[6] and by particularly affecting productive-age persons and skilled workers, has impacted seriously on the economy. At the start of the 1990s, HIV prevalence was just over 10 per cent among adults age 15–49 years. This rose remarkably to 36 per cent by 1995–1997.[7] Since then, the country has recorded a decline in the prevalence, dropping to about 27 per cent in 2001 and further reducing to 15.3 per cent in 2007. Still, in 2003 about two million Zimbabweans were living with HIV.[8] In addition, the decline in prevalence was partly a result of very high mortality rates.[9] In 2010, the HIV prevalence among adults (15–49 years) was estimated to be 13.6 per cent.[10] The epidemic has led to a huge increase in the number of orphans, child-headed households and vulnerable children in the country. By 2003, nearly 10 per cent of Zimbabwe's population was comprised of orphans.[11]

Meanwhile, the broader Zimbabwe public health system has been laid waste by the country's political and economic crisis. By early 2008, Zimbabwe had experienced a mass exodus of its skilled health workforce and only had approximately 800 doctors remaining in the country with a doctor to population ratio of about 1:12,000.[12] Remaining professionals, a large number themselves HIV positive, exhibited low motivation and faced low and erratic pay amid spiralling inflation. Many health facilities were closed down by the end of 2008 due to inadequate staff, lack of basic medical supplies and equipment, run-down infrastructure and, at times, staff harassment by state security personnel.[13] The poor state of health facilities affected the availability of HIV and AIDS services, especially access to anti-retroviral medication, often leaving patients with few options.[14] As a result, Zimbabwe experienced dramatic increases in maternal mortality and under-five mortality. Life expectancy for women, which had reached 56 years, plummeted to 34 years.[15]

The Principles: Human Rights Frameworks on Public Health

Civil and political human rights violations in Zimbabwe (governmental abuse of political opponents and intimidation of the wider population) and neglect of basic social services partly informed the donor community's need to find an alternative to normal assistance programmes. However, HIV/AIDS is a human rights issue, and not just a public health issue.[16] Changing patterns of engagement – and any question of "principled" engagement – by external actors on HIV/AIDS crises in Zimbabwe must therefore be viewed against a broader normative framework, including also the principles of "right to life" and the evolving "right to health".[17]

First, donor engagement must be seen in the light of the general duty of states to take steps "individually and through international assistance and cooperation, especially economic and technical, to the maximum of … available resources, with a view to achieving progressively the full realisation" of social and economic rights.[18] There are particular international legal duties in relation to children and women's health.[19] Second, many argue that the fundamental "right to life" is implicated in deliberate decisions of states on non-provision of life-saving treatment or assistance.[20] Third, the 1948 *Universal Declaration of Human Rights* asserts every person's right "to a standard of living adequate for the health and well-being of himself and his [sic] family".[21] The *International Covenant on Economic, Social and Cultural Rights* of 1966 states that everyone has the right "to the enjoyment of the highest attainable standard of physical and mental health".[22] Fourth, states and multilateral bodies have steadily articulated rights relating to HIV/AIDS, including the centrality of access to treatment, as fundamental to the realisation of the right to health and other human rights associated with health.[23] Fifth, debates about intellectual property and trade-related aspects of life-saving HIV treatment have a strong human rights dimension.[24]

Sixth, in developing the notion of the indivisibility of rights, there is general consensus that non-enjoyment of civil and political rights negatively affects access to and enjoyment of rights to health. In Zimbabwe's case, it has been pointed out that the realisation of the right to health is dependent on the realisation of a much broader range of rights.[25] This is connected to increased discussion over the past decade about how structural factors – problems in the social, economic and political environments – shape, constrain and impact health outcomes.[26] This is particularly relevant for Zimbabwe where violence, intimidation, a collapsing economy, migration, and institutionalised stigma have all limited the reach and effectiveness of the HIV response. Responsive, accountable and democratic governance in southern African countries is strongly linked to fulfilment of health rights,[27] with the lack of a free press particularly affecting a climate of neglect of HIV/AIDS victims in some African countries.[28] The converse is also true: non-enjoyment of health rights tends to affect a population's capacity to advocate for and access political and civil rights. Indeed, one argument might be that a "hierarchy of needs" analysis would privilege social and economic rights over political ones. If accepted, such an argument would have important implications for theories of Ostracism (revolving as they mainly do around external intervention to assure political and civil rights). We return to this in our concluding remarks.

The most immediate duties in international law vested in the Zimbabwean state are to take measures to protect, respect and fulfil the rights of persons under its jurisdiction. The duties on the international community to assist in that process are somewhat more amorphous. While there is a strong moral case for development assistance, access to life-saving medicines and technical support, the legal basis for what is sometimes called a "right to development" and for corresponding duties of assistance are not as clear cut. This is broadly the normative framework relevant to considering what principles may have conceivably been involved in relation to assistance on public health in a climate of political oppression and weak, uninterested or malevolent government.

Donor Engagement on HIV/AIDS 2000–2008

Patterns

The response by development partners after 2000 can be analysed along two relevant axes: the amount of funding provided and the channel through which funding was provided. The funding that was allocated to Zimbabwe, while substantial, was significantly lower than that of similarly affected neighbouring countries and, unlike in other countries in the region, the vast majority of funding was channelled through non-government mechanisms.

Amount of Funding

Funding globally for HIV increased dramatically from less than US$300 million in 1996 to US$10 billion by 2007.[29] Many of the largest and most prominent global HIV funding bodies supported the Zimbabwean HIV response, including the UK Department for International Development (DFID), the United States Agency for International Development (USAID) and the US President's Emergency Plan for AIDS Relief (PEPFAR) and Centers for Disease Control and Prevention (CDC), the European Union (EU), and the Global Fund to fight AIDS, TB and Malaria (Global Fund). The World Bank, one of the largest global donors to HIV programmes, has not had any large-scale grants or loans with Zimbabwe in this sector, but the overall trend in the first decade of the twenty-first century was engagement by HIV donors.

The Global Fund in particular has been a key source of support for HIV and AIDS programmes in Zimbabwe, approving a total of US$136.8 million in funds, with a disbursement to date of US$46.5 million.[30] Between 2002 and 2008, DFID provided Zimbabwe with over £35 million to support HIV and AIDS and other essential health programmes[31] and provided £20 million in partnership with USAID. The Expanded Support Programme for HIV and AIDS is a multi-donor-supported "common funding mechanism" aimed at scaling up access to HIV and AIDS care and treatment services.[32] USAID provided US$33 million over five years and CDC contributed US$50 million between 2001 and 2008. Between 2004 and 2008, Zimbabwe received about US$109 million from PEPFAR as support for a comprehensive approach towards HIV and AIDS prevention, care and treatment.[33] The EU provided €150 million to support the health sector over three years. National government spending on HIV in Zimbabwe was relatively high in 2005, with US$14 million being provided. Due to the enormous inflation rate, however, in 2007 only US$86,000 was provided by the Zimbabwe government.[34]

Funding Relative to Neighbours

While Zimbabwe has received considerable amounts of funding for its HIV response, the funds received by the country are a pale shadow compared to its neighbours.

As shown in Table 7.1, Zambia, which has an almost equal prevalence rate among adults 15–49 years and number of children and adults living with HIV as Zimbabwe, received about eight times the amount of PEPFAR funding received by Zimbabwe, and almost four times the amount of Global Fund disbursed funds. In 2006, while Zambia received US$173 million in external funding for HIV, Zimbabwe only received US$24 million.[35] Looking at 2008 alone, Zimbabwe received about US$26.4 million from PEPFAR – ten times less than Zambia's allocation and a quarter of what Namibia received.[36]

Table 7.1   PEPFAR[37] and Global Fund[38] funding profiles – Zimbabwe and Zambia

Country	Zimbabwe	Zambia
National Prevalence Rate (Adults 15–49 years) %	15.3	15.1
Adults and Children (0–49 years) living with HIV at end of 2007	1.3 million	1.1 million
AIDS deaths (adults and children) in 2007	140,000	56,000
AIDS orphans at end of 2007	1,000,000	600,000
PEPFAR funds received (2004–2008)	US$109 million	US$846 million
Global Fund rounds approved	3	3
Global Fund amount approved	US$136,852,889	US$456,013,161
Global Fund amount disbursed	US$46,545,555	US$182,088,991
Total external funding (2006)	US$24 million	US$173 million

One estimate from 2005 suggested that the average amount of HIV and AIDS support in Zimbabwe was only US$4 per HIV-positive person compared to the Southern African region average of US$75.[39]

In addition to relative scale-down in funding, Zimbabwe missed out on certain funding opportunities altogether. In 2003, the Bush administration initially excluded Zimbabwe from its US$15 billion emergency AIDS plan. In mid 2004 Zimbabwe lost out on a bid for US$218 million from the Global Fund. The *New York Times* reported Zimbabwe's health minister's response: "I am very angry about it because many people are going to die because of these heartless people." The *New York Times* piece exemplifies the competing views in the development assistance and multilateral community at this time:

Officials from the Global Fund and other relief agencies say heartlessness has nothing to do with it. Rather, they say they are trying to save as many lives as possible without channelling money to untrustworthy governments. "They are not spending their money well, so why would they spend ours well?" asked a European diplomat whose government had restricted aid ... "I personally feel this is very unfair" said Bernard Mokam [head of UNDP Zimbabwe] ... "I personally do not comprehend that the donor community could continue to refuse to support people in need for political reasons. HIV/AIDS should be dealt with as a humanitarian issue. This is just unacceptable." Still, no one, including Mokam, disputed that Zimbabwe's government was making life difficult for donors and the charities they subsidized even when, as in the case of AIDS, the government pledged its full cooperation.[40]

In 2005 UNICEF called for an end to the "stark contrast" between the aid given to Zimbabwe and comparative African countries, saying donor isolation was having a "catastrophic effect" on children in Zimbabwe. A UNICEF Zimbabwe spokesperson called on donors critical of Mugabe "to find other means" of pressuring the Zimbabwe government, "rather than doing it through children" and other vulnerable groups.[41] Then UNICEF Executive Director Carol Bellamy expressed the view that the reduced funding on HIV/AIDS was unacceptable, declaring that "the world must differentiate between the politics and the people of Zimbabwe. Every day children in Zimbabwe are dying of HIV/AIDS, every day children are becoming infected, orphaned, and forced to leave school to care for sick parents."[42] These strong statements form the backdrop against which to consider the donor response after 2000.

Channel of Funding

Those agencies that provided funding for the Zimbabwean HIV response after 2000 mostly chose to channel it through UN agencies and NGOs and not through the Zimbabwean government.[43] UN agencies, including UNDP, UNICEF and the United Nations Population Fund (UNFPA), and various local and international NGOs were the major recipients of donor funds instead of the Zimbabwean government. DFID, for example, channelled its funds mainly through UN agencies, especially UNICEF and UNDP, and local NGOs. USAID used NGOs with US-based headquarters and other community-based organisations to channel its funding.

The Global Fund, on the other hand, disbursed some funds directly to the Zimbabwean government through the National AIDS Council (NAC). The NAC was a principal recipient for the first two rounds of Global Fund money together with UNDP.[44] However, in 2008, the government of Zimbabwe was accused of diverting US$7.3 million of Global Fund money for non-directed use. Although the government eventually refunded the money, this strained the relationship between it and the Global Fund. The Global Fund stopped disbursing funds through NAC and decided to use UNDP as the sole recipient for further disbursements.[45] There were fears that disbursing funds through UNDP could lead to delays in programme implementation due to the bureaucracy of the UN system. However, civil society in Zimbabwe appeared to view the UN system as a "lesser evil" and overall appeared confident that funds and services mainly reached those in need.[46]

Assessing Donor Policies 2000–2008

The response on HIV/AIDS by donors after 2000 fits broadly within the wider Western approach of ostracising Mugabe's regime. The response appears to have been rooted, in part, in generalised disapproval of the regime's destructive political and economic behaviour and, in part, in distrust of what the Zimbabwe government would actually do with donor funding.[47]

While a proportion of Zimbabwe's health facilities were run by NGOs and church groups, a majority of patients presented at facilities operated by the Zimbabwean government. As noted, funding was largely channelled through UN or non-government mechanisms, with decreasing direct donor engagement with the government health system.[48] Operational-level practical information sharing and collaboration continued even where higher-level formal interactions between government and donors were limited. For example, the Global Fund Country Coordination Mechanism included representatives of government, NGOs and donors; external donor representatives would meet with district-level ministry officials who were responsible for coordination and delivery. The question that arises is the impact that this "partly engaged" approach might have had on modifying the impugned political or transparency behaviours, what impact the approach had on those living with HIV/AIDS (including the human rights dimensions of this), and whether another approach might have brought better results both for those infected and affected, and in terms of altering the political behaviour. The impact might also be analysed in terms of the impact on health rights (social and economic rights) and the impact on rights pertaining to the wider political arena (civil and political rights).[49]

Impact on Politics

Assessment of the donor attitude has to be done against the backdrop of recognition of just how serious and deadly the HIV/AIDS threat has been in Zimbabwe. Taken to its logical conclusion, there is an argument that political isolation to incentivise a "return" to democratic governance is pointless if the democracy that may result is totally compromised by the virulent effect of this disease on the basic social fabric. To the extent that donor partial disengagement was intended to impact on political decision-making and behaviour in Zimbabwe, and so also contribute to the realisation of civil and political rights, the impact was probably negligible. These are very difficult matters to assess with any scientific accuracy, but there is little evidence to suggest that the reduced level of engagement and funding on HIV/ AIDS led to political progress or to greater protection of political rights. Except to the extent that collapse of the public health system rendered the country less governable, the stance of donors on HIV/AIDS does not appear to have had any effect in either weakening ZANU-PF or influencing overall government policies. Reduction in funds for HIV/AIDS thus had few, if any, tangible political benefits (unless one counts the fact that taxpayers in donor countries felt a reassurance that donors were "doing something" about the problem in Zimbabwe). It might be said that relative to this lack of political benefit, there were opportunity costs in scaling back funding for HIV/AIDS. The statements by UNICEF, UNDP and others reflect this assessment.

Impact on Public Health

Despite the political challenges and caution from donors, Zimbabwe's HIV response achieved some progress, including a decline in prevalence and new infection numbers.[50] Access to services increased.[51] The number of eligible patients on anti-retroviral therapy increased from about 5,000 in 2004 to over 116,000 by mid 2008, including 10,000 children.[52] On the logic that some progress in the HIV response in Zimbabwe was possible despite the increasingly limited engagement of donors (less than a seventh that of Zambia's funding), it may seem arguable that had Zimbabwe received HIV funding in comparable amounts to Zambia, for example, more substantial achievements might have been possible. Instead, a half-generation of Zimbabweans with HIV had very little by way of medical intervention. The true "opportunity costs" in reducing funding can only be properly assessed, however, by reference also to financial transparency issues (discussed further below).

What Could Have Been Done Differently Between 2000 and 2008?

The approaches open to donors concerned about political abuse and financial impropriety in Zimbabwe conceivably included the twin "extremes" of a total cut-off of aid or continued "normal" funding, as well as a compromise "middle road".

    Any discussion of options ought to set donor responses to HIV/AIDS in the historical context of a number of phases of donor engagement and disengagement in Zimbabwe's development. Zimbabwe's modern political discourse has been peculiarly and disproportionately structured around rhetoric concerning donor interference. Zimbabwe has previously experienced international isolation (Ian Smith's Rhodesia between 1965 and 1979) followed by intensive engagement and support from donors after Mugabe was elected by a large majority in 1980. Foreign donor and diplomatic activity has long been a highly visible aspect of Zimbabwean political life. For a time, until attention shifted to Pretoria in the mid 1990s, Harare – the capital of a post-conflict, post-colonial State in the frontline against *apartheid*, engaging with Western powers and actively addressing development challenges – was *the* place to be for donors and diplomats in sub-Saharan Africa. Well before the rhetoric of the last decade, Zimbabwe's political discourse and international interactions have thus been thoroughly run through with the vocabularies of grievance over external actors' roles, dipped wherever necessary in the wider colonial critique. One sees patterns of manipulation of the role of the international community for domestic political purposes: from the energetic responses of white nationalists in Rhodesia to UN sanctions and blockades and the severance of economic, cultural and sporting ties, to the effective ways in which the ZANU-PF government, increasingly over time, sought to avoid responsibility by drumming into the population how various economic or political problems were the fault – or indeed a plot – of neo-colonial Western powers and the international financial institutions they controlled.

It is not unusual for the imposition of sanctions, strong statements from abroad, or withdrawal of support to be manipulated by a political regime eager to portray itself as a victim. However, what makes this historical pattern relevant and what makes Zimbabwe an important study in Principled Engagement is that this tendency has been so peculiarly prevalent and acute in Zimbabwe as to comprise, at times, almost the entirety of public discourse of the Zimbabwean leadership. Our tentative conclusions are made within this wider context. The almost pathological but ultimately pragmatic need of Zimbabwean leaders to fix blame on outsiders must factor into any assessment of "how things might have been done differently" in terms of donor engagement. One of these conclusions might simply be to emphasise how those engaging in Zimbabwe have long faced a dilemma: the more "access" and input they have had (and ability to substantially "roll out" policies and programmes), the less load the government carried and the more exposed donors have been to the government's tendency to blame their helpers. On the other hand, any move to withdraw or modify engagement (or impose sanctions) in order to influence or weaken the State is inevitably portrayed in a manner that – where the propaganda State controls the media – might actually be largely counter-productive to political goals.

In this context, continuing funding and support at levels similar to neighbouring countries with similar epidemics, such as Zambia and Malawi, and committing a proportion of funding through government systems, would likely have carried significant costs. The government would have had no incentive to become more responsive and responsible on the issue; the economic position of certain elites would have been reinforced (through misdirection of donor funds); the regime would have taken credit for service delivery in a way that increased its legitimacy despite its problematic position in the international community. It is highly likely that a considerable proportion of the funds would simply have been appropriated by the state for other ends, or by individuals within the state for personal gain. It is unsurprising that donors did not continue this approach.

Another option available to the international community would have been to reduce aid even further or cut it off altogether. As the above-quoted comments from UNICEF and UNDP representatives make clear (even in the context of some funding), there is little doubt that the HIV response would have been dramatically weakened, with serious consequences for social cohesion. From an analytical perspective, delivery on social and economic rights would have been compromised with little apparent benefit in terms of civil and political rights. Additionally, a total aid embargo would likely have played directly into the regime's hands: ZANU-PF would have argued that the international community was abandoning the Zimbabwean people and that they were the only ones who could assist Zimbabweans. It is not impossible that this would have further entrenched the government and weakened the opposition.

Given the problems with either of these approaches, there might have been an argument for something approaching conditional, accountable or "principled" engagement. After considering the position after 2008, we return to this in our "reflections" below.

Donor Engagement on HIV/AIDS Since 2009

The Zimbabwe case affords an opportunity to consider how Principled Engagement may be called for in situations of formal political transitions. In February 2009, a political agreement between the ruling ZANU-PF party and the main faction of the Movement for Democratic Change (MDC) saw the MDC leader, Morgan Tsvangirai, become Prime Minister.[53] The transitional government is shared uneasily by reformers and reactionaries, whereby the MDC and ZANU-PF each share half the cabinet seats. The challenges faced by the new government are formidable and a quiet but intense power struggle continues. Despite this, at the beginning of the transition there was general optimism that the transitional government would provide a path to a better future for Zimbabwe.

The issue for external actors in this context is: does one stand by and watch the transitional government fail because of the risk that engagement at this early stage will strengthen reactionary elements and legitimise an incomplete transition; or does one accept the risks and engage in the hope of strengthening the capacity and credibility of reformist elements?[54]

Despite the "considerable international scepticism" about whether the political arrangement can succeed overall,[55] since the swearing-in of the transitional government, immediately after the agreement, donors began to test the waters of re-engagement. In 2009, the US announced US$73 million in aid[56] and the UK committed about £60 million, including support for nurses' salaries. Norway, an important contributor to Zimbabwe since independence, increased its aid to nearly US$15 million despite having discontinued its support in 2000.[57] Germany, Denmark, the EU and China, as well as the World Bank and International Monetary Fund, all provided increased or new support to the country. Yet few donors were willing to provide direct assistance to the Zimbabwean government. The European Union and DFID, for example, delivered an increasing percentage of their aid through international organisations and NGOs. The issue for external actors in the Zimbabwean context is how to engage in such a situation where there are evident needs alongside a politically tenuous situation. The challenge is how best to deliver the support to achieve results, support governance and consolidate peace and stability.

Most donors accepted and continue to accept that the cost of inaction outweighs the risks of supporting the power-sharing government. There is a consensus that the present arrangement represents the best chance yet for Zimbabwe to emerge from the political, economic and human catastrophes of the past decade. Tsvangirai himself has stated: "anything positive that comes from this government will be credited to us, and equally the negatives, so we have no choice but to get this inclusive government to deliver. People want the dividend from the inclusive government, and they will demand it from us, not from ZANU-PF."[58]

One way in which the donor community in Zimbabwe has, since the transition, attempted to address the challenges of this environment, has been to establish multi-donor pooled funds. These are managed by international organisations, receive funding from various development partners and maintain policy interaction with the government. They are characterised by agreement between donors and Zimbabwean ministry officials on objectives and targets. Steering committees are set up that are co-chaired by the ministry and a donor representative, with the secretariat often managed by an international organisation such as UNICEF. The international organisation manages all financial resources through pooled funding in accordance with their rules and regulations to promote transparency and trust. The scope of work generally includes a major emphasis on service delivery at the national scale as well as efforts in policy reform and capacity building. It has been found that social sector interventions are generally less controversial than security sector reform or constitutional efforts and are thus more likely to gain wide support across the political spectrum.

Since the adoption of this approach, there have been multi-donor funds in education, essential medicines, water and sanitation, and health. For example, in the education fund, multiple donors contributed to a US$50 million contribution that provided 15 million textbooks (as well as stationery and storage cabinets) to all primary schools in all core subjects, taking the ratio of textbooks to pupils from 10: 1 to 1:1. An estimated 2.8 million primary school pupils benefited from this distribution of materials.

This cautious re-engagement has been true in the HIV arena as well. In August 2009, following a meeting between Tsvangirai and Dr Fareed Abdullah, the Global Fund's regional head for Africa, the Global Fund released US$37.9 million. Abdullah described the decision as a turning point "between a troubled past and what we hope to be a somewhat easier future".[59] In September 2009, the Coordinator of US government AIDS activities, Ambassador Eric Goosby, visited Zimbabwe and met with government officials, stating "we are happy to have an open dialogue with government and civil society that allows us to strengthen and refocus our efforts".[60] Multi-donor funds have strengthened the HIV response as well, with a programme being developed to support more than 500,000 AIDS orphans with school fees and other essentials. Additionally, all 1,500 health facilities in the country have been supported with basic packages of essential medicines, dramatically reducing stockouts.

Based on the approach described above, donor engagement during the post-February 2009 period exhibits some characteristics of Principled Engagement: the donor community is in dialogue with itself, identifying areas and ministries where it can seize a perceived opportunity to re-engage with Zimbabwe and buttress the momentum for reform. The political risks remain high and the trajectory of such political transition is far from certain, but the engagement of donors in this period has a clearer objective of supporting the transition through increased funding and engagement at all levels. It is Principled Engagement in the sense that it involves direct contact with various factions in government, notwithstanding risks, in order to leverage outcomes that go broadly towards fulfilment and protection of the interests of the mass of vulnerable persons.

Reflections

Our reflections on evolving understandings of Principled Engagement fall into two parts: assessing the donor role on HIV/AIDS during Zimbabwe's political isolation and 2009 "transition", and some general remarks on Principled Engagement in a public health context.

Principled Engagement in Zimbabwe

After 2000, donors significantly reduced assistance for HIV and AIDS in Zimbabwe. This appeared to stem both from transparency or governance concerns, and the broader effort of some in the international community to demonstrate political disapproval and engender better conduct by the regime towards its own people. Donor responses did not amount to total disengagement, but they cannot be considered an example of Principled Engagement either. Rather, donors took to delivering support through UN agencies and NGOs, avoiding the government.

It is tempting to make the judgement that, while well intended, remaining levels of donor interaction with government did not seek imaginatively or persistently enough to harness the Zimbabwean public service in promotion of health rights or other human rights. It is tempting to think that there were opportunities, not taken, to seek out middle- or senior-level public service champions and ensure services reached those living with or affected by HIV/AIDS; to negotiate conditional funding arrangements and special dispensations notwithstanding the general hostility of government to external involvement in Zimbabwe; to cooperate with the national government despite its manipulation and misuses of donor funds; to be more "principled" in the use of donor funds by accepting wastage of some proportion of those funds as the price to pay for advancing social and economic rights of otherwise abandoned populations. Certainly, this was the publically expressed view of UNICEF, UNDP and other agencies whose mandate compels them to deliver services to affected populations in support of governments where these exist. Direct dialogue and cooperation on public health between donors and pariah states might suggest a legitimacy that is politically unpalatable, but it can also provide channels for further political communication (public health as a "safe" issue), or provide an example of what normality would look like across other sectors, given further cooperation. Reform-leaning ministry insiders can utilise the engagement of donors (at the risk of politically compromising them). In transitions, delivery and quick impact on public health services can help boost the credibility of reformist elements.

On this analysis, it could be said that the general approach of isolation and sanctions had negative implications for the fight against HIV/AIDS in two ways. First, it is possible that the overall donor stance alienated potential partners in government on public health objectives. Second, and while this is not a general study of the effect of autonomous sanctions on Zimbabwe, it could conceivably be argued that isolation has weakened the economy and in this way undermined public health responses more generally, from government resources to household resilience. This is certainly the Mugabe regime's argument. The signalling effect of the mere existence of sanctions (even if they are simply travel bans on individuals) may have unnerved existing businesses and deterred potential investors.[61] However, sanctions have been highly targeted, individualised measures. The overwhelming consensus is that the significant damage to the Zimbabwean economy has been as a result of the government's conduct and misconduct.

All who consider the issue may have an intuitive sense that more might have been done, and differently, to assist those with HIV/AIDS in Zimbabwe in the 2000s, including by direct engagement with the Mugabe government. As unsatisfying as it may seem, however, we are unable to reach a conclusion that neatly demonstrates the availability of a third, more principled, more engaged way between 2000 and 2008. There may have been opportunities for more robust engagement undertaken with strict safeguards, but this assumes that all the power is with the donor (one just needs to be more robust and regimes will thereupon cooperate), and that the recipients are without agency or passive. It is not at all obvious that a more robust approach would have resulted in the government simply cooperating and agreeing to strict safeguards. To argue otherwise suggests that donor officers in Harare did not try, throughout the period, to reach workable positions with government. Arguably, donor agencies and their staff, including UN agencies, showed significant tenacity, adaptability and humanitarian concern in continuing after 2000 to work with and for Zimbabweans despite the levels of hostility, neglect and corruption at the highest levels in the government.

It seems that many decisions were made simply on the basis that there was no way, where government was actively hostile to NGOs who might otherwise have provided third-party monitoring, to be confident about where funds were going. A determined donor community might have said "let us champion the Health Minister, make him look good, and he will ensure at least some of this gets through." Perhaps politicians needed to inform constituencies of the existence of more nuanced, principled alternatives, so that they could change from a more hands-off approach to one of conditional or "principled" engagement in order to test the outcomes.

Ideas about more robust engagement also assume that there is some receptivity at the highest level. It is not obvious that the Zimbabwean government would have cooperated. In academic analyses there is often an assumption that, in situations like Zimbabwe after 2000, one is dealing with a government with a coherent policy, and that by certain strategic interventions it is possible to persuade or pressurise government into changing that policy. However, these approaches inadequately account for the uncomfortable truth that the isolated regime often does not have anything capable of description as a "policy". The motivational posture of those in control in Zimbabwe was perhaps not particularly susceptible to approaches, whether robust or not. To suggest donors ought to have found policy levers is to deny the reality, to which most of the common citizens in any Harare street could attest, that the only real "policy" of the ZANU-PF leadership was, increasingly, to stay in power or within patronage circles at all costs, while accumulating as much wealth as possible while the sun still shone. In such circumstances it is difficult to talk about Principled Engagement to alter policies. One is really dealing with Principled Engagement to secure some degree of interim cooperation in pursuit of opportunities to make some difference to people's lives on the ground.

This reflection on policy coherence in the "target" state can be made in relation to donors, too. We would argue that, conceptually, one attribute of engagement that is "principled" is that it involves deliberate, proactive and strategically designed approaches in accordance with coherent, shared objectives among donors against a backdrop of universal values: in some ways for engagement to be "principled" it needs to be "considered" engagement, rather than ad hoc or reactive, disjointed policy-making. In the case of HIV/AIDS responses between 2000 and 2008, there is little evidence that donors were operating under such a considered approach. There may be an assumption – entrenched by the tendency to talk of "the international community" or "donors" as a whole – that donors act in a concerted, coordinated manner and with a clear overall objective. In reality, there is often a "wait-and-see" approach to these environments that can, taken to its extreme, be characterised as either abdication of any policy-making, or highly experimental policy-making. Partly because donors were dealing with a lack of policy in government (other than a survival and enrichment "policy"), the continued but modified engagement did not appear to be done in accordance with a considered view about the long-term political objective of the changed policy. There is a corresponding difficulty in assessing whether the "strategy" was either effective or based in considerations of principle.

This is to be contrasted with the response after February 2009, when there was a much clearer goal of early engagement by those donors willing to take the risks. This shared objective was to strengthen the capacity of the government to deliver and, through this, enhance the credibility of the reformist (MDC) element of the "unity" government. Those donors prepared to take the risk by engaging directly with a transitional, partly compromised government subject to certain principled caveats are, we think, to be commended. Apart from substantive benefits, such interventions can help fortify or inspire reformist elements at crucial periods, hold open political space, and engender popular belief in an alternative and viable future. In this sense, and where public health imperatives and norms also require a proactive approach, Principled Engagement of the sort followed by some donors after 2009 in Zimbabwe is, we argue, preferable. There is little to be gained from principled non-engagement during such periods of change. However, it must be noted that, after 2009, donors, while more focused and coherent in their interventions in Zimbabwe, have not been wholly united and a high proportion of funding has continued to bypass government systems. One dilemma is this: trust between donors and the transitional government is essential, but conceptually this requires a degree of extension on the part of donors of faith, credit and support. The risk of embezzlement, funds leakage or other waste is not necessarily as great as the opportunity cost of not engaging in principled but proactive engagement, persuasion, capacity building and progressive programme expansion.

The topic under consideration illustrates, of course, the difficult trade-offs that often are involved in promoting respect for civil and political rights while also aiming to fulfil social and economic rights. In reality, there is no good answer to what the international HIV donor community should have done differently in Zimbabwe from 2000 to 2008. Well-intentioned people were involved in trying to balance the needs of vulnerable Zimbabweans with the political realities and international disapproval of the conduct of ZANU-PF. There was not a cohesive engagement policy. Rather, the approach was in some respects experimental policy along a middle ground that practitioners and policy makers could live with.

Principled Engagement on Public Health Issues

What can be generalised from the Zimbabwe experience in terms of Principled Engagement on public health issues?

First, even if the overall policy on an oppressive regime is one of isolation, public health issues by their nature may compel differential treatment. The humanitarian imperative (and self-interested strategic fears of contagion and destabilisation) point generally towards engagement where there is the chance to mitigate widespread human suffering. Principled Engagement by reference to socio-economic rights might partly displace principled non-engagement that is based on solidarity over political rights abuses. While the trend of global rhetoric is to refuse to differentiate between rights in this way, there will always be powerful constituencies urging response to humanitarian needs despite the claims of stakeholders concerned about the wider context of abuse of political rights.

Second, while there is increasing recognition that humanitarianism in fragile or conflict-affected areas is inevitably deeply politicised, public health emergencies, especially those which constitute or occur within the context of a humanitarian crisis, raise that body of convention or tradition institutionalised in the Red Cross (International Committee of the Red Cross or ICRC) that is perhaps more amenable to some degree of suspension of political claims. Because they are attended by some of their own normative frameworks and conventions, public health emergencies may not necessarily be good or suitable case studies for Principled Engagement.

Third, HIV/AIDS is to some extent a "slow-burning" public health crisis. There may be useful future Principled Engagement research to be done comparing factors for external actors' engagement in delinquent, intransigent countries in acute emergencies (such as cholera) as opposed to chronic emergencies (HIV/AIDS).[62] During the cholera outbreak in Zimbabwe in late 2008 and early 2009, which killed more than 3,000 people, the "international community" quickly allocated substantial funding of more than US$23 million.[63] Funds came quickly and, in the acute nature of the emergency, donors appear for humanitarian and strategic stability reasons to have put aside traditional concerns about the Mugabe regime (rather than stand back and hoped the population blamed Mugabe for its plight, thus in theory adding to domestic pressure for reform). Mugabe nevertheless condemned the donor response, labelling the action as an excuse for the West to invade Zimbabwe and accusing the British of infecting Zimbabweans in the first place.[64] Information Minister Sikhanyiso Ndlovu declared, "The cholera epidemic in Zimbabwe is a serious biological, chemical war force, a genocidal onslaught on the people of Zimbabwe by the British."[65] To the extent that such reactions are sensible as "policy", they represent concern that a less immediately humanitarian reason for donor responsiveness to the cholera outbreak is that the opportunity was taken to re-establish a donor foothold in the country in circumstances where the regime would be reluctant to be seen to resist help. Footholds provide platforms for greater influence in-country. This shows how engagement can, of course, be characterised as "principled" in two ways simultaneously: fulfilling socio-economic rights claims, while (more politically controversially) laying the groundwork for donor presence that can work towards improving political rights.

Fourth, there is insufficient exploration of the role of public health during political crises. By this we mean not just emergencies or natural disasters that are compounded by or highlight the lack of external leverage, but also the role that a strong public health sector can play in enabling community cohesion and sustaining community resistance to triggers for intra-societal conflict. Social issues such as health have been largely absent from the peace-building literature – which emphasises transitional justice, elections and democratic institutions – yet can play a significant role in the development of sustainable, peaceful societies.[66] Then UN Secretary-General Boutros Boutros-Ghali's report on democratisation asserted that "the best way to cultivate a citizen's readiness to participate in the development of his or her country, to arouse that person's energy, imagination and commitment, is by recognizing and respecting human dignity and human rights."[67] Rather than just voting, speaking freely or not being subject to torture, "respecting human dignity and human rights" has as much to do with providing people with access to the means to survive, to gain access to available medicines, to raise healthy children.[68]

Finally, while particular human rights and humanitarian considerations apply to public health issues, donor engagement on public health is likely to be linked to broader political objectives of the donor government or authority. The issue may not be susceptible to being hived off separately. Where objectives remain unclear or merely global ("a change in regime"), it is likely that donors will not seek out innovative, nuanced mechanisms to allow them to continue to engage in helping public health delivery. Opportunities to educate or influence or persuade, in support of continuous improvement on human rights (including health rights) might remain undiscovered or unpursued.[69] Opportunities to temporarily strengthen an otherwise undesired leader by allowing them some success in addressing health issues – in order to give them the courage to move forward – might be lost. Outsiders often assume that Mugabe's regime is monolithic: without efforts at Principled Engagement there may continue to be the assumption that all actors in all ministries are as implacable and undesirable and unmoveable as someone in the peak leadership, thus obscuring opportunities to engage in a principled fashion towards building consensus across the spectrum on uncontentious public health improvements, or assisting at least some government policy that is not highly linked to political debates, or where the price of holding people hostage to their leadership is considered simply too high to pay.

Endnotes

1   See the work of Valerie Braithwaite, mostly in the tax field, on the various motivational postures of actors subject to regulatory and other governmental interventions, from game-playing, to reactance, to disengagement, to lack of capacity; available at http://vab.anu.edu.au/index.php#pubs [accessed 10 July 2012].

2   In this sense the question of appropriate responses to delinquent regimes perhaps bears similarities to debates in criminology where notions of restorative justice, seen as more "positive", effective and justifiable, are contrasted with traditional (and more "negative") retributive justice ideas.

3   We consider the period until December 2009, approximately the first year of the "transitional" or "unity" government. We use these terms conscious that there is no inevitable trajectory away from oppressive, closed society, either generally or in the case of Zimbabwe at the time of writing (mid-2010).

4   Zimbabwe African National Union – Patriotic Front (ZANU-PF): the party of Robert Mugabe. In setting a broad context we do not purport in this section to undertake a comprehensive chronology of international responses to the Mugabe regime.

5   The Zimbabwe National AIDS Strategic Plan (ZNASP) 2006–2010 provides an organising structure to the current national response: Ministry of Health and Child Welfare, Zimbabwe, available at http://www.nac.org.zw/documents/reports [accessed 10 July 2012].

6   For a helpful summary, see http://www.avert.org/aids-zimbabwe.htm [accessed 10 July 2012].

7   USAID/Zimbabwe, "HIV/AIDS Health Profile", 2010, available at http://transition. usaid.gov/our_work/global_health/aids/Countries/africa/zimbabwe_profile.pdf   [accessed 16 December 2012].

8   IRIN News, "ZIMBABWE: Recognition of HIV/AIDS role in humanitarian crisis", available   at   http://www.irinnews.org/Report/42278/ZIMBABWE-Recognition-of-HIV-AIDS-role-in-humanitarian-crisis [accessed 10 July 2012].

9   Government of Zimbabwe, "Zimbabwe Country Progress Report 2008 to the UN General Assembly (UNGASS Report) – reporting period January 2006 to December 2007" UNAIDS, 2008, available at http://data.unaids.org/pub/Report/2008/zimbabwe_2008_country_progress_report_en.pdf [accessed 10 July 2012].

10   USAID/Zimbabwe, op. cit.

11   UNAIDS, "Zimbabwe: epidemiological fact sheet on HIV and AIDS" UNAIDS, 2008,   available   at   http://www.unaids.org/en/Regionscountries/Countries/Zimbabwe [accessed 10 July 2012].

12   Andrew Meldrum, "Zimbabwe's Health-Care System Struggles On", *The Lancet* 371, no. 9618 (2008), 1059–60, available at http://www.thelancet.com/journals/lancet/article/PIIS0140-6736%2808%2960468-7/fulltext [accessed 10 July 2012].

13   Physicians for Human Rights, January 2009, *Health in Ruins: PHR Reports on the Man-Made Health Crisis in Zimbabwe*, available at http://physiciansforhumanrights.org/blog/report-health-in-ruins-zimbabwe.html [accessed 10 July 2012].

14   Brenda Strysko, "Zimbabwe Queues", *Journal of Midwifery and Women's Health* 54, no. 5 (2009), 412; Todd C., Sunanda R., Madzimbamuto F. and Sanders D., "What is the Way Forward for Health in Zimbabwe?" The Lancet 375, no. 9714 (2010), 606–9, available at   http://www.thelancet.com/journals/lancet/article/PIIS0140-6736%2809%2961498-7/fulltext [accessed 10 July 2012].

15   World Health Organization. "The World Health Report 2006 – Working Together for Health", available at http://www.who.int/whr/2006/en/ [accessed 10 July 2012].

16   "HIV/AIDS and human rights: international guidelines" Geneva: UNAIDS and Office of the High Commissioner for Human Rights, 1998 (HR/PUB/98/1); "The protection of human rights in the context of HIV/AIDS", Commission on Human Rights Resolution 1997/33, Geneva: Office of the United Nations High Commissioner for Human Rights, 1997 (E/CN.4/RES/1997/33); "Handbook for legislators on HIV/AIDS, law and human rights" Geneva, UNAIDS and Inter-Parliamentary Union, 1999. See also the work of the UNAIDS Reference Group on HIV and Human Rights.

17   For the purposes of analysing Principled Engagement we consider aspects of the international human rights legal framework, but are conscious that development assistance – particularly humanitarian and emergency assistances from those who "have" to those who "have not" – is situated within other normative but non-legal (moral and ethical) frameworks.

18   Art. 2(1) of UN General Assembly, *International Covenant on Economic, Social and Cultural Rights*, 16 December 1966, United Nations, Treaty Series, vol. 993, p. 3, available at: http://www.unhcr.org/refworld/docid/3ae6b36c0.html [accessed 2 September 2012].

19   See, in particular, Article 24 of UN General Assembly, *Convention on the Rights of the Child*, 20 November 1989, United Nations, Treaty Series, vol. 1577, p. 3, available at: http://www.unhcr.org/refworld/docid/3ae6b38f0.html [accessed 10 July 2012], and Art. 12 of UN General Assembly, *Convention on the Elimination of All Forms of Discrimination Against Women*, 18 December 1979, United Nations, Treaty Series, vol. 1249, p.

13, available at: http://www.unhcr.org/refworld/docid/3ae6b3970.html [accessed 10 July 2012]. Whether or not these norms represent customary international law (binding on all non-parties as well) is not clear.

20   Art 6 of UN General Assembly, *International Covenant on Civil and Political Rights*, 16 December 1966, United Nations, Treaty Series, vol. 999, p. 171, available at: http://www.unhcr.org/refworld/docid/3ae6b3aa0.html [accessed 10 July 2012].

21   Article 25. The right to health was affirmed in the preamble to the 1946 Constitution of the World Health Organization. See also the elaboration of this right through General Comment 14 of the UN Committee on Economic Social and Cultural rights, and the work of the Special Rapporteur on the Right to Health, available at http://www.ohchr.org/EN/Issues/Health/Pages/SRRightHealthIndex.aspx [accessed 10 July 2012].

22   Article 12.

23   See UNAIDS, op. cit. Also, the "Declaration of Commitment on HIV/AIDS" 26th special session of the United Nations General Assembly (A/RES/S-26/2), New York, 2001.

24   See for example, Richard Elliott, "TRIPS and Rights: International human rights law, access to medicines, and the interpretation of the WTO agreement on trade-related aspects of intellectual property rights", Montreal: Canadian HIV/AIDS Legal Network and AIDS Law Project (South Africa), 2001.

25   Amon J.J. and Kasambala T. "Structural Barriers and Human Rights Related to HIV Prevention and Treatment in Zimbabwe," *Global Public Health* 4, no. 6 (2009), 528–45; see too Kevin De Cock, Dorothy Mbori-Ngacha, Elizabeth Marum, "Shadow on the Continent: Public Health and HIV/AIDS in Africa in the 21st Century", *The Lancet* 360 (2002), 67–72.

26   Kim Blankenship, Sarah Bray and Michael Merson, "Structural Interventions in Public Health", *AIDS*, Structural Factors in HIV Prevention June 2000, 14 (supple 1): S11–S21.

27   Hoosen Coovadia, Rachel Jewkes, Peter Barron, David Sanders and Diane McIntyre, "The Health and Health System of South Africa: Historical Roots of Current Public Health Challenges", *The Lancet* 374, no. 9692 (2009), 817–34.

28   Alex De Waal, *AIDS and Power* (London: Zed Books, 2006).

29   UNAIDS, "2008 Global Report on the Global AIDS Epidemic", UNAIDS: Geneva, Switzerland.

30   The Global Fund, Regional Grant Portfolio: Zimbabwe, available at http://portfolio.theglobalfund.org/en/Country/Index/ZIM [accessed 10 July 2012].

31   UK Foreign and Commonwealth Office, Zimbabwe Development Programmes, available at http://ukinzimbabwe.fco.gov.uk/en/about-us/dfid-in-zim [accessed 10 July 2012].

32   Contributing donors are DFID, CIDA, Irish Aid, Norway and SIDA.

33   PEPFAR, "2008 Country Profile: Zimbabwe", available at http://www.pepfar.gov/documents/organization/82009.pdf [accessed 10 July 2012].

34   Government of Zimbabwe, op. cit.

35   Government of Zambia, "Country Progress Report 2008 to the UN General Assembly (UNGASS Report)", 31 January 2008, available at http://www.safaids.net/files/2008%2006%2004%20Zambia%20UNGASS%20Progress%20Report.pdf [accessed 10 July 2012].

36   IRIN Plus News, "Zimbabwe: A Timeline of HIV/AIDS Funding Woes", available at http://www.plusnews.org/Report/85691/ZIMBABWE-A-timeline-of-HIV-AIDS-funding-woes [accessed 10 July 2012].

37   PEPFAR, "2008 Country Profile: Zimbabwe", available at http://www.pepfar.gov/documents/organization/82009.pdf [accessed 10 July 2012]; PEPFAR, "2008 Country Profile: Zambia", available at http://2006-2009.pepfar.gov/documents/organization/81673.pdf [accessed 10 July 2012].

38   The Global Fund, "Regional Grant Portfolio: Zimbabwe", op. cit.; The Global Fund, "Regional Grant Portfolio: Zambia", available at http://portfolio.theglobalfund.org/en/Country/Index/ZAM [accessed 10 July 2012].

39   Zimbablog, "Zimbabwe: Global Fund Accusations a Blow to AIDS Response", 5 November 2008.

40   Sharon Le Franiere, "Donor Distrust Worsens AIDS in Zimbabwe", *The New York Times*, 12 August 2004, available at http://www.nytimes.com/2004/08/12/world/donor-mistrust-worsens-aids-in-zimbabwe.html?pagewanted=all&src=pm [accessed 10 July 2012].

41   Basildon Peta, "Lack of Aid 'hurts Zimbabwe's children'", *The Independent*, London, 22 March 2005, available at http://www.independent.co.uk/news/world/africa/lack-of-aid-hurts-zimbabwes-children-6150132.html [accessed 10 July 2012]. Overall, Zimbabwe was then receiving a total of $14 per person in annual aid, compared with $68 for Namibia and $111 for Mozambique.

42   UNICEF, "Zimbabwe's Forgotten Children", 17 March 2005, available at http://www.unicef.org/infobycountry/zimbabwe_25622.html [accessed 10 July 2012].

43   DFID Zimbabwe, "DFID's Programmes in Zimbabwe", January 2010, available at http://webarchive.nationalarchives.gov.uk/+/http://www.dfid.gov.uk/Documents/publications/programmes-zimbabwe.pdf [accessed 10 July 2012]; USAID/Zimbabwe, "HIV/AIDS Crisis Mitigated", available at http://transition.usaid.gov/zw/html/HIV_AIDS.html [accessed 10 July 2012].

44   The Global Fund, Regional Grant Portfolio: Zimbabwe, op. cit.

45   Cuthbert Nzou, Reliefweb, "Global Fund Channelling Aids Funding Through UN", 19 June 2009, available at http://reliefweb.int/report/zimbabwe/zimbabwe-global-fund-channelling-aids-funding-through-un [accessed 10 July 2012]; IRIN News, "ZIMBABWE: Global Fund Moves to Safeguard Money", available at http://www.irinnews.org/report.aspx?ReportId=85109 [accessed 10 July 2012].

46   The Body: the complete HIV/AIDS resource, "IRIN Examines Government Officials, Advocates Reaction to Global Fund Restructuring in Zimbabwe", 6 July 2009, available at http://www.thebody.com/content/news/art52559.html [accessed 10 July 2012].

47   On the latter, see generally Le Franiere, op. cit.

48   Many of the privately run clinics in Zimbabwe did not experience any donor pressure. Nor could they afford adverse relationships with government and maintained relationships with the Ministry of Health for the purposes of coordination, adherence to policy and treatment guidelines, and procurement of necessary medication and equipment.

49   We are aware that adopting a "rights lens" to health or political situations or strategies is not without conceptual and other problems of its own.

50   Joint United Nations Programme on HIV/AIDS, "Evidence for HIV Decline in Zimbabwe: A Comprehensive Review of the Epidemiological Data", 2005. However, most observers note that a principal reason for the decline in prevalence was the high mortality rate from already-infected persons.

51   Government of Zimbabwe, op. cit.

52 World Health Organization, "WHO Country Cooperation Strategy Document 2008–2013 – Zimbabwe", 2009, available at http://www.who.int/countryfocus/cooperation_ strategy/ccs_zwe_en.pdf [accessed 16 December 2012]; Government of Zimbabwe, op. cit.

53 "Communique", Extraordinary Summit of the SADC Heads of State and Government, 27 January 2009, endorsed by the MDC's National Council on 30 January 2009, available at www.sokwanele.com/thisiszimbabwe/archives/3132 [accessed 10 July 2012]. The "Global Political Agreement" was signed on 12 September 2008 in Harare.

54 Joel Negin and Jolyon Ford, "Rebuilding Zimbabwe: Australia's Role in the Transition", Policy Brief, Sydney: Lowy Institute, 7 October 2009, available at http://www. lowyinstitute.org/publications/rebuilding-zimbabwe-australias-role-supporting-transition [accessed 10 July 2012].

55 International Crisis Group (ICG), *Zimbabwe: Engaging the Inclusive Government*, Africa Briefing #59. Brussels, 20 April 2009.

56 BBC, "Obama Pledges Aid for Zimbabwe", *BBC News*, 12 June 2009, available at http://news.bbc.co.uk/2/hi/africa/8098334.stm [accessed 10 July 2012].

57 Norway.com, "Norway Increases Aid to Zimbabwe", 25 May 2009, available at http://blog.norway.com/2009/05/25/norway-increases-aid-to-zimbabwe [accessed 10 July 2012].

58 International Crisis Group, op. cit.

59 IRIN Plus News, op. cit.

60 PEPFAR, "Zimbabwe: Ambassador Eric Goosby Visits Zimbabwe, Discusses Health Sector", September 2009, available at http://www.pepfar.gov/press/docs/130559. htm [accessed 10 July 2012].

61 Tawanda Hondora, "Economic Sanctions Undermine Zimbabwe's Economy", 13 November 2009, available at http://www.newzimbabwe.com/pages/sanctions32.13170. html [accessed 10 July 2012]; Alex Magaisa, "Zimbabwe: Sanctions, the Economy and Democratic Process", http://www.newzimbabwe.com/pages/magaisa6.13113.html [accessed 10 July 2012]. More recently, both sides of politics have called for the lifting of UK, EU, US and Australian sanctions measures.

62 Perhaps an analogous contrast is between an armed conflict recognised as being one to which the Geneva Conventions apply, and mere State violence or ongoing repression (human rights law applies, but no specific institutions are engaged).

63 UN Office for Coordination of Humanitarian Affairs, Financial Tracking Service, "Other Humanitarian Funding to Zimbabwe 2008", available at http://fts.unocha.org/ reports/daily/ocha_R4_A789___1209020206.pdf [accessed 10 July 2012]. These funds came from the UK, US, EU, the Gates Foundation, the private sector, various national Red Cross societies as well as Canada, Australia, China, Tanzania, Botswana and Namibia.

64 BBC News, "Zimbabwe Cholera is Over – Mugabe", 11 December 2008, available at http://news.bbc.co.uk/2/hi/7777178.stm [accessed 10 July 2012]. Had donors not responded, Mugabe might just as readily have condemned them for not valuing African lives.

65 Sebastian Berger, "Britain Caused Cholera: Mugabe", 14 December 2008, available at http://www.theage.com.au/world/britain-caused-cholera-mugabe-20081213-6xw4.html [accessed 10 July 2012].

66 Negin, J., "The Central Role of Health in Building Peaceful Post-Conflict Societies", *Journal of Peace Conflict & Development* 10 (March 2007), available at http:// www.brad.ac.uk/ssis/peace-conflict-and-development/issue-10/Health-in-post-conflict-societies-FINAL-EDIT.pdf [accessed 28 May 2013]; Kruk, M.E., Freedman, L.P., Anglin,

G.A. and Waldman R.J., "Rebuilding Health Systems to Improve Health and Promote Statebuilding in Post-Conflict Countries: A Theoretical Framework and Research Agenda", *Social Science & Medicine* 70 (January 2010), 89–97.

67   Boutros Boutros-Ghali, *An Agenda for Peace: Preventive Diplomacy, Peacemaking and Peace-Keeping*, Report of the Secretary-General pursuant to the statement adopted by the Summit Meeting of the Security Council on 31 January 1992, paragraphs 17, 18, 22, 24, available at http://www.unrol.org/doc.aspx?n=A_47_277.pdf [accessed 10 July 2012].

68   UN Millennium Project, *Who's Got the Power? Transforming Health Systems for Women and Children*, Millennium Project Task Force on Child Health and Maternal Health, 2005, available at http://www.unmillenniumproject.org/reports/tf_health.htm [accessed 10 July 2012]. See also Amartya Sen, *Development as Freedom* (New York: Anchor Books, 1999).

69   See, in this regard, the work of John Braithwaite, in particular "Responsive Regulation and Developing Economies", *World Development* 34, no. 5 (2006), 884–98.

Chapter 8

Engaging Business in the Business of Human Rights

Justine Nolan and Auret van Heerden

In recent years, much has been written about globalisation and the positive and negative impact of business on human rights and how, why and if the corporate sector should be more engaged in both respecting and protecting rights. The debate has largely moved from the "if" business should be engaged with human rights, to the "how" (although there remains a set of persistent objectors who dispute this paradigm shift). But as the role and influence of corporations have increased globally so too has the confusion around what specifically is required of them. And, if there are expectations that companies should be engaged more substantially with human rights, what is the best mechanism for doing so?

Corporations are not governments (who remain the primary protectors of human rights) but some do assume public functions and all of them need to perform due diligence to ensure that they are respecting human rights within their fields of operation. Although ultimately beholden to its shareholders, a corporation's role in contemporary society – and its "social license to operate"[1] – depends now on its ability to meet the expectations of an increasingly diverse range of stakeholders including consumers, customers, business partners and the community in which it operates. Respect for human rights is now (not unreasonably) one of these expectations.

This chapter examines how and why business needs to be engaged in protecting human rights and considers the particular challenges to human rights stemming from supply-chain production. The development and practices of the Fair Labor Association (FLA) are used as an example of Principled Engagement by business in the field of human rights. However, this is not a story with just one principal actor. The particular path of engagement pursued by the FLA (that is, being proactive rather than reactive and one where accountability and transparency are paramount) involves input and engagement from a variety of stakeholders including: government, business, worker representatives, non-government organisations (NGOs), consumers and workers. Business, while having a critical role to play in improving the human rights of workers in supply-chain production is part of the solution but not the entire solution. A culture of cooperation and proactive engagement are both key elements of the engagement model adopted by the FLA and the glue that binds the disparate stakeholders together in a common goal of reducing human rights violations by the corporate sector. Fifteen or 20 years ago, very few companies acknowledged any affirmative obligation to address workplace conditions in the factories of their foreign suppliers – factories they generally neither owned nor operated – but this concept is no longer an anathema to companies. For companies, the question is no longer "Do we have an obligation to address workers' rights in suppliers' factories?" It is "How do we do it, at what cost, and with whom do we collaborate in addressing the problems that exist?"[2]

Why Business Needs To Be Principally Engaged in Protecting Human Rights

An important aspect of the evolution of the global economic system has been the increased reliance by companies, transnational corporations (TNCs) in particular, on a global supply chain. This reliance is especially obvious in low-wage, labour-intensive industries like apparel and footwear. But it also applies to the manufacturing sector generally, including for example, the car, airline and electronic sectors. In today's global economy, large companies in most industries have come to rely on a series of contractors and suppliers in a range of countries to produce their products. And "in a world of 80,000 transnational corporations, ten times as many subsidiaries and countless national firms, many of which are small and medium-sized enterprises", any attempt to "regulate" corporate behaviour will always be a challenge.[3]

To some extent, transnational business has always been, and is increasingly, conducted in "rights-free zones" – jurisdictions with weak regulatory systems.[4] This has become progressively more complicated given the decentralised supply chains that produce so many of today's consumer goods. Operating in such an environment, one might argue, places an onus, if not a legal obligation, on business to ensure that it does not violate human rights. Business always has an impact but the willingness of a company to engage in a principled manner with human rights issues will more likely ensure the impact is a positive one rather than a negative experience. The question remains how and with whom business should collaborate in order to ensure they avoid negative impacts.

Just as the range of business activity is broad, so too is their potential impact on human rights. Corporations play a fundamental role in domestic and international economies, and both the presence and the absence of business can impact human rights. Through commercial activity driven by corporations, jobs and wages are made available, goods and services are provided and taxes are paid enabling governments to provide further goods and services. Thereby, directly or indirectly, a vast array of human rights may be supported – from rights to work, welfare, food and shelter, health and education, and freedoms of speech, association and movement. In short, not only are corporations central to the provision of many of the things that make human life more tolerable, enjoyable and fulfilling, the work and wages that enterprises bring to all communities are key elements in the establishment and maintenance of the individual human dignity that human rights strive to meet.

However, the influence of corporations on human rights is not all benign. Corporations, both local and multinational, have been and continue to be minor and major abusers of human rights. Some corporations are guilty of treating workers badly – in terms of pay, conditions and working environments; some pollute the environment in ways that have dramatic and serious effects far beyond their immediate surroundings; some discriminate against indigenous peoples, or certain ethnic or religious groups, or against women, or people with disabilities, or on grounds of sexuality; and some work alongside (or inside) governments that perpetrate gross human rights abuses.[5]

Different Models of Engagement

The UN Special Representative on business and human rights, Professor Ruggie, has repeatedly stated that there is no "silver bullet" that will provide a systemic solution to reducing the incidence of business-related human rights abuses.[6] A plethora of tactics have been adopted in attempts to regulate or at least reduce the negative impact business can have on human rights, with varying levels of success.

The engagement of business with human rights was thrust upon some companies earlier than others, with some adopting a proactive approach while others remained essentially reactive. The Body Shop has long promoted itself as much more than just a beauty company. More than 30 years ago, The Body Shop pioneered its simple idea that businesses have the power to do good, and has continued to very visibly promote human rights as one of its essential platforms for doing business. In 1996, when the US television network CBS's *48 Hours* programme broke news alleging sweatshop conditions in Nike's contracted factories in Vietnam, the company's first reaction was to deflect and resist any attempts to be held directly responsible for conditions in a factory that it did not own and for workers that were not direct employees of Nike.[7] However, the publicity backlash that ensued, and a lively debate within the company as to its ongoing role with respect to its contracted factories worldwide, eventually ensured Nike's acceptance of a broader and proactive approach to protecting human rights than might otherwise flow from strict legal liability.

Developments since the 1970s have seen a variety of attempts to "regulate" the impact of business on human rights – whether it be via voluntary international, national or company- or industry-specific guidelines; declarations; codes of conduct or via the threat of lawsuits or public reporting requirements, to name just a few. While each of these mechanisms engages business at some level in "solving" the problem, that is, improving human rights protection, the models of engagement are very different. Some adopt a punitive approach that does very little to comprehensively engage business in human rights but nevertheless may still be effective in changing future behaviour. The threat of litigation or increased legislative regulation is confrontational, reactive and generally focused on a narrow set of human rights violations. Such mechanisms tend to view business as part of the problem to be solved rather than engaging business as part of the solution.

In the last 15 years or so, the development and reliance on "soft law" instruments, such as codes of conduct that guide corporate behaviour but are not necessarily legally binding, has increased. Codes are widely used in supply-chain production as a mechanism for achieving corporate compliance with human rights standards. All codes, to a varying extent, rely on corporate engagement, but they work best when they are multi-stakeholder. The legitimacy, credibility and the potential longevity of the code are dependent on how business engages with other stakeholders in the development and enforcement of such codes.

Three different approaches to the question of how business respects human rights have developed in parallel, with each envisaging a different role for how companies might engage in human rights. At the macro level, the United Nations Global Compact is an example of an attempt to produce a broad but brief, universally applicable code of conduct for all corporations operating in all industries in all countries. The Global Compact is the epitome of a non-confrontational approach to engaging corporations in human rights issues, with business being asked by the UN to "embrace and respect" human rights. While other stakeholders, such as civil society, are involved to a nominal extent in the process, the mode of engagement is largely that of one conglomerate to another – business to the UN and vice versa – with no real performance standards and accountability.[8]

At the other end of the spectrum, at the micro level, a growing number of corporations now have their own voluntary codes that may have been developed in-house with little or no involvement from external stakeholders such as NGOs, trade unions, consumers or workers, and which the corporations implement with no transparency or external accountability.

In between are the collective codes that have been developed particularly in industries with poor social or environmental track records, such as the extractive industries and the clothing, footwear and toy industries. Such code initiatives come in two forms – those which originate from a multi-stakeholder forum and have ongoing accountability to external stakeholders, and those that are industry-only in their governance and accountability structures. Both are seen as a way of tailoring the codes beyond what is possible in the one-size-fits-all approach of initiatives such as the Global Compact, while endeavouring to achieve a degree of consensus, consistency and cooperation that is often lacking in single-enterprise corporate-driven codes. The multi-stakeholder basis for developing such codes (and critically, which stakeholders were involved) and the monitoring, reporting and public verification systems attached to these codes, are two crucial indicators of their long-term sustainability and effectiveness. The FLA is one example of how business can be principally engaged in human rights protection.

The concept of Principled Engagement as discussed by Pedersen and Kinley in this volume, and as exemplified by the FLA in the case study below, delineates a "third way" of protecting human rights. Principled Engagement in this context is delineated by several factors. First, it relies on non-coercive means of advancing rights protection. It emphasises negotiation over confrontation. Second, it focuses on engaging those directly responsible for the human rights situation. In the context of supply-chain production, the question of who bears direct responsibility for rights violations is a complex one. Does responsibility for reducing corporate violations lie with the domestic government (where the production occurs), with the foreign government (where the corporation is headquartered), and/or with the brand who ultimately sells the product, or its agents, suppliers and distributors who are integral to the supply chain? Within this complex web with varying levels of "responsibility" for improving the working conditions are the workers themselves, their representatives, NGOs and the consumers of the product. The model of Principled Engagement, as demonstrated by the FLA case study, is also aimed at improving the practical framework for human rights protection and, while initially focused on an audit-based policing model, has more recently transformed into a partnership model that attempts to involve all of these disparate stakeholders.

The reason that codes and initiatives, such as the FLA, have developed in such numbers over the past two decades is that there remain very few legal obligations dealing with human rights that bind corporations operating trans-nationally. This lack of clear legal liability has been central to the creation of the permissive international "human rights free" environment[9] in which some corporations now operate and the parallel increase in the development of soft law mechanisms to "regulate" corporate behaviour. Those few obligations that do exist are very limited in scope and are in fact merely domestic laws that happen to have extra-territorial (that is, international) application. The traditional vision of both international labour standards (ILO Conventions, for example) and international human rights law is that they focus on and bind only States, as States have long been viewed as the principal protagonists in human rights abuses.

This focus on States as the bearers of human rights responsibilities has meant that TNCs have been able to operate largely in a legal vacuum, devoid of obligations at the international level. International law – whether it be labour standards developed by the International Labour Organization (ILO) or human rights law developed within the UN – does not directly recognise the corporate form as one giving rise to rights and responsibilities. The ILO, because of its tripartite structure involving governments, employers and worker representatives, has long taken a more proactive approach to engaging business as part of its "solution" in reducing violations of workers' rights. The UN, however, has been much slower to adopt an approach of engagement and it was not until the launch of the Global Compact in 2000 and the appointment of Professor Ruggie as the UN's Special Representative on the issue of transnational corporations and human rights in 2005[10] that the UN saw the corporate sector as a significant player that should be fully embraced and engaged in the protection and respect of human rights.[11]

Over recent decades, a variety of soft law instruments have variously attempted to fill or at least partially block this legal lacuna. The use of soft law may be more attractive to business and governments alike because it may simply contain inspirational goals and aspirations that aim for the best possible scenario, with few constraints if such goals are not met. However, soft law can serve as a testing ground for the development of new mechanisms of accountability and also function as a useful and necessary tool for the development of ensuing hard law that legally binds parties to their commitments. It should be noted, though, that characterising soft law as non-binding is accurate only in the strict legal sense. Soft law and the codes developed by organisations such as the FLA reflect varying norms and societal expectations concerning corporations and their responsibilities; while a company may choose to ignore these standards, doing so may impact on the company's social license to operate. For this reason, a significant, if still small, proportion of corporations are engaging in human rights and increasingly adopting a consequentialist approach to human rights issues which recognises that moral liability can have an impact equal to that of legal liability. However, they also recognise that such moral liability will vary widely depending on the particular code of conduct to which the company adheres and the level of enforcement and transparency that is attached to such a code.

As an alternative approach, the Business as Usual model contrasts the path of Principled Engagement by opting to downplay or simply ignore the relevant human rights issues. This approach is market driven and keen to isolate business from a human rights framework. With hundreds of thousands of companies operating around the world and only about 7,000 signed up to the UN's Global Compact, it would seem there is no shortage of examples of companies adopting this approach. Many companies and business lobby groups remain stuck in the era of denial, questioning if companies should be involved in human rights issues, rather than how. In 2003, when the crescendo around the UN Norms was reaching fever pitch, the International Organisation of Employers and the International Chamber of Commerce were highly visible lobbyists campaigning specifically against the UN Norms but more generally against regulation and, one might argue, even engagement on human rights more broadly.[12]

Coercion is another alternative technique sometimes employed in rights protection. Boycott campaigns have long been used in the human rights world as a mechanism to correct a specific wrong. They are essentially the polar opposite of the engagement model adopted by the FLA. The potential positive and negative impacts of boycott campaigns on human rights are a keenly debated topic. The boycott launched in the late 1970s against the Swiss-based corporation Nestlé was prompted by concern about the company's marketing of breast milk substitutes (infant formula), particularly in less economically developed countries. While the initial campaign focused on boycotting the company's products, at various times over the years it morphed into an engagement model whereby a variety of disparate stakeholders sought to influence the company's behaviour, particularly via the adoption of a code of conduct. By 1981, after a series of protracted negotiations and with the backdrop of a continuing boycott campaign, the World Health Assembly adopted Resolution WHA34.22, which included the voluntary International Code of Marketing of Breast-milk Substitutes (which aimed to restrict the marketing of breast milk substitutes). With many countries subsequently converting the Code or elements of it into national legislation, this campaign would appear at first to be a wildly successful example of the power of punishment. However, later evidence[13] suggests that failure to abide by the provisions of the Code is still a significant cause for concern, and in one form or another the boycott campaign against Nestlé continues, as do discussions as to the effectiveness of the boycott model as a means of improving human rights. There are numerous other examples of boycotts that never resulted in any change in behaviour, the campaign against the use of forced child labour in the harvesting of Uzbek cotton being a case in point. Despite the fact that a coalition including governments, business, trade unions and NGOs supported the call for boycott, the export of Uzbek cotton has not been affected.

Securing the engagement of business in human rights issues is not a foolproof method for obtaining success, nor is it a straightforward process. What it does aim to do is provide business with a viable mechanism for responding to the structural and governance gaps that exist in the marketplace in respect of human rights protection. For such engagement to be effective, it must be based on a partnership that involves a variety of stakeholders who all have a keen and mutual interest in ensuring long-term sustainable success in reducing human rights violations. The fact that such a process is likely to be incremental (accepting that achieving something, even if not perfect, is preferable to achieving nothing) and may involve prioritising (or some might argue compromising) some rights over others are valid limitations and criticism of the process, but not necessarily fatal flaws. For some, the FLA is a legitimate and necessary embodiment of the "third way" of engaging with business in respecting and protecting human rights. For others, it is viewed as having conferred legitimacy on business that is unwarranted and unwelcome, it rewards continuing bad corporate behaviour and ultimately makes little difference. Faced with such a dichotomy, a closer examination of the FLA is warranted.

Case Study: The Development of the Fair Labor Association

The FLA emerged as a response to the perfect regulatory storm generated by the decline of the three tiers of labour market regulation – ILO Conventions, national labour laws and labour relations systems. Traditionally, the ILO adopted Conventions, member states incorporated those into their labour law and enforced them, and trade unions and employers struck bargains over their application at enterprise or sectorial level. The growth of global supply chains over the last 40 years, however, has created a rights-free zone that is responsible for increasing amounts of world trade but in which labour inspectors are conspicuous by their absence and representative trade unions are a rare exception.

These global supply chains were first developed to reduce the costs of labour-intensive production processes such as clothing and footwear, but they continue to expand as more products and services – from computer chips to medical research – seek lower-cost production platforms. This has been accompanied by the development of a global labour market that has outstripped the traditional forms of labour market regulation. Global supply chains stretch across multiple jurisdictions but are effectively regulated by none. Consider, for example, a typical scenario whereby an American brand places an order with an agent in Hong Kong, who contracts a Korean supplier in Seoul, who allocates it to their facility in Bangladesh. Once produced, the goods are delivered directly to a retailer in Europe. The brand, the agent, and the retailer do not have an employment relationship with the workers and are often unaware of the terms and conditions of employment at the production facility. They assume that the Korean supplier, as the employer, takes care of all legal obligations, including social, labour and environmental requirements. That is not an assumption one can make. The Bangladeshi labour administration (like many others) is under-resourced and unable to enforce the labour laws. To complicate matters further, the Export Processing Zones (EPZs) are exempted from the industrial relations ordinance that should protect workers' rights. Finally, poverty pushes large numbers of young, rural women into the labour market where they are forced to accept whatever they can get, including terms and conditions that violate the buyer's codes of conduct and Bangladeshi labour law.[14]

These global supply chains are also inherently unstable. The supplier has no assurance of future orders nor the workers of employment, and this insecurity further undermines the full enjoyment of rights at work. Workers and employers often refrain from contributing to social security schemes or joining trade unions or employers' associations because they do not have a long-term view of their employment or business relationships.

This lack of regulation, combined with the vagaries of global competition, has predictably led to frequent abuses of human and labour rights. In response, civil society organisations have used the only weapon they had, namely information, to expose abuses of labour rights and embarrass the brand-name buyers involved. In the early 1990s, reports of child labour in the Bangladeshi export garment industry shocked consumers in the West, as did revelations of bonded child labour in the manufacture of carpets in India.[15] Major brand-name companies, such as Nike and Gap, faced exposés of working conditions in supplier facilities in Asia and Central America. At that time, the standard response of companies confronted with such information was to emphasise that they did not own the factory, were not the employer and had no legal liability for the rights or working conditions of the workers concerned. Given the risk of reputational damage however, brands (whose most valuable asset was often their image) were forced to react to exposés.

However, those reactions were individual, selective and ad hoc, and so in 1996, then-US President Clinton convened a meeting at the White House of leading brands, trade unions, human and labour rights NGOs and the US Department of Labor. He urged them to find a way of preventing labour rights abuses in global supply chains, regardless of whether they owned the factory or had strict legal liability. They formed a White House Task Force known as the Apparel Industry

Partnership and set about negotiating a system to protect rights in global supply chains. They were soon joined by a group of US colleges and universities who were equally concerned about the working conditions at factories making logoed products for sale on campuses. The Apparel Industry Partnership took three years to develop a methodology that involved the companies adopting a code of conduct[16] (based on international labour standards) and attaching the code to contracts with suppliers. This established a floor of standards for production worldwide, the so-called level playing field. The system required buyers to i) conduct internal audits of suppliers to ensure that the code was being applied, and ii) agree to external audits to verify the integrity of the system.

The FLA was set up to conduct those external audits. FLA-affiliated companies submit their supplier lists to the FLA staff who draw a risk-weighted random sample for unannounced external audits. The FLA-affiliated companies are obliged to remedy any non-compliance issues identified in internal or external audits and the results are finally published on the FLA website. In effect, this system of internal and external labour audits mirrors that of the financial audit system, but it is more robust in that the company does not choose the external auditors or know when they will appear at the factory gate. It is also arguably more muscular than government labour inspection because supplier non-compliance with the code can lead to cancellation of the contract, an outcome that would be far more costly to the supplier than the fine a labour inspector could levy. The FLA works in over 30 countries and the levels of labour administration have declined noticeably over the last decade, and not only in failing and failed states.

The Limitations and Potential of Principled Engagement

The FLA is only one of a series of corporate social responsibility initiatives that emerged in the 1990s,[17] but it is unique in that it is the only system that provides for unannounced factory audits with transparent results. This is a crucial difference in that affiliated companies know that they cannot simply "talk the talk" because the unannounced audits will likely expose their lack of real action. Similarly, they have a strong incentive to remedy non-compliance findings because the results are published and the public is able to see the efforts that companies have made to redress the situations uncovered by the auditors. If one considers that in 2012 for example, FLA-affiliated companies, and the FLA itself, conducted some 10,000 factory monitoring visits, uncovering about 100,000 non-compliance issues, one gets an idea of the magnitude and significance of the commitment. All other voluntary initiatives set up to regulate supply chains or hold companies accountable have failed to agree on the need for external audits with transparent results. This shortcoming has arguably made them less effective and credible.[18]

Companies that join the FLA are therefore agreeing to help regulate unregulated jurisdictions. They establish rights in workplaces that would otherwise not enjoy them. To date, some 40 major buyers have brought entire product categories into

the FLA system. Another 3,000-odd companies who supply the FLA's 200 college
and university members have submitted their licensed production to FLA scrutiny.
So is this a new form of global labour regulation? Are private actors going to
have to deliver public goods such as labour inspections from now on? The FLA
is particularly strong in the sporting goods sector, with Adidas, Arena, Asics,
New Balance, Nike, Puma and W.L Gore all participating. It also has a growing
presence in sectors as diverse as agriculture, electronics (Apple), food (Nestlé),
gifts and paper.

Some commentators argue that it is illegitimate for private companies to be
conducting labour inspections and that resources should rather be devoted to
strengthening public labour administration systems. It is the responsibility of the
State to protect rights, they say, and this cannot and should not be usurped by
private actors. The only legitimate and sustainable solution, the argument goes, is
to strengthen the capacity of the State to play its proper role. Unfortunately, years
of ILO technical assistance to countries around the world has not been able to stem
the decline of labour inspections, and the global labour market has quite simply
overwhelmed most national systems of labour market regulation. Even developed
market economies have trouble maintaining adequate levels of inspection.[19]

The need for private actors to take responsibility for labour inspection remains,
and will probably grow. No socially responsible company would want child
labour, forced labour or toxic conditions of work involved in the production of
their goods, so the need to perform due diligence to ensure that labour standards
are respected, even in jurisdictions where labour inspectors are active, is often a
necessity.[20]

Perhaps the ideal situation would be one in which private actors complemented
the work of public agencies by mobilising resources to protect social, labour and
environmental rights. If the private and public actors cooperated and coordinated,
it might be possible to weave social safety nets in countries which have never had
them before. That synergy has been hard to capture and most public agencies are
either in denial or in bad faith about the lamentable state of labour law enforcement
in their jurisdictions. This has certainly stymied ILO action on the topic since no
member state wants to admit publicly that its labour laws are not being enforced and
that it requires assistance from international organisations or private corporations.
This effectively means that the most concerted action to enforce labour laws and
international standards in factories around the world is that undertaken by FLA-
affiliated companies, particularly when they cooperate with local stakeholders.
The FLA is increasingly consulting with local stakeholders to identify priority
issues and working with them on agreed remedial strategies. Those strategies are
developmental, rather than punitive, and the compliance audit is being replaced by
needs assessments and gap analyses followed by capacity building.[21]

So does it work? The FLA has analysed audit results every year since it started
external auditing in 2002 and concluded that while audits are reasonably effective
in identifying violations they are less so in effecting lasting change. The number
of violations (a global average of 13 per factory) has remained stubbornly high,

despite thousands of audits and remedial programmes. Why? One of the reasons is that the system was developed and implemented in a top-down manner. The White House initiative brought together the US parties concerned and they took the unilateral decision to add code standards to their contracts. Suppliers around the world, confronted with those new and exacting requirements, found that it was easier to cheat than to comply.

This is a classic reaction to regulatory efforts which raise the bar too high, too fast. In retrospect, the introduction of the new system was not accompanied by sufficient dialogue along the global supply chain to ensure good faith cooperation from suppliers. This was at least in part a function of the fact that the Apparel Industry Partnership was reacting to a series of labour rights crises around the world. If the initiative had been more proactive it would probably have been more consultative in nature.

The result is that code of conduct audits have provoked a veritable industry of falsified wage and hour records as suppliers attempt to "comply" with code standards. Newspapers in south China, for example, carry advertisements by consultants offering to game audits and by software providers offering programs that fake wage and hour records. Social auditors have become adept at exposing fake records but this cat-and-mouse game has become a treadmill. The overall levels of compliance remain largely unchanged. This does not mean to say that a lot of improvements have not been made; nor does it detract from the hundreds of thousands of wrongs that have been righted as a result of audits. But overall, code of conduct audits are not changing the culture of non-compliance that reigns in many exporting countries.

The FLA has therefore shifted its emphasis from policing to partnership and a more nuanced form of Principled Engagement. Suppliers have been invited to join so that they become part of the solution rather than simply "the problem", and local stakeholders have been included in the definition of issues and responses rather than being left with no option but to name and shame. Sustainable compliance is now pursued through needs assessment followed by capacity building rather than coercion. The top-down enforcement of standards has been replaced by a joint venture between buyers, suppliers, the FLA and local stakeholders and service providers to equip factories with the systems and expertise that they need to be compliant. Capacity building involves not only management and supervisory staff but also workers who are empowered to understand their rights and provided with channels and guarantees that allow them to exercise those rights. The FLA acts as the facilitator and enabler of the collaboration between buyers, suppliers and civil society, providing a "safe space" within which they can engage on a principled basis to address common concerns. The FLA also provides the technical inputs and services necessary for them to make practical progress on those issues.

The FLA therefore engages in very practical terms with a range of interested parties in the supply chain. That engagement is rights based, in that the companies voluntarily commit to the code principles, but it goes beyond that in two important respects. The companies who join voluntarily sign a contract with the FLA in which they agree to the performance requirements of the FLA Charter, and they repeat those requirements in their contracts with suppliers. This contract is renewed annually. The engagement is thus set down in great detail in written form, reducing the risk of whitewashing or co-option. Secondly, the engagement is transparent. This provides an even stronger guarantee of performance than the written contract in that ultimately it is the court of public opinion that holds sway in determining company behaviour. In return, the FLA provides important services. Its verification audits and company accreditation attest to the integrity of the company compliance efforts and its capacity building services provide much needed support to the social responsibility programmes of the supply chain actors. These mechanisms for accountability assumed by FLA companies lay the framework for a principled model for engaging companies in the business of human rights.

Two examples of Principled Engagement by the FLA and its members and stakeholders are illustrative of the practical embodiment of this approach. In 2009, the FLA convened two multi-stakeholder forums in China to discuss socially responsible retrenchment in the wake of the financial crisis. Consumer demand had collapsed and factories were closing or downsizing on a wholesale basis, often violating workers' rights in the process. The FLA brought together government agencies, buyers, suppliers and trade union representatives to discuss how to handle the inevitable retrenchments in a manner consistent with the code of conduct and the law. Similarly, when Nike was confronted by Australian television network Channel Seven in 2008 with allegations of abuse of foreign migrant workers at a supplier facility in Malaysia,[22] the FLA commissioned a report on the employment of foreign migrants and organised a multi-stakeholder forum to seek consensus on practical solutions to the most common abuses of workers' rights. These initiatives provided "safe spaces" in which the stakeholders could meet and seek practical solutions to complex issues of code compliance. There was plenty of condemnation flowing from the media and labour rights groups but it provided no channel for resolution of the issues. The parties concerned, particularly buyers and suppliers, needed a trusted third party to convene and moderate the discussions and to contribute practical proposals for action.

Not everyone agrees that these forms of engagement are principled, appropriate or effective. The FLA is both a facilitator of Principled Engagement and, by virtue of its corporate membership, a "principledly" engaged actor itself. For some, however, the role assumed by the FLA is little more than colluding with the "enemy" with few tangible benefits. The United Students Against Sweatshops, for example, argues that the FLA cannot perform due diligence on companies in an independent manner because those companies are often members of the FLA and their dues are a large part of the FLA's budget, so that the partnership is not set on equal footing.[23] Others argue that "social auditing" is no more than a fig leaf for buyers who are not serious about changing conditions in their supply chains because their very motivation for going offshore was to find unregulated jurisdictions in which standards and costs were lower.[24] Moreover, the arguments go, any change in corporate behaviour is incremental at best and at worst simply a form of corporate "greenwashing" (or "bluewashing" if such corporate responsibility attempts include the UN as a stakeholder). In this context, does the FLA represent a flawed form of Principled Engagement? Or worse, a sophisticated form of Business as Usual?

The first allegation (of a conflict of interest) was carefully considered in the design of the FLA system. The Board of Directors has six company, six university and six NGO seats with an independent chair, and there is a super-majority voting system that prevents any one constituency from dominating. In addition, the audits are arranged by the FLA staff, are unannounced and transparent. A cursory glance at the results will show that the findings are substantial and often involve egregious code violations, something that companies would only accept if they were serious about making improvements (as distinct from seeking "cover"). The fact that those results are published by the FLA demonstrates that the companies are not able to censor or suppress findings, even when they reflect badly on them.

Similarly, companies who go offshore in search of unregulated environments would presumably not join an initiative like the FLA that is attempting to "re-regulate" those jurisdictions. Why engage in private regulation with multi-stakeholder oversight if your real intention is to escape regulation? There are, no doubt, companies using corporate social responsibility and social auditing as a form of "greenwash", but they are generally outside of multi-stakeholder initiatives and such companies certainly could not live with the independent auditing and transparency requirements of the FLA. The danger in the FLA's approach to Principled Engagement is not that it is placing the bar too low but rather that its monitoring, auditing and transparency requirements are too stringent. Relatively few companies are willing to agree to unannounced and transparent independent audits and this challenges the FLA's attempts to reach critical mass in key sectors like apparel. Put simply, if the approach is too "principled", there may be very little engagement from the corporate sector.

In some ways the condemnation employed by labour rights groups and the media supports the engagement activities of the FLA in that it forces companies to look for ways to improve their image. Most of the companies affiliated to the FLA had been through periods of condemnation before they joined. Mere affiliation, of course, does not prevent future bouts of condemnation, but the FLA programme does provide a basis for responding to, and engaging with, critics. Many of the groups employing name-and-shame tactics are in communication with the FLA on specific cases and some have made use of the FLA Third Party Complaints mechanism to defend workers' rights.

One of the toughest challenges facing those companies that choose to undertake some engagement mechanism as a means of protecting rights is proving to be market economics. Global supply chains are characterised by relentless pressures on prices and lead times, and some buyers have contradictory approaches – constant price cutting on the one hand and code of conduct auditing on the other. Price competition is, of course, fundamental to the market economy and does not necessarily lead to declining labour standards, but in global supply chains it is often the case. In developed market economies, companies respond to price competition through innovation and efficiency gains but suppliers in developing countries often lack the management resources to do so. Given that the suppliers' rent and utility costs are generally inflexible, workers' wages and working conditions are often the adjustment variable when prices fall or costs increase. In a free market this should not be the buyers' problem, but the power differentials in global supply chains (between buyers and suppliers, and suppliers and their workers) are so great that buyers should perform due diligence to ensure that the price they negotiate is sufficient to pay workers' wages and benefits.

This risk – of competitive pressures undermining labour standards – has to be approached with considerable caution. Any grouping that sits down to discuss prices runs the risk of contravening anti-trust or competition rules and so the discussions need to be carefully organised and conducted. Second, the buyers and the suppliers have conflicting commercial interests and confidentiality is a major concern. Third, it is well nigh impossible for either party to escape their competitive environment and they have very little room to manoeuvre when it comes to prices. It is therefore hard to see how anything other than engagement in a "safe space" could get companies to adopt more consistent sourcing and corporate social responsibility practices. The FLA provides the brokerage and the assurances necessary to get them to engage, and if they do agree to come to the table, the technical inputs required to realise the adaptive measures to cope with commercial pressures. However, that engagement is not only technical. The FLA is not a business development agency. Its interactions with buyers, suppliers and other stakeholders are always on the basis of the standards contained in the code of conduct. Experience has shown that the achievement and maintenance of acceptable levels of compliance depends on having good management policies, procedures, trained staff, communication, and worker involvement. The FLA provides technical assistance in those areas, but always as part of a clear strategy to achieve better outcomes in terms of code standards.

Factors that Make Principled Engagement Work in the FLA Case

Chronologically, it helped to be convened by government. The fact that President Clinton brought the parties together at the start and supported the process until it bore fruit in the form of the FLA provided a very important moral imperative. It was probably equally important that the US government then withdrew and let the newly formed not-for-profit organisation (the FLA) get on with the job. This allowed the FLA to be more agile and creative than it could have been had government remained at the table. It also allowed the FLA to operate in exporting countries without being challenged as an agent of US foreign or trade policy.

Second, consumer pressure provided another moral imperative. Companies could not ignore or reject the consumer expectations that they "do the right thing".

Third, the risks associated with doing business in many badly regulated jurisdictions provide what might be called the supply-chain imperative. This sometimes takes a legalistic form that strips the meaning from a "rights-based" approach, but it nonetheless provides a basis of standards (the code of conduct) that supply-chain actors can rely on.

Fourth is the very robust framework of performance obligations that provides boundaries within which the staff and participants work. The significance of the transparency requirements in this regard cannot be overstated.

Fifth is the steady flow of information about human and labour rights abuses in global supply chains that obliges companies to perform due diligence and undertake the delivery of what is essentially a state function, namely labour inspection.

And finally, there is the existence of a growing number of civil society actors focusing on market or regulatory failure. These networks of NGOs constitute a new accountability mechanism. Particularly significant is the growth in the number of NGOs that want to be part of the solution and that are willing to engage with companies in the search for those solutions.

Conclusion

Reducing corporate violations of workers' rights is a process of progressive realisation. While a diverse range of initiatives aimed at curbing violations of workers' rights have proliferated in recent decades, it is also clear that such initiatives "have been unable to stem the flow of human rights violations by TNCs".[25] This should not be taken as an indication that such measures are altogether devoid of merit. Initiatives that have relied on the development of soft law via such tools as codes of conduct can play a vital role in internalising human rights norms within corporations and solidifying the notion that corporations have duties with respect to shareholders *and* stakeholders (including workers in their supply chain) alike – a process that in time "can shape the standards of care that are legally expected of business".[26] This is especially so in respect of workers' rights, with corporate codes and reporting guidelines emphasising the importance of environmental and social impacts not only on employees but also on the community in which the company operates, taking into account the workers in its global supply chain. However, not all codes or initiatives are alike and there remains a vast gulf of difference between the aspirations of some codes and initiatives and how they actually engage business in the process of reform. The FLA is one example of how corporations can be both *principally* and "*principledly*" engaged in the business of human rights.

Endnotes

1   John Ruggie, "Protect, Respect and Remedy: A Framework for Business and Human Rights", Report of the Special Representative of the Secretary-General on the Issue of Human Rights and Transnational Corporations and Other Business Enterprises (UN Doc A/HRC/8/5), 7 April 2008, 54.

2   Michael Posner, President, Human Rights First, Testimony before the United States Congressional Human Rights Caucus "Human Rights And Brand Accountability: How Multinationals Can Promote Labor Rights", 8 February, 2006, available at http://digitalcommons.ilr.cornell.edu/cgi/viewcontent.cgi?article=1012&context=codes [accessed 28 May 2013].

3   John Ruggie, "Business and Human Rights: Further Steps Toward the Operationalization of the 'Protect, Respect and Remedy' Framework", Report of the Special Representative of the Secretary-General on the issue of human rights and transnational corporations and other business enterprises (UN Doc A/HRC/14/27), 9 April 2010, para. 82, available at http://198.170.85.29/Ruggie-report-2010.pdf [accessed 16 December 2012].

4   John Ruggie, "Business and Human Rights: Mapping International Standards of Responsibility and Accountability for Corporate Acts", Report of the Special Representative of the Secretary-General (SRSG) on the issue of human rights and transnational corporations and other business enterprise (UN Doc A/HRC/4/35), 19 February 2007, para. 88, available at http://www.globalgovernancewatch.org/resources/business-and-human-rights--mapping-international-standards-of-responsibility-and-accountability-for-corporate-acts [accessed 28 May 2013].

5   David Kinley and Justine Nolan, "Trading and Aiding Human Rights: Corporations in the Global Economy", *Nordic Journal of Human Rights* 25, no. 4 (2008), 358.

6   Ruggie, 2007, op. cit., para. 82.

7   CBS News, *48 Hours*, 17 October, 1996. Transcript available at http://www.viet.net/web/nike/public_html/48hrfmt.htm [accessed 1 May 2012].

8   Other examples with different approaches to enforcement are OECD, *Organisation for Economic Co-Operation and Development Guidelines For Multinational Enterprises*, 2011, available at http://www.oecd.org/daf/inv/mne/48004323.pdf [accessed 28 May 2013]; United Nations, *Norms on the Responsibilities of Transnational Corporations and Other Business Enterprises with Regard to Human Rights*, United Nations Sub-Commission on the Promotion and Protection of Human Rights Res 2003/16 (UN Doc E/CN.4/Sub.2/2003/12/Rev.2), 13 August, 2003, available at http://www.unhchr.ch/huridocda/huridoca.nsf/%28Symbol%29/E.CN.4.Sub.2.2003.12.Rev.2.En [accessed 1 May 2012].

9   Olivier De Schutter, "Extraterritorial Jurisdiction as a Tool for Improving the Human Rights Accountability of Transnational Corporations", November 2006, available at http://www.reports-and-materials.org/Olivier-de-Schutter-report-for-SRSG-re-extraterritorial-jurisdiction-Dec-2006.pdf [accessed 1 May 2012].

10   United Nations, "Secretary-General Appoints John Ruggie as United States Special Representative on Issue of Human Rights, Transnational Corporations, Other Business Enterprises", news release, 28 July 2005, available at http://www.un.org/News/Press/docs/2005/sga934.doc.htm [accessed 1 May 2012].

11   The UN has been grappling, for some decades, with how best to engage business on human rights issues. One of its earlier attempts was in the 1970s: the Centre on Transnational Corporations was established by the UN in 1975, and by 1977 it was coordinating negotiation of a voluntary *Draft Code of Conduct on Transnational*

Corporations. However, no final agreement was concluded. See Jem Blendell, "Barricades and Boardrooms: A Contemporary History of the Corporate Accountability Movement", United Nations Research Institute for Social Development (UNRISD) Programme on Technology, Business and Society, Paper No 13, (2004) 11, available at http://www.unrisd. org/80256B3C005BCCF9/%28httpPublications%29/504AF359BB33967FC1256EA9003 CE20A?OpenDocument [accessed 1 May 2012].

12   International Organization of Employers and International Chamber Of Commerce, *Joint Views of the IOE and ICC on the Draft Norms on the Responsibilities of Transnational Corporations and Other Business Enterprises with Regard to Human Rights*, United Nations Economic and Social Council (UN Doc E/CN.4/Sub.2/2003/NGO/44), 24 July 2003, available at http://www.unhchr.ch/Huridocda/Huridoca.nsf/0/918bbd410b5a8d2 cc1256d78002a535a?Opendocument [accessed 1 May, 2012].

13   Tony Waterston and James Tumwine, "Monitoring the Marketing of Infant Formula Feeds: Manufacturers of Breast Milk Substitutes Violate the WHO Code—Again", *BMJ* 326 (2003), 113–14.

14   A tragic example of the lack of domestic enforcement is the April 2013 collapse of the Rana Plaza building, housing five garment factories, in Bangladesh. Over 1,100 people died illustrating the deadly consequences of a lack of enforcement at the local level. See:, Julfikar Ali Manik, Steven Greenhouse and Jim Yardley, *New York Times*, April 25,   2013,   http://www.nytimes.com/2013/04/26/world/asia/bangladeshi-collapse-kills-many-garment-workers.html?pagewanted=all&_r=0; and Dan Viederman, 'Supply chains and forced labor after Rana Plaza: lessons learned' *The Guardian*, May 30 2013, http://www.guardian.co.uk/global-development-professionals-network/2013/may/30/rana-plaza-bangladesh-forced-labour-supply-chains [accesssed 14 June 2013].

15   See, for example, the history and current work of GoodWeave (formerly known as Rugmark), http://www.goodweave.net [accessed 1 May 2012].

16   *The FLA Workplace Code of Conduct and Compliance Benchmarks*, revised 5 October 2011, is available at http://www.fairlabor.org/labor-standards [accessed 1 May 2012]. Internal and external auditors use a set of benchmarks to test code compliance.

17   Other multi-stakeholder initiatives include Social Accountability International, the Ethical Trading Initiative and the Fair Wear Foundation. The Worldwide Responsible Apparel Production (WRAP) is an industry grouping.

18   See, for example, the Electronic Industry Citizenship Coalition (EICC), Business Social Compliance Initiative (BSCI) and Global Social Compliance Programme (GSCP).

19   Lance A. Compa, *Unfair Advantage: Workers' Freedom of Association in the United States under International Human Rights Standards* (Ithica, NY: Cornell University Press, 2004). Also Human Rights Watch, *Blood, Sweat, and Fear: Workers' Rights in U.S. Meat and Poultry Plants*, 25 January 2005, available at http://www.hrw.org/en/reports/2005/01/24/blood-sweat-and-fear [accessed 1 May 2012].

20   See the emphasis placed on due diligence to mitigate risk by John Ruggie, 'Guiding Principles on Business and Human Rights: Implementing the United Nations "Protect, Respect and Remedy" Framework', Report of the Special Representative of the Secretary-General on the issue of human rights and transnational corporations and other business enterprises, A/HRC/17/31, 21 March 2011.

21   For more information on this approach, see the FLA website: http://www.fairlabor. org/our-methodology [accessed 1 May 2012].

22   The Channel Seven report is available at http://www.youtube.com/watch?v=e9ZktmrGGMU [accessed 1 May 2012].

23   FLA Watch website: http://flawatch.usas.org/about/ [accessed 1 May, 2012].

24   "The basic underlying supply chain model of jumping from factory to factory, of pushing prices down, is simply incompatible with a reasonable level of worker rights", Scott Nova quoted in *Inside Higher Education*, 28 September, 2006. Available at http://www.workersrights.org/press/InsideHigherEd_Sept-28-06_CodesDontWork.pdf [accessed 1 May 2012]. See also, AFL – CIO, *Responsiblity Outsourced: Social Audits, Workplace Certification and Twenty Years of Failure to Protect Worker Rights,* April 23 2013, available at: http://www.aflcio.org/content/download/77061/1902391/CSReport.pdf [accessed 14 June 2013].

25   David Kinley and Rachel Chambers, "The UN Human Rights Norms for Corporations: The Private Implications of Public International Law", *Human Rights Law Review* 6, no. 3 (2006), 491.

26   Halina Ward, "Legal Issues in Corporate Citizenship", *International Institute for Environment and Development*, February 2003, iii, available at http://pubs.iied.org/pdfs/16000IIED.pdf [accessed 1 May 2012].

Chapter 9

Wrestling with Shadows: Principled Engagement with Violent Economies and the Repressive Regimes that Rule Them

James Cockayne

Authoritarian, repressive and violent regimes often share another characteristic: involvement in illicit economic activity, much of which has its own negative impacts on human rights. Organised oppression has to be financed somehow. In many cases, large-scale human rights violations are not the ends of violent economics – they are the means. Large-scale human rights abuse, like conflict, is thus often the continuation of economics by other means.[1] This chapter explores how the concept of Principled Engagement might be applied to efforts to transform today's "violent economies"[2] and the violent regimes – both state and non-state – that rule them.

The sociologist Charles Tilly pointed out over two decades ago that rulers sometimes behave like organised criminals.[3] Like protection racketeers, authoritarian and repressive regimes – and many repressive non-state armed groups – lack popular legitimacy, and so are forced to turn to coercion as a means for revenue extraction and the assertion of their rule. Today, the resemblance between organised crime and repressive rule is more than passing, and has taken on a more transnational, and thus more durable and violent, scope. Violent, repressive and authoritarian groups in places as diverse as Afghanistan, Africa, parts of Asia, Central America, the Middle East and south-eastern Europe have turned to a range of predatory and parasitic activities such as graft, drug production and trafficking, and illicit traffic in natural resources, as a means to sustain organised coercion. The revenues they earn in global markets sustain their rule, while ongoing human rights abuse helps to entrench the system of plunder and profit that underpins these shadowy economies.

Access to illicit revenues can serve as a major obstacle to effective international engagement and pressure on human rights. Yet some recent research and experiences suggest that efforts to control these regimes' illicit economic behaviour – or to hold rulers accountable for it[4] – can provide an important avenue for effective engagement and behavioural transformation. In this chapter both are explored: how Ostracism and Business as Usual approaches to human rights engagement with authoritarian regimes affect their illicit economic behaviour, perhaps even perpetuating violent economies and the human rights abuses they entail; and whether and how tools for transforming violent regimes' engagement with the illicit global economy may serve as vehicles for influencing those regimes towards more human rights compliant behaviour.

The first part of the chapter provides an introduction to the role that illicit economic activity plays in sustaining violent, repressive and authoritarian groups' rule in today's globalised economy. The argument is that the same traits that mark a tendency to human rights abusiveness give repressive regimes and non-state groups a comparative advantage in the production and distribution of illegal goods and services into the global economy. As a result, we are seeing a convergence of "crime", "conflict", "corruption" and human rights abuse that poses conceptual and practical challenges for any policy of engagement.

The second part of the chapter, drawing on the definitions of Ostracism, Business as Usual and Principled Engagement provided in Chapter 1 of this volume, explores how the apparatus of criminalisation, control and punishment that the international community has built in the last two decades has served in some cases to drive those regimes closer to illicit, violent economic actors and activities. Next, the impacts of normal trade and investment on these regimes' interaction with shadow economies is explored, suggesting that this approach in fact seems to offer criminal actors a path to political and financial legitimacy, in turn unwittingly risking the de facto criminalisation of these regimes. This points to the need for a third approach – Principled Engagement.

The third part of the paper explores how the concept of Principled Engagement might be applied in dealing with the connections between human rights abuse by ruling regimes and their access to illicit finance. Reviewing two illustrative cases in Africa – the Governance and Economic Management Assistance Program (GEMAP) in Liberia, and the World Bank's support to the Chad/Cameroon oil pipeline – identifies factors that may impact on the success of Principled Engagement with violent economies and their governing regimes. Drawing on recent literature applying the concept of "mediated states" to contemporary contexts,[5] the conclusion is that effective Principled Engagement may require efforts that transform the *mediating institutions* that sustain such regimes' control of illicit revenues, transforming structural incentives to convert violence into revenue. This will require not only *strategic engagement* by external actors with key leaders – which can take a variety of forms ranging from negotiation to elimination – but also *communicative engagement* – which seeks to transform the normative base and incentive structures that shape domestic actors' choice to use violence as a means of political and economic advancement.

In conclusion, some of the policy implications of this analysis are explored. It is argued that international actors should move away from a system which is based too heavily on the *internationalisation* of control towards a more nuanced approach that combines international control with international capacity building to develop *internal* controls. Finally, I identify four areas where we might usefully direct our attention in attempting to apply a policy of Principled Engagement to violent economies.

Violent Economies and the Regimes that Rule Them

The end of the Cold War removed the major state sources of political, financial and military patronage for repressive regimes and armed non-state actors around the world. These groups were forced to look to sources of revenue and weaponry other than the superpowers, in order to sustain their organised coercion. Many increasingly turned to the shadow economy,[6] participating in or simply covertly taxing drug production and smuggling (Afghanistan, Pakistan, Burma/Myanmar, Colombia, Guatemala, Kyrgyzstan, Tajikistan, Haiti, West Africa, Venezuela, Albania and Kosovo); illicit logging (Liberia, Burma/Myanmar, Indonesia under Suharto); illicit diamond, gem and mineral extraction and trafficking (the National Union for the Total Independence of Angola (UNITA) during the Angolan civil war, groups in the Democratic Republic of Congo (DRC), Uganda and Rwanda, the Revolutionary United Front (RUF) and others in Sierra Leone and Liberia, Burma/Myanmar again, and Zimbabwe); trafficking in nuclear material and expertise (Pakistan, North Korea); cigarette smuggling (Lebanon's Hizbollah, North Korea again, Serbia under Milosevic); oil smuggling (Iraq, Nigeria); and even counterfeiting (North Korea) and credit-card fraud (Liberation Tigers of Tamil Eelam (LTTE) in Sri Lanka).

Improvements in global transportation, communications and financial transfers reduced the barriers to market entry and operating costs for commercial entrepreneurs around the world – including those who wished to engage with criminal markets. Armed groups and governing regimes stood in a good position to take advantage of these opportunities, especially if they were willing to use violence to extract resources and protect illicit trafficking. In some cases – such as Milosevic's Serbia, in parts of Russia in the mid 1990s or more recently in the case of the alliances between military forces and drug traffickers in Guinea-Bissau – this has led to a direct "political-criminal nexus".[7] In other cases, the relationship is more indirect and predicated on collusion, corruption and the extraction of a criminal rent.[8] This has not necessarily required governing metropolitan elites to directly participate in illicit trade themselves: instead it is often enough for them to acquiesce in, or protect, the operations of armed groups operating in the "ungoverned spaces" of rural hinterlands and urban *favelas* and *bidonvilles*, receiving corruption rents as a fee for not enforcing the law. As Ken Menkhaus points out of contemporary African states:

> [S]tate authorities have in some respects pursued a rational strategy by allowing frontier zones to go ungoverned, especially if the frontier has little economic value, the cost of establishing rule of law is higher than whatever revenue can be earned from the area, the state faces a serious shortage of money and capacity, and negative spillover of anarchy in the frontier does not unduly impact the core areas of the state. The result has been enormous tracts of territory in the hinterlands of many African states that are in a condition of de facto state collapse.[9]

In fact, the very absence of the state from those areas may make them *more* economically valuable to *de jure* rulers, since it becomes possible for those areas to be used for riskier – and therefore more profitable – activities, especially crime. The presence of armed criminal groups on a state's territory can create a win–win situation: governing elites can plausibly deny their control over these spaces even as they collect a clandestine "protection" fee from the criminal groups; while the armed, criminal groups are left relatively free to conduct their profit-making activities – whose formal criminalisation serves to allow them to charge a higher price for their services, because of the nominal risks involved.

The result is a system that profits from apparent conflict and instability, while in fact functioning on a basis of hidden crime and collusion.[10] Violence and the abuse of human rights are central to this system. Organised criminal groups are themselves highly authoritarian and repressive,[11] relying as they do on physical, sexual, social and mental violence and coercion for their control and profits. Women and children, in particular, suffer at their hands. But human rights abuse is also central to the collusion of state authorities in these violent economies. The regimes that govern states in which organised crime becomes embedded have strong incentives to limit political speech and openness, use law enforcement institutions to repress political opponents, and to limit the effectiveness of social institutions – while often, themselves, plundering a country's wealth.

From all this emerges a pattern of violent economies that blend crime and conflict, with state-ruling elites and armed groups collaborating and competing for access to illicit revenues in a system that transforms violence and coercion into profit. In such situations, it can be very difficult to distinguish between predatory commercial strategies, politically motivated armed conflict, and authoritarian tactics of repression. Criminal finance as a means to a political end becomes increasingly hard to distinguish from crime as an end in itself – and the results are often portrayed as politically motivated human rights abuses, rather than economically motivated entrepreneurialism.

In cases such as Bosnia and Iraq, sectarian and ethnic organisations have undertaken "ethnic cleansing" operations, clearing territory for military, political *and economic* reasons.[12] Clearing a valley or suburb served, in each case, an important military and political objective. But it also served an important economic objective, allowing the cleansing force to pillage those areas, take control of trafficking routes (in drugs, cars, women and guns in Bosnia; in oil in Iraq), control black markets, and profit from control of housing stock (which rulers rent or dole out to populations under their control). And the context of armed conflict allows the use of violence to commoditise goods and services which would normally be unavailable – such as forced labour, sexual servitude and illegally extracted or plundered resources.[13] Similar patterns can be observed elsewhere, for example in Kosovo, Colombia, Burma/Myanmar, Sierra Leone and Tajikistan, where military and political manoeuvring has at times been difficult to distinguish from criminal strategy.[14]

Violence – and the abuse of human rights – is thus a central component of such economies. And it provides these regimes and groups with a key comparative advantage in the globalised economy: the capacity to produce and distribute illegal goods and services, in particular by encouraging young men to take risks they might not otherwise bear, and by forcing young women and children into positions of subjugation and servitude.[15]

This comparative advantage is amplified by a number of factors that are often present in such states. Often, repressive rule coexists with rentier economies, state domination of the market and under-development. Even with the absence of violence, these factors often lead to the flourishing of an informal economy, partly as a survival mechanism for those who do not have the necessary connections to state rulers, and later as a mechanism for ruling groups to consolidate their informal hold over power. Informal transactions avoid intrusive state extraction and taxation: but they also lack the protections that states nominally offer, making them vulnerable to control through violence, and thus vulnerable to abuse of human rights, from the right to private property to the right to life.

In such circumstances, employment prospects are often meagre, and life expectancies often short – giving young men, in particular, lower risk aversion than actors in other areas, helping to draw them into a life of crime. Current youth bulges in many of these places will only worsen this employment gap. Many of these young unemployed men are likely to have received only minimal schooling, and those exposed to conflict may boast skills primarily as specialists in violence. Rapid urbanisation in such contexts serves also to further break down traditional authority structures, lowering normative and institutional barriers to engaging in violent criminal activity. The reach of the state into urban peripheries is often weak, leaving a gap that local organised crime groups increasingly fill by providing and controlling public goods and services, including security and "rough justice".[16]

How Ostracism and Business as Usual Reward Violent Entrepreneurs

As Pedersen and Kinley explain in Chapter 1 of this volume, in recent years the international community has pursued both Ostracism and Business as Usual approaches in attempting to transform the behaviour of repressive regimes. This section argues that both have failed adequately to grapple with the economic aspects of human rights abuse, and also consider what a better approach might look like.

The Fruits of Exile

Since the end of the Cold War, the international community has built up a complex – and not always coherent – apparatus for ostracising regimes, groups and even individuals that have been involved in terrorism, war crimes or other kinds of human rights violations. These mechanisms include trade embargoes and sanctions regimes imposed multilaterally by the United Nations (UN) Security Council or unilaterally by states, which remove those targeted for sanctioning from circulation in the global economy. The apparatus of Ostracism also includes international investigations and prosecutions conducted through international war crimes tribunals, and through decentralized action by states – leading potentially to conviction, stigmatisation and removal from normal society through incarceration.

Yet little thought has been given to how exclusion from the formal, regulated global economy alters the incentives of such "violent entrepreneurs"[17] to engage with the informal, unregulated global political economy. Efforts to woo authoritarian regimes towards the path of good global citizenship through Business as Usual may also risk encouraging such regimes to simply play a double game – using their control of violence, the mechanisms of internal repression, and their connections to underground international networks to gain market advantage internally – while externally presenting themselves as legitimate, peaceable businessmen. Such a Business as Usual approach, in other words, risks "laundering" the ill-gotten political and financial gains of violent criminal activity.

Let us consider each of these propositions in turn, beginning with the relationship between today's violent economies and the startling new technologies of Ostracism that the international community has developed over the last two decades. As Gerry Simpson has documented at length in his *Great Powers and Outlaw States*,[18] there is a long history of Great Powers seeking to use legal discourse to ostracise revolutionary, non-status-quo and nuisance powers – in other words, to "outlaw" them. But the decentralized structure of international relations has largely ensured that this "crimetalk" has not been accompanied by centralised law enforcement mechanisms. In the past, the rhetoric of criminalisation at the international level was exactly that: rhetoric. States generally lacked the means, beyond their borders, to institutionalise that rhetoric, or to put in place the classic technologies of criminal justice at the domestic level – policing, investigation, criminal trial, and detention.

International criminal justice was, consequently, until recently focused on inter-state cooperation to enforce domestic criminal norms. Those domestic norms were, in turn, somewhat shaped by agreements by states to subject to criminal justice the conduct of private, transnational actors (such as pirates and military recruiters) which states – "moved by selfish but shared interests"[19] – recognised as a common problem. Even after the depravity of the Second World War, when states agreed that there were certain extreme cases in which even the conduct of state officials warranted substantive criminalisation at the international level (such as genocide, war crimes, torture and apartheid),[20] states left the enforcement of these international criminal norms to each other – and as a result these remained largely unenforced.

In the last two decades, however, we have seen a remarkable effort, led primarily by Western liberal democracies, to create systems at the international level that replicate or complement the penal systems at the domestic level. Most attention has been focused on the growth of international criminal trial processes. But we also see a similar trend towards "internationalisation" of domestic regulatory and policing technologies, through the UN Security Council's creation of lists and regimes regulating terrorism, weapons of mass destruction (WMD) proliferation, and states and armed groups using children in armed conflict; the UN Security Council's blessing of anti-money-laundering regimes, controls on the trade in "blood diamonds", and multi-stakeholder groups responding to Somali piracy; and in the increasing reliance on international commissions of inquiry, investigations and expeditionary policing in conflict and post-conflict situations.[21] Although they are deemed "administrative" or "preventive", rather than "penal", the UN Security Council's sanctions regimes also bear many of the hallmarks of these technologies of control traditionally found in domestic criminal justice systems.

What this points to is an attempt – particularly by the Western liberal democracies that have been the driving force in the creation of most of these international technologies of control – to use the UN Security Council to export to the international level the mechanisms growing out of a "culture of control" that has developed in Western democracies in the last four decades, particularly dominating the Anglo-Saxon democracies since the 1980s.[22] As David Garland has explored, this "culture of control" was closely related to a particular penal politics, which used crimetalk and criminal justice mechanisms as instruments of Ostracism, suppression and control – rather than as instruments of social reform, individual rehabilitation or social reconciliation – notions that had been dominant in criminological discourse and practice in an earlier period in the middle of the twentieth century.[23]

In the absence of serious geopolitical opposition in the first two decades after the end of the Cold War, Western states – especially the US, but also the UK and France – took actions on the international level, including in the UN Security Council, that reflected and responded to their domestic political culture, exporting these domestic criminal justice technologies to the international level, and creating a system whereby they could use penal and quasi-penal regulatory instruments to label certain actors – from Saddam Hussein to Osama bin Laden – and exclude them from formal participation in the global political economy. In Chapter 1, Pedersen and Kinley characterise the role of "coercion" in a policy of Ostracism as the threat of or actual deprivation of "value". International criminalisation obviously involves just such "value deprivation", through the incarceration of individuals, or other forms of exclusion from society or access to economic potential – for example through the imposition of bans on an individual's circulation in society (for example, UN Security Council travel bans), or bans on the circulation of their goods and services in the global economy (for example, trade embargoes, commodity bans, commodity certification requirements, asset freezes). It is, in other words, an international apparatus of Ostracism.

The basic problem is clear: the deprivation of access to *legal* value may increase the incentives that violent actors perceive in accessing *illegal* value. Crime and violence-based commerce may become the primary vehicle for value creation and accumulation.

Where international trade sanctions have been imposed, sanctions targets have repeatedly turned to criminal networks and violent entrepreneurs as a source of revenue and material goods.[24] The Haitian *junta* targeted in the early 1990s turned quickly to narco-trafficking. Many ended up in US gaols. Milosevic turned to cigarette and other forms of smuggling, and to plunder under the cover of ethnic cleansing, acting through gangsters like Arkan.[25] Saddam Hussein turned to oil smuggling.[26] The ruling elite of North Korea is deeply engaged in counterfeiting. The Taliban has relied heavily on narco-trafficking.

Repressive rulers and criminal groups have become closer, as smuggling becomes a patriotic or ideological enterprise, an act of resistance to the foreign enemy.[27] Presidents' sons – such as Uday and Qusay Hussein in Iraq, Marko Milosevic in Serbia, Ousmane and Moussa Conté in Guinea-Conakry – frequently become major crime bosses, since they can reliably serve as gatekeepers between the repressive regime and the criminal underworld, while affording the real kingpin an element of plausible deniability. Efforts to disempower such violent actors depend significantly on the effectiveness of international law enforcement – which is often weak, given the trans-boundary, clandestine nature of much of this economic activity, and the international community's fragmented policy-making machinery, which struggles to prioritise between what are seen as competing objectives of enforcing the law and fostering political stability. The overall effect of international sanctions is thus often the localised normalisation of transnational criminal activity, secrecy, the use of violence and coercion in business activities, and collusion between political rulers and criminal elites.[28]

Thus, unadulterated Ostracism in the form of economic sanctions not only seems, as Lektzian and Souva recognise, to increase state rents, rewarding non-democratic rulers who rely more on rents to maintain power[29] – but also to reward a particular exercise of that power, found in black markets: highly violent, repressive, secretive and arbitrary. It seems, in other words, to positively facilitate the development of a human-rights-abusing political economy, pushing violent groups' economic base further towards a model that is more risky – and thus potentially more violent and more profitable. By pushing repressive rulers further into the shadows, Ostracism risks further weakening international oversight and international leverage, thus reducing the prospects of effective human rights promotion and advocacy.

Business as Usual and Moral Hazard

If Ostracism pushes repressive rulers further into the shadows, does it follow that a better strategy would be simply to drag these rulers into the full glare of international society? That may be the case. But what does not appear to work is an approach that reduces "international society" to "the international economy", and seeks to transform violent entrepreneurs into upstanding businessmen, by waving a magic wand of economic liberalisation and openness. Such an approach simply allows violent entrepreneurs to launder their ill-gotten financial and social power, turning a dangerously blind eye to their unclean hands. In the process, the international community risks creating a moral hazard, essentially signalling through policies of amnesty and impunity that such behaviour will ultimately be tolerated. A more nuanced approach may be needed which takes the violent realities of social life under such repressive regimes into account.

In this volume, the process of business-oriented engagement with repressive regimes is described as "Business as Usual": encouraging long-term political liberalisation in repressive and authoritarian states through short-term economic engagement and liberalisation. But integrating criminalised political-economies into the global economy, without first managing their transition away from criminal systems, carries grave risks. In particular, as we have learnt in the Balkans, Russia and even in parts of Latin America and Africa, the Washington Consensus-inspired rush to integrate conflict and post-conflict economies into global financial and trading systems risks simply rewarding those with existing market power in those economies – even if that market power was won at the barrel of a gun.[30] Laissez-faire economic liberalisation in fact allows those actors to launder their assets and their legitimacy, rolling dirty money into acquisitions of privatised state assets or new profit opportunities, and using their financial power and muscle to buy political influence or even office.[31]

The fundamental moral and policy shortcomings of such an approach are obvious: it seems to reward bad behaviour, and may thereby encourage such behaviour in the future. So can we imagine a different, third way?

What Might Principled Engagement with Violent Economies Look Like?

Criminal financing of repressive regimes depends on effective organisation – the organisation of supply routes, financing channels, decision-making protocols and the other shifting rules of this shadow game. Often, this informal organisation exists in the shadows and interstices of more formal organisations: tribal structures embedded within state security apparatus and political parties, or criminal networks penetrating courts and banks, for example. These shadow-filled institutions thus mediate between the official rule of the repressive state and the unofficial power distributed through the shadow economy.[32]

In early modern Europe, state power and administration were centralised in large part to enable the financing and efficient organisation of external war-making.[33] States coerced populations (usually the nobility) in their territory into tax-extraction schemes, providing protection from foreign predators, while using the revenues to enlarge their own territory through aggressive war. Today, the reverse is the dominant pattern in many places: external illicit finance facilitates internal war-making – repression, predation, coercion and parasitism. It is a much less risky arrangement, in many ways, and also requires considerably lower internal expenditures: a state which does not rely on popular consent can dispense with the hassle and cost of managing an effective bureaucracy for the provision of public services, instead relying on corruption payments and threats of coercion to continue its parasitic racket.[34] Once they have tapped into global illicit markets, ruling groups may prove quite happy to rule at arm's length, instead governing portions of their territory and populations indirectly through "mediating" institutions such as local militias, kinship networks, traditional authorities, warlords – and criminal organisations.[35] Ruling regimes' access to illicit cross-border funding streams weakens their incentive to extend the state's administrative reach to peripheral areas. Instead, control of the state and the privileges of sovereignty – including control of security institutions – becomes the ultimate prize for which groups compete, sometimes violently, since it guarantees access to monopolistic profits from criminal rents.[36] In West Africa, for example, a spate of recent coups in Guinea-Bissau, Guinea-Conakry and Niger is considered by many to be a result of competition between different groups within these states to control revenues derived from the burgeoning Latin America–West Africa–Europe drug trade.[37]

This synergy between illicit global commerce and "mediated" states is very significant for how we think about organising efforts to improve human rights in repressive regimes. It suggests that effective strategies will need to deal not only with the nominal leadership of such a regime, and the formal economic "business" sector, but also grapple with the shadowy institutions that underpin regime power. The populations that human rights engagement should benefit may be hidden behind a veil of corruption and crime, with which the international community must wrestle if it wishes to reach them.

Indeed, in many mediated states and violent economies, the populations most vulnerable to human rights abuse exist *physically* separate from nominally ruling, metropolitan "elites": in borderlands and peripheries, and in urban slums excluded from access to the physical and regulatory infrastructure of the state.[38] There, they are bound as much to the informal authorities that control passage across borders – to neighbouring states and between the formal and informal worlds – as they are to the formal authorities. This draws these populations in "peripheral" areas (such as the Kivus in DRC, the Afghanistan–Pakistan border region, large parts of the Sahel, or the *favelas* of Brazil) away from the gaze of the international community and the reach of the state, and deeper into the shadows, where the gun rules. This undermines international efforts to ensure respect for human rights – such as engagement in dialogue with state rulers – since these approaches tend to work through capitals and high-level leaders and formal state institutions, rather than through the mediating institutions – including the corrupted security apparatus and organised criminal groups – which may exert effective control over these populations on a daily basis.

A focus on the transformation of these mediating institutions thus seems likely to be important in engaging with a regime to reform its human rights behaviour. And indeed, this seems in some ways to be what is missing from the "ostracising" and business-oriented approaches. Taken alone, Ostracism seems ill-suited to the transformation of the economic underpinnings of such violent regimes. One form of Ostracism seeks – unrealistically – to cut these regimes off entirely from the world economy, thereby incentivising the violent entrepreneurialism and smuggling that reconnects the regime to the global economy through clandestine channels. Another, more "targeted", form seeks to remove only a small number of leaders from the picture – for example through investigation and prosecution – but risks thereby failing to grapple with the underlying structural incentives for the kind of violent economic behaviour they embraced. Those hydra-heads, once lopped off, are quickly replaced. The first, blanket, approach to Ostracism has proven, in the form of blanket trade bans and embargoes, to be not only impractical and unrealistic but often – as in Iraq and Haiti – downright abusive of populations' enjoyment of human rights. The second, more targeted, approach avoids these pitfalls, but also risks failing as a result to transform the institutions that produce the organised coercion that underpins both systemic human rights abuse and violent economies.

A better approach, therefore, may be to understand targeted Ostracism and Business as Usual as elements in a package of efforts aimed at transforming the whole political economy on which this violent behaviour rests. Ostracism of the leaders of the institutions that wield power within that political economy can then be seen as just one form of "*strategic engagement*" with that political economy – as Ann Kent has described it, distinguishing it from "*communicative engagement*". Strategic engagement can be understood as focused on the agency underpinning a violent economy. Communicative engagement, in contrast, is focused on the economy's constitutive structures – it aims to transform the normative institutions that shape how participants in that political economy understand their own cost–benefit analyses and interests. While Ostracism is a form of strategic engagement, Business as Usual can thus be understood as preoccupied primarily with communicative engagement, aiming to entice large numbers of economic actors to move away from the shadows and towards the legitimate, transparent economic sphere.

Learning from Africa

Which combinations of strategic engagement and communicative engagement, Ostracism and Business as Usual, and when? Two recent experiences in Africa may provide some insights.

Transforming West Africa's War Economies

West Africa – in particular Guinea, Sierra Leone, Liberia and Côte d'Ivoire – has been plagued by interlinked war economies for the past two decades. Much of this conflict has been fuelled by what the Special Court of Sierra Leone has termed the "joint criminal enterprise" of Charles Taylor and the RUF to use war to loot Sierra Leone and Liberia of their precious natural resources. Since the early 1990s, the international community has undertaken numerous interventions, ranging from peacekeeping missions to development projects, yet has struggled to put a stop to the region's persistent violence. At times, it in fact has appeared that the international community has become unwittingly complicit in the political economy that the region's factions have built, spinning violence into gold: in some diplomatic circles, the term "Linas–Marcoussis effect" is now used – after a deal that was struck to create a government of national reconciliation in Côte d'Ivoire in January 2003 – to refer to the notion that rebels may have a *positive incentive* to attack civilians in some cases, since it seems to induce the international community to move more quickly to negotiate a political truce which gives the rebels access to political and economic spoils.[39]

But West Africa has also been a source of positive experimentation in international intervention, some of which may hold important lessons for any attempt to build a theory of Principled Engagement. This section looks briefly at interventions in the interlocking conflicts in Sierra Leone and Liberia as sources of insight for this enterprise.

In Sierra Leone, the 1999 Lomé Agreement promised peace by granting the brutal leader of the RUF, Foday Sankoh, the position of Vice-President and head of a new mineral resources commission, and granting a general amnesty to his fighters. This was, in effect, a bargain struck through strategic engagement between the government of Sierra Leone and the RUF leadership, facilitated by the international community.

The Lomé accord quickly unravelled. It left the RUF in control of large parts of Sierra Leone's diamond and mineral wealth, which it traded with Liberian President Charles Taylor for guns and money. With his access to this violent economy unfettered, Sankoh continued to resort to violence, and his fighters had few economic incentives to participate in the disarmament, demobilization and reintegration (DDR) programme the international community was backing. Tensions escalated, culminating in the abduction of over 500 UN peacekeepers in May 2000.[40] Only after a renewed outbreak of conflict that ensued did the international community and the government of Sierra Leone switch to a policy of Ostracism, with Sankoh being arrested and the government enlisting the support of the UN Security Council to create an international war crimes tribunal, the Special Court for Sierra Leone. Sankoh eventually died in custody, awaiting trial as a war criminal. With him out of the picture, the RUF collapsed. The Special Court for Sierra Leone is often seen as having played a key role in Sierra Leone's path out of conflict, by removing Sankoh and other key militia leaders from the nation's politics. And it may demonstrate the utility of the shadow of Ostracism in any attempt at Principled Engagement.

When the UN intervened in Liberia a few years after the events described above, it seemed to apply a similar combination of Ostracism (or its shadow) and broader strategic engagement with Liberian factional leaders. But this proved, quickly, to be insufficient: instead, a form of communicative engagement emerged.

In Liberia, the initial focus was on Ostracism, when the Special Court for Sierra Leone indicted the President of Liberia Charles Taylor in June 2003. After some negotiation, Taylor agreed to step aside, and went into semi-voluntary exile in Nigeria – though Nigeria later surrendered him to the Special Court for Sierra Leone for trial. Though this decapitation strategy seemed at first remarkably successful in bringing stability to Liberia, it quickly became clear that this was not enough to transform Liberia's violent economy. There was a real risk that Taylor's removal would simply lead to a fight between remaining factional leaders for the spoils, with one of them possibly emerging from this fight to take his place as kingpin, perhaps even using the internationally backed transitional process, including political and economic liberalisation, to launder the wealth and power they had amassed during the war. The UN's efforts to promote a DDR programme faltered badly when factional leaders used their control of violence to attempt to secure themselves plum post-conflict positions, and to control the country's resources and "shadow state".[41]

Liberia's violent economy seemed to be persisting. In August 2004, former combatants in Liberia's civil war were allegedly forcing civilians to tap rubber illegally at the Guthrie rubber plantation, in a relationship some described as "slavery".[42] Other combatants were engaged in illegal mining and cross-border smuggling of gold and consumer goods.[43] Nor was the National Transitional Government of Liberia (NTGL), which ruled in the post-conflict transition to elections, above suspicion. A European-Commission-funded audit of public enterprise financial mismanagement turned up grave mismanagement of a number of national concessions, while an Economic Community of West African States (ECOWAS) investigation suggested serious corruption within the office of the NTGL Chairman.[44] Together, this evidence led funders to threaten to ostracise the entire country by imposing stricter sanctions and withdrawing all development assistance.

Instead, a novel approach to Principled Engagement with Liberia's violent economy was agreed by the NTGL and foreign donors, which seemed to focus more on institutional and communicative engagement than on targeted engagement with Liberia's political elites. To this point, international interventions in Liberia had largely focused on bargaining with and seeking to pressure factional leaders in Liberia, and separately on trying to pay lower-level cadres to disarm and encourage development. The two levels of engagement had not worked in tandem. This did little to reform the corrupt institutions which bound the leadership and lower-level actors together in what the International Crisis Group described as a "shadow state" – a system of corruption, coercion and violent repression. Now, the international community moved to deal with those mediating institutions by taking sole control of revenue collection away from corrupt politicians, and making revenue collectors accountable to the international community. This, it was argued, would make politics less attractive to warlords and empower civil society,[45] so that, in time, Liberia could transition from a period of internationalised control to a more sustained system of internalised control.

The mechanism for this arrangement was the GEMAP. This imposed rigorous controls on public expenditure by placing internationally recruited experts with co-signature authority in key ministries, agencies and state-owned enterprises, including the Liberian Central Bank, the Ministry of Finance in support of the inter-ministerial Cash Management Committee, the Bureau of the Budget, the Forest Development Authority, Roberts International Airport, the Liberia Petroleum Refinery Corporation and the National Port Authority. The Economic Governance Steering Committee, chaired by the Liberian head of state with the US Ambassador to Liberia as deputy chair, provides oversight for GEMAP's implementation.[46]

These arrangements – some of which remain in place at the time of writing – are generally perceived to have reduced corruption opportunities, improved the revenue-collection capacity of the state, and stimulated investor confidence, rewarding effective economic governance. Yet GEMAP has not been without its critics. Some have argued that it has little net capacity-building impact on Liberian institutions and professionals, and that it has failed to communicate effectively with the Liberian population, leading to a sense that it was an imposed solution.[47] And its anti-corruption effect has been hampered by weakness in the Liberian law enforcement institutions, parliament and judicial sectors – another set of key mediating institutions that underpin repressive state and private power.[48]

As a joint UN/World Bank review of GEMAP recognises, action by civil society seems to play a key role in the success of such initiatives:

> The GEMAP experience suggests that civil society is important in helping to create an enabling environment for the negotiation and implementation of robust intervention initiatives, within the host country as well as internationally. Active civil society support could also be important in ensuring that implementation of a robust intervention initiative is actively pursued by government authorities ... Outreach to a wide range of Liberian stakeholders required a communication and information strategy. This aspect was not addressed in the design and initial discussions of [GEMAP] and was raised only when NTGL opposition to the proposed plan was entrenched.[49]

Despite this self-criticism by the World Bank and UN, other commentators have, in fact, suggested that exactly such a communicative effect has emerged, generating real social change:

> The GEMAP program, combined with President Sirleaf's strong pro-reform agenda and endorsements of GEMAP, caused an immediate change in the public discourse on corruption. GEMAP provided responsible government workers an excuse for resisting the inevitable "corruption culture" pressures that skew bureaucratic decisions toward rent-seeking. "GEMAP is watching," became a common statement for avoiding doing things the old way. This has not been limited to the public sector. Private businesses now often count both international agencies and the government among their clients. Long accustomed

to governmental self-dealing, many are encouraged by a new procurement law and the presence of international financial co-signers on the GEMAP-supported Cash Management Committee in the Ministry of Finance to insist on proper documentation when supplying Ministries or Agencies. The reputational risk of becoming known as supportive of corruption has "incentivised" new behavior. Whether as an excuse for doing the right thing, or out of a fear of newfound accountability, the effect has been positive thus far.[50]

What seems to have occurred in Liberia, this suggests, is a "reframing" of the acceptable methods of political and economic advancement – a burgeoning rejection of corruption and the violence that underpins it.[51] The Principled Engagement of authoritative external actors working with authoritative local actors (in this case, President Ellen Johnson Sirleaf, in particular) can reframe what had been normalised behaviour as abnormal and unacceptable behaviour, ostracising it from everyday life.

But we should be mindful of the impact of criminalisation in this reframing process. The language of "crime" and "corruption" may be particularly powerful in mobilising such a reframing; it provides a particularly potent example of what Wocjek Sadurski has called a "rhetorical asset", which can be used to delegitimise strategic actors in the eyes of local populations, and is thus a crucial resource in the dialectic process implicit in the concept of "engagement".[52] Yet it is also a dangerously rigid instrument: once an actor has been labelled a "criminal", it can be difficult to resile from such a characterisation, limiting bargaining options.[53] It thus limits the ability of those engaging with a repressive regime or group to shift frames, treating the regime in different ways in different contexts and when dealing with different audiences – a crucial possibility in this dialectic process.

Still, GEMAP has survived and is largely seen as a success story. One key distinguishing factor that might explain that is the level of unity and commitment from key international donors in support of GEMAP. As Dwan and Bailey argue: "The single most powerful factor in the introduction and eventual signing of GEMAP was the unity of Liberia's international partners."[54] This was a product in part of a "shared diagnosis" of the structural causes of the problem in Liberia; but it was also a product of effective leadership in the development and implementation of an engagement strategy. Then UN Secretary-General Kofi Annan intervened directly with the NTGL Chairman to persuade him to accept GEMAP in 2005, and the UN Security Council issued Resolution 1626 endorsing the initiative just ten days after it was signed; the Security Council also decided to incorporate reporting on the implementation of GEMAP into the regular reporting on the United Nations Mission in Liberia (UNMIL) by the UN Secretary-General, creating an informal monitoring mechanism that helped to put sustained pressure on the Liberian authorities.[55] This was politically possible because GEMAP had the active support and participation not only of the UN but also the US, European Union, African Union, ECOWAS, World Bank and International Monetary Fund (IMF).[56]

Such widespread agreement on the principles of engagement with a violent economy is rare. The Liberian case is notable – and perhaps exceptional – because no major power had any overriding economic stake in its violent economy. The same cannot be said in other cases, such as Sudan, Myanmar or even DRC; in each of those cases, major world powers have public or private economic interests that reap significant benefits from the violent economies currently operating there. Yet the presence of such strategic unity in the GEMAP case may also suggest that coherent and unified support can more easily be secured where the scope of engagement is kept narrow (in this case it was limited to economic governance) and there is hope of a real, identifiable and quick dividend that can be used to sell ongoing engagement to foreign and domestic stakeholders alike.

But it was not just *unity* that appears to have made GEMAP successful – it was unity *behind the threat of effective sanctions*. From the beginning, GEMAP was carefully linked to the international system of Ostracism: targeted sanctions. The UN Security Council had recognised the centrality of good economic governance for Liberia's future stability by maintaining existing sanctions on the export of diamonds and timber from Liberia *even after* the negotiation of the Accra peace accord in mid 2003.[57]

What Not to Do: The World Bank in Chad

Few of these factors were present in the somewhat comparable case of the World Bank's support for the development of an oil pipeline between Chad and Cameroon.

This $4 billion dollar project was originally agreed in June 2000. It aimed to assist the Chadian and Cameroonian governments to develop oil fields in southern Chad, then pipe the oil through a newly constructed 1,070 km pipeline to Cameroon's Atlantic coast. It also aimed, explicitly, to use this process of engagement and development to raise governance standards and improve the rule of law in Chad, through civil society participation in government expenditure decisions, reform of economic governance practices, and external monitoring and dialogue.

Drilling was financed by Exxon, Petronas of Malaysia and Chevron, while the pipeline was owned by two special-purpose vehicles supported by the World Bank and the International Finance Corporation. As a precondition to that support, the World Bank relied on the 1999 passage by the government of Chad – seen as highly corrupt and repressive in many quarters – of a Revenue Management Law that ensured it spent its considerable revenues from the project primarily on poverty alleviation – and strictly limited military expenditure – while also promoting transparency in revenue management, and civil society participation. This provision was deemed crucial because Chad's governments have traditionally used state resources to finance weapons purchases, often used to repress internal political opposition. Amnesty International USA wrote that "[i]n the south in the 1990s, where the majority of the state's oil reserves are found, counter-insurgency operations were particularly brutal. Hundreds of people were summarily executed."[58]

Indeed, in November 2000, just months after the pipeline deal was announced, the government used $4.5 million of a related $25 million oil contract signing bonus to purchase weapons. Civil society voiced strong concern, but the World Bank concluded that the payment was not covered by the deal it had made with the Chadian government to limit military expenditures. Also, notably, this deal only covered the bilateral relationships between Chad and the Bank; it did not control Chad's direct dealings with private sector actors. Exxon, Chevron and Petronas would not have to stop pumping oil if Chad missed its agreed expenditure targets.

That soon proved very significant. The up-swing in violence in neighbouring Darfur in 2003 led to an influx of refugees into Chad, raising tensions. President Idriss Déby's decision in 2005 to attempt to remove presidential term limits did likewise, and was heavily criticised by human rights groups and political opponents of the government. With the security situation becoming increasingly unstable, in late 2005 the Chadian government altered the revenue management law to, amongst other things, allow it to spend oil revenues on security sector activities. This led the World Bank in January 2006 to withhold loans and grants to Chad, and to suspend disbursement of $124 million in other forms of development assistance. But oil revenue – much inflated by a spike in global prices – kept on rolling in.

By April 2006 the World Bank and the Chadian government had agreed to a new formula that allowed the government to reorient spending so that oil revenues were not allocated to security spending – though other government funds were freed up for such spending in the process.[59] This was formalised in a Memorandum of Understanding (MoU) in mid 2006, but it was not until mid 2007 that a group of donors (African Development Bank, the European Commission, France, Germany, the IMF, the UN including the United Nations Development Fund (UNDP), the United Nations High Commissioner for Refugees (UNHCR), the United Nations Fund for Children (UNICEF) and the Food and Agriculture Organization (FAO), the US and the World Bank) travelled to Chad to "normalise" the arrangement through talks with the government. At that point, the parties essentially agreed to overlook Chad's non-compliance with the earlier deal on the basis of "sovereign necessity", while moving in future back towards the earlier-agreed allocation of oil revenues, even as Chad was permitted to double the funds it could allocate to a "general-purpose" fund from which military expenditures were drawn.[60] On the surface, this amounted to something of an uneasy truce but critics suggested it in fact left the government of Chad free to use oil revenues to fund internal repression. One NGO claimed that

> several of the civil society leaders who have played crucial roles in raising awareness of problems with the pipeline in Chad were forced to flee into exile earlier this year when the Déby government used a threatened rebel attack on N'Djamena [in February 2008] to crack down on critics and political opponents.[61]

And indeed, Chad did not stick to the agreed expenditure allocation.[62] Increasingly frustrated, by September 2008 the World Bank had found a way to mount an honourable withdrawal, ending its support to the project after the Chadian government voluntarily paid off its debt from the project early.

A recent evaluation of this experience by the World Bank's own Independent Evaluation Group is instructive in highlighting how and why this attempt at Principled Engagement to transform Chad's political economy failed.[63] It found some gains during the project period in employment, health and poverty indicators, but frequent inefficiency in the project's administration and a significant deterioration of Chad's long-term economic management. And it was damning on governance questions.

> Between 2000 and 2007, while Africa as a whole showed a slight improvement, Chad experienced a marked deterioration against all major governance indicators – with the decline especially sharp in rule of law, control of corruption, and government effectiveness.[64]

In part, it explained, this was due to a rise in oil prices and early completion of drilling and pipeline construction, which sharply altered the leverage offered by the project, in effect freeing the Chadian government from the shadow of Ostracism.

> The larger revenue also generated temptations and competing claims that were in part associated with the re-emergence of political instability and violent rebellion. The slow efforts at capacity building were undercut by the more rapid inflow of oil money. And the oil revenue much greater than the total of foreign aid sharply altered the initial leverage calculus of the program.[65]

Ultimately, the evaluation concluded, this allowed the government of Chad to renege on its commitments to the World Bank – and it was the government's fault, not the Bank's, that rule of law and governance suffered as a result.

> It must be underlined that protection of human rights, control of corruption, enforcement of the rule of law, and the management of the economy for the benefit of economic and human development are the fundamental responsibility of a country's government, and not of the international institutions that may support its stated objectives and intentions.[66]

At the heart of these missteps seems to have been a failure by the World Bank to use the leverage provided by the oil revenue windfall to transform the institutions of governance in Chad. The independent evaluation notes considerable advances as a result of the project in revenue transparency in Chad, but notes the complete absence of expenditure transparency, and the possibility of backsliding on revenue transparency.[67] Moreover, the approach taken by the World Bank led to budgetary fragmentation, with Chad essentially operating four budgets – one based on aid, one on oil revenues, one on Bank grants, and one on domestic revenues. As the evaluation notes, "[t]his was not a prescription for improving the institutional capacity of the budgeting system in the long run".[68] This lcd the evaluators to a broader conclusion which may be of particular salience in thinking about how to operationalise Principled Engagement in a range of sectors.

> [I]nstitutional enclaves generally only work in the short term and, over time, tend to lead to systemic institutional damage and diminished capacity ... Setting up institutional enclaves and special mechanisms to protect resources and accomplish quick results can damage local capacity in the long term. Such enclaves are generally not successful beyond the short term and, even when successful in the short term, they tend to undermine the already weak local systems and thus long-term development.[69]

Overall, then, there is a clear contrast between the perceived success of GEMAP in Liberia and the perceived failure of the World Bank's project in Chad. The different position of the host government in each case is clearly crucial – increasingly supportive of a transformational agenda in Liberia (but only after initially very strong, unified pressure from the international community) – and increasingly defiant in Chad. Yet what this also points to is the absence from the World Bank arrangement in Chad of any strong institutional reform agenda and communicative engagement process with local actors, which might have served – as the GEMAP effort in Liberia appears to be serving – to develop local accountability pressures on the regime to ensure its continued cooperation with the international agenda of liberalisation and pro-human-rights policies. In Chad, the absence of such pressures left the regime free to renege on its deal with international actors, with the only costs to it being reputational. In contrast, under GEMAP, the arrangement was used to change the cost–benefit analysis operating in the relationship between the state and local society and seemed potentially to be removing violence as a legitimate and acceptable method of political and economic advancement.

Conclusion: On Wrestling with Shadows

Externally driven transformation of violent economies and repressive regimes is hard. Internal actors have more to lose than external actors from politico-economic reform and will often use all the means within their control to resist it. For reasons of effectiveness alone, if not others, our aim should therefore be to find ways to move engagement with violent regimes away from the system of *internationalised* control (especially Ostracism) we have built over the last two decades, towards a system which fosters *internalised* control – by protecting the rights of a country's population, unpicking the fabric of violence, and allowing citizens to exert effective accountability over their rulers. In this final section, drawing on the discussions above, four key areas are identified where we might usefully direct our attention in attempting to apply a policy of Principled Engagement to violent economies.

Strategic Clarity Is Crucial – But Very Difficult to Sustain

As the two African cases discussed above suggest, any effort by the so-called "international community" to reform a violent economy depends on unity of purpose and clarity in the shared intervention strategy. It was unity of vision that underpinned the relative success of GEMAP in Liberia. For a contrasting case, we need only look to Afghanistan and the competing visions amongst the NATO allies, UN and others on how best to encourage security, foster development, and protect human rights. Nowhere is this absence of unity more clear than on the question of how to break the hold of the opium economy: the international community's intervention is a tale of strategic incoherence, reversed courses and constantly shifting priorities.[70]

The Afghan counterexample also helps make clear just how hard strategic clarity is to muster and maintain in a multilateral context. But generating such consensus may in fact be made *even harder* if we resort to labels that criminalise certain actors – as we have in Afghanistan. As I noted earlier in my discussion of the role of communicative engagement in "reframing" certain conduct, criminalising labels provide a very rigid frame: once an actor has been labelled a criminal, the appropriate response seems to be punishment – not negotiation and reconciliation. This poses a real theoretical – and practical – obstacle for Principled Engagement. How principled can engagement really be if it involves overlooking past human rights abuses, which international law would seem to suggest require effective remedy and perhaps even criminal punishment – not forgiveness and amnesty? What principles should guide whether we deal with a repressive actor as a partner for peace, or a target for law enforcement?[71]

Multiple Sources of Leverage will be Necessary – Including from the Private Sector

The experiences discussed above also suggest that the transformation of an entire political economy requires multiple sources of leverage, combining both carrots and sticks, and working at the level of grassroots or civil society engagement, as well as at the level of engagement with strategic actors. The shadow of Ostracism seems important in focusing minds, while the prospect of a reward for reform also seems to be important. This in turn may suggest that – notwithstanding the difficulties of strategic coordination discussed above – multi-actor alliances may in the long run be more effective at generating behavioural change in such regimes, unless individual actors with leverage in multiple sectors (such as the US government) play a leading role in driving the process of engagement.

The failed attempt by the World Bank at Principled Engagement with Chad over the last decade points to this need for multiple sources of leverage. The World

Bank's major source of leverage was the access it offered to favourable financing terms. This leverage evaporated as higher-than-expected oil revenues began to flood the government's coffers. Although numerous other actors were involved in a visit in mid 2007 to Chad in an effort to convince the government to abide by the spirit of its agreement with the World Bank, these actors also conducted their engagement solely in terms of their donor relationship with Chad. The possibility of the withdrawal of foreign military assistance was not, for example, put on the table. This was important, because official development assistance was no longer the key source of leverage over Chad. Particularly notable was the absence of any discussion that the private sector partners in the project (Exxon, Petronas and Chevron) might consider withdrawing from the project because the Chadian government had failed to meet the terms of its agreements with the World Bank. Had these private sector actors' support been enlisted in the effort at Principled Engagement, perhaps the World Bank's money might have talked a bit more loudly. Of course, there were a variety of legal and commercial obstacles to involving the private sector in such a way. Yet the absence of any real discussion of such an option – or of how private sector engagement and leverage might be made both more principled and more effective – was telling.

In Liberia, in contrast to Chad, the international community has had more success at Principled Engagement, perhaps in part because it has used multiple forms of leverage, linking together an international criminal trial, the deployment of a peace operation, DDR, access to international markets (through the prospect of removal of international commodity trading sanctions) and institutional capacity-building efforts. Here, the private sector's support has been enlisted more clearly, with a number of private sector actors – notably in the rubber, timber and diamond sectors – accepting the international community's decision to greatly restrict their access to Liberian trade while a process of reform was undertaken.[72]

Such an approach might better place the costs and responsibility for implementing the resulting Principled Engagement on the sector that has the highest incentive to bear those costs – the private sector. In a globalised economy, to be effective, Principled Engagement may need to change local incentive structures by working outside the borders of the state in question, creating international pressures through action with a range of foreign public and private actors. This is the strategic logic that has underpinned, for example, the Kimberley Process on diamond certification; it may now need to be extended to other areas of the global economy.

Institutional Reform Is Key – But Both Enclaves and Excessive Formalism Should Be Avoided

Transforming an entire regime based on violent political and economic activity requires more than just removing the actors at the top: it requires root-and-branch reform of the institutions that structure and shape individual actors' choices, which in turn reproduce these in a system of violence. The more successful engagements among those examined above appear to have been those that dealt with the institutions that mediated between formal state power and law, and informal social power and authority.

Yet institutional reform programmes have a dangerous tendency towards bureaucratic and technocratic fetishism, especially when designed, approved, funded and administered by foreign bureaucrats. The danger is that they focus more on outputs than outcomes, and fail to see the way that formal institutions interact with the informal institutions of the local context, hiding in plain sight from the foreign bureaucrat's gaze. This can lead to ceaseless human rights and rule of law training seminars for government officials and security services – but often little focus on human rights outcomes. As the World Bank's experience with budget reform in Chad demonstrates, the danger is that this simply produces an "enclave" which has little long-term systemic effect. Even in the comparatively successful example of GEMAP in Liberia, the long-term impacts of economic governance seem to be emerging not out of the specific institutions into which international staff have been inserted, or any "legacy" effect they may have generated through direct professional mentoring, but more out of the broader normative impact the process is having in the wider political economy – reframing corruption as an unacceptable aspect of political and economic life, creating a space for local action to foster accountability.

A related danger is that efforts to engage with – and reform – the institutions of an abusive regime will focus too heavily on *formal* institutions – arms of the executive, parliamentary committees, security forces, courts – and fail to wrestle with the *informal* institutions that live in the shadows and interstices of those formal institutions – the kinship, *wantok*, patronage and criminal ties that bind. The danger of such an approach is that it fails to deal with the incentive structures that have the decisive influence over actors' choices within these regimes. Once the external accountability imposed by the international gaze is removed, these hidden forms of accountability come back to the fore. Only by grappling with these structures can we affect the long-term reforms necessary to ensure that populations' enjoyment of civil, political, economic, social and cultural rights is not mediated by some inappropriate intervening variable – tribe, class, ethnicity, religion, family ties, gender, or some other factor. This is the only way to prevent violence and discrimination once again becoming the basis for political and economic action, leading back to repression and into the shadows once more.

Sunlight is the Best Disinfectant: Improving Formal Accountability

Finally, all of the cases discussed above make clear that formal accountability – especially criminal accountability – is a uniquely powerful tool in changing the calculus of strategic actors engaged in violent political economies. The international community has certainly made huge strides in the last two decades in shining a light on the worst excesses of repressive and aggressive rulers, building a system of international criminal accountability which appears to be proving increasingly capable of affecting the decisions of the worst human rights abusers – and even, on occasion, holding them to account. Yet there is still a great deal that could be done to entrench that system, to empower states as enforcers of international human rights law (especially through improved international cooperation arrangements), and to clarify the relationship between global criminalisation regimes (in the areas of human rights, humanitarian law, sanctions and narcotics, amongst others) and the political processes of peacemaking and strategic engagement.

Even more, however, there may be a need for further experimentation with some of the examples – such as the Independent International Investigation Commission and Special Tribunal in Lebanon[73] and the International Commission Against Impunity in Guatemala[74] – whereby the international community assists the accountability efforts of actors *within* states. Ultimately, it is only effective *internal* accountability systems that will protect a population's human rights from abuse by its government – whether for political or economic purposes.

This chapter has attempted to highlight how we might begin more effectively to engage with repressive regimes to realise these honourable principles, highlighting the need to use the space created by the shadow of Ostracism to foster local accountability capacity and institutional reform, which can ultimately replace external pressures. It has pointed to the need to understand the socio-economic function played by human rights abuse and criminal activity, understood against both local context and the globalised economy, arguing for an expansion of the field of human rights engagement from strategic engagement with state regimes and their formal apparatus, to a broader communicative engagement with the mediating institutions which often underpin their power. It has suggested that this ought to occur through engagement with local civil society and the foreign private sector, and warned against the self-imposed straitjacket which unthinking use of ostracising – and especially criminalising – labels at the international level may create.

It may be a long time until we see states and intergovernmental organisations take the economic underpinnings of violent regimes seriously into consideration when designing their human rights intervention strategies. When they do, if they consider the concerns discussed above, they may find themselves better equipped to reduce the profitability and attractiveness of these systems of violence, to wrestle with these shadows and to bring light into the hidden and violent pockets of the global economy in which increasing numbers of humans find themselves trapped.

Endnotes

1   Compare Carl von Clausewitz, *On War* (London: N. Trübner, 1873), 18 with David Keen, *The Economic Functions of Violence in Civil Wars*, Adelphi Paper no. 320 (Oxford: Oxford University Press, 1998), 11.

2   Stephen Jackson, "Protecting Livelihoods in Violent Economies", in Karen Ballentine and Heiko Nitzschke (eds), *Profiting from Peace: Managing the Resource*

Dimensions of Civil War (Boulder, Co.: International Peace Academy/Lynne Rienner Publishers, 2005) 153–82.

3   Charles Tilly, "War Making and State Making as Organized Crime", in P.B. Evans, D. Rueschmeyer and T. Skocpol (eds), *Bringing the State Back In* (New York: Cambridge University Press, 1985).

4   Ellen L. Lutz and Caitlin Reiger (eds), *Prosecuting Heads of State* (Cambridge: Cambridge University Press, 2009).

5   Ken Menkhaus, "The Rise of a Mediated State in Northern Kenya: The Wajir Story and its Implications for State-Building", *Afrika Focus* 21, no. 2 (2008) 23–38.

6   R.T. (Thomas) Naylor, "The Insurgent Economy: Black Market Operations of Guerrilla Organizations", *Crime, Law and Social Change* 20, no. 1 (1993) 13–51.

7   Roy Godson, *Menace to Society: Political-Criminal Collaboration Around the World* (Washington, DC: National Strategy Information Center, 2003).

8   Jean-François Bayart, Stephen Ellis and Beatrice Hibou, *The Criminalization of the State in Africa* (Bloomington: Indiana University Press, 1999); David Keen, *Conflict and Collusion in Sierra Leone*, (Oxford: James Currey, 2005); Florian P. Kühn, "Aid, Opium, and the State of Rents in Afghanistan: Competition, Cooperation, or Cohabitation?", *Journal of Intervention and Statebuilding* 2, no. 3 (November 2008), 309–27.

9   Menkhaus, op. cit., 5.

10   Compare Keen, op. cit., 8.

11   Louise Shelley, "Transnational Organized Crime: The New Authoritarianism", in H. Richard Friman and Peter Andreas (eds), *The Illicit Global Economy and State Power* (Lanham, MD: Rowman & Littlefield, 1999), 25–51.

12   Peter Andreas, *Blue Helmets and Black Markets. The Business of Survival in the Siege of Sarajevo* (Cornell: Cornell University Press, 2008); Phil Williams, *Criminals, Militias, and Insurgents: Organized Crime in Iraq* (Carlisle, PA: Strategic Studies Institute, 2009).

13   Ibid.

14   Keen, op. cit., 8; Gretchen Peters, *Seeds of Terror: How Heroin is Bankrolling the Taliban and al Qaeda* (New York: Thomas Dunne Press, 2009).

15   Bernd Beber and Christopher Blattman, "The Industrial Organization of Rebellion: The Logic of Forced Labor and Child Soldiering", Working Paper no. 72, January, Households in Conflict Network, Brighton, 2010.

16   James Cockayne and Phil Williams, *The Invisible Tide: Toward an International Strategy to Deal with Drug Trafficking through West Africa* (New York: International Peace Institute, 2009).

17   Vadim Volkov, *Violent Entrepreneurs: The Use of Force in the Making of Russian Capitalism* (Cornell, NY: Cornell University Press, 2002).

18   Gerry Simpson, *Great Powers and Outlaw States: Unequal Sovereigns in the International Legal Order* (Cambridge: Cambridge University Press, 2004).

19   Paola Gaeta, "International Criminalization of Prohibited Conduct", in Antonio Cassese (ed.), *The Oxford Companion to International Criminal Justice* (Oxford: Oxford University Press, 2009), 64.

20   Ibid.

21   James Cockayne, "The United Nations Security Council and the Turn to International Criminal Governance", in A. Crawford (ed.), *International and Comparative Criminal Justice and Urban Governance: Convergence and Divergence in Global, National and Local Settings*, (Cambridge: Cambridge University Press, 2011).

22   David Garland, *The Culture of Control: Crime and Social Order in Contemporary Society* (Chicago: University of Chicago Press, 2001).
23   Ibid.
24   Peter Andreas, "Criminalizing Consequences of Sanctions: Embargo Busting and Its Legacy", *International Studies Quarterly* 49 (2005), 335–60; R.T. (Thomas) Naylor, *Patriots and Profiteers: On Economic Warfare, Embargo Busting and State-Sponsored Crime* (Toronto: McLelland and Stewart, 1999).
25   Andreas, op. cit., 340–44.
26   Ibid., 343–56.
27   Naylor, 1999, op. cit.
28   Andreas, op. cit., 335–60; Naylor, 1999, op. cit.
29   David Lektzian and Mark Souva, "An Institutional Theory of Sanctions Onset and Success", *Journal of Conflict Resolution* 51, no. 6 (2007), 848–71.
30   Mike Pugh, "The Political Economy of Peacebuilding: A Critical Theory Perspective", *International Journal of Peace Studies* 10 no. 2 (2005) 23–42; Monika Heupel, "Shadow Trade War Economies and their Challenge to Peacebuilding", *Journal of International Relations and Development* 9 (2006), 140–69.
31   Mike Pugh, "Postwar Political Economy in Bosnia and Herzegovina: The Spoils of Peace", *Global Governance* 8, no. 4 (2002), 467–82.
32   Menkhaus, op. cit., 23–38.
33   Tilly, op. cit.
34   Compare Bayart, op. cit.
35   Menkhaus, op. cit., 23–38.
36   Kühn, op. cit., 309–27.
37   Cockayne and Williams, op. cit.
38   Carolyn Nordstrom, *Shadows of War: Violence, Power, and International Profiteering in the Twenty-First Century* (Berkeley/London: University of California Press, 2004); Willem Van Schendel and Itty Abraham, *Illicit Flows and Criminal Things: States, Borders, and the Other Side of Globalization* (Bloomington: Indiana University Press, 2005).
39   International Crisis Group, "Liberia and Sierra Leone: Rebuilding Failed States", *Africa Report* 87, Freetown/Brussels, 8 December 2004, 21–2.
40   Keen, op. cit., 248–66.
41   International Crisis Group, "Rebuilding Liberia: Prospects and Perils", *Africa Report* 75, Freetown/Brussels, 30 January 2004; International Crisis Group, 8 December 2004, op. cit.
42   International Crisis Group, 8 December 2004, op. cit., 22.
43   Ibid.
44   Renata Dwan and Laura Bailey, "Liberia's Governance and Economic Management Assistance Programme (GEMAP). A Joint Review by the Department of Peacekeeping Operations' Peacekeeping Best Practices Section and the World Bank's Fragile States Group", New York/Washington DC, May 2006, 8; Matt Chessen and Robert Krech, "Post-War Reconstruction in Liberia: The Governance and Economic Management Assistance Program (GEMAP)", paper presented at the International Workshop on Peacebuilding and Corruption, Oxford University, 22–23 March 2007, 56, available at http://mattlesnake.com/Gemap%20paper_files/Peace_Corr_Mar%2022%5B1%5D.pdf [accessed 12 May 2012].
45   International Crisis Group, 8 December 2004, op. cit., 23–4.

46   Raymond Gilpin and Emily Hsu, "Liberia: Gemap – A Model for Economic Management in Conflict-Affected Countries", United States Institute of Peace, Washington DC, 7 May 2008.

47   Ibid.

48   Nicolas Jahr, "Corruption and Reconstruction in Liberia", *Dissent* 53, no. 3, Summer 2006, 24–8.

49   Renata and Bailey, op. cit., 20.

50   Chessen and Krech, op. cit., 10.

51   On the role of discursive frames in peacebuilding, see also Séverine Autesserre, "Hobbes and the Congo: Frames, Local Violence, and International Intervention", *International Organization* 63 (2009), 249–80.

52   Reflecting this dialectical orientation, Pedersen and Kinley in Chapter 1 define Principled Engagement as a process that "seeks to ... 'mediate' the conflict between external norms and internal practices by encouraging and supporting the target to reform".

53   On labelling in the peacemaking context, see James Cockayne and Adam Lupel, "Introduction: Rethinking the Relationship Between Peace Operations and Organized Crime", *International Peacekeeping* 16, no. 1 (February 2009), 419.

54   Renata and Bailey, op. cit., 19.

55   Ibid., 17–18.

56   Ibid., 10–13.

57   Ibid., 21.

58   Amnesty International USA, *Contracting Out of Human Rights: The Chad–Cameroon Pipeline Project*, September 2005, 7, available at http://www.amnesty.org/en/library/info/POL34/012/2005 [accessed 12 May 2012].

59   World Bank, "World Bank, Chad Reach Interim Agreement On Funding, Oil Revenue Management", Press Release No. 2006/383/AFR, Washington, DC, 26 April, 2006.

60   World Bank, *Multi-Donor Mission Visited Chad from June 12 to 23, 2007*, available at http://web.worldbank.org/archive/website01210/WEB/0__CO-12.HTM [accessed 12 May 2012].

61   World Bank, "World Bank Statement on Chad-Cameroon Pipeline", Press Release No: 2009/073/AFR, Washington, 9 September 2008, available at http://web.worldbank.org/WBSITE/EXTERNAL/NEWS/0,,contentMDK:21894530~pagePK:34370~piPK:34424~theSitePK:4607,00.html [accessed 20 May 2013].

62   Independent Evaluation Group (IEG), "The World Bank Group Program of Support for the Chad–Cameroon Petroleum Development and Pipeline Construction: Program Performance Assessment Report", Report No. 50315, Washington, DC, 20 November, 2009, 8.

63   Ibid., 8.

64   Ibid., xiii.

65   Ibid., xiii.

66   Ibid., 24–5.

67   Ibid., 25–6.

68   Ibid., 26

69   Ibid., 26, 45.

70   Peters, op. cit.; Vanda Felbab-Brown, *Shooting Up: Counterinsurgency and the War on Drugs* (Washington, DC: The Brookings Institution, 2010).

71   Compare James Cockayne and Adam Lupel, "Conclusion: From Iron Fist to Invisible Hand – Peace Operations, Organized Crime and Intelligent International Law Enforcement", *International Peacekeeping* 16, no. 1 (February 2009), 151–68.

72   David Bridgman and Robert Krech, "Liberia: Building Peace Through Investment-Climate Reform", in Hany Besada (ed.), *From Civil Strife to Peace-Building: Examining Private Sector Involvement in West African Reconstruction* (Ontario: Centre on International Governance Innovation and Wilfred Laurier University Press, 2009), 248–64.

73   James Cockayne, "Foreword", *Journal of International Criminal Justice* 5, no. 5 (2007).

74   Andrew Hudson and Alexandra Taylor, "The International Commission against Impunity in Guatemala: A New Model for International Criminal Justice Mechanisms", *Journal of International Criminal Justice* 8, no. 1 (2010), 53–74.

Chapter 10

Development as a Vehicle for Principled Engagement on Human Rights: The Implications of "New Aid"?

David Kinley

Engagement is a process, not a destination. It involves exerting pressure, by raising questions and hypothetical possibilities, and by probing the other country's assumptions and thinking. Above all, it involves testing how far the other country might be willing to go. Properly understood, the diplomacy of engagement means raising questions that the other country may wish to avoid or be politically unable to answer. It places the ball in the other country's court.[1]

This is how Chester Crocker, Assistant Secretary of State in successive Reagan administrations, and a key player in the United States' then engagement strategy with South Africa, described the notion in a 2009 *New York Times* article commenting on the Obama administration's various overtures towards Iran.

Crocker goes on to stress what engagement is not. It is not sweet talk; nor normalisation. It is not akin to détente, rapprochement, nor appeasement. One might add that neither is it endorsement nor validation of, nor indifference to, current or past actions of the engaged country. Engagement is none of these. What it is, or could be, in the particular context of protecting and promoting human rights through aid and development programmes, is the concern of this chapter. Principled Engagement, among other things, invests human rights principles in the engagement process; it takes a middle path through Ostracism and Business as Usual, as the two policy extremes available for human rights promotion. This chapter illustrates how human rights and development can and should be mutually reinforcing, each offering a tool for the other to achieve its aims – with development providing an instrument by which Principled Engagement between states on human rights issues can be promoted, and human rights providing a set of guiding principles for engagement on development issues that can enhance the effectiveness of aid.

The phenomenon of "New Aid" reflects the fact that aid and development programmes worldwide have recently undergone certain significant changes, while others are mooted. These changes, it is argued, underscore the need for such an inquiry. This is not just for the obvious reason that with changes in the development landscape, so the content and scope of Principled Engagement is affected, but further, that the changes are themselves to some degree prompted by its very use. New Aid creates challenges for the continuing and expanded employment of Principled Engagement, born of both external seismic shifts, such as the rise of China's economic influence and the militarisation of aid, and taming the more extreme of its own effects, for example, by encouraging private sector involvement in development and identifying the failures of aid engagement. The interplay between Principled Engagement and New Aid brings the relationship between human rights and development into even sharper focus and redefines both the methods and goals of their respective agendas.

This chapter has three objectives: (1) to analyse the conceptual and policy perspectives of the idea of Principled Engagement as deployed in the parallel and increasingly interactive fields of development and human rights; (2) to assess how these perspectives bear out in practice in the context of so-called "New Aid"; and (3) to canvass particular challenges that "New Aid" poses for Principled Engagement.

Conceptual and Policy Perspectives on Principled Engagement in Development and Human Rights

One might expect that engagement on the grounds of development alone – at least to the extent of it alleviating poverty[2] – would necessarily be principled, flying above the tainted waters of economic leverage and geopolitical strategising, and focused on humanitarian fundamentals, including respect for basic human rights. The reality of development, in the past as well as the present, bears some resemblance to these elements, but only if you look hard and long. Even when aid and development initiatives have focused on human rights outcomes, their manner, form or delivery have been far from uncontroversial. Long-stalled efforts to establish a right to development in international law and the political and operational objections that many have with the Human Rights-Based Approach (HRBA) to development are two prominent examples of controversies that have raged between developed and developing countries.[3]

The interrelationship between development that promotes human rights ends and Principled Engagement is inexorable and desirable. Certainly, there must be conceptual room for such a proposition if only because as promoters of human rights we, collectively, have no choice but to do so, if we earnestly believe in protecting and promoting human rights wherever and whatever the nature of their endangerment. Human rights are universal in aspiration and intentionally flexible in design as expressed in international law. They are oriented towards inclusion rather than exclusion, albeit with limitations placed on states regarding how far they can exercise such flexibility. It is true that individually, when faced with human-rights-abusing states, we may choose between disengagement as a consequence of hard-line admonition, indifferent and uncritical engagement, and some third way that is the concern of this book. But the ends of human rights would be detrimentally served if this third way were not a regular complement to the other two approaches. The disengagement and business-oriented approaches are not only appropriate in certain circumstances and at certain times, their very deployment (or even potential deployment) may be crucial to the success of Principled Engagement, as the two extremes bookend the scope of possibilities for a third way.

International Law

Both international development and human rights are mediated to a significant extent through international law, while, on the face of it, Principled Engagement seems more clothed in loose-fitting pragmatic diplomacy than the starched garb of legal stricture. There is, however, less distance between the two than this sartorial characterisation might suggest. The discipline of international law exists in a more or less perpetual state of self-critical analysis of its principled foundations. How much, it is asked, is international law merely a reflection of self-interested, domestic political exigencies and the wielding of international power (whether economic, military or ideological),[4] and how much driven by more nobly collectivist, normative concerns? Whereas the first-mentioned, "apologist", perspective of international law has some truth in it, it is nonetheless taking the point too far. The recourse to politics in international legal argument may be inevitable but that does not mean to say that politics is "*simply* subjective and arbitrary".[5] Political views, as Martti Koskenniemi rightly maintains, "can be held without having to believe in their objectivity and ... they can be discussed without having to assume that in the end everyone should agree".[6] Such views comprise, among other things, taking stands based on principles of justice and morality. International law is similarly variously composed. It too reflects collectivist, normative concerns, even if mixed in with more self-interested motives. To be sure, the scope for argument and contestation may be more limited in the international law than in "politics", but the two arenas nevertheless share the necessity of engagement. Like a harbinger of the notion of Principled Engagement that we are propagating in this book, Koskenniemi counsels utopian and apologist lawyers alike, that the best way to understand politics in the context of international law is "less in terms of ready-made principles clashing against each other than a human practice of continuous criticism of and conversations about present conditions of society and the ways in which to make them more acceptable".[7] This way of conceiving international law is realistic and practical, while remaining normatively sound. It also provides a legal framework that is sufficiently fluid to accommodate the constant interaction between idealism and pragmatism that is a core characteristic of Principled Engagement.

Policy Formulation

As one moves from the framework of a legal (or political) concept to the practice of policy formulation, it is fair to expect that there will be a corresponding flexibility of perspective that Principled Engagement demands. And so there is (or there can be), regarding policy-making in the interlinked fields of economic development and human rights. The intimacy of their association is apparent from the perspective of both parties to the relationship – that is, for example, whether one takes the Amartya Sen perspective of the ontology and broad social purposes of economic development, or the Mary Robinson perspective of the fundamental importance of economic capacity to the fulfilment of human rights.[8]

Over the past decade in particular, donor demands (hard or soft) for improved governance and policy-making processes in host states, including greater respect for human rights, have strengthened the tie despite the ever-present concerns that such demands are tantamount to imperialistic paternalism. As the Overseas Development Institute (ODI) makes clear, there has to be, "a measure of grim realism about the politics of policy in aid-dependent countries. But this does not mean that there is nothing anyone can do. Nor does the insufficiency of the technocratic approach imply that there is nothing useful that donors can do."[9] By way of explanation of the sorts of changes that would help, the ODI continues:

> [I]f the international community were prepared to recognise the role of perverse incentives in the current aid set-up, there would be some hope of more collaborative and therefore more effective actions to take things forward. The country-level changes may appear intractable, but this is only because no one is devoting any brainpower to achieving the transition from political incentives that undermine development to political incentives that promote development. In this respect, a viable alternative to the so-called good-governance agenda is long overdue.[10]

What this suggests is a failure of Principled Engagement modalities, rather than the insufficiency of the human rights principles informing it. The sorts of viable alternatives will stem from the sort of attitudinal policy changes advocated by Arbour and Darrow.[11] In particular, they argue that, "human rights may play a constructive role in the political dialogue by helping to define inner and outer boundaries of acceptable behaviour based on governments' own human rights commitments."[12] To this end they reject the idea that an organisation like the United Nations can be value-neutral in national policy dialogues. Accordingly, they argue, "the United Nations cannot choose to acquiesce in bad policies or priorities that clearly conflict with international human rights treaty commitments of the country concerned"; instead, it should encourage the domestication of such treaty commitments. Indeed, "its effectiveness in encouraging compliance with human rights norms lies in the balance, as does its very legitimacy."[13] In other words, a greater boldness in the marking out of acceptable and unacceptable behaviour, born of an intelligent, nuanced and informed assessment of *both* the relevant political circumstances *and* the demands of international law, especially regarding human rights standards, is needed for all development organisations, but perhaps especially so in the case of those that are UN-affiliated. The boundaries referred to above are those that loosely delineate the space in which human rights promotion strategies – including Principled Engagement – can be employed and thereby prompt a re-examination of the divide between human rights practitioners and development economists.

Bridging the Divide

In the fraught field of aid effectiveness, development economists and human rights advocates are, alas, too often distanced from each other; apparently aiming for the same goals but using different assumptions, methods and targets. Two recent, prominent contributions to the debate – one from an economics perspective and the other a human rights perspective – illustrate the point well.

In the sequel to his "Bottom Billion" thesis,[14] economist Paul Collier goads those whose developmental zealotry for governance reform might lead them to conclude that for some ill-governed folk, it is better to be dead than fed. For Collier there is an overwhelming need to get the economics right, and then such public goods as accountability and security will follow.[15] However, such a corollary assumes too much, especially in the very states that he focuses on – the poorest, smallest and most dysfunctional. Certainly, a robust economy must be established, but not to the exclusion of contemporaneous interventions on institutional and procedural matters and, more importantly, their consolidation as the economy grows and after it reaches its beneficial "tipping point".[16] Human rights in particular are not assured through economic rescue of the poor alone. One of the most important factors in China's growing engagement in global human rights discussions is the oft-voiced assumption that by way of the extraordinary achievement of lifting nearly 235 million people above the poverty line[17] over the last 30 years, the government has thereby helped to secure these peoples' human rights.[18] Without question the alleviation of poverty is an essential prerequisite to the fulfilment of a state's human rights obligations, as it inevitably advances the fulfilment of peoples' rights to basic health, welfare and housing. Yet, for the achievement of other economic and social rights, such as education, safe and fair working conditions, non-discrimination and trade unionism, let alone the protection of such civil and political rights as freedom of movement, association, privacy, speech and fair trial, the intermediary of efficient, fair and open government is required.

On the other side of the ledger, while Irene Khan, in her book *The Unheard Truth*, is rightly keen to elevate human rights within the hierarchy of essential tools and objects in tackling poverty, this cannot be at the expense of dismissing or diminishing the role of economy. Poverty is neither first and foremost a problem of human rights, nor one of economics. There is no league table of disciplines for overcoming poverty; no battle for the supremacy of ideas. Certainly Khan has a valid point to make in chastening those who think that economics is *the* answer or even the first step. And she is right to join the many who draw attention to the need for human rights considerations, especially in respect of economic and social rights, to be part of the package of how best to approach development. But the objective is just that, for human rights to be part of a package, which also indispensably includes strategies for economic development.[19] To overreach the human rights argument sacrifices credibility for political attention. In the long run this serves the interests of neither development nor human rights.

A greater meeting of minds and practices across the divide is essential and the flexibility inherent in Principled Engagement provides one avenue through which this might be achieved. Another phenomenon, in tandem with Principled Engagement, which might provide the catalyst for this more integrated approach, is the changing nature of international development assistance on the ground, which over the past decade or so has heralded an era of New Aid.

Practice – In the Context of "New Aid"

It is possible to read the many manifestations of aid since the Second World War as attempts, with various degrees of success, to construct vehicles for aid delivery that are not just more effective (an enduring preoccupation), but also fairer. These attempts have ranged from rescue and reconstruction in the 1940s, through dealing with the legacies of decolonisation in the 1950s and 60s, and the direct infrastructure grants and loans of the 1970s, to the fiscal conditionalities of the 1980s and the governance conditionalities and host state "ownership" models of the 1990s. No effort has been spared in the planning of aid over this time,[20] and certainly there is evidence of principled, well-intentioned and even wise allocation of aid.[21] But too much of the story is an unedifying tale of exploitation, ulterior motivation, inefficiency and mismanagement, on all sides of the development process.[22]

The New Aid landscape of the 2000s and 2010s has certain still-emerging features which provide both challenges to, and opportunities for, the ways in which Principled Engagement might play a part in achieving better development outcomes. During the past decade new sources and definitions of aid have appeared, as have alternative approaches to understanding its effects and different metrics by which to measure its impact. There are a wide range of features which one could use to sketch the new face of aid and assess the nature of these changes, not all of which can be covered here. I therefore restrict myself to looking, briefly, at four especially prominent features which separately and together exemplify the breadth and depth of the changes afoot, and which also reveal how it is that both development and human rights are being, or can be, promoted through Principled Engagement. One might add, in the specific context of this book, that Mac Darrow's "new aid modalities" discussed in the next chapter could be seen as a fifth (and more refined) feature of the New Aid typology used in the present chapter, distinguished by Darrow's focus on the shifting rationales for development, rather than on its configuration and capacity to deliver.

Not "More Aid", but "No Aid"?

The quantity of aid has long been a matter of contention, in terms of economics, politics and morality, and debates about its quality are equally, if not more, heated. In *The White Man's Burden*, Bill Easterly has estimated that the West has spent $2.3 trillion on foreign aid over the past 50 years and yet has not managed to address the most basic and persistent problems of extreme poverty, disease and preventable deaths to anything like the level that one might fairly expect of such a sum. He has advocated a more market-oriented approach to economic development.[23]

Dambisa Moyo extended this line of argument in respect of Africa in advocating for the removal of dependency-inducing aid by turning off the aid tap altogether and replacing it with the "tough love" discipline that would result should African states be forced to raise funds on the global bond market.[24] The levels of poverty and human rights abuses remain dire in sub-Saharan Africa, despite decades of significant inflows of foreign aid, but Moyo's approach is politically naïve, sensationalist and perniciously irresponsible.[25] There is no doubt that aid has been squandered and, even worse, sometimes invested counter-productively (when directly or indirectly bolstering the power of tyrants), but the answer lies in fixing the plumbing rather than in turning the tap off altogether. Questioning the principles upon which development engagement is effected is no bad thing – indeed it is desirable – but engagement there must nonetheless be.

In fact, it is both flow (quantity) and plumbing (quality, effectiveness and principles of engagement) that need attention if development strategies are to deliver better human rights protections. And it is here that the opportunities and challenges for Principled Engagement arise. In terms of flow, aid totals are pitifully low. The total Official Development Assistance (ODA) budget of the West is approximately $US134 billion.[26] The long-standing, UN-endorsed aid target of 0.7 per cent GNP has been achieved and maintained by only five OECD countries, and most languish around 0.3–0.4 per cent.[27] Even the much-vaunted promises contained in the 2005 Gleneagles Agreement between (the then) G8 nations to massively increase aid budgets for Africa and elsewhere seem now ready to be abandoned as many of those countries struggle to address their own soaring domestic budget deficits in the wake of the Global Financial Crisis.[28]

The problems with the flow of aid and consequent poor results for human rights are exemplified by the patchy progress towards the attainment of the Millennium Development Goals (MDGs) by 2015. Some advances have been made regarding reductions in extreme poverty and child mortality rates, as well as primary education targets, but there has been lamentable progress made in respect of maternal health, combating HIV/AIDS and sanitation.[29] It has been estimated that had the global ODA figure been doubled since 2006 and until 2015 (a relatively modest sum when compared with the cumulative national stimulus packages deployed in response to the Global Financial Crisis in 2008/9) then – plumbing permitting – the MDGs could have been achieved.[30] While there is certainly room for debate over how much, how directly, and how effectively more aid will lead to greater human rights protection, there is no doubt that more aid has the potential to enable individuals, communities and governments to improve the rights standards by which they live or abide.

While the problems with plumbing are equally serious, and even more complex, they present an opportunity for Principled Engagement to be usefully employed. It has been calculated, for example, that approximately one fifth of the global total of development assistance for health (approximately $26.87 billion in 2010) is "unallocable"; that is, auditors are not reliably able to say where and how funding has been spent.[31] This is an enormous problem and one that is endemic across all aid sectors. Improvements in the direction, flow and efficiency by which aid is delivered are dependent on a host of interlocking factors, which together provide ample space for various forms of donor/recipient engagement. One of the most important factors is the relationship between the integrity and capacity of governance structures in host states, and aid conditionality. Aid conditionality is a double-edged sword; on the one hand, advancing governance and self-sustainability, while on the other, promoting host state dispossession and diversions from "real aid" funding, directing funds more towards governance projects serviced by home state professionals, rather than infrastructure, industrial or agricultural projects that engage more host state resources and personnel.[32] Other important factors are whether, and if so, how, donor states restructure recipient states' indebtedness (through, for example, debt-forgiveness or debt-for-development schemes); the manner in which both home and host states manage private sector development (including attracting and regulating foreign direct investment (FDI), the use of public/private partnerships and the nature of corporate social responsibility requirements); and the levels of coordination between donors themselves.

Each of the factors listed above offers opportunities as well as challenges to the quest of promoting human rights through the vehicle of Principled Engagement with developing states generally, and pariah states in particular. From the strategic perspective of Principled Engagement, the key is to focus on the opportunities, as seen by donor and recipients jointly, while accepting that there are problems, rather than be driven to despair of the whole enterprise by a myopic focus on the difficulties.

Innovative Development Financing and "The Age of Philanthrocapitalism"[33]

The increasing role of the private sector, especially by way of institutional philanthropy and innovative development financing, is another feature of New Aid.[34] This is a broad-based phenomenon. It encompasses not only such conspicuous philanthropic entities as the Gates, Ford, Rockefeller, Carnegie, Clinton, Helú, Acumen and Soros foundations, whose impact is increasingly apparent,[35] but also a penumbra of macro- and micro-level private sector initiatives. These range from individual remittances and the now big business of micro-finance,[36] through to Robin Hood taxes and their offspring,[37] debt and equity investments in housing, debt-forgiveness (including debt-for-development swaps) education, health, energy service providers in low-income economies, state-issued "aid bonds",[38] and the novel capital-raising initiatives of bodies like the Global Fund and GAVI.[39]

To be sure, philanthropic institutions are hardly new on the development scene, broadly defined. But dramatic changes in their reach, modus operandi and size[40] have made their impact more significant and their activities more visible. In the field of health care funding – strongly favoured by many private funders – the private sector's share of the global total of development assistance for health has risen from almost nothing in the early 1990s to some $8 billion in 2007, more than one third of health aid from all sources.[41] Much of this has been driven by new ways of raising, allocating and distributing funding, in respect of which the foundations have played a key innovative role; for example, Acumen's promotion of micro-financing and small business investment, and the Clinton Foundation's Procurement Consortium that provides affordable pharmaceuticals. Even straightforward commercial enterprise, such as African retail outlets and mobile phone companies offering services that make remittances quicker and safer, fall under the umbrella of private sector innovations that provide direct developmental and human rights benefits.[42]

These initiatives move beyond mere "responsible" or "ethical" investment (with its philanthropic orientation around what *not* to invest in – for example arms, tobacco and gambling), to embrace an orientation that actively seeks out opportunities which traditional aid and commerce have not taken or have done so inadequately. This has been described as a "messy transition",[43] and is arguably made more so by the global financial crisis.

Messiness is in fact a typical feature of Principled Engagement, and in the development and human rights context this could include such unorthodoxies as embracing profit-seeking enterprise. The above variations of the private sector dimension of New Aid are premised on the notion that aid is amenable to a business-model approach, which opens the door to profit-seeking investment, both in respect of the raising of capital and its expenditure. It is, in short, to provide the poor with market power, as Melinda and Bill Gates argue.[44] It is hardly surprising that the injection of private sector finance and acumen is accompanied by private sector perspectives and preconceptions. This is undoubtedly jarring for those steeped in the orthodoxy of international development methods, and certainly some of the effects are detrimental (and others questionably beneficial) to the interests of the poor and the marginalised, as tends to be the case when essential services such as water and power are privatised. But it is most certainly not all bad. The effective use of Principled Engagement within development must certainly come to terms with the dangers of the privatisation of aid, but it must also actively engage with the potential for great gains to be made through the private sector.

Thus, for example, economists Hubbard and Duggan are right to admonish an overreliance on "charity" as the instrument of aid, when investing in small business can often yield sustainable results. They cite, disapprovingly, situations where local well-digging companies are unable to compete with foreign donors or charities that dig wells for free.[45] That said, it does seem that old style aid-as-charity is disappearing as private sector means, methods and money increasingly seep into development initiatives. The bilateral agencies themselves are beginning enthusiastically to embrace public–private partnerships and other initiatives that provide direct support to local businesses, such as the UK's Department for International Development's (DFID) Private Sector Department, and AusAID's satellite Business for Millennium Development.[46] In any event, the "public" part of aid is concerned to insure against an overreliance on the market by investing in processes that mitigate the disadvantages of private gain without public benefit. That is, to continue the well-digging example, to fund water access for those who are not catered for by the private sector because they are too poor to pay, the profit margins are too thin, the local government is dysfunctional or corrupt, or because of a humanitarian emergency.

Additional human rights concerns over the privatisation of development stem from questions about accountability, where political distortions are born of economic distortions. Thus, there can be distorting impacts of really big investments in certain aspects of the health and education fields, for example, "discriminating" against certain issues, and bleeding talent from certain causes to more favoured ones. In respect of the work of foundations there is a balance to be struck between the claims of home state regulation and scrutiny of their activities (not least because most private foundations are to some degree dependent on (public) tax concessions) and the claims of the host state which must protect itself, and be protected against, the (foreign) private capture of public institutions.

In many ways, the whole notion of invoking the private sector in pursuit of development and human rights goals is an exercise in Principled Engagement. A 2009 Monitor Group Report reflects just this point in its recommendations as to what ought to be the next steps in the field. It notes three market features that need to be addressed if the potential of private-sector-oriented development assistance is to be unlocked: (i) the exploitation of (and not *by*) intermediary services provided by the West's financial services sector; (ii) building the commercial and financial infrastructure in the host states; and (iii) absorptive capacity in the host states' governmental, industrial, legal and financial sectors.[47] Action by development agencies in respect of all three will need to be based on a solid knowledge of local circumstances, an appreciation of the big picture of aid objectives and openness to alternative paths towards their achievement. This illustrates the tailored and flexible approach to achieving development in furtherance of human rights that is the essence of Principled Engagement, demanding the action of host states to ensure that the innovations born of such flexibility stay true to the principles guiding engagement. In this respect it is an ambitious project.

The Militarisation of Aid

Intervention by way of aid has, over the past two decades, become increasingly associated with military intervention, especially when it is being characterised as reconstruction and/or post-conflict assistance. In most recent times, the upward trend in conflict-related aid has become exponential. Thus, for example, in the period 2002 to 2005 alone, the US Department of Defense's share of US ODA disbursements increased from 5.6 per cent to 21.7 per cent.[48] To a considerable degree this is due to the widespread belief among defence strategists that aid can be used in furtherance of military objectives, particularly as a counter-insurgency strategy to "win the hearts and minds" of local communities and thereby secure greater stability. But input is also going the other way. The UK's DFID, for example, has produced a handbook on "Quick Impact Projects", that provides guidance to the British military regarding the funding and implementation of "short-term, small-scale initiatives ... designed to have an immediate impact contributing to post-conflict stabilization or recovery".[49]

These particular developments have occurred within the context of a shift in foreign policy thinking in the US (and the West generally) that places development at the heart of achieving one's geopolitical goals. Thus, in the words of US Secretary of State Hillary Clinton, "[d]evelopment ... [t]oday is ... a strategic, economic and moral imperative – as central to advancing American interests and solving global problems as diplomacy or defense".[50]

As a strategy, military engagement (or campaigns) either does not qualify at all as Principled Engagement, or does so only at the most extreme end of the Principled Engagement spectrum through, for example, so-called "humanitarian intervention" born of the notion that there exists an international responsibility to protect.[51] When aid is deployed as an accompaniment or follow-up to military action it necessarily becomes entangled with the unpredictability of war, which obscures the nature and purposes of the engagement. When, therefore, the unexpected occurs, the conflation of Principled Engagement and engagement for other, military, purposes can have disastrous consequences for both economic development and for human rights. The paralysing conflagration that followed the US- and UK-led invasion of Iraq in 2003, and that lingers still, is an especially poignant example of just such consequences. In his evidence to the Chilcot Inquiry into the UK's involvement in the Iraq war, Tony Blair, the UK Prime Minister at the time, admitted that his government had planned for a non-existent humanitarian disaster after the invasion, but had not foreseen that the Iraqi state would not function.[52] Such a sombre reflection on post-invasion planning failures is an indication of the significant problems of legitimacy (that is, lack of "principledness", despite claims to the contrary) that lurk within efforts to combine developmental and military goals, problems which are exacerbated by the size of their attendant budgets.

In the present context there are two interrelated levels of concern – one strategic and the other operational. Strategic concerns centre on the debilitating effects on human rights standards of the diversion of aid and development resources to conflict areas in preference to those areas that are equally in need, but are of less (or no) military importance to the donor states. The top four recipients of USAID funding in the 2009 financial year,[53] for example, were Afghanistan, Pakistan, the West Bank/Gaza and Egypt, all countries of especial military and geopolitical concern to the US. Egypt is also the second largest recipient of "foreign military funding" from the US State Department, receiving nearly $1.3 billion in 2011, which amounted to nearly three times what it received in official aid from the US in that year. The largest recipient – Israel – received almost $3 billion in military funding in 2011, which was equivalent to approximately 20 per cent of the total US aid budget for 2011.[54] The strategic importance of the security/aid axis in the US was institutionalised inside the State Department with the establishment of the Office of the Coordinator for Reconstruction and Stabilization (CRS) in 2004.[55] The stated mission of the CRS is "to lead, coordinate and institutionalize U.S. Government civilian capacity to prevent or prepare for post-conflict situations, and to help stabilize and reconstruct societies in transition from conflict or civil strife, so they can reach a sustainable path toward peace, democracy and a market economy". Its activities have been various and widespread including, for example, assistance in the health, justice, agriculture and commerce sectors of Afghanistan, Pakistan, Congo and Somalia.[56] The significance of the role of the CRS in US foreign policy as a whole has been further entrenched by the Obama administration as reflected in Secretary of State Clinton's views quoted above, such that now it is viewed as an almost indispensable companion to the Defense Department's contemplation of military objectives. And while the CRS does not expressly purport to promote human rights protections, there is an assumption that the nature of CRS's engagement in post-conflict situations will be to advance human rights standards.[57]

Operational concerns over the militarisation of aid centre on objectives and means of delivery. It is argued, for example, that in its very essence (and not just because of the capriciousness of conflict as noted earlier), it compromises the neutrality of humanitarian aid workers as aid delivery is defined by military objectives rather than developmental aims.[58] Further, it is argued that it interrupts aid delivery by exposing aid recipients and humanitarian workers to security risks – if they become politically associated with a belligerent force, aid workers are more likely to become military targets.[59] There are also concerns that transparency is reduced as the military is generally less accountable to public scrutiny, and that an over-powerful presence of the military shrinks the space available for local, community-based development initiatives.[60]

As a matter of fact, such operational concerns are inseparable from the strategic concerns, reflecting the unavoidable intertwining of the questions of legitimacy and efficacy of aid delivered through or alongside military operations. As such, and in the context of the pragmatic nature of Principled Engagement, it is especially instructive to consider the differences in opinion at ground level as to the impact of the militarisation of aid, for there is no consensus. Thus, Nicolas de Torrente (a former Executive Director of Médecins Sans Frontières) worries about the role of coalition forces in providing humanitarian assistance in Iraq, arguing that

> [t]he manner in which the US-led coalition made the minimization of harm
> and the provision of relief for Iraqis an integral part of its political and military

agenda contributed significantly to the hostility towards humanitarian action and those who deliver it … the US government failed to preserve space for the politically independent and principled role of humanitarian organizations.[61]

Responding directly to de Torrente, Advocacy Coordinator for CARE in Afghanistan Paul O'Brien argues that it may be both "principled and pragmatic" for humanitarian agencies to accept funding from belligerents in war,[62] an opinion that reflects the expectations of a number of UN guidelines and policies covering the use of militaries in humanitarian crises and disaster relief operations.[63]

The challenges and opportunities for development posed by its increased militarisation are here to stay, and envisaging a role for Principled Engagement within this context is unquestionably difficult since such principles as human rights protection and military or national interests are used interchangeably to describe the same, complex process. Peace building is seen as a vital ingredient in nation building by the development and military communities, as well as, importantly, their political masters. While at the same time the time-honoured conundrum of waging war to beget peace will remain as poignant as ever, not lessened by claims of humanitarian or other developmental motives.

Chinese Aid – The 800 Pound Panda in the Room

Over the last ten years, the perfect storm of China's exponential economic growth, ballooning capital reserves and its commensurate demand for raw materials, has led to a huge expansion in its overseas aid and trade activities, especially in Latin American, south-east Asia and (most strikingly) Africa. A 2009 US Congressional Research Service paper reported "that PRC foreign assistance and government-supported economic projects in Africa, Latin America, and Southeast Asia grew from less than $1 billion in 2002 to $27.5 billion in 2006 and $25 billion in 2007".[64]

Examples of the impact and leverage of Chinese aid and trade are now regularly reported in the media[65] and China's economic footprint in developing countries is increasingly featured in broader international relations, as illustrated by the fact that the flow of outward Chinese FDI grew by over seventy times to US$68.8 billion per annum in the decade prior to 2010.[66] More particularly, agreements made in 2009 during the fourth meeting of the Forum on China–Africa Cooperation (FOCAC) – an official forum dedicated to Sino-African cooperation and dialogue – included a promise by China to provide US$10 billion of preferential loans to African countries over the next three years, for use, mainly, to support infrastructure and social development projects. By May 2012, China had indeed approved loans of US$11.3 billion for 92 projects in Africa.[67] Furthermore, at the 2006 FOCAC, another pledge had been made to increase trade value between China and Africa to $100 billion by 2010. Despite the financial crisis, this commitment was also honoured in 2008, when trade hit $107 billion, marking a ten-fold increase since 2001. The trend, moreover, seems set to continue, as bilateral trade between China and Africa exceeded \$160 billion for 2011, representing a 28 per cent increase from 2010.[68]

But what, one might ask, are the human rights consequences of Chinese investment in Africa? Is it just the latest in a long line of debilitating foreign invasions – after the gun came the shackle and chain, the Bible, and now the Yuan? Well … "yes and no"! "No" because it does provide badly needed infrastructure, jobs, some technology transfer (but only sparingly so, it is argued),[69] and foreign currency for African state coffers. But, at the same time, "yes", as such investment generally takes too much and leaves too little and, specifically, may occasion human rights abuses, both directly through poor work conditions and environmental despoliation and indirectly by entering into joint ventures with governments who abuse human rights.[70] In any event, such economic engagement is necessarily accompanied by some level of political engagement, if only by "placing new pressures on Chinese [foreign] policy".[71]

The staggering acceleration of Chinese investment into Africa is matched by the veritable library of commentary on all aspects of the venture – political, economic, sociological, cultural, environmental and human rights (though the last mentioned is relatively neglected as yet). Gareth Le Pere (Institute of Global Dialogue, South Africa) astutely notes that it has typically provoked two reactions: "one of awe, and the other of trepidation and paranoia".[72] The reality of events on the ground is more nuanced than either of these poles, and engenders both palpable human rights benefits as well as problems. In light of the history of colonial and post-colonial exploitation of Africa by European powers for economic gain, geopolitical advantage, religious and cultural proselytisation, one must be careful not to be hypocritical with respect to China's newfound presence and influence on the continent. The *en vogue* China-bashing in the West may be more to do with what Denis Tull labels as the "respite" it provides Westerners "from reflecting on their own deficient policies towards Africa".[73] Whatever the metric, the West's history does not measure up well. But, of course, this by no means excuses continuing human rights abuses by any foreign government and by any means.

The human rights abuses that are typically associated with China's economic aid, FDI and corporate presence in developing countries comprise exploitative and discriminatory employment practices, unsafe working conditions, detrimental health consequences of environmental degradation, and antipathy towards trade unions.[74] There are also other, more systemic, abuses that flow indirectly from the Chinese presence, such as arms sales and the turning of blind eyes to host government tyranny, repression and corruption. China, it is claimed, has an "all-weather friend" attitude towards its bilateral African partners. This is born of its two fundamental principles of international engagement (as restated in the 2006 White Paper on Defence) – namely, that the object of the relationship is mutual benefit; and that the manner of the engagement is non-judgemental and respectful of each other's sovereignty.[75] Here again there is potential to distort or limit local capacity to adhere to constitutionally protected human rights or obligations under international human rights law. An indication of how insidiously damaging this can be is gained from certain initiatives that seek to combat the effects of such diminished capacity, like the Norwegian government's promulgation of a model Bilateral Investment Treaty that underscored the parties' commitment to international human rights and labour rights laws.[76] Moves by the African Union and even the Economic Community of West African States (ECOWAS) to adopt interventionist stances regarding circumstances of extreme political or economic unrest caused by the actions or inactions of member state governments are further examples of the same concerns.[77] While Principled Engagement does not require coordinated policies, the lack of any governance (let alone human rights) principles in China's engagement – or its "principled engagement with Chinese characteristics", if one takes into account the importance it places upon mutual benefit and non-interference with sovereignty – adds a layer of complexity and a potential limit upon the effectiveness of Principled Engagement.

Challenges Posed by the "New Aid" Landscape

Like all the incarnations of aid philosophy and practice before them, the four features of New Aid outlined above are centrally concerned with the questions of the objectives of both donor and recipient states, the quantity and quality (impact and/or efficacy)[78] of aid. What they also highlight are questions regarding the source and delivery of aid. Together, these are the metrics that both define New Aid and provide a means by which we can evaluate the extent to which it promotes Principled Engagement and lifts human rights standards.

One of the most striking features of New Aid is how collectively its component parts traverse the traditional lines of distinction and separation in the field. Private sector investment is enmeshed with public sector funds. Trade and aid deals can be indistinguishable, as exemplified by China's investments in Africa. The means and objectives of military intervention have become tied up with those of development in some situations. Institutionalised philanthropy has expanded into development assistance, both in tandem with traditional methods and actors, and in ways that redefine them. And in parallel to all four of these features of New Aid, the ingratiation of human rights imperatives into the methods and goals of development adds to the blurring of its boundaries.

The challenges for developmental economists, human rights activists, policy analysts, politicians and international lawyers are first, to understand more fully the parameters and dynamics of New Aid generally, and specifically in respect of its impact on human rights; and second, to formulate the regulatory frameworks (domestic and international) that enhance its potential and mitigate its human rights contradictions and detriments. These frameworks will update the space in which Principled Engagement operates and better equip it to meet the particular pathologies of New Aid.

This chapter has focused upon the first of these, and can at best only project what might be done in respect of the second, as New Aid is just that, still new. But at the broadest level, some projections can be made. Here, four are suggested:

The Need to "Civilise" New Aid

Too much "private" in public–private partnerships will distort the objectives of aid in such undesirable ways as stressing the short term, focusing on home state commercial benefits, and repatriating profits. The "public" in public–private partnerships will have to be insistent on the OECD definition of Official Development Assistance – namely, that primarily it promotes the economic development of the host state[79] and thereby creates the conditions within which human rights may be better protected.[80] The arms-length treatment of human rights in the International Finance Corporation's recent review of its Performance Standards provides an example of how this public/private tension can play out.[81]

Pluralistic Engagement

Engagement is needed on political, economic, governance and human rights dimensions and must be pluralistic, as well as principled. That is, the interrelations must be (at least) three-way – not just bilateral – involving the new (non-Western) donors. In terms of global influence and impact there is no longer an option not to engage new donors such as China. Such pluralistic engagement is promoted by the Monterrey Consensus,[82] and is already occurring tentatively between China and both the EU and the Development Assistance Committee (DAC). Of course, there are limits as to what such engagement can achieve in terms of harmonising donor policies, especially where opinions on the principles for aid engagement diverge, but it opens another front for Principled Engagement to achieve better development and human rights outcomes.

The New World Order

At the level of the ordering of international relations, the New World is represented by the creation of the G20, the changed voting quotas in the IMF and World Bank, and the new *un*conditionality of IMF interventions. Here, the challenge is to see whether and how individual (or interpersonal) benefits in terms of equality and development (if not expressly human rights) can be gleaned from the new accords at the inter-state level. On the face of it at least, there are grounds for optimism. For while neither the 2011 Cannes nor the 2012 Los Cabos G20 Communiqués[83] mentioned human rights, both did stress the importance of their derivatives and prerequisites – namely: the need to exploit the beneficial impacts of economic development in the poorest and least well-governed states; the need to curb the hyperventilation of global economic cycles; recognition of the intimacy of the relationship between economic health and global, regional and national security;

progression towards achieving the MDGs; the need to promote employment with labour rights and social security protection; and the pursuit of trade policies that promote least developed countries,[84] coupled with the imperative to find the "political energy" to close the Doha Round of trade talks.[85]

Rights Realism

There has to be greater recognition and acceptance of human rights as ends of development, more than practical means for its achievement. A human-rights-based approach to development, whether policy based or legally sanctioned, is for many developing states a sideshow, while too often constituting a self-indulgent delusion for Western development specialists.[86] The ongoing attempts to resurrect the notion of a right to development in international law are emblematic of the problem, as they are doomed to fail no matter their noble intentions.[87] The manifold difficulties faced by the enterprise are as entrenched as ever – that is, in defining "development" and the "right" to it; in clearly identifying the rights bearers and duty holders; and in negotiating the practicalities of its enforcement.[88] As with Charters of Rights in domestic laws, better human rights outcomes are, above all else, dependent on the politics of bureaucratic will and community culture, not on the instantiation of a treaty, a statute or a policy. By this, I do not mean to say that human rights instruments and institutions do not play an important part in the broader attitudinal changes – they do, but it is only a part. They are symptomatic not dispositive. The institution of a legal regime as a development goal (local or global) offers an arena to contest the perplexing political and economic choices that make development work and human rights respected, but it cannot be a substitute for them by predetermining those choices.[89]

Conclusion

There is no doubt that development aid can be used as a vehicle for Principled Engagement between states, and as such the enjoyment of human rights in recipient states can be advanced. Neither development nor human rights, however, is achieved through science, but rather by art. Development aid is fundamentally a crude tool; susceptible to the proclivities of those who use it and abuse it. The various components of New Aid illustrate the positives and negatives of this circumstance.

At base there has to be engagement on aid issues – "no aid" is not an option. The key to the success of such engagement – the speed and sustainability of results, in terms of social and political, as well as economic development – lies in the principles that guide it. Human rights, by way of their enunciation in international law and, importantly, their limited adaptation in practice,[90] provide one set of widely recognised, ready-made principles for the job. In fact, it is in this role – the provision of principles – that human rights are of the most use to development, rather than the offering of solutions as to how to make aid more effective or efficient.

Endnotes

1   Chester Crockcr, "Terms of Engagement", *New York Times*, 14 September 2009, available at http://www.nytimes.com/2009/09/14/opinion/14crocker.html?_r=0 [accessed 11 July 2012].

2   Consider the definition of Official Development Assistance (ODA). ODA refers to official, rather than private, flows of aid from donor to developing countries, with the main objective of promoting economic development and welfare. ODA financing is concessional in character with a grant element of at least 25 percent. Organisation for Economic Co-operation and Development (OECD), "Glossary of Statistical Terms", available at http://stats.oecd.org/glossary/index.htm [accessed 11 July 2012].

3   See OHCHR, "Right to Development", http://www.ohchr.org/EN/Issues/Development/Pages/DevelopmentIndex.aspx [accessed 11 July 2012]; *Declaration on the Right to Development*, UNGA Res 41/128 (UN Doc A/RES/41/128), 4 December 1986; *UN Statement of Common Understanding on Human Rights-Based Approaches to Development Cooperation and Programming* (2003), adopted by United Nations Development Group.

4   Jack L. Goldsmith and Eric A. Posner, *The Limits of International Law* (Oxford: Oxford University Press, 2005).

5   Martti Koskenniemi, *From Apology to Utopia: The Structure of International Legal Argument* (Cambridge: Cambridge University Press, 2006), 536.

6   Ibid.

7   Ibid., 537.

8   See Amartya Sen, *Development as Freedom* (Oxford: Oxford University Press, 1999) and Mary Robinson, "Development and Rights: The Undeniable Nexus", UN Office of the High Commissioner for Human Rights (26 June 2000), respectively. Sen's perspective is the inspiration behind the United Nations Development Program's (UNDP) annual country development rankings on the basis of both social and economic indicators: see especially UNDP, *Human Development Report 2010 – The Real Wealth of Nations: Pathways to Human Development* (2010); UNDP, *Human Development Report 2000 – Human Rights and Human Development* (2000).

9   David Booth, "Aid Effectiveness after Accra – How to Reform the 'Paris Agenda'", ODI Briefing Paper No. 39 (London: ODI, July 2008), 2, available at http://www.odi.org.uk/resources/docs/2549.pdf [accessed 11 July 2012].

10   Ibid., 4.

11   See Louise Arbour and Mac Darrow, "The Pillar of Glass: Human Rights in the Development Operations of the United Nations", *American Journal of International Law* 103 (2009), 446.

12   Ibid., 489–90.

13   Ibid., 490, 461.

14   Paul Collier, *The Bottom Billion: Why the Poorest Countries are Failing and What can be Done About It* (Oxford: Oxford University Press, 2007).

15   Paul Collier, *Wars, Guns and Votes: Democracy in Dangerous Places* (New York: Harper, 2009), 189–96.

16 In another part of the book Collier notes that his studies show that such a point is reached for many states when average income per head reaches approximately $2,700 per annum, after which evidence indicates that countries are likely to break the cycles of internecine violent conflict and chronic dysfunctional government. Ibid., 20–22.

17 There are in fact different interpretations of what the "poverty line" constitutes, that necessarily lead to different figures. Consider, for example, the PRC's own analysis, which sets the rural poverty line at 2,300 yuan (approximately 349 AUD at current exchange rates) annual per capita net income, which 122.38 million people fail to earn. National Bureau of Statistics of China, "Statistical Communiqué of the People's Republic of China on the 2011 National Economic and Social Development", 22 February 2012, available at http://www.stats.gov.cn/english/newsandcomingevents/t20120222_402786587.htm [accessed 9 September 2012]. The World Bank sets the poverty line at $1.25 per day, or approximately $450 per annum: World Bank, "World Bank Updates Poverty Estimates for the Developing World", 17 February 2010, available at http://econ.worldbank.org/WBSITE/EXTERNAL/EXTDEC/EXTRESEARCH/0,,contentMDK:21882162~pagePK:64165401~piPK:64165026~theSitePK:469382,00.html [accessed 11 July 2012].

18 See for example, Wang Chen, "Remarks at the 2nd Beijing Forum on Human Rights", 2 November 2009, available at http://www.china.org.cn/china/human_rights/2009-11/05/content_18834804.htm [accessed 28 May 2013], in which this figure is quoted. Wang, who is the Minister of the State Council Information Office, adds that as such China has become "the first country in the world to reach the poverty alleviation goal of the UN Millennium Development Goals".

19 David Kinley, *Civilising Globalisation: Human Rights and the Global Economy* (Cambridge: Cambridge University Press, 2009), 104–19.

20 Indeed, for Easterly it is precisely the emphasis on planning that is at the root of the problem. In the alternative, Easterly argues for the construction of a lightly regulated, largely unplanned and certainly private-sector-led economic canvas upon which the development can paint itself. William Easterly, "Introduction: Can't Take it any More?", in William Easterly (ed.), *Reinventing Foreign Aid* (Cambridge MA: MIT Press, 2008), 1–43. Even so, such free-market circumstances that favour "searchers" over "planners" do not occur spontaneously, but require planning.

21 See Hans-Otto Sano, "Development and Human Rights: The Necessary, but Partial Integration of Human Rights and Development", *Human Rights Quarterly* 22, no. 3 (2000), 734, 739–40.

22 See Deepak Nayyar, "Learning to Unlearn from Development", *Oxford Development Studies* (September 2008), Section 2.

23 William Easterly, *The White Man's Burden: Why the West's Efforts to Aid the Rest Have Done So Much Ill and So Little Good* (New York: Penguin Press, 2006).

24 Dambisa Moyo, *Dead Aid: Why Aid is Not Working and How There is a Better Way for Africa* (London: Allen Lane/Penguin, 2009).

25 Sachs and McArthur (among others) for example, contend that Moyo's analysis of historical statistics on poverty is inaccurate, especially as she ignores the advances in child mortality, adult literacy and children's primary education, as well as the fact that FDI has also risen significantly over the last five years in Africa, all, in part, as a result of development aid initiatives. Jeffrey Sachs and John W. McArthur, "Moyo's Confused Attack on Aid for Africa", *Huffington Post,* 27 May 2009. Owen Barder argues that Moyo has misunderstood or misrepresented the literature showing a positive correlation between aid and growth regardless of good government and promotes already-mainstream alternative

policies for which the evidence of effectiveness is no more conclusive than for aid: Owen Barder, "Review of *Dead Aid* by Dambisa Moyo", 31 March 2009, http://www.owen.org/wp-content/uploads/review-of-dead-aid.pdf [accessed 9 September 2012]. Paul Collier also takes issue with Moyo's suggestion that aid is responsible for all of Africa's woes and argues that the Global Financial Crisis undermines her suggestion that private markets are the better solution to African development. Paul Collier, "Dead Aid, By Dambisa Moyo", *The Independent*, 30 January 2009, available at http://www.independent.co.uk/arts-entertainment/books/reviews/dead-aid-by-dambisa-moyo-1519875.html [accessed 11 July 2012].

26   ODA is estimated to have decreased by 2.7 per cent since 2010 to $133.5 billion in 2011: OECD, "Development: Aid to Developing Countries Falls Because of Global Recession", 4 April 2012, available at http://www.oecd.org/dac/aidstatistics/developmentaidtodevelopingcountriesfallsbecauseofglobalrecession.htm [accessed 9 September 2012].

27   OECD, "History of the 0.7% ODA Target" Information Note, June 2010, available at http://www.oecd.org/dataoecd/16/38/45539274.pdf [accessed 11 July 2012]. For ODA as a percentage of GNI for individual OECD countries, see OECD, "Aid Statistics: Donor Aid at a Glance 2009–10", available at http://www.oecd.org/dac/stats/donorcharts.htm [accessed 28 May 2013]. It seems that other exigencies nearly always get in the way of the apparently earnest intentions by governments to achieve the 0.7 per cent target, typified, for example, by the UK government, which pledged in the 2009 Queen's Speech to enact legislation mandating the target in the national budget. The draft bill lapsed upon the calling of the 2010 UK general election and has not been reintroduced by the Coalition Government, although it retained a policy commitment to meet the 0.7 per cent target by 2013 and quarantined the aid budget from otherwise drastic spending cuts: see Aruni Muthumala, *The 0.7% Aid Target*, The House of Commons Library, Standard Note, SN/EP/3714 (17 September 2012), available at http://www.parliament.uk/briefing-papers/SN03714.pdf [accessed 13 October 2012].

28   There is no reference to the Gleneagles targets in the Muskoka Declaration. Larry Elliot and Patrick Wintour, "G8 Seeks to Divert Attention from Broken Aid Pledge", *The Guardian*, 25 June 2010. See also "G8 Muskoka Declaration: Recovery and New Beginnings", Muskoka, Canada, 25–26 June 2010, available at http://www.canadainternational.gc.ca/g8/summit-sommet/2010/muskoka-declaration-muskoka.aspx?lang=eng [accessed 11 July 2012].

29   United Nations, *The Millennium Development Goals Report 2010*, 2010, 4–5.

30   UN Millennium Project, *Investing in Development: A Practical Plan to Achieve the Millennium Development Goals (Overview)*, 2005, 58.

31   The Institute for Health Metrics and Evaluation, University of Washington, "*Financing Global Health 2010: Development Assistance and Country Spending in Economic Uncertainty*", 2010, 80, available at http://www.healthmetricsandevaluation.org/sites/default/files/policy_report/2010/FGH_2010_REPORT_FINAL_051111.pdf [accessed 16 December 2012].

32   Peter Uvin, *Human Rights and Development* (Bloomfield, CT: Kumarian Press, 2004), does a fine job of charting the contents and contours of this dilemma. Compare with the World Bank's 2009 Nordic Trust Fund Knowledge and Learning Program on Human Rights, the stated objectives of which are: "The program seeks to provide Bank staff and management with up-to-date knowledge in four areas: (a) how human rights and economic development relate to each other in national economies and in key sector/thematic settings;

(b) how the Bank's operational work relates to human rights; (c) what the legal and institutional frameworks of human rights outside the Bank are; and (d) how the Bank could or should respond to external interest and queries about its work and human rights." World Bank, "Nordic Trust Fund Knowledge and Learning Program on Human Rights", *Approach Paper*, 25 September 2009, para 2.

33   Matthew Bishop and Michael Green, *Philanthrocapitalism* (New York: Bloomsbury Press, 2008), Chapter 1.

34   A 2009 Monitor Group concluded that "using profit-seeking investment to generate social and environmental good is moving from a periphery of activist investors to the core of mainstream financial institutions": Monitor Group, *Investing for Social and Environmental Impact* ("Monitor Report"), 2009, 5, available at http://www.monitorinstitute.com/impactinvesting/ [accessed 11 July 2012]. The Report goes on to say, "no one can know for sure how much money has been invested or is seeking investment that generates both social and environmental value as well as financial return. But a good guess is that the total size of the market could be as big as $500 billion within the next decade", 5.

35   For example, the annual expenditure on development projects by the Melinda and Bill Gates Foundation (more than $3 billion for many years, though dipping to $2.47 billion in 2010) – Gates Foundation, *2010 Annual Report*, 7, available at http://www.gatesfoundation.org/annualreport/2010/Documents/2010-annual-report-ceo-letter-english.pdf [accessed 12 September 2012] – is not far behind that of the Australian Government's overseas development agency, AusAID – total budget in 2010 of approximately $3.85 billion. AusAID, *Annual Report 2010–11*, v, available at http://www.ausaid.gov.au/anrep/rep11/pdf/anrep10-11entirereport.pdf [accessed 12 September 2012].

36   With total assets worth $60 billion worldwide by the end of 2008. Greg Chen, Stephen Rasmussen and Xavier Reille, "Growth and Vulnerabilities in Microfinance", Focus Note No 61, Consultative Group on Assisting the Poor, February 2010. There has been an average growth of 21 per cent in borrowers and 34 per cent in loan portfolios between 2003 and 2008: Adrian Gonzalez, "Is Microfinance Growing too Fast?", Microfinance Information Exchange Data Brief No 5, available at www.themix.org/publications/mix-microfinance-world/2010/06/microfinance-growing-too-fast [accessed 11 July 2012].

37   Including "voluntary" travel taxes. See, for example, the MASSIVEGOOD campaign: UN Department of Public Information "Press Conference on 'MASSIVEGOOD', Innovative Health Financing Initiative", 4 March 2010, available at http://www.un.org/News/briefings/docs/2010/100304_MASSIVEGOOD.doc.htm [accessed 11 July 2012].

38   For example, since 2006, the International Finance Facility for Immunisation (IFFI) has raised over $3 billion in triple A-rated bonds for the provision of vaccines. See International Finance Facility for Immunisation, "Bond Issuances" (2010), available at http://www.iffim.org/bonds/previous-issuances [accessed 11 July 2012].

39   The GAVI alliance raises aid bonds against 10–20 year commitments of donor governments through IFFI to provide sustainable, predictable financing, and is piloting the use of Advance Market Commitments, through which donors guarantee a long-term affordable vaccine price in advance of its development to overcome initial financial barriers to immunisation aid. GAVI Alliance, "Innovative Financing", available at http://www.gavialliance.org/about/in_finance/index.php [accessed 11 July 2012]. The Global Fund's Debt2Health initiative, in partnership with creditors, grants recipient countries debt relief in return for their investment in Global Fund approved health initiatives: The Global Fund, "Innovative Financing", available at http://www.theglobalfund.org/en/donors/innovativefinancing/ [accessed 28 May 2013].

40   Efforts such as the "Giving Pledge" Campaign launched by Bill and Melinda Gates in June 2010, which seeks to persuade more than the estimated 15 per cent of US-based billionaires who currently give away significant proportions of their fortunes to do so by writing a letter pledging to donate at least 50 per cent of their accumulated wealth, are indicative of these changes. See "The Giving Pledge", http://www.givingpledge.org [accessed 3 May 2013].

41   See Diagram: *Raising It: Development Assistance for Health, By Source*, The Institute for Health Metrics and Evaluation, University of Washington in "A Spoonful of Ingenuity", *The Economist*, 7 January 2010, 52.

42   "Uncaging the Lions", *The Economist*, 10 June 2010, available at http://www.economist.com/node/16317978 [accessed 11 July 2012].

43   Monitor Report, op.cit., 5.

44   Bill Gates, "2009 Annual Letter from Bill Gates: The Role of Foundations", Bill and Melinda Gates Foundation, available at http://www.gatesfoundation.org/annual-letter/Pages/2009-role-of-foundations.aspx [accessed 11 July 2012].

45   R. Glenn Hubbard and William Duggan, *The Aid Trap: Hard Truths about Ending Poverty* (New York: Columbia University Press, 2009), dust jacket commentary.

46   See Business for Millennium Development website, http://www.b4md.com.au/part_2.php [accessed 11 July 2012].

47   Monitor Report, op. cit., 43 *et seq.*

48   See Centre for Strategic and International Studies, *Integrating 21st Century Development and Security Assistance: Final Report of the Taskforce on Nontraditional Security Assistance* (2008), vi, available at http://csis.org/files/media/csis/pubs/080118-andrews-integrating21stcentury.pdf [accessed 25 September 2012]; citing OECD DAC, *Peer Review of the United States: Full Report* (2006), 12, available at http://www.oecd.org/dataoecd/61/57/37885999.pdf [accessed 11 July 2012].

49   Department for International Development, *Quick Impact Projects: A Handbook for the Military*, 7, available at http://webarchive.nationalarchives.gov.uk/+/http://www.dfid.gov.uk/Documents/publications/qip/booklet.pdf [accessed 11 July 2012]. According to DFID, the handbook was developed because the "growing awareness of the linkages between conflict prevention and poverty reduction, the political context in which humanitarian disasters are addressed, and the importance attached to helping rebuild countries emerging from conflict all serve to emphasize the need for DFID to work effectively with the military", 6.

50   Hillary Rodham Clinton, "Remarks on Development in the 21st Century", Remarks to the Center for Global Development, Washington DC, 6 January 2010, available at http://www.state.gov/secretary/rm/2010/01/134838.htm [accessed 11 July 2012].

51   Gareth Evans, *The Responsibility to Protect: Ending Mass Atrocity Crimes Once and for All* (Baltimore: Brookings Institution Press, 2008).

52   Tony Blair, transcript of evidence given before the Chilcot Inquiry, 29 January 2010, available at http://www.iraqinquiry.org.uk/media/43909/100129-blair.pdf [accessed 11 July 2012], reported in Patrick Wintour and Richard Norton Taylor, "Righteous, Responsible but no Regrets: Tony Blair's Day in the Dock", *The Guardian*, 29 January 2010, available at http://www.guardian.co.uk/uk/2010/jan/29/responsible-no-regrets-blair-iraq [accessed 11 July 2012].

53   See USAID, "Where does USAID's Money Go?" (2010), available at http://transition.usaid.gov/policy/budget/money/2010 [accessed 11 May 2013]. Afghanistan was also the top recipient for the fiscal year 2012, receiving nearly $2.2 billion, which was more

than double what the second largest recipient, Pakistan, received for that year. USAID, "Where does USAID's Money Go?" (2011), available at http://transition.usaid.gov/policy/budget/money [accessed 11 May 2013].

54   For USAID figures see ibid., and for foreign military funding statistics see US State Department, *Executive Budget Summary, Function 150 and Other International Programs, Fiscal Year 2013*, 172, available at http://www.state.gov/documents/organization/183755.pdf [accessed 11 July 2012].

55   The intersecting roles of the Defense and State Departments in this area is further underscored by the regularised transfer of funds from the former to the latter for the provision of reconstruction, security and stabilisation assistance to countries in post-conflict situations or at risk of conflict ("section 1207 authority": *Fiscal Year 2006 National Defense Authorization Act* Pub L No 109–163, § 1207, 119 Stat 3136, 3458–9) which authorised the Secretary of Defense to transfer funds to the Secretary of State between 2006 and 2010. The "section 1207 authority" was not renewed after it expired at the end of 2010. Authority for crisis prevention and response funds was transferred to the State Department over the course of 2010, with the establishment of a Complex Crises Fund to fulfil the functions previously carried out by the Pentagon under s 1207. The Obama Administration sought $100 million funding for the Complex Crises Fund in the 2011 fiscal year budget. Nina M Serafino, "Peacekeeping/Stabilization and Conflict Transitions: Background and Congressional Action on the Civilian Response/Reserve Corps and other Civilian Stabilization and Reconstruction Capabilities", Congressional Research Service Report, 17 February 2010. By July 2010, some $442 million had been transferred under this authority to the Department of State and was being used to support 33 projects in 28 countries: "1207 Funding", State Department (USA), available at http://www.fas.org/sgp/crs/natsec/RL32862.pdf [accessed 11 July 2012].

56   See US Department of State, Office of the Coordinator for Reconstruction and Stabilization, *2009 Year in Review: Smart Power in Action*, 1 March 2010, available at http://www.state.gov/j/cso/scrsarchive/releases/183741.htm [accessed 11 July 2012].

57   Especially in respect of its governance and rule of law activities; see ibid., 9.

58   Stuart Patrick and Kaysie Brown, *The Pentagon and Global Development: Making Sense of the DoD's Expanding Role*, Centre for Global Development, Working Paper No.131 (November 2007), 5, 14.

59   Lara Olsen, "Fighting for Humanitarian Space: NGOs in Afghanistan", *Journal of Military and Strategic Studies* 9, no. 1 (2006), 11–12.

60   See Centre for Strategic and International Studies (2008), op. cit., 25–6, 35.

61   Nicolas de Torrente, "Humanitarian Action under Attack: Reflections on the Iraq War", *Harvard Human Rights Journal* 17 (2004), 1, 3.

62   In Paul O'Brien, "Politicized Humanitarianism: A Response to Nicolas de Torrente", *Harvard Human Rights Journal* 17 (2004), 31–9.

63   See the UN Office for the Coordination of Humanitarian Affairs, "Policies, Guidelines and Related Documents", available at http://ochaonline.un.org/OCHAHome/AboutUs/Coordination/HumanitarianCivilMilitaryCoordination/PolicyGuidelinesRelatedDocuments/tabid/4938/language/en-US/Default.aspx [accessed 11 July 2012].

64   Thomas Lum, Hannah Fischer, Julissa Gomez-Granger and Anne Leland, "China's Foreign Aid Activities in Africa, Latin America, and Southeast Asia", Congressional Research Service Report, 25 February 2009, available at http://www.fas.org/sgp/crs/row/

R40361.pdf [accessed 11 July 2012]. The reported study was from the NYU Wagner Graduate School of Public Service, 2008; see Summary.

65   For example, on 17 October 2009, *The Economist* concluded its commentary on the massive Chinese investment in Guinea, West Africa (exemplified by a recent $7 billion deal with the China Investment Fund), despite the ruling junta's appalling human rights record (including the slaughter of 150 demonstrators calling for a democratically elected civilian government barely two weeks before the above China Investment Fund deal was signed) by stating, ruefully, "As Guinea may show, China's unconditional approach to doing business may reap benefits, except perhaps for Africans who cherish democracy and human rights." More recently, the *Financial Times* reported that, according to its own research, China has lent more money to developing countries over the past two years than the World Bank, in pursuit of energy security and a more prominent role for the Renminbi in international finance: Geoff Dyer, Jamil Anderlini and Henny Sender, "China's Lending Hits New Heights", *Financial Times*, 17 January 2011.

66   Denise Leung and Yingzhen Zhao, "Environmental and Social Policies in Overseas Investments: Progress and Challenges for China", World Resources Institute, April 2013, pp.4-5. available at http://pdf.wri.org/environmental_and_social_policies_in_overseas_ investments_china.pdf [accessed 15 June 2013].

67   FOCAC, *Implementation of the Follow-up Actions of the Fourth Ministerial Conference of the Forum on China–Africa Cooperation*, 18 July 2012, available at http:// www.focac.org/eng/ltda/dwjbzjjhys/t952532.htm [accessed 25 September 2012].

68   See He Wenping, "More Soft Power Needed in Africa", *China.org.cn*, 27 February 2012, available at http://www.china.org.cn/opinion/2012-02/27/content_24740629.htm [accessed 11 July 2012].

69   See Paul Hubbard, "Chinese Concessional Loans", in Robert I. Rothberg (ed.), *China Into Africa: Trade, Aid and Influence* (Baltimore: Brookings Institution Press, 2008), 217–29, at 225, for a poignant example of how the PRC is concerned above all with promoting Chinese commercial interests.

70   And are, as a consequence, "subject to intense scrutiny and evoke strong criticism regarding an alleged lack of corporate social responsibility": Jing Gu, "China's Private Enterprises in Africa and the Implications for African Development", *European Journal of Development Research* (2009), 583. This positive/negative dichotomy in the specific context of outward FDI is explored by Denise Leung and Yingzhen Zhao, above, note 66 [accessed 15 June 2013]...

71   Thomas Wheeler, "China's Development Diplomacy", *The Diplomat*, 4 March 2012, available at http://thediplomat.com/2012/03/04/china%E2%80%99-development- diplomacy [accessed 11 July 2012]. Wheeler stresses the fact that no matter China's professed foreign policy credo of "non-interference", any significant level of commercial engagement in another state by Chinese companies backed (or indeed directed) by Beijing will inevitably favour some power elites – most likely the incumbent rulers – and so consolidate their position at the expense of others. Thereby, "China's economic role may inadvertently exacerbate instability", especially, as Wheeler notes, in post-conflict developing states.

72   Garth Le Pere, "The Geostrategic Dimensions of the China–Africa Relationship", in Kweku Ampiah and Sanusha Naidu (eds), *Crouching Tiger, Hidden Dragon?: Africa and China* (Scottsville, South Africa: University of KwaZulu-Natal Press, 2008), 20.

73   Denis M Tull, "The Political Consequences of China's Return to Africa", in Chris Alden, Daniel Large and Ricardo Soares de Olivera (eds), *China Returns to Africa* (London: Hurst, 2008), 127.

74   See, for example, Bates Gill and James Reilly, "The Tenuous Hold of China Inc. in Africa", *The Washington Quarterly* 30, no. 3 (2007), 37, 46–7.

75   Ministry of Foreign Affairs (People's Republic of China), *China's African Policy*, January 2006, available at http://www.fmprc.gov.cn/eng/zxxx/t230615.htm# [accessed 11 July 2012]; Information Office of the State Council (People's Republic of China) *China's National Defense in 2006* (Beijing, 2006), available at http://www.china.org.cn/english/ features/book/194421.htm [accessed 11 July 2012].

76   See Preamble and Article 23 of the Model, American Society of International Law website, available at http://www.asil.org/ilib080421.cfm#t1 [accessed 26 September 2012]. The proposal was abandoned in 2009. Damon Vis-Dunbar, "Norway Shelves its Draft Model Bilateral Investment Treaty", *Investment Treaty News*, 8 June 2009, available at   http://www.iisd.org/itn/2009/06/08/Norway-shelves-its-proposed-model-bilateral-investment-treaty [accessed 11 July 2012].

77   See Tull, op. cit., 127–8.

78   As exemplified by the *Paris Principles on Aid Effectiveness* (2005) and their augmentation by the *Accra Agenda* (2008), which adopts a more holistic approach to the issue.

79   See OECD, op. cit., n. 2.

80   Tony Addison and George Mavrotas (eds), *Development Finance in the Global Economy* (Basingstoke, Hampshire/New York: Palgrave Macmillan, 2008); George Mavrotas and Mark Gillivray, *Development Aid: A Fresh Look* (Basingstoke, Hampshire: Palgrave Macmillan, 2009).

81   The IFC's new Performance Standards were finalised in January 2012, after extensive stakeholder consultation and the release of two drafts. See http://www1.ifc. org/wps/wcm/connect/115482804a0255db96fbffd1a5d13d27/PS_English_2012_Full-Document.pdf?MOD=AJPERES [accessed 28 May 2012]. The new standards have not added a standalone human rights performance standard, instead incorporating them into social and environmental standards. While human rights are also referenced in the objectives of community health, safety and security standards, as well as indigenous peoples standards, some consider this outcome to be a dilution of the human rights message and a missed opportunity to civilise IFC development financing by skewing its public–private balance in favour of the latter. See Bretton Woods Project, "IFC Updated Performance Standards: Weak on Human Rights and Other Shortcomings", 14 September 2011, at http:// www.brettonwoodsproject.org/art-568878 [accessed 12 October 2012].

82   *Monterrey Consensus* (22 March 2002), paras 49–50.

83   See "Los Cabos Summit Final Declaration", 18–19 June 2012, and "Cannes Summit Final Declaration", 3–4 November 2011, both available at http://www.g20.org/ index.php/en/previous-leaders-summits [accessed 11 July 2012].

84   To which end the "aid for trade initiatives" within the "Enhanced Integrated Framework", under the auspices of the WTO, are designed. See Pascal Lamy on the place of the Enhanced Integrated Framework in Doha: Pascal Lamy, "Enhanced Integrated Framework: Building Capacity to help Least Developed Countries Weather the Crisis", Opening Statement, WTO Ministerial Breakfast on LDC Issues, 1 December 2009, available at http://www.wto.org/english/thewto_e/minist_e/min09_e/ldc_lamy_opening_e. doc [accessed 11 July 2012]; and Patricia Francis on private sector enhancement and

acceding LDCs: Patricia Francis, "Trade Capacity for Acceding LDC's", Statement, WTO Ministerial Breakfast on LDC Issues, 1 December 2009, available at http://www.wto.org/english/thewto_e/minist_e/min09_e/ldc_francis_e.doc [accessed 11 July 2012].

85   See WTO, "Day 3: Ministers Show 'Political Energy' for Ending Doha Round", *WTO News*, 2 December 2009, available at http://www.wto.org/english/news_e/news09_e/mn09a_02dec09_e.htm [accessed 11 July 2012], and as reiterated more recently, "Members Confront Doha Round Deadlock with Pledge to Seek Meaningful Way Out", 29 April 2011, available at http://www.wto.org/english/news_e/news11_e/tnc_dg_infstat_29apr11_e.htm [accessed 12 October 2012].

86   See the *UN Statement of Common Understanding on Human Rights-Based Approaches to Development Cooperation and Programming* (2003), adopted by United Nations Development Group, available at http://hrbaportal.org/the-human-rights-based-approach-to-development-cooperation-towards-a-common-understanding-among-un-agencies [accessed 11 July 2012]. More promising perhaps is the UN's current review of the *Draft Guiding Principles on Extreme Poverty and Human Rights* (DGPs 2004), which seeks to establish the DGPs as interpretive and practical tools in striving for development goals: Office of the High Commissioner for Human Rights, *Draft Guiding Principles on Extreme Poverty and Human Rights: The Rights of the Poor – A Technical Review* (2009), 3, available at http://www2.ohchr.org/english/issues/poverty/consultation/docs/Technical_Review_DGPs.pdf [accessed 26 September 2012]. Yet still, even here, the Review reveals continuing misplaced belief in the value of imposing international *legal* obligations on the international community at large for the alleviation of poverty – see discussion in ibid., para. 7 (at 6) – regarding Section 3 of the current DGPs (2004) on international cooperation, "which does not reflect the current understanding in the political realm nor in mainstream human rights scholarship of the notion of international assistance and cooperation and the obligations incumbent on a variety of actors". To the extent that intergovernmental organisations may have such responsibilities, see International Law Commission, *Draft Articles on Responsibility of International Organisations*, Report of the Fifty-Eighth Session (A/61/10), 2006, ch. VII.

87   A High Level Task Force on the Implementation of the Right to Development was established in 2004 by the (then) UN Commission on Human Rights (CHR Res. 2004/7) with the objective "to provide the necessary expertise to the [UN] Working Group [on Development] to enable it to make appropriate recommendations to the various actors on the issues identified for the implementation of the right to development", which, given the opaque and contested nature of the purported right, represents a thoroughly Panglossian viewpoint. See http://www.ohchr.org/EN/Issues/Development/Pages/HighLevelTaskForce.aspx [accessed 11 July 2012].

88   Which were the very same issues that placed the *Declaration on the Right to Development 1986* into a coma; see David Kinley, *Civilising Globalisation: Human Rights and the Global Economy* (Cambridge: Cambridge University Press, 2009), 106–108. Their intractability is perhaps one of the reasons why some have made ever more surreal attempts to overcome them. The prize in this category must go to Arjun Sengupta (a former UN Independent Expert on the Right to Development) and his incomprehensibly tautologous formula presented as (of all things) a "rewrite [of] the definition of the right to development … in a form that can be operationalized". "The Human Right to Development", in Bård Andreassen and Stephen Marks (eds), *Development as a Human Right*, 2nd edition (Cambridge: Intersentia Publishing, 2010), 18 *et seq.*

89   A vital point well made by David Kennedy in *The Dark Sides of Virtue* (Princeton, NJ: Princeton University Press, 2004), 152, and too often missed in eager efforts to lay claim to the existence and authority of the right to development. See, for example, Margot Salomon, *Global Responsibility for Human Rights: World Poverty and the Development of International Law* (Oxford: Oxford University Press, 2008), in which the realpolitik of international political and economic relations are marginalised in the face of the prevailing rules-based multilateralism of international law (32–40). There may be good arguments why this *ought* to be so – why, in other words, the politics and economics should be tamed by regulation – but one cannot proclaim that this is the *existing* position, and certainly not so in respect of the anaemic legal standing of human rights and duties regarding poverty alleviation and economic development.

90   See David Kinley, "Bendable Rules: The Development Implications of Human Rights Pluralism", in Brian Tamanaha, Caroline Sage and Michael Woolcock (eds), *Legal Pluralism and Development Policy* (Cambridge: Cambridge University Press, 2012), 50–65.

Chapter 11

"New Aid Modalities":
An Opportunity or Threat to Principled
Engagement on Human Rights?

Mac Darrow[1]

The "new aid modalities" are shorthand for the policy reforms introduced at the turn of this century, encapsulated in the 2005 Paris Declaration on Aid Effectiveness.[2] Traditional aid modalities, according to the stereotype, were predicated upon "donor–recipient" roles that exacerbated asymmetries of political and economic power between richer and poorer countries,[3] ratcheted up poor countries' burdens in administering aid, bypassed national planning and budget processes, undermined already weak state capacities, and promoted accountability only from the recipient government to the donor.

The Paris Declaration sought to correct these historical and structural biases based upon the idea of aid partnerships rather than "donorship". The Paris Declaration promotes "national ownership" of aid programmes in recipient (or "partner") countries, and alignment of aid with partner countries' development priorities, administrative and public financial management systems. The Paris Declaration also encourages greater harmonisation of donor countries' aid policies and activities, a clearer focus on development results, and strengthened "mutual accountability" between donor and partner governments. In practical terms this requires donors to act in concert and redirect financial support from their own standalone projects towards what is known as "programmatic" or sector aid and direct support to the national budget of partner countries. This occurs through basket fund arrangements in which grant aid is often combined with credits from an international financial institution.[4]

It is difficult to quibble with the need for changed donor/recipient roles and accountability arrangements, given the well-documented shortcomings in the aid industry in recent years. But there is more to these reforms than meets the eye. While the Paris Declaration commitments may appear modest and eminently sensible on their face, and while they are expressly limited to improving the efficiency and results-based management of bilateral and multilateral aid relationships, the practical implications of the "new aid modalities" are in fact deeply political, reflecting shifting currents in the geopolitics of aid and developing countries' increasingly insistent demands for a better deal from richer countries. As this chapter will show, the silence of the Paris Declaration on the substantive objectives of, and values implicit in, aid partnerships risks entrenching an unduly technocratic, managerialist and depoliticised development policy agenda.[5]

Some might argue that an exclusive or literal focus on the Paris Declaration is not necessarily a bad thing, that technical aid fixes are challenging enough, and that human rights would only compound and politicise these challenges. Introducing human rights concerns might, on this view, be perceived as political conditionality, leading to confrontation and withdrawal rather than sustained engagement on the basis of an equal partnership. However, the assumption that aid is "apolitical" is deeply suspect. Moreover, states and aid organisations have committed themselves in many forums to respecting international human rights in aid and development relationships, however poorly these commitments have been reflected in practice.

As this chapter will show, the failure to explicitly recognise human rights in aid relationships, far from ostracising partner countries, may undermine development objectives in their own terms, expose donor states and organisations to complicity in human rights violations, and erode the foundations for Principled Engagement based upon the internationally agreed human rights commitments to which all countries have to varying degrees subscribed. Principled Engagement, in the present context, means bringing human rights programming and advocacy to the front and centre of aid policies and partnerships in order, at a minimum, to avoid complicity in human rights violations, as part of a programme for strengthened, predictable and sustained engagement towards improved development results.

This chapter analyses the policy and institutional framework of the "new aid modalities" and explores the potential policy consequences for efforts to promote more principled human rights engagement in aid relationships. It examines these issues in connection with the UN's recent moves towards "Delivering as One", as well as in their application to donor harmonisation efforts on land reform in Cambodia. A particular focus is given to joint (or, in aid effectiveness jargon, "harmonised") UN human rights advocacy and its relationship with the Paris Declaration principle of "national ownership". Human rights advocacy has often been associated with traditional "donorship" roles and modes of behaviour, linked to democratic governance policy conditionalities and a narrow spectrum of human rights concerns commensurate with market liberalism and deployed as a blunt instrument rather than as an integrated component of broad-based and sustainable partnership strategies for social change. Yet, as we will see, with certain preconditions, recent developments in policy and practice help to show how these stale stereotypes and underlying ideological controversies may be overcome.

Policy Framework for the "New Aid Modalities" and Human Rights in the United Nations

The Paris Declaration, signed on March 2005, marks an important turning point in international efforts to improve the effectiveness of aid. Over 100 representatives of governments and international organisations, including those from more than

50 developing countries, put their signatures to a set of 56 action commitments which, while built on previous global agreements on aid effectiveness, represented an unprecedented comprehensive and broad-based consensus among donor and partner countries. The UN was among the signatories to the Paris Declaration, and has embarked upon numerous reform programmes relating to aid effectiveness as well as human rights in recent years.

However, the principles of the Paris Declaration are not, of themselves, in all respects internally consistent. There is said to be an "implicit program logic" within the Paris Declaration that is yet to be properly teased out, explaining how the Paris Declaration principles are expected to improve development results. But these putative explanations are based as much on "widely shared hunches" as research or analysed experience,[6] without which the Paris Declaration risks being reduced to an aid *efficiency* – rather than aid *effectiveness* – policy agenda. More particularly, some observers have noted that a high degree of harmonisation among donors may be damaging for "national ownership" and thus alignment. In the UN context, for example, it has been pointed out that joint programmes sometimes run the risk of being supply driven, thereby undermining national ownership and alignment.[7] There are almost certainly potential conflicts between aspects of mutual accountability and the objective of maximising the use of country systems and public financial management, oversight and audit procedures.[8]

There are also a number of very specific concerns that the Paris Declaration, however well intended, may have the effect of undermining human rights guarantees. For example, the office of the UN High Commissioner for Refugees (UNHCR) recently expressed concern "that the country-driven nature of the [UN aid effectiveness reform] process, coupled with the close alignment with national priorities, could result in a shift away from a human rights-based programming framework".[9] A focus on concrete and time-bound "measurables" in line with "new public management" theory has reportedly led to a reduced interest in goals that are more difficult to measure, particularly in the short term, such as the promotion of human rights, participation and democracy.[10] Progress towards direct budget support (where the UN's financial contribution compared to other donors will often be modest), reduced earmarking of aid, and increased use of country systems may in some circumstances come at the cost of the UN's leverage and ability to advocate for the poorest and most marginalised groups of people.

Increased harmonisation may in some circumstances lead to "lowest-common-denominator" advocacy positions on sensitive issues. This raises the stakes for the national human rights dialogue, and the UN's role in national donor coordination forums and technical working groups. Moreover, the Paris Declaration's disproportionate preoccupation with efficiency gains may inadvertently promote an excessively technocratic approach to donor–partner relations that could undermine domestic accountability and governance. A preponderant focus on financial and budgetary processes and institutions may in effect empower interest groups which are insensitive to the significance of equity and rights issues for development effectiveness, and marginalise actors and duty bearers in key policy areas with important roles for sustainable development and the realisation of human rights.[11] Therefore, notwithstanding their distinctive historical tracks, discourses, constituencies and institutional settings, human rights have entered the aid effectiveness debate as part of the proposed solutions to these kinds of specific problems.

This is not to deny potentially valuable synergies and opportunities that the Paris Declaration and new aid modalities might bring for human rights. There is a growing body of empirical evidence on the role that human rights can play in improving development processes and improving results, as well as how human rights relate to aid effectiveness principles.[12] On available anecdotal evidence, at least (human rights not being formally included in many official evaluations of the UN's development work), joint programming by UN development funds, programmes and agencies makes it easier to bring human rights within a single coherent country strategy, supported by joint resource mobilisation arrangements and integrated programme delivery mechanisms. Increased harmonisation of UN programmes has reportedly resulted in a greater focus on horizontal policy priorities such as gender, human rights, HIV/AIDS, the environment, and employment and decent work.[13] These possible benefits must be seen alongside the risks, although the dominant (even if unspoken and unproven) assumption seems to be that the former outweigh the latter.

The legal mandate of the UN's development agencies to integrate human rights within development and aid policies is clear, although the tenor and temperature of human rights debates on the UN's intergovernmental bodies can be unpredictable.[14] Participating states (from both donor and developing countries) and international development organisations at the third High Level Forum on Aid Effectiveness in Accra, Ghana, in September 2008, reached an unprecedented agreement that human rights should be an integral part of aid partnerships.[15] Under the banner of "Delivering as One" (or DaO), the UN and partner governments launched a set of eight pilot country initiatives to promote more coherent and harmonised business practices, joint programming and advocacy, as part of a wider move towards system-wide coherence consistent with the Paris Declaration.[16]

Human rights (except for gender equality and women's empowerment) are not part of the official intergovernmental oversight criteria for DaO pilots, or UN operational activities for development more generally. Nevertheless, human rights principles and programming approaches have been taken up in all DaO pilots, to varying degrees. The UN Development Group (UNDG, the inter-agency body responsible for oversight and coordination of the UN's development operations) and Organisation for Economic Co-operation and Development – Development Co-operation Directorate (OECD-DAC) have produced statements and policy guidance on human rights and the new aid modalities,[17] and human rights guidance has been provided for UN leaders in the field – including UN Resident Coordinators and Humanitarian Coordinators.[18] Yet further specific guidance still seems to be needed to ensure that the "new aid modalities" are implemented in a manner that is respectful and supportive of human rights, and that technical efficiency gains are more directly and systematically translated into "effective" aid relationships, good development processes, and more equitable and sustainable results.

Translating Policy to Practice

The tensions and disconnects between human rights and new aid modalities, as well as possible synergies, can be brought out through an appraisal of the UN's human rights joint advocacy in the context of aid relationships. UN leaders are expected to advocate for the values and fundamental objectives expressed in the UN Charter, including human rights. Joint advocacy within the donor community is critical, symbolically, as well as from the standpoint of leverage and impacts. But how can a principled advocacy role for donors be reconciled with the imperative to remain constructively engaged with national partners? Do "aid effectiveness" principles help or hinder us in navigating this tension? Experience will be sampled first from a few of the eight DaO pilot countries, as well as efforts to increase donor harmonisation on forced eviction and resettlement problems in Cambodia.

The UN's Human Rights Advocacy in DaO Countries

The UNDG has reported that joint UN-wide advocacy task forces and coordination mechanisms have helped UN Country Teams in DaO pilot countries to integrate so-called "cross-cutting issues" (including human rights) within advocacy strategies, and that a cohesive UN can play a more influential role in advocacy and policy support.[19] The UN's credibility in advocating for human rights at country level is seen to be linked to the organisation's universal membership and impartiality. While the traditional caricature of human rights advocacy presupposes a focus upon governance, democracy and civil and political rights issues (elections, arbitrary detention, torture and the like), in practice, socio-economic rights advocacy has been equally prominent.

By way of example, the UN Country Team in Mozambique, a heavily aid-dependent country, collaborated with civil society partners in 2008 and 2009 to develop budget briefs for submission to parliament analysing the draft national budget in relation to various children's rights issues, disparities and social protection concerns. It also participates actively in the "Programme Aid Partnership" multi-stakeholder working group structures at national level, and as at October 2009 was promoting a common policy position on the evaluation of Mozambique's national development plan.[20] The UN Country Team's guidelines for "Communicating as One" in Tanzania highlight the importance of all human rights for the UN's joint advocacy, arguing that a joint response to particularly critical issues – including gross violations of human rights and deliberate breaches of UN Conventions to which Tanzania is party – will enhance the UN's image as a coherent and well-coordinated organisation at country level. Interestingly, its joint programme document makes specific provision and budget allocation for research and evaluation connected with its communications strategy. Donors' approaches to human rights in Vietnam have reportedly not always been especially well harmonised.[21] However, in recent years the UN Country Team has pursued joint advocacy on topics including children's rights, HIV/AIDS and sexual and reproductive rights (although not civil and political rights, which are considered too sensitive). Advocacy has been pursued publicly as well as behind closed doors, and the Country Team has used human rights treaty reporting processes and the Universal Periodic Review process of the UN Human Rights Council as vehicles for joint advocacy as well as technical and capacity building support.[22]

While avoiding categorical conclusions, these cases suggest that donor harmonisation can support the promotion and protection of a wide range of rights (economic, social, civil, political and cultural), and that human rights advocacy may be pursued without any contradiction to the principle of national ownership. Advocacy need not always be public, and need not be confined to naming and shaming tactics. Correspondingly, donor harmonisation need not result in lowest-common-denominator advocacy positions. Human rights advocacy may usefully be integrated within the UN's joint development programming frameworks, consistent with and complementary to the UN development system's capacity-building role, and pursued in a principled way within the framework of aid partnerships.

Responding to Human Rights Violations in the Land Sector in Cambodia

Cambodia makes for an intriguing case study in which a number of international donors have, in effect, sought to give effect to a philosophy of Principled Engagement, walking a fine line between withdrawal from the aid partnership, on the one hand, and complicity in human rights violations on the other. As a preliminary issue, it seems open to doubt whether the Paris Declaration principles should apply in Cambodia. In the International Development Association's view, Cambodia's relatively weak institutional and policy environment warrant its inclusion in the "fragile state" list of countries,[23] subject to the OECD-DAC's "principles for good engagement in fragile states",[24] thereby calling into question the viability of programme aid, direct budget support, national ownership, alignment and other principles and assumptions reflected in the Paris Declaration. Yet at the same time, Cambodia has formally committed itself to implementing the Paris Declaration aid effectiveness reforms, with support of the large donor community in the country, implying the existence of adequate capacities, systems and commitment to use aid effectively. The latter assumptions have been challenged by numerous commentators, including with respect to donor support in the land sector.[25] It is not necessary to resolve this contradiction here, save to say that building effective aid management capacities can be a very long and uncertain undertaking, calling for flexibility and intelligence in the application of any set of global principles.

Cambodia is an aid-dependent country, where gender and human rights issues are heavily influenced by culture and the legacy of conflict. Social and economic inequality is acute, and economic growth tends be concentrated and captured by formal urban areas in a context of a very low tax base.[26] While ostensibly a multi-party political system, the ruling party dominates political and economic life and there are few serious constraints on executive power. Land tenure is among the biggest development challenges facing the country. Human rights violations in the land sector in Cambodia have been the subject of local and international concern for many years.[27] Land grabbing, expropriations and forced evictions are commonplace in both urban and rural areas, backed by powerful and opaque webs of elite political and economic interests, exacerbated by a climate of impunity, lack of an independent judiciary and weak rule of law. There is increasing inequality in the distribution of land holdings in Cambodia, with an estimated 20 per cent of the poorest families having no land and around 20 per cent of the richest families holding 60 per cent of available land.[28] The poorest and most marginalised groups have not so far proved able to mobilise or have their interests represented effectively at the political level. This is a clear instance where sustainable development and human rights imperatives neatly intersect.

Donor interest and involvement in the land sector has been prominent for many years, although in the assessment of some commentators, donors have sometimes been part of the problem insofar as efforts to safeguard security of tenure and promote more equitable distribution of land are concerned.[29] Traditional OECD-DAC donors are well established in the country, along with emerging donors such as China and South Korea. The rising influence of South–South cooperation – in Cambodia as well as globally – has complicated efforts towards greater harmonisation on human rights and governance questions, although traditional (OECD-DAC) donors have only selectively adhered to human rights, corruption and governance benchmarks in practice.[30] Notwithstanding the landmark human rights commitment reflected in paragraph 13(c) of the Accra Agenda for Action, paragraph 19(e) strikes quite a different tone:

> South-South co-operation on development aims to observe the principle of non-interference in internal affairs, equality among developing partners and respect for their independence, national sovereignty, cultural diversity and identity and local content. It plays an important role in international development co-operation and is a valuable complement to North-South co-operation.[31]

China has accordingly proclaimed a "no strings attached" policy to aid for Cambodia, although as with the wider donor community, does not consistently back up its policy commitments in practice.[32]

Recently, however, the UN and certain other bilateral and multilateral donors have taken steps to address directly some of the more serious human rights shortcomings in the land sector. Local and international housing rights NGOs have lobbied actively to this end. In an effort to consolidate and harmonise its advocacy, in 2007 the UN Country Team developed and approved a joint position on resettlements and evictions, with guidance from the Office of the High Commissioner for Human Rights (OHCHR) country office and in consultation with civil society groups. Called the "UN Common Viewpoint", this statement spells out Cambodia's obligations under international treaties and conventions and establishes an agreed foundation for intensified joint UN advocacy on human rights in connection with land tenure and forced evictions problems, as well as humanitarian responses to evictions in specified conditions. The UN Viewpoint has reportedly served as a useful tool for dialogue with government and other partners, has raised awareness among a wide array of stakeholders of the relevant laws and standards, and contributed to a common understanding among all actors (government, donors and the UN Counter Team) of international standards pertaining to eviction and resettlement.

Besides serving as policy support, the UN Viewpoint led to UN action in 2009–2010 in response to the forced eviction of 44 families living with and affected by HIV from Borei Keila, central Phnom Penh, to harsh conditions in a relocation site 25 kilometres away from the city centre. In response to this eviction, UN agencies (United Nations Development Program (UNDP), United Nations Children's Fund (UNICEF), the United Nations World Food Programme (WFP), the Joint United Nations Programme on HIV/AIDS (UNAIDS) and OHCHR) first advocated for the eviction to be postponed or cancelled, then advocated for an improvement of housing and living conditions at the resettlement. This advocacy resulted in the Municipality of Phnom Penh agreeing to a fundamental change in the housing structure, supported financially by UN agencies and Caritas, as well as support in relation to food and home-based care, coordinated with national AIDS counterparts and relevant services providers. UNAIDS, together with OHCHR, played an important human rights advocacy function with national counterparts, backed by civil society pressure.[33] The UN clarified that its humanitarian support should not be taken as endorsement of the eviction, and advocated publicly that future eviction processes should observe human rights standards and not discriminate against persons with HIV or other vulnerable groups.

Interestingly, the World Bank, a long-time supporter of the government in the land sector, has recently played an active role in advocating for a rights-sensitive response to land reform, prompted by civil society pressure and its accountability for safeguards compliance through its Inspection Panel.[34] In July 2009 the World Bank published a critical review of the government of Cambodia's "Land Management and Administration Project (LMAP)", a major land-titling programme designed to improve land security and promote efficient land markets, highlighting forced evictions and land insecurity problems for poor urban communities and indigenous populations, among other problems.[35] This report led the government of Cambodia to abruptly terminate cooperation with the World Bank on LMAP, on the grounds that "the World Bank set many conditions which make it difficult to cooperate".[36] The World Bank's measured response highlighted the importance of adhering to international treaties.[37] In November 2010, the World Bank's Inspection Panel (an independent body established to oversee compliance with the World Bank's operational policies) issued a damning report in response to forced evictions and human rights complaints concerning LMAP, which – in a rare even if partial human rights victory in Cambodia – reportedly led to the government granting legal title to 800 of the estimated 3,500 displaced families.[38] The international human rights mechanisms – treaty bodies as well as Special Procedures of the UN Human Rights Council – have supported development partner and civil society advocacy for equitable land reform. But donor harmonisation in the land sector has been a persistent challenge, which limits the prospects for more widespread and enduring gains.

The Cambodia case underscores the importance of harmonised, coherent system-wide advocacy on politically charged human rights and development issues, even in circumstances where OHCHR or other specifically mandated "protection" agencies are present in the country. But even so, the results achieved on the ground have been modest in the context of the scale of violations, with apparently little cause for optimism about the future. Principled human rights action in the land sector remains the exception to the rule, running up against deeply entrenched political and business interests. Certain influential donors have stood apart from this effort, even within the OECD-DAC grouping, let alone among the emerging donors. Until this changes, and until the political climate admits free expression and more effective organisation around human rights concerns, housing and land rights for the powerless will likely remain precarious.

Other Hard Cases

The UN has developed a considerable body of experience on human rights advocacy in some of the most challenging operating environments, although this has not yet been comprehensively analysed. By way of example, in 2002, under considerable international pressure, the government of Uzbekistan agreed to a country mission of the then UN Special Rapporteur on Torture and other Inhuman or Degrading Treatment or Punishment. The UN Resident Coordinator and UN Country Team gave substantive support to the Special Rapporteur's mission, which resulted in a highly critical report cataloguing the systemic and institutionalised practice of torture. The UN Country Team thereafter negotiated a capacity building programme with the government including, for the first time, civil society participation and a proposed prison monitoring regime.[39] The UN system in Iran, too, under the leadership of the Resident Coordinator, has maintained consistent active engagement with government on human rights issues in recent years in the areas of children's rights, refugees' rights and human rights defenders, along with gender and HIV/AIDS issues, within an overarching capacity development framework. Human rights complaints and petitions received by the UN Country Team in Iran have regularly (and appropriately) been transmitted to OHCHR, Special Procedures and relevant bodies with specific mandates for investigation and follow-up, without prejudice to the UN's development partnership.[40] And the

UN system's response to the military crackdown on popular protests in Burma/ Myanmar in September 2007 is an especially noteworthy example, involving joint public advocacy and strategic interactions with UN human rights mechanisms in a situation where the UN's *raison d'être* and legitimacy were, in the view of UN Country Team members themselves, put directly on the line.[41]

As in Cambodia's case, the impacts of human rights advocacy are not always easy to quantify. Ambitions obviously need to be tempered with a healthy dose of pragmatism in operating environments such as these, with the modest minimum aims of avoiding complicity in human rights violations, respecting and protecting human rights within the sphere of the UN's influence, and helping to broaden political space and create an enabling environment for human rights fulfilment in the longer term. Harmonised policy positions and creative divisions of labour are all the more vital in these settings, in concert with specialised human rights mechanisms and agencies.

Capacity Constraints and Institutional Barriers

As noteworthy as the above cases are, within the constraints and caveats mentioned, they do not appear to be typical. Regrettably, the more discernible tendency in the development field generally appears to be risk aversion. Peter Uvin, speaking from considerable experience within and beyond the UN development system, pulls no punches on this point: "It is amazing to what extent in most countries the entire official aid rhetoric and all the written documents tiptoe around the key human rights challenges, preferring silence, insinuation, self-censorship, and gentle neologism to any frank mention of the stakes, the problems, and the unfulfilled challenges."[42] It is often difficult to find an objective justification for this. International aid workers are, by and large, Uvin argues, "free from risk; their political mortality rate is close to nil worldwide". While the politicisation of aid and risks confronted by aid workers have undoubtedly increased in recent years,[43] it is difficult to quibble with Uvin's assertion that "[t]he internalized fear for negative repercussions in the donor community is based much more on passivity and habit, on a general desire not to rock the boat, than on a realistic assessment of the scale of negative repercussions. Aid workers get socialised in the art of whispering, of gently brushing under the table, of looking the other way, and in so doing they jointly create the very silence they individually decry."[44]

There are a number of institutional and capacity constraints that need to be recognised and addressed, in order to improve performance. First, there does not appear to be a well-developed or consistent understanding about what human rights advocacy, or alignment of UN values and actions with the human rights purposes of the UN Charter, actually means in practice. There is insufficient guidance about how "national" priorities, as distinct from government priorities, can objectively be identified, and what to do when these clash with the UN's value system. Governments do not always enjoy democratic legitimacy, they do not always coordinate internally, and do not always subscribe to the UN's value system and hence may need to be brought in. While considerable innovation and progress on advocacy has been evident in recent years, much of the experience has been ad hoc in nature, often lacking clear country-specific goals or strategies and lacking feedback loops into joint programming and institutional learning. With certain exceptions, such as the DaO pilot in Tanzania, there appears to be comparatively little available experience on how advocacy strategies might be more rigorously and systematically monitored and evaluated.

Clear guidelines are needed for the UN's human rights advocacy, including mechanisms for the reliable and fair assessment of advocacy priorities tailored in accordance with varying socio-economic and other national conditions. The national policy dialogue must be undertaken openly and transparently, on the basis of objective human rights criteria and benchmarks established by reference to the government's own treaty obligations and consistent national laws, in order to minimise perceptions of subjectivity, double standards and arbitrariness. Socio-economic rights should be treated on the same footing as civil and political rights, to help avoid the ideological baggage of "political" conditionality. In these challenging undertakings, the UN's legitimacy as standard bearer for global human rights values may well provide greater strength, credibility and leverage than its relatively modest financial clout ever could.

Updated policy guidance is needed in other respects as well. Clarity of roles, expectations and institutional support are critical ingredients for effective public advocacy on sensitive issues, where circumstances so require. Yet there has been a considerable degree of confusion on these basic questions in practice, as UNHCR remarked:

> There is currently a significant degree of reliance on agencies such as UNHCR and OHCHR to promote the importance of human rights and freedoms within the DaO pilots, and a certain degree of tension between developmental and human rights-oriented work has emerged in this respect ... This is the case despite the fact that all UN bodies [under the UN Charter] should be dedicated to mainstreaming human rights as well as advocating their observance, whether this is an explicit and particular mission of each body or not ... [H]uman rights still fail to appear on the agendas of some UN agencies involved in the DaO initiatives at country level.[45]

The experience sampled earlier affirms the intuition that Principled Engagement by the UN and internal divisions of labour should be worked out flexibly, penetrating binary distinctions and popular caricatures of "development" and "human rights" issues, "promotion" and "protection" work, and "good cops" (development actors) and "bad cops" (human rights actors). A flexible, country-specific and needs-driven approach can create space for agreement on effective divisions of labour that draw upon the specialised mandates and comparative advantages of all members of the UN system in a position to influence the given situation.[46]

Practical guidance may also be needed to help UN Country Teams engage more effectively in human rights policy dialogues on donor coordination bodies and national policy coordination structures including General Budget Support donor groups and performance assessment reviews; sectoral policy dialogues and annual sectoral reviews (which are often more open to civil society participation); and technical working groups associated with Sector-Wide Approaches, Joint Assistance Strategies, poverty reduction strategies and national development plans. Effective advocacy in such forums requires a high level of expertise, leadership and political sophistication, notwithstanding the UN's comparatively modest contribution to Official Development Assistance (ODA) in most countries.[47] These are critical levels of intervention if "national ownership" and alignment principles are to be taken seriously. Experience in certain of the DaO countries (for example Mozambique, sampled above) could be drawn upon in helping to frame system-wide guidance.

The tenor of policy guidance in this field needs to transcend discredited "donorship" modes and suggest a framework for flexible, nuanced and tailored responses to serious human rights problems. The OECD-DAC has set down some important markers for Principled Engagement in aid relationships, suggesting that donors should take a "harmonised and graduated" approach to deteriorating human rights situations as the optimal means of safeguarding human rights while respecting partners' legitimate concerns about conditionality. According to the OECD-DAC:

> In responding to serious human rights situations, the focus should be on harmonised, clear signals and targeted actions that do not penalise the most vulnerable in society. Rather than reducing aid in response to human rights concerns as a first resort, donors should seek to deliver aid through a range of aid instruments and channels to continue supporting poverty reduction, and where possible, targeting their assistance to achieve progress on human rights. Establishing human rights as part of the development partnership will help enhance predictability, and provide a basis for open and transparent dialogue where needed.[48]

Recent policy guidance of the UK's Department for International Development (DFID) sets out a similar principled framework for country human rights dialogue. Human rights are an explicit part of DFID's policy, pursuant to statutory duties under its Human Rights Act. A set of "benchmarks" should be agreed with government, and discussed with civil society and parliament as well as other donors, in order to provide a transparent indication of what aid and national actions are expected to achieve and provide a focus for discussions between donors and partner governments. Success in meeting benchmarks is not intended to be used as a mechanism for triggering disbursements. Similarly, failure to meet benchmarks should not automatically lead to interruption of aid flows, although it may lead to decisions to change the way aid is delivered, including switching some or all aid towards non-government channels. The explicit objective is to establish a clear and transparent framework for structured dialogue with the partner government about the progress with reforms and how constraints to implementation might be resolved.[49]

The UN, among other bilateral and multilateral donors, does not come value neutral into national policy dialogues.[50] There are limits on the extent to which many donors will passively acquiesce to bad policies or priorities that clearly conflict with international human rights treaty commitments of the country concerned, quite apart from more hard-nosed national interest calculations. With its explicit human rights mandate, multilateral character, universal membership and impartiality, it is the UN's role in particular to encourage that agreed international human rights obligations be domesticated or socialised through national laws and integrated within national development goals. The national dialogue on UN-supported aid and development will inevitably require agreement not only on the substantive and empirically justifiable preconditions for good development results, but also on the human rights "bottom lines" that would trigger remedial action of some kind including, at the outer limits, withdrawal from the aid relationship. These are self-evidently not easy decisions, especially given the UN's relatively modest financial leverage in most cases, and the possibility of a principled stand unwittingly visiting a double punishment upon the rights-holders themselves. However, a transparent, coordinated, harmonised and graduated approach, as reflected in OECD-DAC and DFID policy guidance, suggests a principled yet practical framework within which adverse human rights outcomes may at least be anticipated and mitigated, if not always eliminated.

Technical guidance is also needed on how to assess the national situation and identify a small number of key human rights priorities for any given advocacy strategy. Human rights assessment is not an exact science, particularly insofar as socio-economic rights are concerned. Household and demographic survey data and statistical and analytical capacities at country level do not always afford the basis for clear, confident shared advocacy positions on complex issues, and neither in many cases do the outputs and recommendations from international human rights expert bodies. Certain DaO countries, for example the Mozambique case already mentioned, carry out rights-based analysis of national budgets in order to furnish inputs and empirical foundations for socio-economic rights advocacy. But this kind of practice does not appear to be widespread.

Nevertheless, there are numerous human rights indicator-setting and benchmark-setting initiatives presently under way which could be factored into updated guidance on human rights policy dialogues and benchmarking efforts.[51] State parties to the International Covenant on Economic, Social and Cultural Rights and the Convention on the Rights of the Child (162 and 191 states parties, respectively) are legally obliged to move progressively forward in realising socio-economic rights, avoid arbitrary retrogression in the realisation of rights, undertake maximum efforts to realise rights within all available resources with priority given to the most excluded or vulnerable, ensure a core minimum level of rights for all, and – where best efforts are not sufficient – request international assistance.[52] A minimally even-handed application of these process criteria may provide objective grounds for privileging the claims of those lower-income countries better able to demonstrate authentic efforts towards human rights realisation, while at the same time increasing the legal and moral impetus for the international community to provide aid when it is both needed and requested. Foreign policy imperatives can never fully be screened out of aid policies and practices; however, framing aid policies more explicitly around shared international legal requirements might at least help to temper the excesses. Human rights practitioners and economists have been working in closer collaboration in recent years to develop quantitative assessment tools and methodologies that, together with qualitative data and more traditional human rights monitoring methods, can import a further measure of objectivity to the task of agreeing human rights priorities, expectations and benchmarks, and to call the bluff of states seeking international support for human rights realisation without first having demonstrated "maximum" effort at home.[53]

But there are other important gaps that policy guidance and capacity building support, of themselves, will not solve. Human rights leadership can be controversial, requiring sound political judgement and, at times, personal courage, as the Burma/Myanmar and Uzbekistan cases exemplify. Yet questions have been raised on the extent to which UN Resident Coordinators, who are expected to advocate on behalf of the UN system, have so far been vested with authority to match their responsibilities and accountabilities.[54] At least anecdotally, many Resident Coordinators do not genuinely feel empowered to advocate on the UN system's behalf at the country level. Their ability to do so effectively depends on a potentially wide range of variables, including human resource and capacity constraints in Resident Coordinators' offices, institutional support and backup within the UN system, and the level of internal cohesion and mutual accountability within UN Country Teams.

Other institutional or structural constraints are also evident to varying degrees. Recent independent evaluations of the UN's common development programming process (known as UN Development Assistance Framework, or UNDAF, which can be viewed as a programmatic expression of the Paris Declaration's harmonisation requirement), and of bilateral and multilateral aid efforts more widely, have highlighted a number of financial, political, institutional and individual disincentives to more effective harmonisation, alignment and strategic prioritisation. The reported problems include internal conflicts over resource mobilisation, the alleged dominance of programme management and disbursement imperatives over more substantive development aims, disincentives to innovation, competition for visibility between donor agencies, and lack of alignment between individual performance incentives and aid effectiveness goals.[55] Problems of this nature are regrettably not new to development, and may go some way to explaining what some perceive as donors' (including the UN's) self-censorship on human rights in many cases. Without continuing improvements at these levels, and without effective and independent accountability mechanisms (noting, for example, the important role played by the World Bank Inspection Panel in the Cambodia land sector case), it will be difficult to make any set of human rights and aid effectiveness policy reforms and internal capacity development measures effective.

Concluding Comments

Principled Engagement in aid relationships should entail, at a minimum, avoidance of complicity in, and explicit respect for, international human rights treaty obligations to which all countries have to varying degrees subscribed. Integrating these principled commitments should not be seen as an extraneous political conditionality; aid – however well intentioned – *may* undermine human rights, and *efficient* aid may do so more efficiently. Withdrawal need not be the inevitable consequence.

The new aid modalities were not conceived with human rights in mind: very far from it. While the discourse of human rights and development (if not the practice) has a long history, it is only since the Third High Level Forum on Aid Effectiveness in Accra, Ghana in 2008 that states and aid organisations have explicitly agreed that human rights should be integrated within aid policies. This commitment certainly appears very timely, in view of the internal contradictions within the Paris Declaration principles and their ambiguous relationship with human rights. But it is not self-executing, and it is not without its internal contradictions, bearing in mind the Accra Agenda for Action's silence on human rights in relation to South–South cooperation. Specific operational and policy implications need to be drawn out into clear guidance for UN aid workers, in order to harness the positive potential of the Paris Declaration as well as expose and safeguard against the latent human rights risks.

The new aid modalities are concerned with generating efficiencies in the delivery of aid per se, rather than advocacy. Yet as the practical experiences surveyed in this chapter show, advocacy cannot be understood by reference to tired and traditional stereotypes. Advocacy, including on human rights issues explicitly, is increasingly part of the UN development system's efforts to "deliver as one" at the country level, and a central element in many "One Programme" strategies. Advocacy, or policy dialogue, is also a logical correlation of ambitions to strengthen national ownership of aid processes and ensure a greater degree of alignment of donor support towards nationally defined priorities. In the absence of an explicit advocacy strategy with clear agreed benchmarks it will prove difficult in most cases to progress towards a situation where donors' and partner governments' priorities are more genuinely aligned, with potentially damaging results for the predictability and impacts of aid. At the same time, national ownership can on no sensible or defensible interpretation be reduced to "government" ownership alone. While active government leadership is vital, advocacy is often needed to encourage broad-based participation in national development processes, on legal and ethical as much as instrumental grounds, and to ensure that "national" priorities take into account the rights and interests of all, especially the most marginalised.

Animated and bound very directly by the human rights purposes of the UN Charter, UN development agencies arguably bear a special onus to ensure that aid partnerships respect internationally recognised human rights standards, an exacting requirement in view of the UN's declining contributions to ODA in global terms and the diminishing influence of official versus private financial flows overall. Yet harmonised human rights advocacy will only be effective when the incentives are present for a critical mass of donors to act in concert, driven by domestic political constituencies in partner countries as well as at home. The challenges faced within the UN are compounded considerably by the constraints to effective harmonisation across the wider spectrum of bilateral and multilateral aid agencies, including emerging donors and international financial institutions. These facts should act as a spur to bottom-up demand, strengthened coalitions and independent institutions for increased transparency and accountability in aid relationships, as a priority for capacity-building support.

It may seem hard to draw much encouragement from such a *problematique*. Yet the sampling of experience reflected in this chapter suggests that certain parts of the UN system are swimming determinedly against the tide, harmonising the UN system's human rights messaging and integrating advocacy on agreed human rights priorities within longer-term strategies for broad-based and sustained country engagement, even in complex operational settings. The challenge now is to take this to scale, through human resource policies, accountability structures and incentive systems that more effectively reward harmonisation, joint programming, and intelligent risk-taking.

Endnotes

1   This chapter is written in a personal capacity, and does not necessarily represent the views of the United Nations or OHCHR. The author expresses his appreciation to the Faculty of Law, University of New South Wales, for valuable support and assistance in the preparation of this chapter through its Visiting Fellowship programme in 2009.

2   For background on the history and purposes of the Paris Declaration on Aid Effectiveness, see OECD, http://www.oecd.org/document/18/0,2340, en_2649_3236398_35401554_1_1_1_1,00.html [accessed 1 May 2012].

3   See for example, Rosalind Eyben, "The Power of the Gift and the New Aid Modalities", *Institute of Development Studies (IDS) Bulletin* 37, no. 6 (2006), 89: "while the gift [of aid] is understood by the donor as an expression of social solidarity and the way it is given attempts to deny difference between the donor and the recipient, a gift in practice reinforces or even reinvents these differences."

4   "Programmatic/sector aid" is the financing of a whole span of activities, for example the education sector, rather than a specific project. "Budget support" is when the donor gives money to the recipient to manage rather than retaining the money and managing it through a donor-controlled project. A "basket fund" is a single fund containing the contributions of

several donors managed by the recipient against a pre-agreed plan without each donor's contribution being earmarked for specific activities. See ibid., 91.

5   On the origins of "new public management", see David Osborne and Ted Gaebler, *Reinventing Government: How the Entrepreneurial Spirit is Transforming the Public Sector* (Reading, MA: Addison-Wesley, 1992). For a political-economy analysis of results-based management, see David Hulme, "The Making of the Millennium Development Goals: Human Development Meets Results-Based Management in an Imperfect World", Working Paper No. 16, Brooks World Poverty Institute, Manchester, 2007.

6   Marta Foresti, David Booth and Tammie O'Neil, *Aid Effectiveness and Human Rights: Strengthening the Implementation of the Paris Declaration*, Overseas Development Institute, October 2006, 3, available at http://www.oecd.org/dataoecd/35/24/38284443.pdf [accessed 1 May 2012]. The "hunches" include the belief that results-based management is good for aid alignment and country ownership, and that aid harmonisation is invariably consistent with country ownership.

7   UN Development Group, Working Group on Programming Policies, *Final Report: Task Team 2 on One Programme*, January 2008, 5, available at http://www.undg.org/index.cfm?P=1211 [accessed 1 May 2012].

8   Foresti et al., op. cit., 5–6.

9   UNHCR, *UNHCR's Engagement in the Delivering as One Pilots: An Informal Stocktaking*, UNHCR Doc. Ref. No. PDES/2008/01, December 2007, available at http://www.unhcr.org/47f242472.html [accessed 1 May 2012].

10   Hulme, op. cit.

11   Foresti et al., op. cit.; Oxford Policy Management and Social Development Direct, "Making Aid More Effective Through Gender, Rights and Inclusion: Evidence from Implementing the Paris Declaration", Analytical Summary, June 2008, iii.

12   See, for example, Robert J. Barro, *Determinants of Economic Growth: A Cross-Country Empirical Study* (Cambridge, MA: MIT Press, 1997); Daniel Kaufmann, "Human Rights and Governance: The Empirical Challenge", in Philip Alston and Mary Robinson (eds), *Human Rights and Development: Towards Mutual Reinforcement* (Oxford: Oxford University Press, 2005), 352–402; Foresti et al., op. cit.

13   UN Development Group, *Statement of Outcomes and Way Forward*, Inter-Governmental Meeting of the "Programme Country Pilots" on "Delivering as One", Kigali, Rwanda, 19–21 October 2009, 4, available at http://www.un.cv/files/Outcome%20Statement%20Kigali%20FINAL%2020091021.pdf [accessed 28 May 2013].

14   For an analysis of intergovernmental debates on human rights mainstreaming, see Mac Darrow and Louise Arbour, "The Pillar of Glass: Human Rights in the Development Operations of the United Nations", *American Journal of International Law* 103, no. 3 (2009), 446.

15   Accra Agenda for Action, Third High Level Forum on Aid Effectiveness, 4 September 2008, available at http://siteresources.worldbank.org/ACCRAEXT/Resources/4700790-1217425866038/AAA-4-SEPTEMBER-FINAL-16h00.pdf [accessed 28 May 2013]. In paragraph 13(c) of the Accra Agenda for Action, donor and partner countries undertook to "ensure that their respective development policies and programmes are designed and implemented in ways consistent with their agreed international commitments on gender equality, human rights, disability and environmental sustainability". The outcome document of the fourth High Level Forum on Aid Effectiveness in Busan, Korea, 29 November to 1 December 2011, specifies that the Accra Agenda for Action remains in effect. See http://www.oecd.org/document/12/0,3746,en_2649_3236398_46057868_1_1_1_1,00.html

[accessed 10 June 2012]. The Paris Declaration has been signed by many, if not most, DaO countries (as well as the UN), and Paris Declaration indicators are incorporated in several of the DaO countries' joint programming (also known as "One Programme") activities.

16   The pilot country initiatives are Albania, Cape Verde, Mozambique, Pakistan, Rwanda, Tanzania, Uruguay and Vietnam, although numerous other UN Country Teams have since adopted the "DaO" joint programming modality.

17   See UN Development Group, *Key Messages*, Third High Level Forum on Aid Effectiveness, Accra, Ghana, 19 August 2008, available at http://www.undg.org/index. cfm?P=631 [accessed 1 May 2012]; OECD, DAC Action Oriented Policy Paper on Human Rights and Development, 2007, Principle 6 ("Consider human rights in decisions on alignment and aid instruments"), available at http://www.oecd.org/dataoecd/50/7/39350774. pdf [accessed 1 May 2012]; and OECD, *Human Rights and Aid Effectiveness: Key Actions to Improve Interlinkages* ("DAC Update"), 2008, available at http://www.oecd.org/ dataoecd/13/63/43495904.pdf [accessed 1 May 2012].

18   The Administrative Committee on Coordination (ACC), *The United Nations System and Human Rights: Guidelines and Information for the Resident Coordinator System*, 2000, available at http://www.undg.org/archive_docs/1-The_UN_System_and_Human_Rights__ Guidelines_and_Information_for_the_Resident_Coordinator_System_-_The_UN_System_ and_Human_R.pdf [accessed 1 May 2012], and Inter-Agency Standing Committee, *Human Rights Guidance Note for Humanitarian Coordinators*, 2006, available at http://www2.ohchr. org/english/countries/field/docs/HRguidance-coordinators.pdf [accessed 1 May 2012]. While in serious need of updating, the existing guidance makes it clear that Resident Coordinators and UN development operations do not have a mandate to undertake individual human rights monitoring, investigations or casework. Rather, they are intended to establish a framework for principled, coordinated and flexible responses to human rights problems.

19   UN Development Group, *Communicating as One: Lessons Learned from Delivering as One in 2007*, 1 August 2008, 2, available at http://www.undg.org/docs/9571/ Communicating-as-One-Lessons-Learned-2007.pdf [accessed 1 May 2012].

20   Personal communication from UN Country Team, Mozambique, to the author on 23 October 2009. See also UN Development Group, *Mozambique Stocktaking Report 2008 "Delivering as One" – Progress and Challenges*, United Nations Mozambique, March 2009, available at http://www.undg.org/index.cfm?P=1129 [accessed 1 May 2012].

21   Oxford Policy Management and Social Development Direct, op. cit., 10–11.

22   Personal communication from UN Country Team, Vietnam, to the author on 22 October 2009. See also UN Development Group, 1 August 2008, op cit., 6; UN Development Group, *Delivering as One Pilots: One Leader and UN Country Team Working Arrangements/Codes*, Summary, 1 October 2007, available at http://www.undg. org/docs/8040/Leadership%20in%20One%20UN%20pilots%20Oct%201%202007.doc [accessed 1 May 2012].

23   So-called "fragile states" (or what were previously called "Low Income Countries Under Stress", or LICUS) are defined by reference to institutional and public sector management criteria established by the International Development Association (IDA, the concessional financing arm of the World Bank Group). For discussion, see Wim Naudé, Amelia Santos-Paulino and Mark McGillivray, *Fragile States*, Research Brief No. 3, United Nations University, 2008, available at http://unu.edu/publications/research-policy-briefs/2000-2010/fragile-states [accessed 1 May 2012]. The normal assumption would be that "fragile states" lack the institutional capacity to use aid effectively, although development partners appear to consider Cambodia as an exception to this rule.

24   See OECD, *Principles for Good International Engagement with Fragile States*, April 2007, available at http://www.oecd.org/document/46/0,3343, en_2649_33693550_35233262_1_1_1_1,00.html [accessed 1 May 2012]. The Fragile States Principles are designed specifically for conflict and post-conflict countries and weak governance environments. They contain several explicit and implicit references to human rights, including principle No. 3 on state-building (promote democratic governance, human rights, civil society engagement and peace-building) and No. 6 on non-discrimination. According to the World Bank's Country Policy and Institutional Assessment ratings, however, Cambodia is on the threshold of a transition out of the "fragile" category.

25   Douglas Gillison and Kay Simsong, "A Decade of Donor Meetings: Donor Discontent May Not Lessen Donor Largesse", *The Cambodia Daily*, 3 March 2007.

26   Chhau Somethea, Country Presentation: Cambodia at OHCHR, UNICEF and University of Oslo, "MDGs and Human Rights: Dialogues for Action", Asian Regional Dialogue, Bangkok, Thailand, 16–17 October 2008, cited in Malcolm Langford, *Human Rights and MDGs in Practice: A Review of Country Strategies and Reporting*, Norwegian Centre for Human Rights, University of Oslo, 2008, 25, available at http://www.ohchr. org/Documents/Issues/MDGs/Human_rights_and_MDGs_in_practice_ML.pdf [accessed 1 May 2012].

27   For a useful overview, see the joint NGO submission to the UN Committee on Economic, Social and Cultural Rights, on review of the period report of Cambodia under the International Covenant on Economic, Social and Cultural Rights, *Land and Housing Issues: Additional Issues and Supplemental Questions*, November 2008, available at http:// www2.ohchr.org/english/bodies/cescr/docs/info-ngos/COHRECambodia_41.pdf [accessed 1 May 2012]. See also Cambodian Human Rights Action Committee, *Losing Ground: Forced Eviction and Intimidation in Cambodia*, September 2009, available at http:// indigenouspeoplesissues.com/index.php?option=com_content&view=article&id=1916:1 osing-ground-forced-evictions-and-intimidation-in-cambodia&catid=62:southeast-asia-indigenous-peoples&Itemid=84 [accessed 1 May 2012].

28   NGO Forum on Cambodia, "Sharing Experiences About ODA Japan from a Human Rights Perspective", in *Fifty Years of Japan ODA: A Critical Review for ODA Reform*, Reality of Aid Asia-Pacific 2005 Report, 77, available at http://www.realityofaid.org/wp-content/uploads/2013/02/ROA_Asia_2005_Full_smll.pdf [accessed 27 May 2013].

29   Ibid., 79; Natalie Bugalski and David Pred, *Formalizing Inequality: Land Titling in Cambodia*, Land Research Action Network (LRAN) Briefing Paper Series, July 2010, available at http://www.landaction.org/IMG/pdf/LRAN-9_Formalizing_Inequality.pdf [accessed 1 May 2012].

30   Gillison and Simsong, op. cit. For a critique of the impact of aid on governance and corruption problems in Cambodia, see Sophal Ear, *The Political Economy of Aid, Governance and Policy-Making: Cambodia in Global, National and Sectoral Perspectives*, PhD Dissertation, Faculty of Political Science, University of California, Berkeley, January 2006, available at http://www.aad.berkeley.edu/mcnair/Ear.Sophal.dissertation.2..pdf [accessed 1 May 2012].

31   Accra Agenda for Action, op. cit.

32   See, for example, Seth Mydans, "Twenty Uighurs, $1 Billion and a Clear Signal", *International Herald Tribune*, 23 December, 2009, reporting on a generous bilateral aid deal signed just two days after Cambodia summarily deported 20 ethnic Uighur asylum seekers back to China. More generally, see Stephanie Kleine-Ahlbrandt and Stephen Small, "China's New Dictatorship Diplomacy: Is Beijing Parting with Pariahs?", *Foreign Affairs*

87, no. 1 (January/February 2008), 38, analysing the realpolitik behind China's human rights diplomacy with authoritarian regimes.

33   See Human Rights Watch, *Open Letter to the Government of Cambodia Regarding the Treatment of HIV-affected Families in the Community of Borei Keila*, 27 July 2009, available at http://www.hrw.org/en/news/2009/07/25/open-letter-prime-minister-and-minister-health-cambodia [accessed 1 May 2012]; CNN, *HIV Families Relocated to Cambodia's "AIDS colony"*, 29 July 2009, available at http://edition.cnn.com/2009/WORLD/asiapcf/07/28/cambodia.hiv/ [accessed 1 May 2012].

34   The Inspection Panel is a three-member independent expert body charged with ensuring that the World Bank complies with its own operational "safeguard" policies, including on environmental assessment and resettlement issues.

35   World Bank, "Cambodia Land Management and Administration Project: Enhanced Review Report", 13 July 2009, available at http://siteresources.worldbank.org/INTCAMBODIA/147270-1174545988782/22303366/FINALERMREPORT.pdf [accessed 1 May 2012].

36   See Norbert Klein, "Hun Sen: Cambodia Stopped the Partnership in Land Titling with the World Bank First", *The Mirror* 13, no. 629, 8 September 2009, available at http://www.cambodiamirror.org/2009/09/08/hun-sen-cambodia-stopped-the-partnership-in-land-titling-with-the-world-bank-first-tuesday-8-9-2009/ [accessed 28 May 2013].

37   Ibid. In the course of reiterating the World Bank's continuing commitment to partnership, the World Bank Country Director for South-East Asia, Annette Dixon, said, "We are encouraged by the Government's statement of its commitment to continuing reforms in the land sector and working towards an improved policy and legal framework for resettlement that reflects their commitment to international treaties." World Bank, *Statement From the World Bank on Termination By Royal Government of Cambodia of the Land Management and Administration Project*, 6 September 2009, available at http://web.worldbank.org/WBSITE/EXTERNAL/COUNTRIES/EASTASIAPACIFICEXT/CAMBODIAEXTN/0,,contentMDK:22303344~menuPK:293861~pagePK:1497618~piPK:217854~theSitePK:293856,00.html [accessed 1 May 2012].

38   The Inspection Panel, "Investigation Report No. 58016-KH, Cambodia: Land Management and Administration Project" (Credit No. 3650-KH), 23 November 2010. For the fuller history of this case, see Inclusive Development International, "BKL case", at http://www.inclusivedevelopment.net/bkl/ [accessed 10 June 2012], and the list of references there.

39   For a more critical appraisal of these capacity building proposals, see David Lewis, *The Temptations of Tyranny in Central Asia* (New York: Columbia University Press, 2008), 23–6, alleging that technical fixes were ineffectual and deflected attention from underlying political obstacles and associated root causes of impunity. The Andijan massacre in 2005 was among the factors which ultimately curtailed this UN-supported initiative.

40   UN Development Group, UN Resident Coordinator Annual Report for Iran, 2006, available at http://undg.org/rcar.cfm?fuseaction=N&ctyIDC=IRA&P=490 [accessed 1 May 2012], arguing that: "One of our key concerns is the tendency for isolation, both driven by certain internal policies, and by certain member states' policies. We believe that an isolation of Iran does not contribute to solution of any of the geopolitical or regional issues that are raised in international debates." See also UN Development Group, "UN Resident Coordinator Annual Report for Iran", 2008, available at http://www.undg.org/rcar08.cfm?fuseaction=RCAR&ctyIDC=IRA&P=1095 [accessed 1 May 2012], noting: "The UN Country Team believes that it is important to continue to engage in a constructive

manner, in collaboration with Iranian counterparts, on capacity building for human rights and limited advocacy activities, as and when opportunities arise. The 60th anniversary of the Universal Declaration of Human Rights was one such instance which gave us a good opportunity to do advocacy on human rights."

41   Darrow and Arbour, op. cit., pp. 446–7 and 451–2. The UN Resident Coordinator was expelled from the country notwithstanding the moderate tone of the UN's public advocacy. However, the UN's senior leadership was supportive of the UN Country Team, and there was no disruption to the UN's humanitarian access on the ground.

42   Peter Uvin, *Human Rights and Development* (Sterling, VA: Kumarian Press 2004), 81.

43   Abby Stoddard, Adele Harmer and Victoria DiDomenico, *Providing Aid in Insecure Environments: 2009 Update*, Overseas Development Institute, Humanitarian Policy Group, Policy Brief 34, April 2009, available at http://www.odi.org.uk/resources/download/3250.pdf [accessed 1 May 2012]. Attacks against humanitarian aid workers have increased sharply since 2006, with Darfur, Afghanistan and Somalia accounting for 60 per cent of violent attacks. This is symptomatic of a growing politicisation of violence against aid operations in a small number of highly insecure contexts. The rise in attacks on UN aid workers is mainly attributable to the heavy casualties suffered by national staff and contractors, particularly truck drivers. The incident rate for the UN's international staff declined slightly, indicating that the marked rise in the casualty rate among international staff was borne primarily by NGOs.

44   Ibid., 81–2.

45   UNHCR, op. cit.

46   For example, the UN Resident Coordinator Annual Report for Iran, 2008, observes: "Like the previous years, the human rights situation continues to be subject to strong criticism, as indicated by the General Assembly resolution 62/168 and the General Assembly's Third Committee resolution A/C.3/1/63/L.40. Even though this is considered a sensitive subject by the Government, the positions taken by the General Assembly as well as other parts of the UN system present an imperative for the UN development system in Iran to continue engaging on this subject. The mandates of the various UN agencies on the ground offer only very limited opportunities for engagement in direct monitoring or follow-up of individual cases. However, the strong cooperation with relevant authorities at UN Headquarters offers opportunities to address a number of issues without overstepping our mandates. Perhaps even more important for the UN development system in Iran are the opportunities to continue its work in national capacity building and advocacy on these issues. These should be fully utilized as and when they emerge. Furthermore, the dialogue on establishing further Technical Assistance programmes on human rights in the country should be continued." Available at http://www.undg.org/rcar08.cfm?fuseaction=RCAR&ct yIDC=IRA&P=1095 [accessed 1 May 2012].

47   See David Kinley, *Civilising Globalisation: Human Rights and the Global Economy* (Cambridge: Cambridge University Press, 2009), 99–101, noting also the rising influence of foreign direct investment (FDI) and bilateral investment treaties, compared with official aid flows.

48   OECD, DAC Action Oriented Policy Paper on Human Rights and Development, op. cit.

49   Department for International Development (DFID), *How To Note: Implementing the UK's Conditionality Policy*, DFID Practice Paper, March 2009, 12–16, available at http://www.ukan.org.uk/fileadmin/user_upload/HTN_Implementing_the_UKs_Conditionality_Policy__May_09.pdf [accessed 1 May 2012].

50   Values may, of course, be imported implicitly as well as explicitly. Numerous donors have explicit human rights policies based upon their own charters, national laws or constitutional arrangements, including the European Union and the European Bank for Reconstruction and Development. For a sampling of donor policies see Laure-Hélène Piron, *Integrating Human Rights into Development: A Synthesis of Donor Approaches and Experiences*, Overseas Development Institute, September 2005, available at http://www. odi.org.uk/rights/Publications/humanrights_into_development_execsumm.pdf [accessed 1 May 2012]. There are also strong legal arguments that international financial institutions are bound by international human rights law in several important respects. See, for example, Mac Darrow, *Between Light and Shadow: The World Bank, The International Monetary Fund and International Human Rights Law* (Oxford: Hart Publishing, 2003).

51   See, for example, OHCHR, *Report on Indicators for Promoting and Monitoring the Implementation of Human Rights*, HRI/MC/2008/3, 6 June 2008, available at http:// www2.ohchr.org/english/issues/indicators/docs/HRI.MC.2008.3_en.pdf   [accessed   1 May 2012]; and the "Indicators Benchmarks Scoping Assessment" (IBSA) initiative, a participatory framework for the identification of nationally relevant indicators and benchmarks to facilitate the review of national reports under the International Covenant on Economic, Social and Cultural Rights, available at http://riedel.uni-mannheim.de/inhalt/ unterdokumente/downloads/ibsa/ibsa2/2_the_ibsa_procedure_as_a_tool_of_human_ rights_monitoring_1_1.pdf [accessed 1 May 2012], although the latter initiative has so far focused upon the right to food.

52   See, for example, OHCHR, Committee on Economic, Social and Cultural Rights, General Comment No. 3: The Nature of State Parties Obligations, E/C.3/1991/3 (1990), available at http://www.unhcr.org/refworld/pdfid/4538838e10.pdf [accessed 1 May 2012]; and Committee on the Rights of the Child, Day of General Discussion on "Resources for the Rights of the Child – Responsibilities of States", 2007, available at http://www2.ohchr. org/english/bodies/crc/discussion2008.htm [accessed 1 May 2012].

53   See, for example, Edward Anderson and Marta Foresti, "Assessing Compliance: The Challenges for Economic and Social Rights", *Journal of Human Rights Practice* 1, no. 3 (2009), 469–76; Terra Lawson-Remer, Sakiko Fukuda-Parr and Susan Randolph, "An Index of Economic and Social Rights Fulfillment: Concept and Methodology", *Journal of Human Rights* 8, no.3 (2009), 195–221, available at http://papers.ssrn.com/sol3/papers. cfm?abstract_id=1361363 [accessed 1 May 2012]. For more detailed discussion on quantitative assessments, see Eitan Felner, "A New Frontier in Economic and Social Rights Advocacy? Turning Quantitative Data into a Tool for Human Rights Accountability", *Sur International Journal of Human Rights* 5, no. 9 (December 2008), 109, available at http:// www.surjournal.org/eng/conteudos/pdf/9/felner.pdf [accessed 1 May 2012].

54   UN Development Group, *Statement of Outcomes and Way Forward*, op. cit., 5.

55   Richard Longhurst, *Review of the Role and Quality of UN Development Assistance Frameworks*, Overseas Development Institute, 2006, available at http://www.unep.org/delc/ Portals/119/8770-Review_of_the_Role_and_Quality_of_UNDAFs.pdf [accessed 28 May 2013]; Paolo de Renzio, David Booth, Andrew Rogerson and Zaza Curran, *Incentives for Harmonisation and Alignment in Aid Agencies*, ODI Working Paper 248, 2005, available at http://www.odi.org.uk/resources/download/1374.pdf [accessed 1 May 2012]; David Kinley and Tom Davis, *Human Rights Criticism of the World Bank's Private Sector Development and Privatisation Projects*, Sydney Law School Research Paper No. 08/53, 2008, 85–102, available at http://papers.ssrn.com/sol3/papers.cfm?abstract_id=1133179 [accessed 1 May 2012].

Index